The Complete Guide to
SELF-PUBLISHING

*Everything You Need to Know
to Write, Publish, Promote, and
Sell Your Own Book*

Tom and Marilyn Ross

Writer's
Digest
Books

CINCINNATI, OHIO

93 92 91 90 89   5 4 3 2 1

Library of Congress Cataloging in Publication Data

Ross, Marilyn Heimberg.
    The complete guide to self-publishing.

    Updated and expanded ed. of: The encyclopedia of self-publishing, cl979.
    Includes index.
    1. Self-publishing—Handbooks, manuals, etc.
2. Publishers and publishing—Handbooks, manuals, etc.
I. Ross, Tom, 1933-   . II. Ross, Marilyn Heimberg.
Encyclopedia of self-publishing. III. Title.
Z285.5.R668 1985   070.5   85-8224
ISBN 0-89879-354-8

ACKNOWLEDGMENTS

Thanks to our many students and clients for the contribution they've made to this work. Without their thirst for information and their faith that we could quench this thirst, we wouldn't have been challenged to dig so deeply—to probe so many crannies—to look beyond the readily available answers for true solutions. Nor would we have had the motivation or the opportunity to test these findings and document the results.

We also wish to express special gratitude to our editor, Carol Cartaino, whose editorial suggestions showed remarkable sensitivity and depth of knowledge. To the entire staff we say a hearty "Bravo!" You are a unique group of caring and competent people. Jean, Beth, Nancy, Jo, Mert, Budge, Howard, Marylyn, and all the others . . . thanks for being who and what you are.

Additionally, we wish to acknowledge the countless individuals, organizations, and companies who so generously offered ideas, information, review copies of books and software programs, and hardware evaluation units. *The Complete Guide to Self-Publishing* grew out of people's experiences—our own and many others'. Sincerest thanks to all those gone before . . . from the pioneers who cut trails . . . to the engineers who paved the road, so that our travels might be easier.

This book is dedicated to self-publishers
throughout the ages
—from the Ben Franklins and Sam Clemenses,
and Zane Greys of yesteryear
to the Louise Hayses, Ken Keyes, Jrs.
and Richard Nelson Bolleses of today.

Most of all, it's dedicated to our readers
—the self-publishing superstars of tomorrow.

Here's what reviewers had to say about the original self-published version of *The Complete Guide to Self-Publishing*:

A handbook stuffed with essential information on how to get into print, and beyond.... The authors are fully prepared; they have self-published and successfully marketed several books. With realism and extraordinary thoroughness, every practical topic is covered: how to organize for research and writing; mastering the ISBN, ABI, and CIP formalities; developing necessary business procedures; finding the right printer and format; advertising and promoting (including some very inventive approaches); and pushing distribution. Under the rubric "Other Alternatives" there are chapters on agents, conventional trade publishers, and vanity presses. Current lists of helpful organizations, reviewing media and syndicated columnists, bookstore chains, selected wholesalers, buyers of subsidiary rights, a bibliography, glossary, and index pack riches right up to the last page.

Booklist

Besides telling how to write, publish, promote, and sell one's own book, the authors provide key names and addresses, book production guidance, sample sales letters, tips on business procedures, and suggestions on organizing and implementing a publicity campaign.

Publishers Weekly

... a sound overview of self-publishing.

Los Angeles Times

One of the most useful and comprehensive books available on this subject.

Richard Morris,
COSMEP Coordinator

This oversized book ... could save writers a dramatic amount of time. There are guidelines for book production, business procedures, publicity, marketing strategies, pointers on agents and outlets.

"Scanning the Bookshelf,"
Copley News Service

Complete information on all aspects of successfully publishing your own book ... and a reference section that is worth its weight in gold bullion—key names and addresses of important book reviewers, major bookstore chains, selected department and variety store buyers, syndicated columnists, wholesalers and subsidiary rights buyers. I've read a lot of books on this subject. This is the most comprehensive, practical guide I've ever seen.

Daniel S. Kennedy, Editor
Marketing Your Services

This book is not only innovative and informative but delightful reading as well. Thank you for all the time and energy you have taken to share your experiences and knowledge with your colleagues.

Diane Tuggle,
Forerunner Press

If you've ever had the urge to write, publish, promote, and sell your own work, here's a fabulous book to guide you successfully through every step of the way. . . . It can save you thousands of dollars and be the difference between having a successful book or a flop.

Sid Asher's World

This is one book you'll need if you're planning to publish your own book. In 75 fact-filled sections, it covers every phase of self-publishing.

Mail Order Digest
National Mail Order Association

Here's a practical work by a couple who have gone the standard route and have prepared a bookful of hints on how to go about publishing your own book. The text offers sound advice on all the basic aspects of publishing.

John Barkham Review

Recommended reading.

Business Opportunities Journal

The Complete Guide to Self-Publishing would be a helpful tool to most any would-be self-publisher.

Tom C. Drewes, President
Quality Books, Inc.

. . . loaded with excellent practical advice, plus forms to fill out and models to follow. The authors are energetic yet irreverent, and their attitude is refreshing . . .

San Francisco Chronicle

This definitive book has become the "bible" for small publishing, and it's easy to see why. It's also easy to see how much good hard work and "hands-on" experience went into making this book. The table of contents alone is overwhelming! Virtually every aspect of small publishing is covered, from the business side to the all-important publicity and promotion. The resource section of the book is worth the cover price alone. A book you will want for constant reference and for dipping into at random. A classic!

Cliff Martin
COSMEP Newsletter

This book is available at special quantity discounts for bulk purchases for sales promotions, premiums or fund raising.
For details write to Attn: Marketing Dept., Writer's Digest Books, 1507 Dana Ave., Cincinnati, OH 45207.

TABLE OF CONTENTS

PREFACE

Self-publishing is a perfect example of the American dream. It is stimulating, demanding, and rewarding. For many it has proven to be the do-it-yourself way to fame and fortune.

This book developed out of the nationwide writing and publishing seminars we have given over the past decade. During these workshops we were barraged with questions. What, should I write about? How do we handle book production? What are the secrets for getting nationwide publicity and distribution? And people who couldn't attend our seminars wanted a guide to help them successfully navigate the risky waters of private publishing. These needs motivated us to write and publish *The Encyclopedia of Self-Publishing*, the forerunner of the first edition of *The Complete Guide to Self-Publishing*, and the updated and greatly expanded paperback edition you're now reading.

The Complete Guide to Self-Publishing has been researched not in the quiet halls of institutions, but in the bustle of the everyday marketplace. This isn't a book of fancy theory; it's a practical handbook of state-of-the-art specifics. We've used ourselves and our own books as guinea pigs, refining our craft and sharpening our expertise. We share many personal experiences in these pages and let you know what works . . . and what doesn't. It is not just our story, but the stories of many of our clients and students, and dozens of other prosperous self-publishers.

Over the last several years we've not only published our own titles but also served as consultants. Our company, About Books, Inc., has helped people and organizations from all over the United States publish and promote their own books. We've dealt with all kinds of nonfiction; and with novels, poetry, children's books, family histories, and autobiographies. We've had the pleasure of working with some of the nicest people on the face of God's green earth. Although we've never met many of these clients face to face, we feel a real kinship with them after helping give birth to their books.

No less real is the sadness we've felt for some self-published books and their authors—authors who have asked us to promote self-published works that simply weren't marketable. The message was unclear or uninteresting or the book itself amateurish and poorly produced. We had to say no far too often. We hope that this book will help prevent these kinds of mistakes.

Done properly, self-publishing is an exciting and viable way to get your book into print. We hope this guide will show many thousands how to do just that!

FOREWORD

Self-publishing has come of age. According to industry records, some five thousand new small presses are founded annually, of which perhaps a third are operated by authors publishing their own work. Mainstream book publishing is dominated by fewer than a hundred large houses, whose number is constantly being diminished by acquisitions and mergers, and it is now apparent that self-publishers are playing an increasingly significant commercial and cultural role on the American book scene.

The explosion in the number of small and self-publishers is a recent development. Few of us have recognized or understood the confluence of factors that brought the phenomenon about during the last fifteen years: the excessive commercialization of mainstream publishing, which aggravated its traditional deficiencies; the massive surge of small business enterprises in the U.S.; and the wide availability of computer-based, desktop publishing systems. Yet that confluence of forces has revolutionized the book world, shattering the monopoly of mainstream publishing, introducing new concepts and techniques, and significantly broadening book distribution. Everywhere barriers have come down: Geographical barriers that once established the hegemony of a few giant New York houses. Editorial barriers that allowed the giants to set the fashions of popular taste. And marketing barriers that limited the efforts publishers would make in promoting books to consumers. In little more than a decade book publishing has been transformed from an elitist endeavor dominated largely by an Eastern establishment to a wide open, burgeoning, grassroots phenomenon radiating the populist energies that created it.

Populist movements, however, also have weaknesses—notably the tendency to be amateurish. The U.S. Constitution guarantees freedom to publish, but does not provide everyone with the talents, skills and resources necessary to publish successfully. Publishers must possess or acquire such skills and resources; otherwise, as Tom and Marilyn Ross sadly note, even their most worthy projects will fail to capture their audiences.

In this volume, the Rosses provide a comprehensive, down-to-earth *vade mecum* for budding self-publishers anxious to understand and learn the entire process. *The Complete Guide to Self-Publishing* offers orientation, perspective, guidance, instruction, and insight on all phases of this complex endeavor, from the conception of an idea for a manuscript and its most effective presentation, to the physical manufacture and distribution of the finished book. Successively, readers as self-publishers will learn to become: writer, editor, designer, typesetter, production supervisor, salesperson, advertiser, promoter, public relations specialist, financier, business manager, and bookkeeper. The authors furnish solid counsel yet write with refreshing informality. The text is enriched by the Rosses' own experiences as self-publishing pioneers, lecturers and consultants—which they recount with an unabashed flair for self-promotion—and permeated with their contagious enthusiasm. The work is colorful enough to intrigue and amuse even the veteran.

The Rosses are particularly strong in areas in which the traditional mainstream book industry has always been weak: marketing, promotion, advertising, publicity and public relations. Page after page in this book bristles with bright ideas and clever ploys for bringing books and readers together. The authors wisely advocate, furthermore, that awareness of readers and their needs should dominate publishers' thinking throughout the publishing process to ensure a responsible and successful outcome.

But do I really need to go into so much detail, you ask? I'm not looking for a career; all I want is to have fun and give people who are genuinely interested in my work a chance to lay their hands on it. Perhaps my book won't be as well edited, designed, typeset, printed, bound, marketed, advertised or sold as the Rosses advocate. But is that really necessary?

You alone know how seriously to take your publishing project. I suggest that if you respect your work and have consideration for your readers, you will edit and design your book as well as possible. A poorly edited book is difficult to read, confusing and unconvincing. A poorly designed or printed one is hard on the eye, unattractive and boring. Furthermore, if you fail to publicize and promote your title, no one will ever find out about it. Even with a vigorous PR program it is difficult to gain attention for one of the more than 50,000 titles published each year, which add to the more than 600,000 titles in print. Remember that publishing costs and the time spent with your project will not diminish significantly if you try to get by with only a minimal effort. Having already invested in bringing the title into print, don't you owe it to yourself to obtain the best possible response for it by marketing it properly? Anything worth doing, it seems to me, is still worth doing well.

Self-publishing, like all enterprises, is likely to benefit you in proportion to your investment in it. If in addition to a fair profit and an author's pride, you can reap from it the satisfaction of having done a professional publishing job, you will experience the magical glow prized by those for whom publishing has become a unique joy and a life's vocation.

After that, who knows?

John P. Dessauer

INTRODUCTION: WHO IS THIS BOOK FOR?

First, let us identify the three routes to publishing and clarify some terminology. A writer can be self-published, subsidy-published, or commercially-published.

Self-publishers are sometimes called private publishers, independent publishers, small presses (though usually this denotes a publisher of several titles), or alternative publishers. But whatever label they may wear, they are, in a word, "mavericks." And they are part of a larger whole known as the small-press movement, which, by the way, is growing at a breathtaking rate and has achieved complete respectability.

We have just received notification that the R. R. Bowker Company is now making available mailing lists of new publishers. This list contains 1,200 new publishers each quarter. That means almost 5,000 new publishers are starting up each year—far in excess of previous industry guesstimates!

So that no one is confused, let us make it clear that we are not talking here about "vanity" or "subsidy" publishing. In subsidy publishing, the author who pays a special kind of publisher to do his or her book is stigmatized because book reviewers and bookstores usually shun subsidy titles, and usually finds that the book's sales are next to nothing. In the last chapter of this guide we explore subsidy publishing in detail.

Commercial publishing houses are those that offer writers royalties on their work. The vast majority of them are located in New York City. Surprisingly, there are only about three hundred large-scale trade publishers. Many medium-sized houses dot the country and often specialize in specific subject areas such as gardening, health, or cookbooks.

Interestingly, the employees of many of these houses will find this book of great use. It will open exciting new vistas for interns—giving them a quick, broad overview of the industry. Even seasoned personnel will find within these pages answers to various questions, plus innovative marketing strategies often ignored in the rush to meet conglomerate demands.

And because self-publishing is but a microcosm of the whole publishing industry, universities offering publishing courses will find *The Complete Guide to Self-Publishing* an unequaled textbook.

Who self-publishes?

Over the years there have been scattered reports of private literary accomplishments. Many of the folks responsible for these success stories were courageous writers who, after being turned away by traditional publishers, have published their own books.

Self-publishing is an exciting alternative to the millions of rejection slips authors collect each year. Repeated rejection can smother the hopes of ordinary men and women. But for the hearty, the courageous, it serves as a challenge. They decide to launch their own work. They become self-publishers. This book is for them.

It is also for entrepreneurs seeking to exploit their own knowledge. Here they will discover proven methods for packaging and promoting ideas, concepts, experience, and skills. And it's been shown time and again that authoring a book gives a businessperson fresh visibility and credibility.

A book is the ideal "product." Unlike a gadget or process that others can modify only slightly and pass off as their own, your book is protected by a copyright. You have an exclusive; no one else can market an identical product. Another reason a book can be preferable to an invention is that a patent only runs for seventeen years, whereas an author's copyright is good for life plus fifty years. Fortunes have been amassed by average people who wrote a book or booklet, then merchandised it through direct marketing techniques. This guide shows businesspeople how to establish a publishing venture to sell their specialized information.

The Complete Guide to Self-Publishing is also for doctors, ministers, educators, counselors, attorneys—any professional who wants to share knowledge or philosophies. Many men and women are opting to capitalize on their expertise this way.

Associations, professional societies, churches, and other non-profit entities will find this manual of great value. Such groups often discover that publishing a book builds their reputation, expands their sphere of influence, and is an effective fund-raising tool. For associations, a book provides an ideal forum for lobbying efforts.

A low-key book about their business, a corporate history, or a colorful chief executive's story can also benefit corporations. Many have found that such a publication stimulates interest in their product or service. A book can also help to establish corporate identity and attract investors. And many corporations are finding that it makes sense to publish information previously used solely in-house. This product gives them a new revenue base.

But what of authors who currently have a book placed with a regular commercial publisher? Will this handbook be of any help to them? It's indispensable! Statistics show that of all the titles put out by commercial houses, only three out of ten are financial successes. It's imperative that authors take the initiative to help their books stand out from the herd! Bowker's Books in Print reports that over 665,000 books are currently in print. And some 53,000 more are ground out each year.

Moreover, unknown writers are hurt by the fact that a disproportionate chunk of advertising dollars is spent for authors with established track records or those with celebrity status and a "name." The Gospel According to Publishers' Row says that you market one in every twenty books hard, take a few healthy swipes at one out of every three, and wait and see about the rest.

This wait-and-see attitude is death to the average author's work. Happily, it needn't be. A book that is perceived as strong in the marketplace will command the necessary resources to become strong. That's where you can play an enormously vital role! This guide will give you the savvy and clout needed to leverage yourself and your book to a position of power.

Noted industry analyst John Dessauer wrote in the October, 1987, issue of *Small Press* magazine, "It appears inevitable that frustrated authors will in the future make far greater use of small publishers, or even of self-publishing, to bring their work to market. The impact of this development is likely to be massive and profound."

And for the author whose title has already languished to out-of-print status, herein are tips on how to bolt from the trade publisher that has let your work die. Books that were neglected through disinterest or blundering have later soared to great profits or acclaim through the efforts of their authors. Here you'll learn how to regain the rights to your book and how to republish and market it successfully.

Lastly, this guide is for people considering paying to have their book produced by a subsidy (vanity) press. We examine the realities of this form of publishing, and offer thought-provoking comments on this controversial method of getting into print.

While certainly not a new field, self-publishing is becoming increasingly popular. The *Los Angeles Times* stated, "Self-publishing has become respectable and even fun" (not to mention a money-maker for those who approach it properly). *Writer's Digest* magazine called it "the do-it-yourself way to success."

This is more than just a growing trend. With computer technology becoming cheaper and easier to use, there's an exciting revolution brewing in self-publishing. The information explosion is fully upon us. Good news, indeed, since how-to and self-help are the bread and butter of publishing.

Publishing is not an act of God; it is a series of actions. To receive the greatest benefit from the information contained in *The Complete Guide to Self-Publishing*, we suggest you first read the whole manual *before* starting to apply any of it. Then go back and take things one step at a time. This is the point when you'll be able to use the "publishing timetable" on page 350. The timetable shows you each of the major steps you must take in the order they are taken.

To simplify things, we'll be referring to a "book" throughout. If you're doing booklets, reports, monographs, or chapbooks, please substitute the appropriate word. For additional clarity and ease, a list of resources and marketing contacts, a bibliography, a glossary, and a comprehensive index are included.

To our knowledge no other reference work contains so much detailed information for authors, publishers, and entrepreneurs . . . nor so many examples of things that work. We hope you find the reading interesting, the material helpful, and your endeavors pleasurable and profitable. To your success!

CHAPTER 1

THE PLEASURES AND PITFALLS OF SELF-PUBLISHING

Are you the type of person who wants to be behind the wheel rather than go along for the ride? Then you have the stuff self-publishers are made of. They choose to control their own destinies. Piloting a plane is much like driving a car, except that in flying, the operator's sights are set higher. So why don't you step into the cockpit, get your publication airborne, and pilot it to success! The feeling is exhilarating, the rewards are great, and it is a lot simpler than it may seem. Not necessarily easy, mind you, but simple. Of course, as everyone who has gone before can tell you, the ride can sometimes get bumpy. Self-publishing, much like flying, offers exciting highs and some worrisome bumps ... the pleasures and pitfalls of the trade.

Success stories from yesterday and today

Self-publishing—the act of privately producing and marketing your own work—is an American tradition as old as the thirteen colonies. Ben Franklin is credited as the first American to take this bold step. Tom Paine was another early American self-publisher. Since then, many famous men and women have first appeared on the literary scene through their own publishing efforts.

Fiction has often been successfully self-published. We might not have the marvelous story of *Huckleberry Finn* if Mark Twain hadn't become a self-publisher. The reception that traditional publishers gave Zane Grey's first novel, *Betty Zane*, was as cool as the backside of a pillow. Consequently, he decided to produce it himself. Among others who have been successful through self-publishing are Anaïs Nin, Walt Whitman, Virginia Woolf, Gertrude Stein, Edgar Allan Poe, even James Joyce with his classic *Ulysses*. Another name not normally associated with self-publishing is Carl Sandburg. Sandburg not only wrote poems but set them in type, rolled the presses, hand-pulled the galley proofs, and bound the books himself.

Can you guess what novel was printed in Florence, Italy? It was too controversial for its time, but D. H. Lawrence realized that the Italians couldn't read what they were printing, so that's where *Lady Chatterley's Lover* was first produced. And what of the Tarzan series? Think of the jungle drama that might never have been if Edgar Rice Burroughs hadn't taken matters into his own hands.

Some of the reference works that we value today were introduced years ago by their authors. This is how *Robert's Rules of Order* and, in 1855, *Bartlett's Familiar Quotations* came to be. Most writers are familiar with a small but superb book titled *The Elements of Style*. William Strunk, Jr., breathed life into it himself when he had it printed in the early 1900s as a text for his English classes at Cornell.

In 1969 when John Muir came out with his classic *How to Keep Your VW Alive*, he had no idea he was launching a publishing empire. On *VW*'s heels came more books from this prolific author. Today, though John has passed away, he left a legacy, John Muir Publications, Inc., that has spread its publishing wings to include titles in such diverse areas as travel, gardening, flea markets, self-defense, computers, guitars, sports, and books about birth and death.

The phenomenally successful *What Color Is Your Parachute?* began its trek to best-seller status as a self-published book. Richard Nelson Bolles, an Episcopal clergyman, originally wrote it for other clergy contemplating a return to secular life. When Ten Speed Press took over this career-counseling handbook, Bolles was asked to make a few revisions to give the book broader appeal. Broad appeal is putting it mildly: *What Color Is Your Parachute?* has sold 3.5 million copies and is good for about 300,000 a year for as long as it's in print. It's been ordered in bulk by the Pentagon and General Electric and used as a textbook in countless classes.

Vicki Lansky submitted her book *Feed Me! I'm Yours* to no fewer than forty-nine publishers before she and her husband, Bruce, got fed up (no pun intended) and decided to publish it themselves. This little book is a guide to making fresh, pure baby food at home. It contains some two hundred recipes for sneaking nutrition into infants and toddlers.

Because they lived on a street named Meadowbrook, the Lanskys dubbed their publishing company Meadowbrook Press. Was the decision to self-publish wise? *Feed Me!* sold 300,000 copies in the original edition; Bantam bought the paperback rights and moved another 500,000 books; and Meadowbrook now has 622,000 copies in print of their comb-bound edition. Not too shabby for a book the trade publishers wouldn't touch! Next Vicki wrote *The Taming of the C-A-N-D-Y Monster,* which headed the *New York Times* best-seller list for trade paperbacks. Meadowbrook, under the creative hand of Bruce Lansky, has gone on to join the ranks of trade publishers, with fifty-eight titles listed in its catalog.

Robert Ringer is a name that has become almost a household word due to the efforts of none other than Mr. Ringer himself. His *Winning Through Intimidation, Restoring the American Dream,* and *Looking Out for Number 1* brought him both fame and fortune. Having mastered the technique of catapulting his own books to best-seller status, he launched an imprint, QED, which publishes books by other authors.

Another self-published book captured the number 10 spot on the *New York Times* best-seller list in February 1980. *On a Clear Day You Can See General Motors* was written and published by a free-lance journalist, J. Patrick Wright. The book is a classical muck-raking job in the Ralph Nader tradition. Press coverage and word of mouth in the business community put it on the best-seller list. But that was only the beginning of this self-published bonanza. Avon bought the paperback rights for a hefty $247,500; it was picked up by a Macmillan book club and by the Conservative Book Club; and Japanese translation rights were sold.

Beverly Nye gathered together some notes from a homemaking class and put out a book called *A Family Raised on Sunshine.* After selling 15,000 copies herself, she turned the rights over to Writer's Digest Books, which peddled another 100,000. Nye went on to write *A Family Raised on Rainbows,* which WDB also took over and merchandised to best-seller status. Ultimately, the rights to these two titles were sold to Bantam. After positive results with *Sunshine* and *Rainbows,* Bantam contracted with Beverly for another book and is discussing a fourth.

Few people know that Gale Research Company began as a self-publishing venture in the bedroom of Frederick G. (Gale) Ruffner. Today this highly respected book publisher has some 500 employees and is a leader in producing library reference works of all kinds.

The Handbook to Higher Consciousness, written and published by Ken Keyes, Jr., stands tall in the annals of success; it has sold more than one million copies. It is the flagship book of a publishing organization that currently has ten titles in print. Keyes has even gone on to establish a college offering courses in the "Science of Happiness."

A book lodged firmly on the *Publishers Weekly* Bestseller List as we go to press is Louise Hay's *You Can Heal Your Life.* Sales are currently at the 600,000 mark. Louise has refused offers from several large publishers for mass-market paperback rights. Smart lady, that one.

But perhaps the biggest contemporary self-publishing all-star is Peter McWilliams and his Prelude Press of Los Angeles. Peter's track record is astonishing for a self-publisher: He has sold nearly 3 million books! Poetry was his first endeavor, followed by a number 1 *New York Times* best-seller on transcendental meditation. Then came the early eighties and popularized computers. McWilliams began by writing articles about The Word, a spell-checker program. Next he was asked to do a 3,000-word piece on word processing. When his 3,000-word article mushroomed to 25,000-plus words, he knew he had a book. Thus *The Personal Computer Book* was born. Soon after, it had siblings named *The Word Processing Book, The Personal Computer in Business Book,* and *Questions and Answers in Word Processing.* McWilliams put Prelude Press up for sale in 1983. The *Wall Street Journal* reported he was offered $1 million in addition to royalties!

Rewards vs. stumbling blocks

Self-publishing offers the potential for huge profits. No longer do you have to be satisfied with the meager 6 to 15 percent royalty that commercial publishers dole out. For those who use creativity, persistence, and sound business sense, money is there to be made.

Self-publishing can be the road to independence. What motivates entrepreneurs to launch their own business? They want to be their own bosses. So said 82 percent of those surveyed in a recent study. More personal freedom was the second most important reason. Most people dream of becoming self-employed. You can turn that dream into reality. Here is a dynamic, proven way to shape your own destiny. It is an answer not only for city folks but for homesteaders seeking a way to make a living in remote areas. (Do we ever know about *that*, living and working in a lonely secluded town of only 2,000.)

Becoming a self-publisher also provides a helpful tax shelter. After forming your own company and meeting certain requirements, you can write off a portion of your home and deduct some expenses related to writing and to marketing, such as automobile, travel, and entertainment costs.

Another advantage is that you can begin your business on a part-time basis while keeping your present job. Why risk your livelihood until you've refined your publishing activities and worked out any bugs?

Want control over your work? In self-publishing *you* guide every step. You'll have the cover you like, the typeface you choose, the title you want, the ads you decide to place. Your decision is final. Nothing is left in the hands of an editor or marketing person who has dozens (or hundreds) of other books to worry about. You maintain absolute control over your own book. (Along with this advantage, however, comes the fact that you also get stuck *doing* everything.)

Privately publishing your work also gives you the advantage of speed. Big trade houses typically take from a year to a year and a half to get a book out. Self-publishers can do it in a fraction of that time. Zilpha Main, who self-published her book *Reaching 90 — My Way*, commented when asked why she took that approach, "At my age I can't wait for New York publishers to make up their minds." Most SP-ers agree. Peter McWilliams readily admits he self-publishes "out of self-defense." Had he waited for Publishers' Row to get his book out, his phenomenal story would have had a very different ending.

If your venture blossoms and the company expands by publishing others' work, you have fresh opportunities to join the growing small-press movement. You can set policy, serve as a spokesperson, and bring deserving writers to the public's attention.

The publishing business is a constant flow of exciting events. You will never forget that supreme moment when you hold the first copy of your very own book, just off the press. When the book starts making the rounds, things happen. There's a domino effect. One day you get your first fan letter (most likely read with blurry vision). Then a prestigious person gets wind of the book and requests an examination copy. Magazines or newspaper syndicates inquire about subsidiary rights. Library orders start flowing in.

And, lo and behold, the biggies — those publishers that previously rejected your work — just may decide to reverse their decision. Self-publishing can be the springboard to lucrative contracts with traditional publishers who were afraid to gamble before. Once the marketability of your book has been proven, they will be eager to take it off your hands.

That's what happened to Roger Von Oech. After writing and publishing *A Whack on the Side of the Head*, which shows how to be a more creative thinker, he sold some thirty thousand copies himself. Then he allowed Warner Books to get into the act. Says Roger, "It was a good deal for both of us." One of the things he negotiated into his contract was a commitment from Warner to spend $75,000 on promotion. Von Oech has traveled to more than twenty-five cities and appeared on 110 shows.

Freda Morris sold her first privately published book, *Self-Hypnosis in Two Days*, to E. P. Dutton for a $5,000 advance. Her next book was gobbled up by Harper & Row shortly after it, too, was self-published. And after Ernest Callenbach sold 35,000 copies of his novel *Ecotopia* under his own imprint of Banyan Tree Books, Bantam took it over and printed another 130,000. Well-known paperback houses also pick up the rights to reprint self-published softcover books that do well in the original edition.

In an interesting switch, Putnam picked up the rights to one of our client's books, *Why Jenny Can't Lead*. The self-published paperback version sold 20,000 copies at $10 each. Then Putnam slapped a new title on it, used the same interior pages we had prepared for our client, and put it out as a hardcover for $14.95. After paying the authors a substantial advance, that is.

Of course, like any business, self-publishing has some stumbling blocks you should be aware of.

Contrary to what Mama always said, you must become a braggart. You'll need to learn to toot your own horn. Since you — and you alone — will be promoting this book, it is up to you to tell anybody and everybody how great it is! (Later chapters will show you how to do this without revealing that it is actually *you* doing the bragging.)

It is an investment; an investment in yourself. As in any business, you will require start-up capital. There must be enough money to print the book, send out review copies, sustain an advertising campaign, and so forth. How much depends on many variables. How long will your book be? Will it have photographs inside? Will the cover be full-color? Will you type it, do it on a computer, or have it typeset? How many copies will you print and on what quality of paper? See what we mean? The costs vary drastically. You might skimp by on a few hundred dollars for a booklet on which you do most of the work yourself. On the other hand, you could spend over $30,000 on a coffee-table book with lots of color photographs. Generally speaking, to produce a professional-quality book and promote it properly, you'll be in the range of $10,000 to $15,000 in today's marketplace. But be forewarned: Lack of market analysis, careful planning, budgeting, and persistence has caused some people to lose their investments. (Don't despair if your budget's as tight as fiddle strings. We'll be showing you some innovative ways to generate working capital in a later chapter.)

You should be willing to devote a substantial block of time to your publishing project. While this can be spread over a long period, there is no getting around the fact that to have a dynamite book, you must spend much time writing it, revising it, producing it, and promoting it.

The many hats of a self-publisher

A basic truth for most self-publishers is that they start out alone. That being the case, you will find yourself wearing many hats. Just because you may be an amateur doesn't mean the book you produce will be flawed. By studying and applying yourself, you can wear the various hats well. Many self-publishers never draw on outside help to do their books — and you can do it all yourself, too, if you choose.

• Writer. The basic foundation for your enterprise. Study your craft and refine your product. Good, readable works sell much more readily than disorganized garble or lofty dissertations.

• Editor. If you're not lucky enough to have a qualified friend or relative to edit — one who knows the English language and will be objective —

the task falls to you. Do it well.

• Designer/Artist. Many books and book covers are self-illustrated or -designed. Even if you decide to get professional free-lance help it would be foolhardy not to get somewhat involved personally.

• Typesetter/Compositor. If you decide to type the finished manuscript yourself or use a computer to prepare camera-ready copy, you become a typesetter. More and more authors are opting for this choice. We discuss the pros and cons in the later chapter "Computers in Publishing."

• Printer. You may even be your own printer. Thousands of booklets are created each year at copy shops. In this case you are also the printer. Learn what will and will not provide crisp copies. Avoid wasted time creating masters that will not provide an acceptable end result.

• Financier/Accountant. You are the chief accountant, bookkeeper, and company representative to your banker. You must keep good records for yourself . . . and for the IRS.

• Marketeer. It doesn't matter how well all other hats fit if you don't wear this one well. Be imaginative and creative. Go ahead and slip into flamboyance when you don this hat. Shrewd promotion and sales strategies will do much to ensure your publishing project's success.

• Shipper/Warehouser. It doesn't do any good to get book orders unless you can fill and ship them. While this is a routine job, it takes time, space, and energy.

• Legal Adviser. Many times attorneys collect sizable fees for answering simple business questions. Take a good look at the question. The use of common sense and comparison to similar situations will often save a fee. There are instances, however, where you definitely need an attorney — you've been accused of libel or copyright infringement, for instance.

• Business Manager. This hat has been saved for the last, but not because it's a low priority. Quite the opposite. You can do a fantastic job on all other aspects of the business and still lose your shirt if this hat isn't secured firmly on your noggin. In fact, a recent Small Business Administration study showed that 93 percent of the businesses that failed did so because of poor management practices. The job of business manager can be a piece of cake or an absolute nightmare — it's up to you. Managing a company is fun if you establish and adhere to operating procedures designed for that business.

Be prepared to fall and skin your knees occasionally. No one has all the answers; certainly not a new self-publisher. While we have compiled this reference to help you avoid mistakes, there will be times when you'll goof or when nothing seems to be going your way. Hang in there! Soon things will take a positive turn. As in anything, there are pitfalls, but there are also many pleasures. Move ahead with passion and conviction and you will succeed.

Identifying your motivation

Not everyone self-publishes for the same reason.

Probably most SP-ers, however, choose this alternative for financial gain. They recognize that here is a potential for much greater returns than any other publishing avenue offers. Take Jim Everroad, for instance. Everroad was a high school gymnastic coach in Columbus, Indiana, before he published a thirty-two-page booklet called *How to Flatten Your Stomach*. It sold a whopping 1.5 million copies and was number one on the best-seller list for so long that many thought it had taken up permanent residence. Now the ex-coach has gone on to endorse and market an exercise device called the Belly Burner, which is advertised on national television.

Bernard Kamoroff, having retired from his CPA practice, found himself seeking something to boost his self-esteem. He put together a book originally called *How to Be a Small-Time Operator and Stay Out of Trouble*. It has since been shortened to *Small-Time Operator*. This little beauty grossed its owner $300,000 the first four years it was out. And it's an ideal ongoing money-maker. Kamoroff updates it annually and has an extensive chain of distributors. Having attained his goal of creating a project that would give him purpose, he now spends about twenty hours a week on his publishing venture.

Literary contribution is an important facet of self-publishing. As trade publishers become more and more preoccupied with celebrity books and sure bets, good literary writers turn more and more to self-publishing. Here they find an outlet for their novels, poetry, and other serious literary works.

Many sensitive men and women are not concerned with making a profit. Instead, they need to see their work in print—to hold in their hands a book with their name as author. Some have spent arduous years submitting and having manuscripts returned, cutting and rewriting and sending again, vainly trying to please an editor, any editor. Often those few who do sell find their work whittled and changed beyond recognition. Even more frustrated are those with a strong belief in their work, who have not been willing to alter it and have thus found themselves without a market. Often these are people who want to share their personal adventures, experiences, and feelings with generations to come. Or perhaps they are the more creative artists and poets whose work is too innovative to be appreciated by the regular markets.

Some people and organizations publish to espouse a cause they feel strongly about. Many alternative publishers use their books to tout anti-establishment political views or to talk about gay rights. We had a client who was vehemently opposed to abortion. A gifted writer, she published a poetic book extolling the right of unborn children to live.

We recently consulted on a book for the National Buffalo Association. *Buffalo Management and Marketing* not only offers unique information about the buffalo but also served as an effective national attention-getter for the NBA. Through our book promotional efforts, we were able to get the organization's executive director on seven hundred radio stations, where she talked about the book, the association, and the benefits of eating buffalo meat.

Your book can have an impact on the lives of thousands—maybe even millions—of people. You have the opportunity to influence the thoughts and actions of your readers ... to sow the seeds of hope, to motivate, to entertain, to inform. Your words are preserved for posterity.

To some, self-publishing is simply fun. They embark on kitchen-table publishing like kids with new toys. Their motive is simply to enjoy themselves. Alas, some also end up making money, too.

Another less widely admitted reason for producing your own book is for ego gratification. It's downright satisfying to see your name emblazoned across the cover of a book. And your friends and associates immediately regard you as a celebrity. "Oh, he/she is an author," they whisper in reverent tones.

For those more practically minded, publishing your own book can be a springboard to other revenue-generating activities. Roger Von Oech says candidly that his book is great advertising for his consulting business. One of our clients who did a guide on how to find a mate—and who also happened to run a dating service—found his matchmaking appointment calendar overflowing when word of his new book got out. Many authors discover paid lectures and seminar programs open to them once they've established their expertise between book covers.

A surprising number of our current clients are Ph.D.'s or other professionals. They've discovered that being an author gives them added visibility and credibility.

Whether your desire is to cart bags of money off to the bank or to etch a new line in the face of literary America, it's time to set some goals.

Setting goals

Before you move ahead on your self-publishing venture, establish concrete goals. Over and over, it has been proven that those who take the time to think through and *write down* the desired results in terms of specific steps are the people who achieve success. Experts tell us that we can program our subconscious to help bring about something we genuinely want.

There are two things you must know to reach a goal. First, it must be clearly identified and quantified. Second, goals should be written and affirmed as though they already existed. To affirm something, you write and/or state it repeatedly, *sincerely believing it has already been accomplished.* You can do this even before you've written your book.

Your affirmation might go something like this: "I have sold five thousand copies of *My Story* as of January 1, 1991. Gross income from these sales is $45,000, and the net profit is $10,000." Or you might say, "I have written a book that is being very well received. It is helping hundreds of people every month." By expressing what you want to happen in the present tense, you condition your subconscious mind to accept it as fact. This method is taught by most success motivators.

Write your affirmation several times each morning and evening. Tack it up on the refrigerator, on the bathroom mirror, on the car dashboard; tuck it in your top desk drawer or in your wallet. Refer to it often. Repeat it aloud. Believe it! By planting this seed of positive expectancy, we condition ourselves to move toward our goals swiftly and unswervingly.

To further promote positive goal setting, we'd recommend adding two books to your library: *Psycho-Cybernetics,* by Maxwell Maltz, and *Think and Grow Rich,* by Napoleon Hill. This type of reading helps form the goal-setting, success habit needed to build a solid business foundation.

Now that you've set your overall goal, what steps will most effectively get you there? As we said earlier it would be wise to read this whole guide before you map out the route that will best lead to your long-range destination. You may decide that mail-order sales hold the key to success. Maybe selling to schools will get you there the fastest. Which avenue you choose for self-publishing sales is up to you, so long as it brings you to the desired results.

What is important is that you lay out the course. Write the steps involved. Break down the overall process into easily digestible chunks. Chew on them. Spit out those that don't work. Take more generous bites of those that are satisfying. Set your goals and plan carefully for a successful journey.

The first leg of your trip has to do with developing a winning manuscript. Your book is your product. How can you assure that it is a good one?

CHAPTER 2

CHOOSING A MARKETABLE SUBJECT

As a self-publisher, you will go into business. The first and most important step any potential businessperson takes is to decide what product or service to offer customers. So, too, you must determine your "vehicle." Some forms of writing hold more promise for commercial success than others. Many people dream of turning out a volume of poetry, writing a novel, or telling their life story. They feel a deep commitment to good literature. If making money is their primary aim, however, they face an uphill climb. There are some tips that will help, though, and they are discussed in this chapter.

Whether you've already written your book, know what you are going to write about, or have yet to pick a subject, there are several steps you can take to assure the salability of your manuscript. A marketable subject is vital both for commercial publication and self-publishing. In this chapter we'll be exploring how to choose a salable topic; how to tap into your personal storehouse of knowledge and write about what you know. We'll look at using cookbooks as fund-raisers and discuss ways to develop titles that "hook" readers. Writing novels, poetry, and other literary works for self-expression and the pure joy of it will also be covered.

Some books quickly establish phenomenal sales records and rocket to best-seller status, while others sit in warehouses awaiting unceremonious last rites. Why? There are two reasons: The winners are usually about hot, timely subjects, and they've been soundly promoted.

Subject matter greatly influences your book's track record. Choosing a marketable topic is the first step toward the best-seller dream to which all authors cling (secretly or admittedly). But how do you know what's marketable?

Nonfiction tops the list. Americans are hungry for information. It can take the form of a book that shows how to do or make something or gives a formula for self-improvement. Books that show readers how to be wealthier, healthier, or sexier lead the pack.

But perhaps the thought of writing a whole book seems as ambitious to you as scaling Mount Everest. Then climb a smaller peak. You might prepare and sell a booklet, report, or chapbook.

Capitalizing on new trends

Beyond the general hunger of Americans to be skinny, rich, and popular, certain specific topics are more salable than others. Catching the tide of current or anticipated trends is certainly one good way to find a salable topic. By staying alert you can recognize a hidden need for information before others. Bingo! A timely, marketable subject.

Such was the case of the first book about cooking in crock pots. The author attended a trade show and noticed that several manufacturers were introducing these new devices. Presto! The lights flashed. Would cooks need new recipes and guidance on how best to use their new cookware? You better believe they would! Since Mable Hoffman's *Crockery Cookery* came out in 1975, over 3 million copies have been sold.

In 1978 when we wrote *The Encyclopedia of Self-Publishing,* the forerunner of this book, we stated, "An opportunity we see on the horizon is in the field of home computers . . . potential buyers need advice in layman's terms on how to select a computer best suited to their needs." (We should have taken our own advice!) Adam Osborne and Peter McWilliams jumped on that bandwagon early, published how-to books, and made a mint. Osborne's *An Introduction to Microcomputers* sold out its first run of 20,000 in three months. It was adopted by dozens of universities as a text, and Adam became the darling of the home computer industry. But today there is a glut of computer books. To be successful in this arena now, an author must find an ingenious approach to the subject.

Take the advice of Mark Van Doren: "Welcome all ideas and entertain them royally, for one of them may be king." Tune in to hot topics. But be careful not to be trapped by a fad. When it comes to "fad-itis," no one is immune. The trick lies in determining the difference between a fad, which can be here today and gone tomorrow, and a genuine trend. Ignore the transient fads. Don't let a turkey gobble up your time and money. As we go to press, regional books are especially active, indicating a trend.

In fact, we've had so many client inquiries on how to do books about a specific geographic area that we recently wrote and published *How to Make Big Profits Publishing City and Regional Books*.

And the *New York Times* reports that several genres have made comebacks recently, including the crime classics of the thirties, forties, and fifties, as well as science fiction/fantasy serials.

Children's books are also hot. The number of hardcover children's books sold in 1987 increased 23 percent over 1986; paperback sales were up 16 percent, says the president of the Children's Book Council. Ambitious yuppie parents and adoring grandparents with more spendable income can be thanked for this trend.

How can you tell a genuine ongoing trend from a mere novelty? The best you can do is a shrewd guess. Ask yourself if it's a single, freaky happening unrelated to anything else — say, a pet rock — or an eruption into wide popularity of something of longstanding interest — fitness, maybe, or organically grown foods. Ask yourself if a lot of people are likely to still be interested in it in a year or two. Think whether other ideas in this field have tended to flash and die or whether they've lasted at least long enough for a book on the subject to be written, published, and find an interested readership. You can't really know for sure, but you can do your best to see that the star to which you've hitched your hopes isn't bright just because it's falling.

The current craze is New Age literature. There are books on channeling, crystals, self-actualization, you name it. Shirley MacLaine touched off this fire with her books and TV special; it has burned unabated ever since. Even publishers who had old books that could fit this label have dusted them off and brought them back into the spotlight to capitalize on the public interest.

Americans continue to be caught up in the running craze. There are scores of books on this pastime. It would make no sense to come out with another run-of-the-mill (pardon the pun) tome on jogging. If you are clever, however, you may find a new way to ride the wave of interest others have generated. That's what Kenneth Cooper did with *New Aerobics*.

How many books on a subject are too many? Look closely at the competition. Do the existing books leave a gap your book could turn into a target? Remember, if your book is to stand out from the pack, it must have a fresh angle, offer a unique approach or information to persuade a prospective reader to buy it, rather than one of the others. Ask a few bookstore managers how well your competition is selling; if it's one a month, maybe you ought to choose another project. If bookstores are reordering frequently and getting lots of requests, then maybe your book will do well, too.

When searching for a marketable subject, one trick is to look at what type of book is selling well, then take a different approach. Figure out how to be better than the pack. For instance, books on securing a job are in great demand — and in abundant supply. So what about a book on how to cope if you think your present job may be threatened? Sorry, it's been done. It's called *The Termination Trap: Best Strategies for a Job Going Sour.* Author Stephen Cohen provides instructions on job-keeping skills, job-saving skills, and job-leaving skills.

Yet another approach was selected recently by Price Stern Sloan. As a takeoff on *Smart Women Foolish Choices*, they published a spoof entitled *Smart Women Stupid Books*. Their parody defines the problem (too many worthless men) and offers the solution (date them anyway).

For a self-publisher it's important to select a specific, clearly defined market. Write for dog lovers, organic gardeners, two-career families. By purposely ignoring big, general groups and targeting a select audience, you can discover a ready market, which is easier to reach.

Evaluate the market. People may be willing to buy and own several cookbooks or gardening guides, because these subjects are broad and of general interest. But how many books on hang gliding or training your pet gerbil to do tricks would *you* want to own? If one would be enough (or too much!), your entry into an already crowded field could not be expected to do very well. Take these things into account and remember that your book's success isn't just dependent on how good a book it is of its type; it'll depend on how many people need and want it. Don't let your enthusiasm for bringing out a complete guide to bee-keeping blind you to the limited appeal of the subject.

As you climb the sheer cliffs of self-publishing, look for tiny crevices that have been passed over by the "big guys." You're a lot less likely to be outscaled by the competition if you define a small niche and address yourself to that audience. For instance, major trade publishers weren't inclined to do a children's guide to San Diego, but a private publisher tackled this topic very successfully.

"Positioning" for profit

Positioning your product can give you extra sales clout. To "position" means to give your book a competitive edge by making it different or special in some way. Let's use cookies as an example. They are positioned in the following ways: chewy, crunchy, nutritious, like Grandma used to make, etc.

In our seminars, we tell the story of the *Starving Students Cookbook*. Its sales were lagging until the author decided to try packaging the book with two inexpensive skillets, shrink wrapping them together, and offering them in Price Clubs and K Marts. When 150 sold in a test store the first two days, everybody knew they had a winning idea on their hands.

And a cookbook was positioned as a gift item by dressing it up with a scarlet ribbon and some cinnamon sticks — then placing it in the house-wares department. By the way, while it languished at $5.95 in bookstores, it sold feverishly for $10 in department stores.

You can position your book in other ways as well: We advised one client who was producing a nautical book to use water-resistant paper so boating enthusiasts could use his manual on the seas without fear of ruining it. One small press in California doubled their sales by adding a "workbook" to their self-help publication. And a Texas small publisher put out *Your Housekeeping Cookbook* as a bilingual presentation giving recipes and menus in both English and Spanish, thus setting themselves apart from other cookbooks.

Some publishers position their books by virtue of price. A $9.95 paper-back edition may be slanted for bookstores or specialty retail outlets, while a $29.95 version (called a *kit*, packaged in a three-ring binder, and perhaps containing some inexpensive related doodad tucked in the binder pocket) is targeted for sales direct to the consumer.

Creative, product-engineered strategies such as these, when used in the early stages, can pay big dividends later on.

Write what you know

Of course, you can also hook up to your own personal knowledge. Joe Karbo, king of mail-order self-help books, commented before his death, "You bet your sweet patootie I've made a bundle sharing my information. And why not? I invested a lot more time and money in my 'education' than most doctors and lawyers."

There are things you can write about effectively and profitably even if you've never written anything in your life. No matter who you are, where you live, or how old you are, you know more about *something* than most other folks, and therefore you possess special knowledge that other people will pay for. All you have to do is write what you know! People from all walks of life, not just professional writers, do it all the time.

A man who designed company symbols and did advertising layout wrote a book on logo design. He sells it as a "minicourse" and gets fifty bucks a crack for it. A young woman successfully sued her former employer for sex discrimination. Then she documented the steps taken and made her information available to help others fight similar injustices.

A businessman who holds exclusive import rights to a small water pump wrote and markets a booklet telling how to build ceramic fountains — which just happen to use his pump. A plastic surgeon does a book, complete with before and after photographs, on the wonders of cosmetic surgery. A lesbian who has come out of the closet writes of her experiences and adjustments to publicly admitting her homosexuality.

Venus Andrecht cultivated an interest in herbs into a multichannel business that includes a career as an author and self-publisher, lecturer, expert on herbs, and entrepreneur extraordinaire. Her book, *The Outrageous Herb Lady,* is subtitled "How to Make a Mint in Selling and Multilevel Marketing." She sells it to her existing network of herb buyers, dealers, distributors, customers, clients, and students.

And that's just the tip of the iceberg. Each year thousands of people add substantially to their income by putting together a book, booklet, or monograph, then merchandising it through direct-marketing techniques. We have one associate whose mailbox is full of orders each month as a result of a book she wrote after cruising the Caribbean for four months. Her cookbook for sailors gives practical boating hints, some two hundred galley-tested recipes for canned goods, and oodles of information on provisioning for long voyages.

But Shirley didn't stop there. She has gone on to write and publish a Spanish book and a book of sea chanties. One thing has led to another. She now does a column for *Sea Magazine,* writes occasional book reviews for the *San Diego Union,* and has established a business delivering yachts.

Another friend, a management consultant, is putting the final touches on a manuscript to show individuals how to develop their personal management potential. After tottering on the verge of bankruptcy, one man wrote a detailed report on his findings. Not only did he *not* go bankrupt, but by sharing the things he learned on the subject, he has sold over 100,000 copies of the book. Many folks establish a self-publishing business to provide a healthy ongoing income during their retirement years.

Okay, you're convinced these people are making money selling their knowledge. "But what do I have to write about?" you ask. First grab a pad of paper and a pencil. Start listing your hobbies and interests. Write down the jobs you've had, and especially note any job functions or procedures that you particularly enjoyed or were good at. For instance, if you're in the field of credit and collection, you may be a very good skip tracer. Many small-business men and women would love to discover how they can crack down on customers who don't pay their bills—instead of shelling out 50 percent to a collection agency or, as often as not, writing deadbeats off as a bad debt.

Now think about your successes. Have you won any honors or contests? Received special recognition for something? Do people always praise you for a characteristic or skill? That could contain the germ of a book, because if you are successful, you're better than most people, and thus you're an "expert" with information to sell. But know-how is worthless without "do-how." What's do-how? It's action. Catalyst. Innovation.

Before jumping into a project, however, the smart person does some homework. Find out what books are already available on the subject and what they are titled. An impossible task? Not really. Your local library is ready to supply all the answers. Look under all possible versions of your topic in the current Bowker's *Subject Guide to Books in Print*; also check *Forthcoming Books in Print*. (See the example below to learn just how to interpret the listings.) It's a good idea to photocopy the relevant pages for future use. Look in the library for any titles that sound like they compete, or order a copy from the publisher.

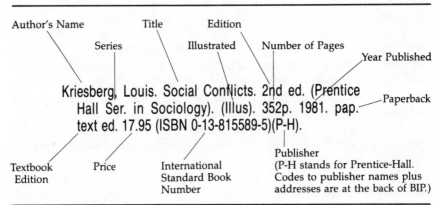

Sample excerpt from *Books in Print*.

Alternatives for entrepreneurial types

Perhaps rather than writing a book in the typical sense, you may choose to bring together a collection of information which you edit into a consistent format, then publish. That's what a San Diego advertising man did. In the late seventies Gary Beals put out the first edition of the *San Diego SourceBook*, which is a directory of country clubs, groups, local associations, organizations, and speakers. Beals didn't stop there, however. He capitalized on the fact that this sort of information quickly becomes obsolete. Soon there was a second edition, and a third. (One of the nice things about annual editions is that you can solicit standing orders from certain customers for each new volume.)

Since entrepreneurial blood pulses rapidly through Gary's veins, he decided that other cities could also use such resources. This led to a network of more than a dozen directories across the nation. But Gary doesn't try to do them all. He franchises given areas to other self-publishers who put out their own *SourceBooks*.

Directories can be big business. One of our previous students, Jacqueline Thompson, pulled together information on specialists in speech, dress, personal public relations, color, executive etiquette, and motivation. Then she put out the *Directory of Personal Image Consultants*. Thompson garnered plugs for her directory in the *Wall Street Journal, Publishers Weekly, Media Decisions,* the *New York Times, Signature,* and *Gentlemen's Quarterly.* Jackie, realizing she had a bull by the horns, immediately decided to make it an annual edition, thereby creating built-in obsolescence and an ongoing revenue base of previous customers. Directories have an added advantage. You not only reap financial rewards by selling the books but can also charge those listed a fee for being included and/or for advertising within the directory. Jackie sells her directory for $35. In addition, she has 290 paid listings in the current edition.

Dottie Walters is an extraordinary businesswoman. In addition to her own international speaking career, she runs a booking agency and training program for speakers, publishes an excellent newsletter called *Speakers & Meeting Planners Sharing Ideas,* and heads Royal Publishing Anthologies. These anthologies have proven extremely lucrative for Dottie and helpful for the people featured in them.

She started out with *Success Secrets,* in which eighteen everyday women tell you how to build a business and a life. The last time we chatted, Dottie said she had twenty-seven anthologies in print. Topics for the books range from motivation to humor and from sales to management. Such luminaries as Dr. Norman Vincent Peale have done the forewords.

Dottie invites participants to write an overview of their topic (assuming it fits the theme of a current book) in about twelve double-spaced typed pages. This then becomes a chapter in the book, complete with the contributor's photo and information on how to reach her. A quantity of the books is produced with elaborate foil covers featuring individual pictures of each contributor.

In turn, participants are expected to purchase a minimum of 250 of the anthologies at around $9 each, which amounts to about $2,250. (And many purchase 1,000, 5,000, even 10,000 books at more reduced prices.) This appears to be a win/win proposition. Those featured in the books have a great sales tool, a promotional angle to leverage for local publicity, and the help of all the other people in the collection who work in a similar field and will be peddling books. And if you compute the figures, it becomes obvious that at $2,250 from each of the eighteen to twenty-four people who participate in each anthology, Dottie is making a sweet profit. And it couldn't happen to a nicer lady.

Put on your creative thinking cap if such big bucks sound appealing. Can you create a book concept that would lend itself to this anthology idea?

Cliff Hillegass is another example of a dynamic self-publishing entrepreneur. He started out twenty-five years ago printing pamphlets for harried college students. Swathed in jarring yellow-and-black-striped covers, they gave summaries of *Macbeth* and *Hamlet*.

Cliffs Notes, as his company is called, has gone on to summarize 220 of the world's great books. These summaries are often the salvation of students long on reading lists and short on methods for cutting their work load. Has it also been Cliff's salvation? Decide for yourself. One year, he sold 3 million copies and brought in almost $9 million!

Cookbooks as money-makers

Cookbooks are another ideal independent publishing vehicle, both for individuals and for volunteer groups. They have flourished ever since 1742, when the early settlers in America started experimenting with ways to prepare the often-unfamiliar foods they found. The first one was published in Virginia and called *The Compleat Housewife, or Accomplished Gentle-woman's Companion.* Since that time thousands of cookbooks on such topics as zucchini, woks, and bananas have sprouted. There are also ethnic cookbooks and appliance cookbooks. In fact, two creative authors capitalized on the self-sufficiency craze and wrote *The Airtight Woodstove Cookbook.*

One of the most successful current titles is *The UNcook Book.* This refreshing combination of text and recipes offers raw-food adventurers a new health high. With our guidance it was self-published by its authors, Elizabeth and Dr. Elton Baker, in 1980. Since that time it has gone through five printings, established the Bakers as nutritional experts, opened up an international lecture tour, and led them to write and publish *Bandwagon to Health* and *The UNmedical Book.*

They are not alone. Ken Haedrich has sold thousands of copies of his self-produced menu manual titled *Good Food/Good Folks.* Pam Williams, the proprietor of a small chocolate shop, collaborated with Rita Morin to self-publish *Oh Truffles by Au Chocolat.* This pair of Vancouver, B.C., entrepreneurs sold out their first printing of ten thousand copies, and worked out a deal with Stein & Day to release the book in the United States in the fall of 1984.

For many churches, temples, women's groups, and other nonprofit organizations, sponsored cookbooks have established themselves as excellent money-makers. Volunteers find this one of the easiest ways to earn a substantial sum in a short period of time.

The Baton Rouge Junior League put together a collection of lip-smackin' goodies and dubbed it *River Road Recipes.* This little fund-raising beauty earns profits of $100,000 to $150,000 a year! And the sequel, *River Road Recipes—a Second Helping,* has also been tremendously successful. In Washington, D.C., the Congressional Club, comprised of wives of government officials, self-publishes continuing editions of *The Congressional Club*

Cook Book. It churns out $75,000 a year in earnings.

Did you know that the classic *Joy of Cooking* originated in 1931 with the First Unitarian Women's Alliance in St. Louis, Missouri? Bobbs-Merrill bought the rights and has been peddling thousands of copies every year since. *In the Beginning* is a taste-tempting collection of hors d'oeuvres that the ways-and-means committee of a Temple Sisterhood put together. Through aggressive marketing it has been reviewed in several hundred newspapers, been merchandised successfully via direct mail, and was purchased by over fifty Waldenbooks stores.

Why are these cookbooks so successful? Because every woman who has a recipe included is an automatic salesperson. Of course, as in any self-publishing venture, there are drawbacks. It is often difficult to work on such a project by committee. Fortunately, there are several valuable sources for help. Sara Pitzer's *How to Write a Cookbook and Get It Published* is a treasure trove of sound advice. There are also two companies that specialize in printing cookbooks. Even if you decide not to use their services, write for general information. They are Cookbooks by Morris Press, P.O. Box 1681, Kearney, NE 68848; and Circulation Services, Inc., P.O. Box 7306, Indian Creek Station, Shawnee Mission, KS 66207.

A case for novels, autobiography, and poetry

You'll notice that the examples we've given are primarily how-to or self-help nonfiction. There is a good reason for that. Only about 10 percent of the books published in the United States today are novels. And of these about one-sixth are done by small presses, according to a recent Arizona State University Library survey. Fiction writers have many obstacles to clear. If they depart from the "average" novel, they're considered by the trade to be eccentric, arty, or simply unsellable. If it weren't for the small-press movement, new and innovative books would entirely dry up.

Those who come through like thoroughbreds frequently hitch their stories to current events, especially events they themselves were or are involved in. John Ehrlichman's *The Company* was inspired by Watergate. And the Egyptian attack on Yom Kippur served as the basis for *Three Weeks in October*, a tale by Yael Dayan.

Dorothy Bryant, a Berkeley, California, woman who self-publishes her novels, began in 1971 by giving away her first novel to generate word-of-mouth sales. (It apparently worked, as Random House now carries the book.) Dorothy admits that it is slow building an audience. But her books have achieved a measure of success. *Killing Wonder*, a literary murder mystery, was sold to a mass-paperback house. Lippincott previously published another of her works, but let it go out of print. However, they proved to be premature in measuring this novel for its literary casket. Not one to be daunted, Dorothy got back the rights and reissued it herself. She sold over three thousand copies within the first year. *Ella Price's Journal,* which Dorothy published under her Ata Books imprint, is doing well as a text in women's reentry programs. On another of her books, *Prisoners,* film rights have been optioned for a TV "movie of the week."

Dorothy's advice to self-publishing novelists is "Put it through another edit." She feels the quality of writing can often be improved and uses literate friends to read and edit her work. It has been her experience that first-year sales will be around three thousand books, tapering off to seven hundred to one thousand per year thereafter.

Autobiography is another area appealing to self-publishers. And if you truly have lived through a unique experience, have rich historical fare to share, or were associated with a "name" person, this may be a prudent move. Otherwise, it can be an expensive ego trip. *How to Write the Story of Your Life,* by Frank P. Thomas, offers helpful guidelines.

Marilyn wrote an "as told to" book about an adventurous modern cowboy who rode horseback and took a pack string from the Mexican border to Fairbanks, Alaska, in less than six months. Tom Davis' impressive 4,500-mile journey set several world records. *Be Tough or Be Gone* is his story. It was an excellent candidate for self-publishing, as he plans to duplicate the trip and peddle books along the way. While this title rolled off the presses, we were able to convince Ripley's Believe It or Not to feature Davis in a column syndicated to three hundred newspapers across the country. Of note is the fact that Tom tried to interest Ripley's in his adventure before we did a book—and had no luck whatsoever. Just another example of how a book gives you fresh credibility and visibility.

In another case a trade-published author chose to breathe life into her book after Little, Brown & Company had let it die. *Snatched from Oblivion: A Cambridge Memoir* is a reminiscence of growing up in Cambridge, Massachusetts, in the early years of the century. It describes Cambridge characters, the local politics, college life, and a period and way of life that have virtually disappeared. Its author, Marian Cannon Schlesinger, decided to be in charge and do it herself when the hardback went out of print and the rights reverted to her. Only four months after publication she had recouped three quarters of her investment. More and more trade-published authors are electing to recapture their work and publish it themselves after it has been allowed to go out of print.

It has been said of writing: "You don't choose it, it chooses you." Nowhere is this more true than for the poet. Poets are compelled to capture their self-expressive messages for the joy of it—and for the sadness of it. Although poetry is perhaps the most difficult thing to self-publish successfully, it can be done.

The work of Susan Polis Schutz is a dynamic example. She and her artist-husband began by publishing a book of poetry. They bundled their books into their car and set out across the country, touting them to anyone who would listen and selling many along the way. Today Susan is one of America's best-selling living poets, having sold over 10 million copies of her poetry books! While continuing to write and edit, she heads a successful publishing venture called Blue Mountain Press.

Not many people know that contemporary best-selling poet Rod McKuen originally published his own book of poems and sold 40,000 copies before his talent was recognized by Random House. They ultimately sold over a million copies of his *Listen to the Wind*.

A collection of poems can be gathered into a chapbook, which is a small paperbound book containing poems, ballads, tales, or political or religious tracts. In Chapter 13, "Publicity," we'll investigate many sources that review poetry and novels and look at some innovative ways of marketing such literary works.

Titles that hook readers

Now that you've isolated your subject, how will you tempt potential readers to partake of this offering?

Christen it with a zesty title! Just as "uncola" sold 7-Up, a dynamic title will motivate people to sip the sparkling prose of your pages. The best ones are brief—certainly no more than six words and preferably two or three. (Yes, we know *If Life Is a Bowl of Cherries, What Am I Doing in the Pits?* is more than six words. When you reach Erma Bombeck's status, you can break the rules, too.)

Your title should also be descriptive and lively. A case in point: *The Traveller's Guide to the Best Cathouses in Nevada.* (Wouldn't you know it was put out by Straight Arrow Publishing!)

In titling fiction let's see what approaches some trade-published books can show us. Sometimes an object or living thing told about within the book lends itself to appropriate symbolism, to stand for the whole book. *Thornbirds* and *Valley of the Dolls* are examples of this method. Sometimes a new twist snaps a title into place. Mary Stewart's *Touch Not the Cat*, with its poetic switching of normal word order, communicates a sense of mysterious danger. If she had titled it *Don't Touch the Cat*, it would have lost that charm and mystery and sounded more like a children's story, or maybe even humor, like Jean Kerr's *Please Don't Eat the Daisies*.

Sometimes a play on words can have a dramatic effect. Capitalizing on the vastly popular *What Color Is Your Parachute?* Price Stern Sloan came out with *What Color Is Your Parody?* The subtitle of a book about finding your perfect mate? "A Guide for *Two*getherness in the '80s."

Other ways to stimulate ideas are to check magazine article titles on your subject to see what thought-ticklers they provide. Look within the book itself for catchy phrases that might make a captivating title. Listen to songs and read poems to find a phrase that's just what you want. Toss around clichés and common sayings to see if a slight change of wording would yield an appealing title.

Just as there are guidelines for good titles, there are also some negatives to avoid. Stay away from trite titles like "All That Glitters Is Not Gold," "Mother's Little Helper," or "To Be or Not to Be." Profane or controversial titles usually spell disaster—you'd have made at least some potential readers dislike your book on sight. And don't choose a title that gives misleading signals: Consider the monk who returned a copy of *From Here to Eternity* to the library, saying, "This isn't what I thought it would be."

Start jotting down some ideas. Don't be judgmental. Write down every idea that comes to mind. Let your thoughts hopscotch across all possibilities. Now settle back with a thesaurus and look up synonyms for likely candidates. Check any fuzzy definitions. Cast out those with no possible application. String the remainder together in various combinations. You may end up with ten or twenty possibilities. All the better.

Next, do some preliminary market research. Big corporations spend hundreds of thousands of dollars to test people's reactions. You can sample public opinion for free. Carry your list of suggested titles everywhere you go. Ask co-workers, relatives, friends—even strangers—which they like best, and least, and why. Capitalize on every opportunity to discuss your potential titles. Keep accurate records of what folks say and additional suggestions they may make.

One caution: Be aware that feedback from friends and relatives will reflect your own opinions more than general public evaluations will. Why? We tend to surround ourselves with people of our own socioeconomic level. This can be a real problem if, for example, you are a doctor writing a book for blue-collar workers and you only test the titles on your peers.

Especially if you're going after bookstore and mass distribution, a title with zap sells books. Here's a case in point: Two different newspaper ads told of new books. One was called *The Art of Courtship*; the other *The Art of Kissing*. Which do you think sold best? *The Art of Kissing* outsold courtship by 60,500 to 17,500! Why? Kissing is fun; it's about a specific benefit we all like. Courtship is general and sounds like work. Then there was *The Squash Book*, which sold 1,500 copies. When it became *The Zucchini Cookbook*, sales zoomed to 300,000 copies. The right title is like the aroma from a French pastry shop: It creates instant hunger for the goodies within. A new book by Nat G. Bodian, *How to Choose a Winning Title: A Guide for Writers, Editors and Publishers* covers this subject in depth.

Now it's time to recheck the photocopied pages of *Subject Guide to Books in Print* and *Forthcoming Books in Print*. Even though titles are not copyrightable, it is not to your advantage to publish a book that carries a name identical to that of another work.

Why should you do a fantastic job promoting your book and then run the risk of customers getting the names confused and ordering the other one instead?

In certain instances, titles can be protected by a registered trademark. The small ® you sometimes see by a product name lets you know it's protected in this way against being used by others. Getting a name registered is a complicated procedure requiring one to plow through a thicket of legalese, but in rare cases it may be warranted. If you have an exceptional title presented in a particularly catchy and appropriate graphic way, you might want to discuss, with an attorney who specializes in handling such matters, your acquisition of a service mark registration.

In rare cases legal action can be initiated on the grounds that the second work is trying to masquerade as the first.

As favored titles begin to emerge, play with them. See if by tossing two together you might mix in an appropriate subtitle. That's what happened with our book *Creative Loafing*. "A Shoestring Guide to New Leisure Fun" emerged as the ideal subtitle. This choice was painstakingly selected over numerous other candidates. *Creative Loafing* won over rivals such as "How to Be a Pleasure Pirate" and "The Joy of Just About Everything." It was the victor because people perked up when they read or heard it. It was intriguing. It sounded like fun. "Boy, do I need that!" was a typical comment. Folks found the contrast of "creative" and "loafing" provocative. They wanted to know more.

"A Shoestring Guide to New Leisure Fun" was chosen because "shoestring" connotes free or cheap activities. "Guide" sounds less stuffy than "handbook" or "manual." "New" is always a selling word, and it suggested that these were unusual forms of entertainment. "Leisure Fun" summarized the theme of the book.

It is wise to subtitle your books. Why? For two very good reasons. *Books in Print* and other important listing sources enter both the title and the subtitle, so you get more mileage out of your listing. It's like getting a brief sales message free. It also gives you more opportunity to describe the book. If you were looking to get a book on mail order, which would you buy: *Eureka!* or *Eureka! How to Build a Fortune in Mail Order*?

Now that we've examined the ingredients that go into choosing a marketable subject and talked about ways to pinpoint an intriguing title, let's proceed to the actual development of your book.

CHAPTER 3

PRODUCT DEVELOPMENT

In this chapter we'll be investigating research sources and tips. We will also explain permission guidelines for using copyrighted materials. You'll learn the easy way to organize a book; how front and back matter can be powerful persuaders; and ways to "plant" editorial material for more sales clout. And we'll advise you how to write tight, snappy copy and offer techniques for editing your own book. Finally we will look at alternate ways to acquire manuscripts if you don't want to or can't write the whole thing yourself.

Research sources and tips

Before sailing out too far in the waters of self-publishing, it is wise to surround yourself with a few navigational guides. By including some basic reference works in your personal library, you can steer clear of reefs and make your journey much easier.

Here's the minimum you will need: Obtain a copy of *LMP (Literary Market Place.* This is a valuable annual directory that puts at your fingertips important "who's where" information on book manufacturers, reviewers, publishers, book clubs, wholesalers, important publishing conference dates, radio and TV contacts, etc. It's an expensive bugger: around $95. But it's an indispensable aid for the serious writer-publisher. If *LMP* is out of your league—or as an ideal supplement—get a copy of John Kremer's *Book Marketing Opportunities: A Directory.* And we've recently published *Marketing Your Book: A Collection of Profit-Making Ideas for Authors and Publishers.* A current copy of *Writer's Market* will take the burden out of locating magazine promotional sources. If the price of these books, which are updated annually, is a deterrent, they're available in the reserve section of most public libraries. You can photocopy pages you need until your business gets going well enough to let you afford your own personal copies.

You'll also want a good up-to-date dictionary—such as *Webster's Ninth New Collegiate Dictionary* or *The Random House College Dictionary*—a thesaurus, and a copy of *The Chicago Manual of Style*, put out by the University of Chicago Press, or one of the other accepted style guides. (Of course, no personal library would be complete without a copy of *this* book.)

And if you can swing it, subscribe to *Small Press* and *Publishers Weekly*. As the trade magazines of the industry, they contain much valuable information. Our bibliography lists other helpful books and newsletters.

Treasures in your library

Are you aware that millions of dollars' worth of free information awaits you? You can locate the names and addresses of prospective buyers all over the country, command the free services of researchers to help you negotiate this maze of data, even pick up your phone and get immediate answers. This reservoir of information and services is located at your main branch public library. It's to your advantage to make optimum use of library facilities and personnel.

Chances are you're well acquainted with the main branch of your library. If not, become friends. Find out about special departments and the names of the librarians in the sections you will most likely frequent. Become familiar with the card catalog, where you can locate books and magazines the library owns. Learn the Dewey Decimal System so you can find books easily. Get a library card so you can borrow material.

Certain periodical (magazine) indexes will be extremely beneficial. These can help you find out what has already been written on a subject, locate experts you may want to interview or have comment on your book, find articles that will give you more insight into a given subject, or help you get a feel for which magazines are prime candidates to review or sell your book. Unfortunately, not all periodicals are represented in one handy index. In fact, the amateur researcher can feel as frustrated as a robin hunting for worms in Astroturf. But there is help. *Ulrich's International Periodicals Directory* tells in which indexes any given periodical is logged. Another valuable resource is the *Standard Periodical Directory*.

The granddaddy of indexes is *Reader's Guide to Periodical Literature* with its references to 185 magazines of greatest general interest. This is an invaluable source when you're researching a particular topic. A new kid on the block is the *Magazine Index*, which lists 400 current popular periodicals, including *all* titles indexed in *Reader's Guide*. There is a long string of specialized indexes, such as *Business Periodicals Index*, the *Applied Science and Technology Index*, and *Index Medicus*. To find out which one applies to your needs, check *Ulrich's* and talk with your librarian.

And don't overlook newspaper indexes for timely help. The *New York Times Index* comes out at two-week intervals and is consolidated annually. The *Wall Street Journal Index* catalogs corporate news in the first section and general news in the second. Frequently a date, location, or spelling of a name can be found in the index without ever seeing the complete news story.

An additional suggestion is the *Encyclopedia of Associations*. Virtually every interest has a society, association, or group dedicated to it. Here is the place to track down technical "insider's" information, locate experts, find out what publications they publish, or perhaps buy mailing lists of their members. (In Chapter 13 we'll show you how to build important lists for publicizing and selling your book.) And don't overlook *Directories in Print*. It contains over ten thousand entries of business and industrial directories, professional and scientific rosters, and other lists. An easy subject index covers some three thousand topics. A couple of helpful books to aid you in using the library are *Finding Facts Fast*, by Alden Todd, and *A Writer's Guide to Research*, by Lois Horowitz.

The public library is not the only keeper of knowledge; university libraries are often more complete. In a school specializing in medicine, law, or business the library is likely to be comprehensive in that area. And their hours often include Sundays and more evenings than public libraries offer. The general public is typically allowed to use college and university library facilities. To check out material, however, you will probably need to become a "friend of the library." This friendship has a price; but the cost of a year's membership is usually modest—often $25 or less.

An exciting resource at universities is unpublished theses. You may find that a student has saved you months of research by writing a comprehensive thesis on the same or a similar topic. Find out what is available and what restrictions—if any—there are on its use.

Moreover, most libraries now offer a computer research service. The speed of computer technology can trim months from your research schedule. Be sure to spell out specific parameters for the information wanted or you could pay for a lot of irrelevant data. Don't request a printout on "birds" if all you want to know are the nesting habits of the peregrine falcon.

There is yet another resource in addition to public and academic libraries. Across America numerous specialized collections exist. Some are part of large companies, others are maintained by associations. Still others are devoted to specific subjects such as genealogy. Find out if there is a library dedicated to your topic and contact the people in charge for assistance. The *Directory of Special Libraries and Information Centers* can point you in the right direction.

And even if you can't visit the collection in person remember that you can lay your hands on almost any book in almost any library through the interlibrary loan system. Librarians have obtained books for us out of specialized libraries that would never loan part of their collection to us as individuals. Just because a book isn't in your local library doesn't mean it is unobtainable.

Yet another avenue to obtain needed research materials is open to you. If approached professionally, many publishers will send you complimentary copies of their books relating to your subject. Remember that copy of the page you made from *Subject Guide to Books in Print?* Drag it out again and scan it for pertinent titles. Also look for reviews in newsletters and trade magazines devoted to your topic. We developed a form letter while researching this book, typed in the title we were requesting, added a couple of powerful enclosures to further establish our credibility, and made clear the subject of our work-in-progress. Thousands of dollars' worth of regular books and reference texts were sent to us free because the publishers hoped we'd find some of the books so good and useful that we'd mention them in our text and give them some free, authoritative advertising among readers specifically interested in the field. That kind of recommendation is worth money to any publisher, so the books weren't just sent for nothing: to the publishers, they were an investment in hopes of future sales.

Since these books really did prove invaluable in providing information for this guide, we recommend many of them throughout the book and list them in the Bibliography—just as the publishers had hoped. So we, and they, both benefitted. In fact, we were so impressed with the selection that we began a special Maverick Mail Order Bookstore of publishing-related titles. To get your free copy of this catalog, simply send an SASE with 45¢ postage to us at About Books, Inc., Box 1500-MOB, Buena Vista, CO 81211. Many of the books cited throughout this guide are available from this one-stop-shopping source.

Another reference source is the Federal Information Centers located in every state. By calling one of them you can gain access to an abundance of federal and state government materials and statistics. Not just legislative stuff, but oddball things like forestry conditions, details from government survival guides, even old weather reports. Smart novelists often use the Federal Information Centers to provide obscure facts and details. For your convenience we've included a list of the various centers in the Appendix.

You can also find a wealth of help in various government documents. As the country's largest publisher, the U.S. Government Printing Office issues a phenomenal amount of information. To find out what is available, write the Superintendent of Documents, U.S. Government Printing Office, Washington, DC 20402. If your local library doesn't have the publication you need, it can probably be borrowed from one of the Federal Depository Libraries in your state. Ask the librarian.

You can secure information by simply letting your fingers do the walking. That's right. Call and ask for it. Suppose you need the address of a wholesaler in a distant town. Libraries can probably locate it in their out-of-town telephone books. Want to know when and where the next meeting of the American Booksellers Association is? They can tell you. Whenever possible, use the phone to save you time and money when doing research. The telephone can serve you well for interviews and surveys also. After introducing yourself, it's a good idea to say, "I'd like to include your thoughts in my study of . . ." and move right into the first question. Studies show this technique is better than requesting permission to ask questions; then you're more likely to be refused.

Whatever vehicle you use to obtain the information you need, be sure you are thorough and accurate. Rex Alan Smith observed that "faulty research is like a faulty septic tank. Sooner or later the evidence will surface and become embarrassing."

Now let's turn our attention to rights and permissions. Your research will no doubt turn up passages or comments from other published works that you would like to use. What are the rules?

Permission guidelines for using copyrighted material

First, let us discuss "fair use." Using material without the need to obtain permission is called fair use. *The Chicago Manual of Style* says that "quotations should not be so long that they diminish the value of the work from which they are taken." In the case of books, experts estimate you can use an aggregate of up to 300 words freely. If you quote just a paragraph from a book and mention the author and title, you don't need to obtain permission. For magazine articles 50 words is the maximum (that's assuming it isn't a 500-word filler). Brad Bunnin and Peter Beren, in their excellent *Author Law & Strategies,* say that straight news articles from newspapers (not features) of any length can be safely used after three months. This does not include any article that is syndicated, under a byline, or individually copyrighted. To use as little as a single line from a poem or song, you need permission. Photographs, artwork, and cartoons will also require the permission of the copyright holder.

One way to circumvent copyright problems is to paraphrase what was said. Ideas are not copyrightable—only the specific words used to express them.

The best rule is to use good common sense. Don't take from another something you would resent being used if you were the author.

RE: PERMISSION TO REPRINT MATERIAL

August 20, 1984

Dear:_____

    My husband and I are writing a book tentatively titled THE
COMPLETE GUIDE TO SELF-PUBLISHING, which Writer's Digest Books
plans to publish in the spring of 1985. The book will retail for
about $19.95.

    We would like to request your permission to include the
excerpt(s) as outlined below in any and all editions of our book.
(And in any derivative or subsidiary works, including paperback
and book club, and special editions for the handicapped such as
Braille, large type, and tapes, in all languages, and in the
advertisement and promotion therefor non-exclusively throughout
the world.)

    We are looking forward to receiving your permission and
giving your material greater exposure. Please indicate the
acknowledgement you wish printed in the book.

For your convenience we've enclosed a duplicate copy of this
letter and a stamped, self-addressed envelope. We thank you in
advance for your cooperation and prompt response.

Sincerely,

Marilyn Ross

MATERIAL TO BE REPRINTED:

TITLE:_____

AUTHOR:_____

COPYRIGHT DATE & HOLDER:_____

PAGE_____, LINE_____ TO PAGE_____, LINE_____.

Permission granted by:_____Date:_____

Acknowledgement to read:_____

415 Fourth Street, P.O. Box 213, Saguache, Colorado 81149-0213   303-655-2504

Permission form to reprint material.

34

When in doubt, formally request permission to quote. See the adjacent copy of the letter which was used for this book, or devise your own. Write the publisher stipulating the following in your request:
- The title and type of your book (i.e., nonfiction, novel, poetry)
- The estimated date of publication
- The title and author of the work you wish to quote
- Its publication date
- The page(s) on which the desired material is located
- The total number of words or lines of poetry or song lyrics you wish to use
- A transcript or photocopy of the exact quotation (or the first and last few words if lengthy)
- A statement about "any and all editions" (See paragraph two of our letter for the wording.)
- A request for exactly how the copyright holder wishes the acknowledgment to read

Send your letter in duplicate, asking that the authorized holder sign and return the original giving you a release and keep the duplicate for his or her files. Including a stamped, self-addressed envelope is a prudent touch. Then be prepared to wait. And follow up. And wait. Obtaining copyright permissions often takes several months, so handle your requests early in the creation process. If you have a large volume of permissions in the works, it would be wise to set up a control log so you know the status of each one. Also, code the letters in some way—for instance, by noting in a separate log the manuscript page(s) on which each piece of permissionable material will appear and from whom the permission will come, with the date you sent your original request. Then you'll find it simpler to integrate the material into your manuscript and check off the item as received when each permission comes. And if too much time passes and one or another of the permissions still hasn't come in, you'll easily notice the fact and begin follow-up.

Often a fee will be involved. If so, you must decide if the quote is worth the asking price. Charges range from a token five or ten dollars to several hundred dollars. These fees are frequently negotiable, however, so don't feel compelled to pay what is stated without trying to arrange a smaller amount.

When you receive permission, pay attention to how they want the acknowledgment to read. When this material appears in the book, you must cite the permission exactly as stipulated.

Of course, some things are not protected by copyright. They are considered to be in the "public domain." Works enter this status via several means. Copyright lapses if the copyright owner allows a work to be published without the proper copyright notice. Material also goes into public domain if its original copyright was not renewed or if copyright protection has been exhausted.

Government publications are also typically in the public domain, but this can be a gray area. If you plan to use extensive sections verbatim, it is wise to have a copyright search performed. When you are using just portions, no permission is needed, but it's a good idea to cite the specific source. Also be aware that government publications often contain illustrations and other materials that are covered by individual copyrights. Read the fine print carefully.

The easy way to organize a book

When confronted with the task of organizing all your research, perhaps you feel a bit like the mosquito that wandered into the nudist colony. He knew exactly *what* to do . . . but *where* should he begin? We usually begin on the floor with a handful of 3" by 5" cards labeled with possible subject areas. The best approach for nonfiction is to sort through your ideas or research material like a deck of cards, dealing them out to the various subject areas. Once they are in what appears to be the appropriate stack, look for the common denominators. When these patterns begin to emerge, you can often see the best way to order them. As you begin to group thoughts and materials, the book's skeleton takes shape.

Now use file folders to represent chapters, placing appropriate data in each folder. This way, you start to flesh out the book's skeleton. Review what you have gathered to see where you're rich with material—and what areas are thin and need further research or perhaps reshuffling and combining of chapters. We were once asked how long a chapter should be. Tom's answer? Long enough to reach from beginning to end. Seriously, there is no way to say ten pages or twenty pages. Organize the material carefully and make logical breaks. Some topics will naturally be more meaty than others. Of course, if you end up with one chapter out of all proportion in length to the rest, see if there isn't a natural break where it could be divided. Once you've grouped material this way, either refine it further with a formal outline or establish a consecutive flow and begin writing.

Writing tight, snappy copy

It has been said, "There are two things wrong with most writing. One is style; the other is content." The way a writer strings words together either grabs the reader by the scruff of the neck and shouts, "Read me!" or hangs as limp and uninteresting as tattered sheets in a tenement window.

Let's examine the writing process and see how we can become better word crafters to improve our chances with readers . . . or editors. Here are some guidelines to help give your work momentum and sparkle. At the end we've included some specific suggestions for novelists.

• Communicate, don't try to impress. The comfort zone of the average reader is at about the eighth-grade level, so practice the old rule of KISS ("Keep it simple, sweetheart"). Studies show that eighth-grade readers can understand fairly easy sentences with an average of fourteen words. Remember, we said "average." You may have a one-word sentence and then a whopper. Just be sure it is basically a simple declarative sentence. If a sentence becomes too long and unwieldy, break it in two. You can use such words as "and," "but," "additionally," "consequently," "therefore," or "accordingly" to divide sentences easily. Use short words instead of long ones. For many writers who typically pride themselves on a strong, versatile vocabulary, this is difficult. Stickler three-, four-, and five-syllable words should be avoided whenever possible. "Recondite" slows down most anyone; yet "family" and "company"—also three-syllable words—are totally acceptable. It comes down to using good judgment.

The late Robert Gunning, an American writer and editor, concocted a readability formula called a "Fog Index" to determine how difficult a given piece of writing was to read. The longer the sentences and the bigger the words, the higher the Fog Index. If you want to avoid "foggy writing" in which a reader may get lost between the punctuation marks, use your good judgment and keep your writing simple and direct.

• Word choice is vitally important. Mark Twain observed, "The difference between the right word and the almost right word is the difference between lightning and the lightning bug." Are your words colorful? Specific? Descriptive? Don't have a man "walk." Rather let him amble, stride, stagger, or shuffle along. Avoid beginning most of your sentences with "the." Try not to develop "I" trouble; overuse of "I" quickly bores the reader. Rephrase the sentence to do away with this repeated reference. Watch for repetition of words within close proximity. Using the same word over and over again (unless it's for emphasis) is a sloppy way of writing.

• Avoid ambiguity. Rewrite anything that is unclear. The story is told that FBI Director J. Edgar Hoover decided he didn't like the margin format used for a letter he had dictated to his secretary. So he scribbled "watch the borders" on it and gave it back to her. She dutifully retyped the letter and sent it off to the top FBI agents. For the next two weeks dozens of agents were placed on special alert along the Canadian and Mexican borders. Think through any confusing areas. What do they mean? Could they be misinterpreted? Take the word "terminal," for instance. It means entirely different things to a computer operator, an electrician, a bus driver, and a physician.

• Keep a wary eye on overall language. Foreign words and unfamiliar jargon confuse the reader. Likewise, "vogue" terms will date your manuscript and may appear ridiculous five years hence.

• Guard against clichés. These are the overused, trite bits and pieces of speech that are part of everyone's conversations. "Money hungry," "sly as a fox," and "grows by leaps and bounds" are all clichés. When we write, it's important to pare away worn phrases; replace them with more original phraseology. Clichés are a sign of lazy writing. Think of a fresh, new way of saying it.

• Delete redundancies and needless words. Why say: He stood up to make the announcement? (Have you ever seen anyone stand *down?*) *Early pioneers* should be simply *pioneers; in the not too distant future = soon; due to the fact that = because; until such time as = until; combined together = combined.* Get the idea? Watch your writing for conciseness. Have you pared away all unnecessary words? Eliminated repetition? Trim words like "very," "really," and other qualifiers that don't serve a definite purpose. Brevity is beautiful. Train yourself to shed the "padding" that comes from years of cranking out student papers.

• One excellent tool for injecting your writing with liveliness is similes or metaphors to show comparisons. A simile uses "like" or "as": "His personality is as bland as oatmeal." A metaphor suggests resemblance. "Her face blossomed with affection." Such additions help readers relate to what you've written.

• Analogies also put zip in a manuscript. They help make or illustrate a point. An example of an analogy would be "Life is a hundred-yard dash, with birth the starting gun and death the tape."

• Anecdotes are another important facet of nonfiction writing. They are little stories or examples that illustrate the points you wish to make. We've sprinkled true anecdotes throughout this book. Sometimes an author makes up an anecdote to fit the occasion.

• To further excite your reader, appeal to his or her senses. Let the aroma of paint, tar, freshly brewed coffee, or jasmine bring reality to your story. Allow the reader to hear locusts chirping, a trumpeter practicing, the crunch of dried leaves. Offer a taste of the delicate flavor of veal Oscar . . . or soggy french fries cooked in stale grease. Sit in a chair that's coarse and scratchy . . . or luxurious and soft. By appealing to the senses, you give a piece mood, texture, and color.

• Another way to achieve readability is to use the "active" voice. In the active voice the subject of the sentence performs the action. Here's an example:

The active voice says: *The wind slammed the door shut.*

The passive voice says: *The door was slammed shut by the wind.*

How much more powerful that statement is in the active version!

• For additional horsepower, be specific! Look for ways to support general statements with details. Think of your writing as a funnel. At the top is the general statement, then it narrows down to a specific incident. This targets the reader's attention toward one given example. Rather than saying the woods are full of trees, say the woods are full of aspen, spruce, and pine.

• Smooth transitions are another hallmark of good writing. Are there graceful bridges between sentences, paragraphs, and chapters? Some words and phrases that serve as transitions are: still, on the other hand, another, next, however, of course, then, finally, but, unfortunately, in short, once again.

• Being sensitive to sexism in writing is especially important today. The least whiff of sex discrimination is an immediate turnoff for some people. We certainly don't advocate such contortions as "shim," "heshe," "herim," or "hisers"—all of which have actually been used in print. But we do feel you should be careful not to use discriminatory pronouns, such as "he" or "his," when referring to both sexes. One easy way around this is to use the plural form of "they" or "their." When dealing with work titles, there are many options: "Policeman" becomes "police officer"; "mailman" becomes "mail carrier"; "salesman" becomes "salesperson." "Mankind" can just as easily be expressed as "humankind." What is important is to maintain the dignity of all people by avoiding stereotypes.

• Avoid bad taste of any kind. Racist statements, gory photographs, sexual overtones, and other undesirable materials are bound to offend some readers. Don't preach religion in a nonreligious book, and keep your politics to yourself unless that's your theme. The one exception to this could be fiction, where you might use a touch of the above to characterize someone in the story. Of course, obscene or pornographic material will be objectionable to the vast majority. In every case it's important to consider your chosen audience, their mores and values, and edit or develop your material accordingly.

Here are some additional considerations for fiction writers:

• Plot. Developing a strong plot is the first ingredient of a good novel. Be sure it's believable and appropriate to the genre. A helpful book for novelists is Lawrence Block's *Writing the Novel,* which gives a good overview of fiction methods.

• Premise/Theme. Is your message clear? Can you summarize it in one simple sentence? (If not, the reader will surely be confused.) Focus on a single well-defined theme.

• Dialogue. Conversation adds depth to your characters and moves the story forward swiftly. But is it realistic? Do people really talk that way? In real life we use contractions in conversation, talk in incomplete sentences, and use slang. To see if your dialogue plays well, read it aloud.

• Pacing. Does the material move smoothly—or does it get bogged down like a car stuck in sand? Remember to alternate points of high and low action so the reader isn't kept at a constant peak.

• Mood/Tone. Is the mood appropriate to your theme? Are you consistent throughout? Starting a murder mystery with a humorous anecdote, for instance, would be misleading.

• Tense/Viewpoint. Are they the same throughout? If your book is in the present tense, don't accidentally wander into the past. Likewise, if your story originates out of Cathleen's head, to suddenly tell how John feels is to switch viewpoint. While many popular contemporary novelists do this, it is a tricky technique to carry off. What you might consider is devoting whole chapters to different characters and alternating them, as was done in *The Other Side of Midnight,* by Sidney Sheldon.

• Settings. Be sure you are familiar with your setting or are prepared to do extensive research so it will ring authentic. Establish the setting early so your reader can grasp what is happening. A conversation taking place in jail has very different overtones from one taking place at a picnic grounds or in bed.

• Description. Good description elevates a book from the pack. Here are two tricks that may help you create more powerful description. If you're talking about a place or a thing, consider giving it human characteristics. As Dick Perry says in *One Way to Write Your Novel,* "The hotel room had lost its youth. Its floors creaked with middle age. It had not bathed in years." Conversely, if you are describing people, give them the characteristics normally reserved for houses, streets, or things. Perry gives these examples: "She was, to children, a haunted house they dare not visit" and "Everyone else was an expressway, racing somewhere, full of purpose; she was a street labeled dead end."

• Characterization. Good characterization has been called the ability to create characters readers care about—ones who seem real, with qualities we can sympathize and identify with. But how does one achieve such people on paper? A vehicle we've found useful is the character sketch. In this sketch you detail every conceivable thing about each character. Not only such obvious things as sex, age, and physical description but the less tangible aspects as well: mannerisms, education, philosophies, family background, religious history, passions, and pet peeves. These are the things memorable characters are made of. Once *you* know your characters well, it's much easier to make them come alive for the reader.

Front and back matter: the powerful persuaders

While you're working away on your chapters, don't forget they're not going to be the whole book. Assuming your book is nonfiction, it will be enclosed, not just by its covers, but by "front and back matter," which can have a dramatic impact on your book's review potential and sales record. The front matter we'll be discussing here includes such things as the foreword, preface, and introduction.

A foreword by an important person can boost your book's sales considerably. Often it comes from the same authority you will ask to look over the completed manuscript for input in general. With a little polishing and expanding, this feedback may well provide a perfect foreword (assuming, of course, the authority liked your work). Don Dible's *Up Your Own Organization* is an excellent example of using a "name" person to help promote a book. He had such favorable response from experts who reviewed his early manuscript that he ended up with three of them writing commendations for his book. This handbook on how to start and finance a new business has an introduction by Robert Townsend, who brought Avis Rent a Car to fame; a foreword by William P. Lear, chairman of the board of Lear Motors Corporation; and a preface by John L. Komives, director of the Center for Venture Management. Being the businessman that he is, Don splashed the names of these three gentlemen across the cover, as they had much greater name recognition than he did.

Typically, you will write your own preface. It outlines your reasons for doing this book and helps establish your credibility. Reviewers frequently draw their material from the preface, so be sure you give them good ammunition. Let your warmth and personality come through. Reviewers and readers alike respond more favorably to a book if they like its author.

The introduction is where you lay the groundwork for the book and give any specific directions (like "read the whole thing before attempting to implement any part of it"). It often falls in with the other front matter. We feel this is a mistake. Readers are likely to ignore it there and start reading with Chapter 1. So list your introduction first in the table of contents, where people are sure to see it, and place it immediately before the first chapter.

Back matter is exactly what it says—material in the back of the book. It can include an appendix, bibliography, glossary, index, even an order form.

An appendix is used for lists of sources of additional information or for quick-reference summaries. The inclusion of appendixes adds greatly to a book's overall usefulness. It can also have a more practical purpose. If your book is too skinny, adding a detailed appendix is an easy extender. One book we know of was stretched from 150 pages to more than 240 by adding a tremendous directory of additional reference material on the subject covered. This was turned to an advantage by promoting the fact that the book included a free directory of business information. Moreover, if your work has an extensive appendix, it may be accepted for listing in the *Directory of Directories*, as this guide has been.

Bibliographies are helpful additions for readers who want more in-depth information on your subject. You may want to list not only those publications from which you drew material but also other relevant works.

Most nonfiction books can benefit from a glossary. When a reader comes across an unfamiliar term, it is comforting to be able to turn to the glossary for a quick explanation. Glossaries are also used later in the book's life, when a ready source for a technical definition is needed.

Indexes are to nonfiction books what butter is to bread. You can use the one without the other ... but it's so much better with the added ingredient. Acquisition librarians in particular are more likely to purchase your book if it is indexed. They know that patrons prefer such books and that they are more useful to the library itself. If you hope to sell to educational markets, an index is almost mandatory. An index is particularly helpful when you first use a book, as it allows you to obtain answers to specific questions. Later, after you've retired the volume to your personal library, the need for an index emerges again when a quick reference on a specific point is wanted.

Planting editorial material for more sales clout

Before we leave the writing stage let's talk a little about how you can introduce material into your book that will later serve as a sales or promotional hook.

Millions of books are sold each year on the basis of commercial tie-ins. For instance, if you have a book on gardening and mention the W. Atlee Burpee Company in a favorable way, you may be able to sell a special edition of the book to that company. (We'll be exploring this aspect of special sales in depth in Chapter 16.) Within reason mention brand names or service companies. A bulk purchase will more likely be considered if you're specific.

Let's say you have a book on missing children. If you have only a couple of paragraphs on how teachers might prevent this problem, you'll be too limited to use it for advertising leverage. But if you expand your coverage to a full chapter, you'll have a whole new market base: the educational community.

Giving editorial space to specific geographic areas or points of interest can also provide valuable sales leads. So can name-dropping. People like to see their names in print. One book we know of included the names, titles, and brief blurbs about the achievements and talents of some two thousand businesspeople. With a cover price of $24.95 can you imagine how fast the publisher's bank balance soared after each of these executives was approached about buying a copy of a book that features him personally? This approach no doubt accounts for the success of the various "who's who" directories.

So don't overlook the possibility of adding editorial matter that will help you downstream in the sales department. (Putting actual advertisements in your book is covered in the next chapter.) It could very well mean the difference between a publishing venture that breaks even or loses money—and one that prospers.

Editing your work

Your manuscript is finally written. You breathe a great sigh of relief. But hold on, you aren't done yet! Even the best writers can benefit from a good editor working behind them. Editing is a special skill that the average author doesn't perform well. And since, in spite of their expertise, editors are notoriously poorly paid, the expense of getting professional help for your work won't normally be too large.

A poorly edited book is harder to read, harder to believe, and less likely to be reviewed. It is shameful to see a good book cut to ribbons by a reviewer because of poor grammar or spelling. Such was the case with *Three Days in November,* published by St. Martin's. While the plot was praised, the reviewer noted, "Unfortunately, the reader also has to detour around some disasters in editing and proofreading."

Because the author knows the subject so well, he or she may be too close to it, losing his or her objectivity. A professional editor can help detect passages that are unclear or poorly organized. This is called content editing. During a second reading your editor will do copyediting—whisking out grammar, spelling, and punctuation errors.

Short of hiring a pro, enlist the help of several literate friends or associates to go over your work. It's a good idea to give them some instructions. Ask that they underline any misspelled or questionable words, circle unclear passages, and note rough transitions with a question mark. Also encourage them to jot any suggestions in the margins. Encourage them to be specific. Specific, constructive criticism is like surgery; it cuts out the malignancy and spares the rest of the body. Vague criticism is like chemotherapy; it causes the copy's hair to fall out and makes the whole thing look sicker than it really is. Even best-selling authors like James Michener use others to refine their work. Says Michener: "I invite four outside experts—a subject-matter scholar, editor, style arbiter on words, and a final checker—to tear it apart. . . . "

Now let's use the following checklist to evaluate your finished work and pinpoint any potentially weak area.

- Title. Is it catchy? Short? Appropriate?
- Opening. Does it arouse interest and hook the reader?

• Organization. Do you tell readers what you're going to tell them, then tell them, and then tell them what you told them? Is the book logically presented? Have you used headings and subheads to help communicate your nonfiction message?

• Credibility. Is your manuscript built on a foundation of accurate information? Are the facts the most current available? Names and places spelled correctly? Figures right? Can the reader sniff the unmistakable aroma of authenticity in the pages? Have you avoided issues which could be too quickly dated?

• Sentences. Are their lengths varied? Their structure and meter? Mix 'em up, shrink 'em, stretch 'em, make 'em gallop, let 'em be languid.

• Conclusion. Does it just stop, or is the package tied together and truly finished?

• Spelling. Pleez spel krecktly! Check questionable words in the dictionary or call the library for clarification.

• Punctuation. Does it clarify what is written? Give impact? Do you add zest by using varied types of punctuation such as semicolons, colons, dashes, ellipses, parentheses, quotation marks, and underlining? Or do you simply stub your toe on a comma over and over again? One word of caution: Don't go wild for exclamation points, underlinings, or other exotic punctuation. Used to excess, these distract people.

• Grammar. Is it correct, yet alive? Use common sense when applying the rules and don't be inhibited by old forms that have become obsolete. For instance, in spite of what your stern English teacher taught you, starting a sentence with "and" or "but" is acceptable practice today. Even slang has its place. Carl Sandburg observed that "slang is language that rolls up its sleeves, spits on its hands, and goes to work." In particular, be sure you haven't used plural nouns with singular verbs, and vice versa.

• Consistency. In preparing your book to be typeset, it is important that you observe uniformity. If you spell out "California" in Chapter 1, abbreviate it as "Calif." in Chapter 6, and use "CA" in Chapter 11, you have no consistency. To avoid this problem, why not try a trick used by many professional editors? They establish a "style guide." It typically covers such things as abbreviations, how numbers will be expressed, and other points relevant to each manuscript. When we edit a book, we create a Style Sheet like the adjacent sample. When we come across something that could be expressed more than one way, we enter our choice for how to express it on the Style Sheet. Then when we run across the same thing, or a similar example, later in the manuscript, we can see how it appeared before. For more information on copyediting in general, we recommend *Copyediting: A Practical Guide*, by Karen Judd.

• Presentation. The physical appearance of your work is also important. You want a manuscript you can be proud to send out for advance comments or for editing. Dirty copy is likely to result in more errors and greater typesetting costs.

The Style Sheet below can be used to keep track of formatting, etc.

Each of us has an innate style of expression. The more we practice the writing craft, the more distinct that style becomes. Your style may develop to the point that people reading unbylined work will recognize it as yours because of your unique way of expressing yourself. Style wears many faces. It can be as simple as Hemingway or as complicated as Faulkner; as lighthearted as Nancy Stahl or as profound as Margaret Mead. The more you write, the more compelling your style will become. By practicing and using the guidelines in this section, you can turn a manuscript that is like a mild processed cheese into copy with the bite of sharp cheddar.

Alternative ways to acquire manuscripts

If you have identified your subject and want someone else to do the writing, hire a ghostwriter. You can find people in a wide range of pay

Style Sheet for Editing

ABCD	EFGH
IJKL	MNOP
QRST	UVWXYZ

scales. If you're willing to go with an unpublished writer (who will probably accept five cents a word), ask around in creative writing classes, check librarians for referrals, or seek members of local writers' clubs. Or you might run a classified ad in the newspaper.

If you want a professional, you have several options. You can look in *Working Press of the Nation* under your general subject category, check "Editorial Services" in *LMP*, or contact "Dial-A-Writer" — a referral service of members from the American Society of Journalists and Authors (ASJA). Another publication that might be helpful is *Freelancers of North America.* When working with a ghostwriter, be sure you have firmly in mind what you want done. Will the person work from your notes and other written material, or will he or she use tapes or personal interviews? Is the writer expected to do a lot of research to flesh out the book? The more specific, organized, prompt, and cooperative you are, the less expensive and happier this experience will be. Believe us, the process can be as smooth as silk ... or as rough as burlap. We've ghostwritten several books, with both joy and frustration.

Sometimes we have to add to our fees simply because we realize in talking with a potential client that he or she will be difficult to work with and require a lot of time-consuming hand-holding. When dealing with a professional, proven ghostwriter, expect to pay at least half of the agreed-upon fee at the beginning. The original thinking process, material organization, and research usually take longer than the actual writing. Interim payments are made as the manuscript is delivered.

Ghostwriting is considered "work for hire." You as the employer contract via written agreement with an individual or company to produce a particular work. If you don't have such an agreement, the writer can claim the copyright belongs to him or her. This can be a technical area. We'd suggest you refer to one of the books listed in the Bibliography or consult a competent copyright attorney if you have questions.

Another way to generate a book is to put the word out that your publishing company is seeking manuscripts. Send information on your specific requirements to *Writer's Digest, The Writer,* and appropriate writers' newsletters, a list of which is included in the Bibliography. Your notice, which will be inserted free as space permits, should be brief and to the point. Study the "markets" announcements in *Writer's Digest* for help with constructing a call for manuscripts. Or—if you're aware of several good articles on a central theme—you might contact their authors and investigate the possibility of putting them together in an anthology. After gaining copyright permission, let the original writers update, shorten, or lengthen the material as needed. You could even string together a group of your own past articles with a central theme if the rights have reverted to you.

For a few hundred dollars you might even buy outright a booklet-length manuscript from a talented but unpublished writer. This not only helps you but gives the struggling writer encouragement, a financial boost, and a published sample of his or her work.

As a point of clarification, international standards say that a publication must be at least forty-nine pages without the covers to be classified as a "book." The U.S. Postal Service is much more lenient. It rules that eight or more pages are eligible for "book rate" postage. This is helpful for poets who may want to put together a short collection of their work as a chapbook. Sometimes people purposely break up a book and sell it in booklet form. Mail-order correspondence courses do this a lot. After you've purchased so many booklets, you're provided with a binder to hold the complete series. Monographs, which are short reports on a particular subject, lend themselves to self-publishing. Usually done in an 8½" by 11" format, most are not even typeset and are merchandised by direct mail.

A still different way to acquire a book is to track down one that is out of copyright. Perhaps you know of an old volume of recipes or quaint household hints, or you come across an intriguing old book while rummaging in the library, at garage sales, or in a used book store. If the copyright has expired, it is now in the public domain and literally up for grabs. What you may want to do is annotate the book, thus bringing it up to date and making it unique.

Malcolm Margolin, of Heyday Books in Berkeley, California, offers yet another alternative. When he learned that the book *Stickeen* had gone out of print, it led him on a merry chase. Margolin felt that the small once-popular book—a story John Muir wrote about himself and a mongrel dog named Stickeen who set out together to explore an Alaskan glacier and got stranded—should be resurrected. Originally brought out in book form in 1909 by Houghton Mifflin, a more recent edition had been published by Doubleday "under license," but sales had been sluggish and it had gone out of print. Heyday Books bought the reprint rights for the duration of the copyright term from Doubleday, then set about reissuing *Stickeen*. The book has been doing well and has gone into a second printing with Heyday's TLC. They often approach backpacking and mountaineering stores to sell the book—a marketing ploy major publishers would consider far too labor-intensive.

Books published before September 19, 1906, are automatically in the public domain. Some that were issued after that are also "reusable," as their original copyright was not renewed. To check on a title's status, contact the Copyright Office at 1921 Jefferson Davis Highway, Arlington, VA 22201. They charge ten dollars an hour for a copyright search and can typically check on three titles in that time.

You can locate old books through antiquarian dealers. Those who specialize in out-of-print books are listed geographically in *American Book Trade Directory*. Once you get your hands on a copy of an old book, it's usually a simple matter to have a printer photograph the pages onto plates. Presto—you're in the publishing business.

Now that you've researched, written, and edited your masterpiece, let's move along and find out how to begin establishing the business framework needed to manage a publishing company.

CHAPTER 4

CONDUCTING BUSINESS

When you embark on a self-publishing journey, you also become a small-business person. This doesn't mean you must go out and rent office space or scale a mountain of red tape. But there are some questions to be answered and things you'll have to do to satisfy the local regulatory agencies. This chapter discusses business location (operating out of your own home and elsewhere), naming your company, how to form a legal business entity, licenses and permits, your company image, and ways to generate working capital.

Business location

Where are you going to operate? In the beginning, working out of your home usually makes the most sense. It helps keep down overhead. Ideally, you will have a bedroom or den which can be used as an office. If not, a corner of the garage, basement, or even the kitchen table will suffice. Before starting, check with your local business licensing agencies to assure that it is legal to operate from your home. Your local chamber of commerce can tell you whom to contact for this and other requirements for setting up a new business.

Get a post office box so your publishing company will have an address different from that of your home. You'll look more professional if you don't seem to be operating out of your basement or garage, even if that's really the case.

Of course, as your business grows and prospers, the office-in-home may become impractical. Most locales forbid employees or heavy pickup and delivery activities at businesses operated in residential areas. Consequently, if you are planning on starting out with one or more employees, it may be wise to rent commercial office space. Perhaps you can share an office at first to minimize expenses. Check the classified ads under "Office Space for Rent" to see what's available.

Naming your business

Notice that we referred to your venture as your "publishing company." The second point to consider is the right name for your new venture. It's prudent to tack the words "press," "publishing company," "books," or "publishers" on the name to help eliminate any doubts about what you do.

Be wary of choosing a name that is too specific. While a company called Wildlife Publications would be fine for your first book on wildflowers of the Northwest, what happens when your second title, *How to Be a Good Stepparent*, is ready to be published? Likewise, geographic names can be limiting. Don't you agree that Tampa Bay Books sounds much less substantial than Windsong Books International? Your choice can also influence how easy it is to sell your company downstream and how receptive vendors are in letting you establish credit. Looking big has definite advantages.

If you want to spark your thinking about press names, try leafing through *Writer's Market, Fiction Writer's Market, LMP,* and *The Small Press Record of Books in Print* directory. So many names of existing small presses, conventional or unusual, are listed in these sources that one or another is likely to help you come up with one that will be all your own.

Be sure you do *not* include any part of your own name in the company title. Why? Because you want to come across as an official publishing entity, not as a writer who publishes his or her own work. Including your personal handle would be a dead giveaway. John Martin publishing a book as Martin Press leaves little to the imagination.

When you arrive at a name, always check in *LMP, Small Press Record of Books in Print,* and the publishers section of *Books in Print* to avoid duplicating an existing publisher's name. (Duplication could cause numerous errors and missed sales.)

To use your new name legally, you'll probably need to file a "fictitious name statement." In most locales this is done by paying a small fee and advertising on four consecutive weeks your intention to "do business as" (dba) XYZ Publishing Company. You'll receive instructions when you apply for your dba. (By the way, you can save money by looking for a little weekly neighborhood paper instead of inserting your notice in the major daily newspaper.)

Forming your business entity

The third consideration is what type of business structure to use.

Sole proprietorship

It is best to start as a sole proprietor, meaning you alone control the business. It is also the simplest to set up and operate. Profits or losses are considered part of your personal income. Funds can easily be transferred between personal and business accounts. The sole proprietorship allows flexibility for freewheeling operations. Of the 15 million businesses in America, over 11 million operate in this fashion.

Partnership

Occasionally writers team up as partners, or a self-publisher gets a financial backer and forms a partnership. Partnership agreements are somewhat complicated, and we recommend that you have an attorney create or review any agreement. This will assure that the agreement accomplishes your intent and protects all parties. Also be aware that in a partnership each person is completely responsible for the debts and obligations of the whole partnership, not just half of them. Additionally, your partner can make promises and incur debts about which you have no knowledge, but for which you *do* have financial responsibility! A tricky business unless you know and trust the other person totally. A better solution could be to incorporate. (Also see the *limited* partnership explained later in this chapter under "Generating Working Capital.")

Corporation

As your business grows, it might be in your best interest to incorporate. In the beginning, however, the drawbacks will usually outweigh the advantages.

Drawbacks include more regulations from state and federal authorities. You will not be able to operate in the same freewheeling way that a sole proprietor often does. Social Security tax for yourself will be somewhat more, too. Unemployment taxes must be paid to the federal and state government covering yourself as an employee. Accounting procedures become more complicated, and personal and corporate funds cannot be intermixed. Your salary is watched closely by tax offices.

Advantages become significant after your business is established. You can set up and be included in employee benefits, such as insurance, tax-sheltered pension plans, profit sharing, and bonus plans. These are not available to the unincorporated owner-operator. Your personal assets cannot be attached by creditors. If you decide to publish other authors, the corporate shield protects against liability suits. The corporation can fully deduct medical insurance and charitable contributions, reducing the amount you personally spend. But you yourself are still allowed the standard deduction. You can also sell shares to help fund your publishing venture. Corporate shares are more attractive to investors than interest in unincorporated businesses. We'll be talking more about this shortly under "Generating working capital." The subject is rather complex, and readers interested in selling shares are encouraged to seek fuller details in the books noted in that section.

Authors could also consider a Subchapter S Corporation. This provides the legal protection of a corporation but permits the profits or losses to flow directly through to the shareholders as though it were a partnership. It is especially useful as a tax shelter when there are losses, provided there is other income to shelter.

A corporation has a permanency not available to sole proprietorships or partnerships. When a sole proprietor or partner dies, the business is legally dissolved and must be reorganized to continue.

Should you decide to incorporate, remember that attorney fees are costly. Why not save several hundred dollars and do it yourself? We've discovered several good guides: *Incorporating Your Business*, by John Kirk, *Inc. Yourself*, by Judith H. McQuown, and *Incorporating Your Talents*, by Robert A. Esperti and Renno L. Peterson. Some people set up nonprofit corporations, a time-consuming and complicated process in some states that, among other advantages, makes possible greatly reduced postage rates and access to grant money. However, these are strictly regulated and closely watched by federal and state agencies, and you probably will require an attorney's assistance.

Legal advice

If you need an attorney, here are a couple of suggestions.

Lawyer referral groups include: The California Area Lawyers for the Arts, Fort Mason Center, Building C, Room 255, San Francisco, CA 94123; and 315 West Ninth Street, Los Angeles, CA 90015.

Also check with your local Lawyer Referral Service, listed in the white pages of the telephone directory. This is a nationwide service that will refer you to an attorney who handles your type of legal question. You will receive a thirty-minute consultation for about $20. (Sometimes the session is even free.) If your consultation exceeds thirty minutes, the maximum fee will be $30. Not bad for the services of a $100-an-hour lawyer. However, before wasting your time or that of the attorney, be sure he or she specializes in literary work or can handle your general business question.

Another time you may want legal advice is when you're negotiating with a trade publisher to sell reprint rights. There are many aspects of a book publishing contract that are "flexible" — if you're savvy enough to know how to effectively mediate certain clauses. Often an attorney or consultant who is conversant with publishing contracts can be less expensive than paying an agent to evaluate/negotiate your contract.

Licenses and permits

The fourth point you want to investigate is what licenses and permits are necessary. In most parts of the country the laws require people who operate businesses to have a business license. Check with your city officials as to regulations.

If your state has sales tax or a similar form of taxation, you'll also need a seller's permit. Here's a bit of advice: When you go to get your seller's permit, be a most *humble* person. If you tell them you're going to sell thousands of dollars' worth of books, they'll tell you to leave a hefty deposit against future taxes and report your taxes quarterly. On the other hand, if you meekly comment that you're going to print a couple of hundred books and sell them to friends, you'll probably duck the deposit completely and only have to report annually.

While you're there, be sure to get a sales tax chart so you know exactly what percent of tax to charge on all retail sales made in your state.

Your company image

Now that you have located, named, established, and licensed your new baby, it's time to send out birth announcements. Key places that are important to your operation should start hearing about you as soon as possible.

Of course, you will want to get company letterhead, envelopes, and probably business cards before you start your announcement campaign. Spend some time and thought on your letterhead design. You may want a distinctive logo. A logo is the company's special identifying mark or symbol. Perhaps your company name lends itself to a graphic. For instance, a flying bird, Pegasus, or even the Winged Victory would be a good logo for Winged Publications, Inc. Your local printer can steer you to a graphic artist who will be able to suggest an appropriate design for your letterhead. Remember that your stationery and business card make the first impression. Don't skimp here. Be sure it is uncluttered, professional-looking, and printed on quality paper.

It's a good idea to also include the new four-digit ZIP code addition. It will eventually be mandatory. For details, contact your local postmaster.

Company image, like personal integrity, is of great value. In building a company image, it is important that the industry start hearing and seeing the name. Send news releases announcing your company and its focus to potential vendors, suppliers, and local news media. Further, it's a good idea to make friends with your mail carrier or the folks at the post office. They will become important "unofficial" company members.

You will want to start building a good company credit rating immediately. To qualify for accounts with various suppliers, it may be necessary to use your personal credit history at first. But in general it's easier to establish business credit than personal credit. Of course, you should open a separate business checking account and pay commercial credit accounts promptly. In addition to building a solid company credit rating, prompt payment often allows you to take a percent discount.

We believe you'll profit by joining COSMEP, the International Association of Independent Publishers. You can do so by sending $50 to P.O. Box 703, San Francisco, CA 94101. As a COSMEP member, you team up with over a thousand writers, editors, and publishers who are committed to preserving vigor, experimentation, diversity, and excellence through free expression in print. This organization publishes a monthly newsletter with market information for writers; technical articles on management, printing, and marketing; distribution outlets; grant information; review sources; and general information about the small-press scene. Members also have access to mailing lists at reduced rates, logos showing that they belong to this trade association, access to group insurance, and other useful support services. And their annual conference is top drawer.

There are also two places you should now contact for information that will be helpful in establishing and managing your enterprise. The Small Business Administration offers a wealth of guidance; much of it is available free. Call its toll-free number, (800)368-5855, and ask for the *Directory of Business Development Publications*.

The SBA has another arm, called SCORE, which could benefit you. It stands for Service Corps of Retired Executives and is made up of some very high-powered men and women, many of whom were corporate officers or successful small-business people before their retirement. They will consult with you free of charge, except for occasional out-of-pocket expenses like travel. While it is unlikely you'll find someone in your area who knows publishing, a SCORE volunteer can still be mighty helpful on general management practices or perhaps in helping create a direct-mail campaign.

The Bank Of America also publishes material you will find useful. You can get a copy of their list of reports by writing the Bank Of America, Dept. 3631, P.O. Box 37000, San Francisco, CA 94137.

Something else of benefit to a new SP-er is Dan Poynter's *Business Letters for Publishers*. It contains a collection of almost eighty creatively written letters covering sales, promotion, finance, information-seeking, and general categories.

Generating working capital

Now you can cash in on another value of a good company image and positive credit rating. A basic truth of business is that it takes working capital (money) to operate. Right now we are going to discuss sources of money. How to determine how much you'll need is in the next chapter.

One of the most obvious is your savings. Don't be too quick to use it, however. In fact, tapping your savings may be the most expensive capital you could use! Let's examine that premise.

Business experts and economists tell us that it is better to use OPM (other people's money) than your own. Why? Here's an example: If you have $5,000 in savings, you can always borrow $5,000. The lending institution will probably not even insist that you use your account as collateral. (Back away if they do.) So you have $5,000 in OPM, plus your initial $5,000 in savings which is still intact. Now $10,000 is available. Turn it around. Suppose you use your $5,000 savings, then try to borrow $5,000. Good luck. Using your own money was costly in this case.

An excellent book on OPM and leveraging is *How to Borrow Your Way to a Great Fortune,* by Tyler G. Hicks. Add it to your business library. Another good source is *Up Your Own Organization,* by Don Dible. *How to Start, Finance, and Manage Your Own Small Business,* revised edition, by Joseph R. Mancuso, is also a valuable guide.

Examine the following money sources to decide which make sense for you. With a good book, a solid business plan, and your strong commitment, money is available.

• Loans/investments from friends or relatives. Forget all the old clichés. Just because you are fond of certain people should not mean that you *protect* them from a good investment! They wouldn't loan you a penny? Have you asked? Shared your manuscript? Explained your marketing plans? That's how Bernard Kamoroff got started. He raised money for his business book from seven friends and relatives. They formed what's called a "limited partnership": They would earn a percentage of profits if there were any, nothing if the book went bust. The agreement was in effect for two printings only; after that the book was 100 percent Kamoroff's. Everyone lucked out on this arrangement. All the investors profited handsomely; and Kamoroff has been raking in the dough on all the annual editions since.

Don't overlook the possibility of relatives or friends cosigning a note. Just be sure that they know this is a business transaction and that their investment doesn't give them carte blanche to tell you how to run things.

• Commercial banks are the backbone of the small-business community. They are conservative, as well they should be. The money they loan belongs to folks like you!

Don't get the idea, however, that business loans are never made to small publishers. It isn't a frequent practice, but it does happen. Although we can't make you a financial wizard within the context of this book, let's examine the basic approach to acquiring a business loan from a commercial bank, venture capitalist, or any other institution or individual.

First, be aware that there are different levels of bank officers. While a regular loan officer at a branch may have a limit of $10,000, a senior loan officer at the main office can go much higher without getting involved with committee approval. The higher you begin, the better your chances.

Second, put together the best possible sales pitch for your book. What makes it special? Why will people buy it? If you are not clear on these issues, you shouldn't be approaching a lender. Use third-party support (what someone else says about it). If the book is nonfiction, what problem does it solve? Don't overlook the approach of having your banker read it. If he or she thinks it's great, you're on your way. Refer to Chapter 14 for more ideas.

Now go over the company's two-year business plan with your banker. (Preparation of this business forecast is explained in the next chapter.) In short, sell your product—explain your plan of action—and ask for the needed cash. If you sincerely believe that this venture is a good investment, you will be hard to resist.

Banks are funny. You never know what will happen when you begin talking to a loan officer. One bank officer Tom spoke with suggested that it was easier to get a personal loan for a European vacation than the same amount of money for a business loan for start-up capital. We don't recommend not telling lenders the truth but that was an interesting observation.

• Savings and loan associations are sources for long-term equity loans. If you decide to finance the business personally and you have equity in your home (you'll be surprised how much it could be), here is a good source. Consider a second or third mortgage. But remember you're going to have higher monthly payments. Will your book sales support them? If not, can you or your mate?

• Credit unions offer low-interest personal loans.

• Life insurance companies are looking for solid business investments. And don't overlook the cash value of your life insurance policy. Cash value loans require no qualification, and interest rates are hard to beat. For instance, if you took out a policy before 1965, you can typically borrow an amount equal to the policy's cash value for about 6 percent interest.

• Retirement funds (pensions) often make loans at very reasonable interest rates. If you participate in such a fund, investigate this as a revenue source.

• Private investors look for high-return investments. Don't overlook this vast pool of funds. Outside investors could buy part interest in your book. After you recover the manufacturing, overhead, and promotion costs, you and the investors would share the profits. One word of caution: Be sure you and your investors are personally compatible or they could thwart you at every turn.

• Venture capital companies are a vague possibility. Usually they seek a situation which allows participation as a major stockholder in return for advanced moneys. While they most often invest in high-tech companies, John Kremer recently did a survey of nineteen firms outlined in his *Venture Capital Sources for Book Publishers*. Get everything in writing and review the proposition with your attorney.

• Suppliers give the small business a tremendous opportunity for what amounts to free thirty- to sixty-day "loans." This is because payment terms are usually "net thirty or sixty days," meaning that you don't have to pay the bill until then. Your company's good credit pays off again. You might even entice your printer into becoming your financier. In this case the printer absorbs the printing costs in exchange for 10 to 20 percent of the sales.

• Corporate stock offers one of the most popular ways to get private investors. Although this method is free enterprise in action, it can only be used by an incorporated business. And it has other drawbacks. When you sell part of the company, you're stuck with whoever buys it; you lose much of your control. Your stockholders may want to have so much input on corporate policy that you become hamstrung in the process.

• Copublishing is another option. In fact, it can be viewed in two ways. In one form of copublishing you join with several other people and divide the actual work and financing of the book project. The other form of copublishing is more sophisticated. Here you work with another entity such as a publisher, association or business. If you work with a publisher, you "package" the book yourself. This involves writing the manuscript, editing, designing, and typesetting. Then the publisher takes over and handles the actual manufacturing, marketing, and fulfillment responsibilities. For your efforts you receive something like 35 percent of the net receipts. To do this you would have to locate a publisher producing books similar to yours and convince them of the viability of your title. You can identify possible publishers by studying *Writer's Market* or *LMP*.

When you copublish with a business or association, like-mindedness is again the key. We'll also explore the subject of premium books in detail in Chapter 16, but be aware that such an arrangement can be used to negotiate money up front for your printing expenses.

• Does the idea of having bucks in advance reassure you? Perhaps selling advertising in your book should be considered. You can sell the inside front cover, inside back cover, plus quarter, half, or full interior pages. If you decide to run with this idea, put together an advertising rate sheet and realistic figures on how many books you expect to sell. You must be a good salesperson and have reassuring information if you expect potential advertisers to part with their cash. (We go into detail on how to do this in our *How to Make Big Profits Publishing City and Regional Books*.) This works well for certain kinds of books where commercial product or service tie-ins coincide with the subject matter. Including advertising will knock you out of fourth-class book rate if the post office scrutinizes your book, however, so be prepared to fork over more postage.

• Another innovative way to generate working capital is to presell your book. We will cover this approach in more detail in later chapters. Briefly, you can do a prepublication special mailing to your personal mailing list — you know: friends and acquaintances, people who've given you their business cards, your Christmas card list, fellow alumni, and any other similar groups whose addresses you have. To special sales outlets or wholesalers, offer a generous discount for cash-in-advance early orders. Run mail-order ads that collect money for future book fulfillment. By using such tactics, many self-publishers earn enough to pay their printing bill before a single book has rolled off the press.

• Subscribers could also be your answer. Years ago in England poets used this approach to cover the costs of printing books of their poems. More recently, it was employed by David McCann, an assistant director of foundation relations at Cornell University. McCann put together a collection of his poems, titled it *Keeping Time*, then put out a classy announcement offering subscriptions. Many of his family, friends, and colleagues were delighted to participate. For a nominal sum, their names were listed in the back of the book and they received a copy upon publication. By using this patron approach, McCann was able to cover the majority of his self-publishing expenses.

• Attending a writers' colony or retreat may also be helpful. While it will not likely provide you with working capital, it may help get your book written. They often supply free room and board — and sometimes a fellowship which can help with book publishing expenses — to budding authors and artists. Stays range from as short as a week to several months. Such places offer unencumbered time and valuable association with talented people in the same field. *Writer's Digest* magazine publishes lists of such retreats from time to time.

• Grants can offer small presses (not necessarily self-publishers) another money source. As a rule, they are designed either to support a general work-in-progress or to fund a particular project. In most cases the small press must either have nonprofit, incorporated status and an IRS tax exemption, or find a sponsoring organization to provide such a conduit. Grants, like ice cream, come in three main flavors: national governments, state governments, and private foundations and corporations.

The vanilla of grants is represented by The National Endowment for the Arts, the largest single granting agency. The NEA's Literature Program is headed by Stephen Goodwin. In fiscal 1987, the Literature Program awarded 190 grants in literary publishing for a total of $1.5 million. The NEA's Assistance to Small Press grant program currently offers awards of from $2,000 to $25,000. Individual fellowships are also available.

While past emphasis has been to support poetry projects, today there is a more balanced program. The NEA has been the road into print for poetry, fiction, creative prose, and contemporary creative literature. If your book has more literary merit than commercial appeal, this is a particularly intriguing funding source. To get more information, write the Literature Program at the address below. They will send you a booklet containing guidelines, application instructions, and an application form.

State funding is next in volume, the chocolate of grants. It is given via state arts councils. New York State leads this pack. A recent annual budget for literature was a whopping $940,000. California and, surprisingly, Massachusetts have the next largest budgets. To get information on what is available and how to apply, contact the state arts council in your state capital.

Foundation and corporate fund-raising is the strawberry flavor of grants. It is extremely difficult, however, to determine who might have money available for your book. If you decide to pursue this course, talk to your librarian about listings of foundations and other private organizations that have grant money available for research. Sometimes you can be lucky and dovetail with a specific program that one of these foundations is concentrating on, such as an educational or ethnic-oriented project.

Another source of information is the Grantsmanship Center. It conducts workshops, employs a research staff, maintains a library, and publishes a magazine. The Center's article "Program Planning and Proposal Writing," gives clear, explicit guidance for the novice grant hunter. Creating a good proposal is over half the battle. This is one place where good writing skills pay off royally. Another helpful tool is *Grants and Awards Available to American Writers,* published by PEN American Center, which recently completed a new edition of this comprehensive list of prizes, grants, fellowships, and awards. You can obtain a copy by sending seven dollars to the address below.

The *Washington International Arts Letter (WIAL)* is yet another reservoir for grant information. It publishes literature covering patronage, support programs, and developments in the arts and government. WIAL offers many interesting books and publications on grants for individuals as well as companies. (See address below.)

Lastly, for our friends to the north, there are a couple of Canadian grant resources that may be helpful. The Writing and Publications Programme of the Multiculturalism Directorate is designed to encourage, support, and develop projects of a historical and literary nature. In 1982/83 it funded more than sixty projects and about fifty publications. Recent policy changes have extended its criteria to include individuals and publishing houses. For more information, write Adrian Papanek, Programme Officer, Multiculturalism Directorate, Ottawa, Ont. K1A 0M5. Another place to look for suitable donors is the *Canadian Directory of Charitable Foundations and Granting Agencies.*

Grant Information—Literature Program
National Endowment for the Arts
Nancy Hanks Center
1100 Pennsylvania Avenue N.W.
Washington, DC 20506

The Grantsmanship Center
1031 South Grand Avenue
Los Angeles, CA 90015

PEN American Center
568 Broadway
New York, NY 10012

Washington International Arts Letter
P.O. Box 12010
Des Moines, IA 50312

Going after grants is time-consuming hard work. But when you click, the rewards—like a big bowl of ice cream on a hot day—make it all worthwhile. There *is* money available for a good investment. Your role is to ferret it out. The job of finding the right means to supply your working capital is, however, only one of the many challenges of self-publishing. Now let's go on to investigate some of the others.

CHAPTER 5

OPERATING PROCEDURES

This chapter is an overview of the essential operating procedures of your self-publishing venture—determining monthly expenses, order fulfillment, inventory control, and the secrets of proper pricing and discounts. We also explain tax deductions. Many shortcuts for conducting your business are included.

Understanding operating procedures

It would be as irrational as trying to cross the Atlantic in a kayak to set up your business and expect it to run without operating procedures. More companies fail from aimless drifting than from any other reason. Make sure you have your destination (goals and objectives) firmly in mind and steer an unerring course. Goals and objectives provide the basis for generating your business plan. (See the section on goal-setting in Chapter 1.) Nothing, however, takes the place of action. A business plan is simply the "how to do it" plan of attack.

When we set our goals in Chapter 1 the "hows" were ignored. No evaluation or judgment was made on the ways in which we would accomplish them. Rather, the goals were intuitively established. The chance of reaching these goals without a plan is like navigating without a compass. A business plan provides the necessary navigational tools.

Scheduling is the first consideration in developing a business plan. Create a detailed schedule of each task or event and when it must occur to reach your goal. Determine the "whats" and "whens" that must be done. The Publishing Timetable in the Appendix will be helpful in doing this.

Next comes the "who" analysis. Decide which activities and events you will personally handle. Do you have helpers? What will they do?

While such things as preparing labels or envelopes for a mailing list or packaging books for shipment can be safely delegated, you will personally want to handle such vital functions as final proofreading and developing a nationwide marketing plan. Then consider which functions will be accomplished by vendors such as designers, typesetters, and printers. When this step is completed, a "who" will be assigned to each "what."

Now that the who, what, and when of the plan are integrated, it's time to consider feasibility. What is the probability of tasks reaching completion as outlined? Determine how many hours each task is estimated to take. Then to be safe, double it. Is the needed time between events available? Make the necessary adjustments to ensure that all steps are feasible. If you can only spend twenty hours per week on your part-time publishing venture, don't schedule thirty hours. Perhaps some part-time help must be added. Or you may need to delay or stretch certain functions. Perhaps you'll need longer to write the book. Maybe if you're pasting it up yourself, you'll do that over a longer period of time. You may even have to stall awhile on some of the more imaginative promotional angles you want to try. Or, as many busy professionals do, hire consultants like us to relieve you of the burdens.

Be aware of schedules that create sudden needs for additional people. The fact that it takes one woman nine months to have a baby doesn't mean a nine-woman co-op can produce a baby in one month. When such scheduling inconsistencies occur, the plan may need to be revised. Review it thoroughly. Make any adjustments necessary to have the pieces fit together. All of the parts must add up to a whole. Perhaps you need to reevaluate your goals. Are they too ambitious? A little tailoring will soon yield the desired—and achievable—result.

Determining monthly expenses

If these results could be achieved without regard to cost, the plan would be complete. But for most of us, part of the goal is to make a net profit. This means expenses must be determined and integrated into the plan. To ease the job of establishing cost factors for each task, figure out your monthly operating expenses. At this point do not include "cost of sales" (any money expended for production or sale of your book). Be sure to include the following items in the recurring monthly expenses or overhead:
- Payroll, employees' total earnings
- Rent
- Operating supplies
- Taxes and licenses
- Automobile expenses (gas, repairs, tires, insurance, parking fees)

- Interest
- Utilities
- Telephone
- Advertising
- Insurance
- Equipment rental and repair
- Duplicating and printing
- Postage

Note: Money drawn from the business by the owner and payments for capital equipment purchased on credit are not considered expenses. These are listed as other payments. Even so, they should be included as part of monthly outlay for this exercise.

After arriving at a total of our recurring monthly expenses, it is simple to figure weekly or hourly overhead rates. (Weekly = 12 × monthly ÷ 52. Hourly = 12 × monthly ÷ 2080.) These figures must be added to cost of sales to arrive at actuals for each activity.

To develop your cost of sales, you must arrive at figures for:
- Contract labor (typing, editing, order fulfillment, marketing consulting, etc.)
- Design
- Typesetting
- Printing
- Binding
- Shipping (Ask your printer for estimated costs.)

These items are considered cost of sales because money is spent (a) to create the product or (b) only when sales occur.

Combining all the cost and expense figures you developed gives you your profit and loss projection for the goal period. It's wise to project a minimum of two years. This will make any banker or financial backer feel more comfortable. It shows that you have done your homework, know what is going on—and what will be going on—in your business. See the following P&L Projection for 1989 example.

Let us review the components of the business plan. We have identified and scheduled those activities that must occur so that our goal can be accomplished. The doer has been named. Hours required to complete tasks have been estimated. Finally, costs were analyzed and applied. All that is needed now is to devise some method to monitor, control, and provide feedback on performance.

Bookkeeping

Bookkeeping/Accounting provides this vital monitor of performance. "I'm definitely not a bookkeeper," you say? Neither were we. But with the help of the local office supply store, we located *The Ideal System, Book-keeping and Tax Record for Manufacturers Number 3131.* Although 3131 is not for publishers per se, it comes close. A few expense heading modifications and it works fine. *Ideal* provides easy-to-follow instructions and examples. Or you might want to use one of the many computerized bookkeeping systems available. This topic is addressed in our later chapter "Computers in Publishing." With a minimum of time and effort, you will become an adequate bookkeeper. The most difficult thing will likely be the discipline to make entries once a week. Daily entry is not required unless you have a great volume of daily transactions.

When entries are kept up to date, it is a simple matter to complete the monthly summary. This summary gives the information needed to compare what you planned to do with what you actually did. Take time to make this analysis to ensure that you're on course.

Order fulfillment

The term used for the entire order entry, invoicing, and shipping process is "order fulfillment." There are basically two ways by which orders are received by self-publishers. One is face-to-face contact, wherein the product is presented, an order placed, and merchandise delivered in one call. If the delivery point is also the billing address, the invoice is left with the buyer. The second method is mail order. Mail call is a daily "high" for the self-publisher because it brings credit orders, orders with checks enclosed, and payments for previous credit orders. Imagine: money in your mailbox!

The face-to-face sale need only be entered into the bookkeeping records after you return to the office. But mail order sales involve other complications. Let's examine the entire order fulfillment procedure and take a credit step by step from the mailbox through shipping and invoicing.

The first step is credit approval. Frankly, we've become much more conservative since the recession in the early eighties. Too many bookstores and little distributors went belly-up and left us holding worthless invoices. If you intend to sell to bookstores or wholesalers, you may want to establish a policy of running a credit check on all orders over fifty dollars. To do this, ask prospective customers for their banker's name and phone and their firm's account number. Also request two or three accounts with whom the firm has done business for a year or more. Call these people and find out if the bookstore or distributor pays promptly and has a good financial reputation. Another clue to financial stability is if their order is on preprinted P.O. (purchase order) forms or letterhead: The theory is that if a firm has invested in official stationery, it's slightly less likely to either go broke or disappear, your valuable books still unpaid

PROFIT & LOSS PROJECTION
Fiscal 1985

GROSS SALES

BOOKS	MY STORY Retail 2,500 @ 8.95	22,375
	MY STORY Wholesale 2,500 @ 3.975	11,185
CONTRACT LABOR	Editing 50 hrs. @ $20/hr	1,000
	Typing 36 hrs. @ $12/hr	432
TOTAL SALES		34,992

COST OF SALES

Payroll	1,200
Rent	480
Office/Operating Supplies	240
Taxes & Licenses	200
Auto Expenses	600
Interest	1,200
Utilities	120
Telephone	600
Advertising	14,000
Insurance	100
Equipment Rental & Repair	240
Xeroxing & Printing	5,600
Postage	1,200

TOTAL EXPENSES	25,780
NET PROFIT	9,212
LOAN REPAYMENT	(1,200)
CAPITAL EQUIPMENT PURCHASES	(240)
OWNER DRAW	(7,200)
SPENDABLE GAIN	572

P&L projection chart.

for. If you get a large order from some outfit you can't otherwise check, there's nothing wrong with asking for payment in advance "until credit is established." Many self-publishers do this as a matter of course on *any* order.

Incidentally, there do exist swindlers who order books from small presses without having any intention of paying for them. They order in large quantities and then sell the books to used-book stores.

We once received an exciting first order for 420 books from an unknown distributor in Michigan. It was typed on a standard P.O. form anyone can get at the dime store. There was no listing for this distributor in *LMP;* that was the first tiny red flag. When Marilyn called to check the company's credit references, she was given a bank reference that proved to be only three months old and already had experienced a bounced check. Needless to say, we declined to ship books to this source. Unfortunately, many other small publishers did not. This particular distributor filed for bankruptcy and was investigated for mail fraud. Still, there's no need to become paranoid: Businesslike caution ought to be enough protection.

For the biggies like Waldenbooks and B. Dalton you may want to ship any amount. Why? Because they aren't likely to go out of business and because credit checks cost money. However, we've discovered that dealing with the big chains costs money anyway. Inevitably, their accounts-payable department loses our statements, fails to respond to repeated billings and letters, and causes us many frustrating and expensive long-distance phone calls before a bill is paid. Additionally, they are famous for trying to return books long past the stated deadline.

Once you feel comfortable with credit approval procedures, you must create an invoice for the orders. We previously used a fancy four-part preprinted form for this purpose. Now we use the one shown adjacent which we had typeset. We simply duplicate a quantity, write in sequential numbers, and type them up as needed. It also serves as a packing slip and mailing label when folded into an "invoice enclosed" envelope. We photocopy the finished invoice for our records and that's all there is to it. If you don't have easy access to a photocopier, one of the multi-sheet preprinted forms we just mentioned will provide you a copy of each completed invoice for your files.

Either immediately as the orders arrive or once a week enter the order, including the invoice number, under the "accounts receivable" and "sales" sections of the company books. Enter any face-to-face sales the same way. Create a "quantity shipped" column and record the number of copies that go out the door. Since you made careful count of your books and logged them when they arrived from the printer, your running inventory will let you know exactly how many copies of the book you

PURCHASE ORDER

No. *608*

This number must appear on all invoices, packages, & correspondence

Date *6/18/84*

THESE ITEMS ARE FOR RESALE

Bill To: SAN *120-1662*

BANBURY BOOK SHOP
20929 VENTURA BLVD.
WOODLAND HILLS, CA 91364

Ship To: SAN *120-1662*

BANBURY BOOK SHOP
20929 VENTURA BLVD.
WOODLAND HILLS, CA 91364

Vendor: *DRELWOOD PUBLICATIONS*
% COMMUNICATION CREATIVITY
P O. BOX 213
SAGUACHE, CO   81148

SHIPPING INSTRUCTIONS

Ship via: *BOOK POST*

Ship ( ) at once   Cancel back orders if not
( ) on _____ 19 ____ shipped: ( ) at once
                                   ( ) within ___ days
( ) Do ( ) Do NOT insure at our expense.

If this order requires clarification, contact:
Name *Jackie LaLline*   Phone No. *818 348-1644*

Please furnish _____ invoice copies

ISBN	Quantity	Author	Title or Description			
0-937766-08-9	1	E. BAKER	BANDWAGON TO HEALTH:			
			THE ALL NATURAL WAY TO EAT,			
			THINK AND EXERCISE			6.95
0-937766-05-4	1	E. BAKER	UNCOOKBOOK; RAW FOOD			
			ADVENTURE TO A NEW			
			HEALTH HIGH			5.95
			— less discount			
FC D						

rec'd
6/21/84

Jackie LaLine
Authorized Signature

Purchase order.

have on hand.

State sales tax is collected when you make retail sales in your own state. (Current legislation before Congress aims to change this, but we hope it will be defeated!) Tax is *not* charged when bookstores and whole-salers purchase merchandise for resale purposes (get their resale number on file) or when books are shipped to individuals out of state. How much to charge, and how and when to hand these taxes over to the appropriate governmental agency, will be explained when you apply for and obtain your own resale number.

COMMUNICATION CREATIVITY *a colorado corporation*
County Road FF38
P.O. Box 213
Saguache, CO 81149
(719) 852-4123 or (719) 589-5995

INVOICE

INVOICE DATE: INVOICE NO:

BILL TO

SHIP TO (IF DIFFERENT)

P.O. NUMBER	SALESPERSON	TERMS NET 30 DAYS	SHIPPED VIA	DATE SHIPPED

QUANTITY ORDERED	SHIPPED	ISBN NUMBER	DESCRIPTION TITLE	AUTHOR	LIST	%	NET
		0-918880-00-9	Discover Your Roots	Heimberg	3.95		
		0-918880-05-X	The Encyclopedia of Self-Publishing	Ross-Ross	29.95		
		0-937766-05-4	The UN!cook Book	Baker-Baker	5.95		
		0-936890-05-3	How to SINGLE Out Your Mate	Soules	4.95		
		0-936944-00-5	Signing Off	Homer	3.95		
		0-918880-03-3	Buffalo Management & Marketing	Jennings-Hebbring	19.95		
		0-937766-08-9	Bandwagon to Health	Baker-Baker	6.95		
		0-935378-00-6	Does God Still Bless America?	Armstrong	5.95		
		0-89879-167-7	The Complete Guide to Self-Publishing	Ross-Ross	19.95		
		0-399-13326-7	Breaking Into the Boardroom	Melia	14.95		
		0-918880-11-4	National Survey of Newspaper Op-Ed Pages	Ross	15.00		
		0-918880-12-2	How to Make Big Profits Publishing City & Regional Books	Ross-Ross	14.95		
		0-918880-14-9	The UN!medical Book	Baker-Baker	8.95		
		0-918880-15-7	Book Promotion & Marketing (tapes)	Ross-Ross	69.95		
		0-918880-18-1	Lotto: How to Wheel a Fortune	Howard	14.95		
		0-918880-21-1	Marketing Your Book	Ross-Ross	9.95		

PLEASE PAY FROM THIS INVOICE.
SORRY, NO DISCOUNTS ON SINGLE TITLE ORDERS.
AFTER 60 DAYS 1½% INTEREST PER MONTH WILL BE CHARGED.

BOOK TOTAL	
TAX	
SHIPPING CHARGE	
TOTAL	

Federal ID #84-0834372

Okay, it's on to the shipping desk . . . which may well be your kitchen table. About 85 percent of all books are shipped fourth-class book rate (book post), which is an inexpensive way to disseminate information. Even with recent increases, it remains the most economical method for shipping. It is not, however, the most reliable. On larger orders, we now ship UPS because the U.S. Postal Service has lost too many cases of books.

But you must first determine where all those books will be stored. They certainly won't fit under the bed! Some options are your garage, a large closet, or renting space in a small storage facility. Or perhaps you have a friend with warehousing space in his business establishment. Be sure that wherever you warehouse them it's *dry*. Nothing would be more disastrous than to discover you had case after case of soggy books. You may also want to insure them by having a rider attached to your home-owner policy. Library rate, even cheaper than book post, is available for books sent by a publisher to a school, college, or library. Because postal rates change so often, you should ask the Postal Service for a table of current rates.

Standard procedure is for the buyer to pay the shipping charges except on prepaid orders. When individuals order a book, they usually expect to pay a postage-and-handling charge of about two dollars. Often the general public reads a review about a book that doesn't mention the shipping costs, however, so the consumer sends only the cost of the book. What do you do? We've found the simplest solution is to type up a little form such as the one shown and indicate the amount owed. Send this form along with the book. In most cases the person remits the additional amount.

P. O. Box 213
Saguache, Colorado 81149

YOUR ATTENTION PLEASE

Thank you for your order. However, you overlooked the amount indicated below. So as not to hold up your order, we are shipping it anyway. Please return this note with the balance due listed below so we can clear your account.

Customer names: _____
Titles ordered: _____

_____ Credit Card Processing Fee (CCPF)
_____ Colorado sales tax
_____ Postage and handling
_____ No discount on one-book orders

BALANCE DUE $ _____

Remit to: Communication Creativity, P. O. Box 213, Saguache, Colorado 81149
PLEASE RETURN THIS NOTE WITH YOUR PAYMENT. WE APPRECIATE YOUR COOPERATION.

Money due form

There are some rather odd requirements that apply to items shipped by book post. To qualify, it used to be that a booklet had to contain at least twenty-four pages, twenty-two of which had to contain *printed material*. In November 1984, however, the U.S. Postal Service reduced the requirement to eight pages. Another requirement is that a booklet be saddle-stitched (stapled) in at least three places. A student in one of our recent seminars learned about this the hard way. Her book was assembled with two staples. She received a call from the postmaster informing her that her shipment of several dozen books did not qualify for book post. She wound up at the main post office, stapler in hand, opened each package, added a staple, and sealed the packages again.

Additionally, you cannot include general advertising in your book and get the benefit of book post. Only incidental announcements of books (flyers and catalog sheets) and order blanks may be included to comply with postal regulations. Although these requirements may seem nonsensical, compliance saves a hassle and costly unproductive hours.

If you want to get books across the country quickly, book post is not the best way. According to one study, book post averages twelve days. One shipment took thirty-seven days. Freight also averages twelve days, whereas UPS (United Parcel Service) typically takes eight days. Average cost per pound in this study showed book post at 14.8 cents, freight at 12 cents, and UPS at 22 cents. All costs have since gone up. To speed things up somewhat, UPS Blue Label (a rush service) is another option. Of course, if you're really in a hurry, there is now Express Mail, Federal Express, UPS red, and several other overnight options, all of which probably cost more than the book itself.

As of April 1988, for Special Fourth Class Book Rate, it's 90¢ for the first pound, 35¢ more per pound for pounds two through seven, and 20¢ more per pound for weights over seven pounds.

Library rates and first class also rose as of that date. The twenty-four page book limit has been reduced to eight pages to qualify for book rate.

International postage is a whole different ball game. Surface mail is naturally much less costly than airmail, but also takes months to arrive. International rates are also due for an increase, so check with your post office for costs and regulations.

Careful selection of shipping containers can cut your costs. As an example, we found that one copy of *Creative Loafing* shipped in a jiffy bag weighed slightly over one pound. Marilyn started a campaign to find a shipping container that would drop weight under the one-pound mark. After some fancy spadework, the weight was reduced by using Sentinel brand shipping bags, which resulted in a savings of 18¢ per single-copy shipment. The bubble-type bags are usually your best bet. For larger multiple-copy orders, use a sturdy box. You can find odd-lot boxes by checking in the yellow pages (the business-to-business yellow pages if your community has them) under "boxes." It is wise to encourage full case purchases since you can then use the cased books just as they came from the printer and avoid laborious unpacking and repacking. You can offer special discounts and do your best to sell the idea of ordering full cases when writing or talking to the buyers who are ordering many copies at a time.

We've been asked by students about insuring the books shipped out. This would be prohibitively expensive. Yes, when you send book post, you will eventually lose some books, but it's cheaper in the long run than insuring every copy that's mailed.

Have a rubber stamp made that states "Fourth Class Book Rate—Return Postage Guaranteed." (Self-inking stamps cost a little more but save time.) Stamp each package and firmly affix the delivery address label or invoice. Weigh the package and use the correct amount of postage. Packages can be carried to the post office counter for weighing and postage. But remember, time is valuable and standing in line is nonproductive, so you may want to invest in a scale that goes up to twenty-five pounds.

Now file the remaining invoice copies in an accounts-receivable file (an accordion-style alphabetical file works great), and you're finished with this order until monthly billing time.

Monthly billings

Monthly billings are used to get in front of credit buyers and jog their memories. We recommend that end-of-the-month reminders be routinely sent to all credit customers over ten dollars. Get the statements in the mail early enough to allow them to be in the customers' accounts-payable file on the first day of the month.

Most credit customers are happy to pay bills from invoices. You simply send a photocopy or an extra carbon of the invoice from your accounts receivable file. However, a few demand monthly statements (an itemized list of all outstanding invoices, plus credits from any payments or returns during the billing period).

It makes sense to send copies of invoices in lieu of statements to any accounts that have no more than one or two unpaid purchases. However, for customers who have three or more orders per month, the monthly statement is preferable. An example of a monthly statement is shown on the following page.

Hold a hard line with very slow-paying customers. It is a sad fact in this industry that it isn't unusual for a bill to go ninety days without being paid. We suggest you take the following steps when a bill is ninety days past due (assuming it is large enough to warrant your time—perhaps over twenty dollars. Always remember that time is money. It's a lot smarter to spend fifteen minutes opening up a new sales channel than it is to devote that time to sending a dun letter for a five-dollar book.) On seriously delinquent accounts call and discuss the problem with the accounts-payable supervisor or the store manager. If that doesn't shake loose some money, send a letter restating your standard credit terms and saying that discounts will be forfeited—that is, the buyer will be charged full list price—if the bill is not paid within ten days. If payment is not received within that time limit, invoice the customer for the difference between the discounted price and the retail price. Or you can inform the buyer that you will begin charging the unpaid account 1½ percent interest per month. Or you can state that unless full payment is received promptly

YOUR COMPANY NAME AND ADDRESS

STATEMENT   12/29/79

B. DALTON BOOKSELLER
9340 James Avenue
P.O. Box 1268
Minneapolis, MN 55431

PLEASE RETURN THIS STUB WITH YOUR REMITTANCE. YOUR CANCELLED CHECK IS YOUR RECEIPT $_____

DATE	Your #	DESCRIPTION	Our #	CHARGES	CREDITS	BALANCE
10/17	15628		1044	61.77		
10/25	58800		1059	146.45		
11/22	69630		1068	63.42		
11/23	122968		1070	10.61		
12/4	57333		1085	95.06		
12/5		payment on account			279.31	
12/16	25766		1096	61.77		
12/18	64206	return CM 934			[59.70]	100.07

PAY LAST AMOUNT IN BALANCE COLUMN ▲

Rediform 8K872

Monthly statement.

(perhaps within an additional ten days), legal collection procedures will be initiated. But assuming that you want your money and the customer's goodwill and continued business, not a lawyer and a court hearing, this final threat should perhaps be reserved for a last resort.

If the account still ignores payment, notify the customer that the delinquency will now be reported to credit agencies and that small-claims or civil court action will be initiated unless response is immediate. If there is still no response, you have a nasty choice. Either carry through . . . or forget it and write off the sale. We've had very little success in getting judgments or financial satisfaction at this point. Sure, you can get an attorney to send a general collection letter or turn the account over to a collection agency, but don't expect much. That's the main reason we've tailored our operation to a cash basis whenever possible.

Accounts receivable

Received on account payments are always exciting. When a payment on account is received, it is matched to the invoice in the accounts-receivable file, entered into the sales section of the books as cash received on account, and as a separate line entry under the accounts-receivable section of the books as a credit. Locate the entry in the existing accounts-receivable section which created the charge and mark it paid. This will avoid confusion in the next month's billing cycle. Mark the invoice paid and record the check number and date received. File this with income records. Once again, this paperwork can be handled on a weekly basis if preferred.

Returns

Returns represent a much less exciting type of credit with which every publisher must contend. It is an undeniable fact that a certain quantity of books shipped will be returned.

Some dealers will ask for a return authorization. If the request is within the time limit specified in your company's terms and conditions of sale (which we'll discuss later in this chapter), it should be approved. Send the customer a credit memo showing how much will be credited for the returns. Use an invoice and show the credit allowed against the original billing invoice. Reinforce the requirement that all returns must be *unblemished* to qualify for a refund. This means the covers are not torn and the interior is like new. Remember, you want to sell these books again!

If you find the returned books damaged and therefore unsellable, issue no credit memo. Require that the account be paid. If the books were damaged in the return process, it's the buyer's business to collect from the shipper, not yours. If the damaged books are hardbound, it may be possible to re-jacket them. If not, or if you don't have extra jackets to spare, donate such books to your favorite hospital or library. Remember, they've already been paid for!

Enter the credit for returns in the sales section as a bracketed negative sale, (e.g., 49.50), and the quantity as a negative, (e.g., 10), and as a separate line item in the accounts-receivable section. Locate the original entry and note "returned" and the quantity. Record the credit on the accounts-receivable file invoice and return the invoice to the system. In cases where you do not do ongoing business with the returning company, you will be expected to send a refund. Unlike large publishers, who can offer credit against other titles, you must ante up.

Inventory control

Inventory control can be very simple . . . or a source of frustration. Remember that one of the entries in the sales section of the company books was a column entitled "Quantity Shipped." Returns are also shown as negative entries in this column. That way you have at your fingertips complete information on shipments and returns — almost!

How about the freebie review and promotion copies you send out? In a later chapter there is a discussion of control cards for these complimentary copies. The cards show quantity shipped and to whom. By simply making a line entry showing "comp copy," date, to whom sent, and a tally in the Quantity Shipped column, however, you have a perfect inventory control. Recording each outgoing book provides a dependable cross-check on other records.

At your local office supply store you can buy inventory sheets in the Ideal Bookkeeping System under the "Proprietor" section. When books are first received from the manufacturer, enter the total received in line one. To establish the inventory "price," add up all the first-run production costs. First-run production costs should include all fees paid for manuscript typing, editing, design, typesetting, printing, and binding. If you personally do one or more of the tasks, use the overhead rate developed under "Determining Monthly Expenses" plus any "draw" taken from the company.

At the end of each month add any new quantities purchased, subtract the net monthly shipments (shipped minus returns), and update the inventory sheet. For the publishing business it makes sense to carry only one title per inventory page. And so we have simple, convenient inventory control as the last of the company operation procedures.

Secrets of proper pricing and discounts

One of the dilemmas every self-publisher faces is how to price the book. Industry estimates say it should sell for anywhere from five to eight times the first-run production costs. Often a greater markup is established for mail-order titles, as people are willing to pay dearly for valuable information. Sometimes mail-order books, especially those based on business topics or how-to-get-rich ideas, are sold at ten, fifteen, even twenty times production costs. Joe Karbo openly stated that his ten-dollar paperback cost him fifty cents to produce.

After much research and testing we have arrived at a *minimum* figure of five times first-run production costs to be profitable. The quantity of the first run should never be more than you are confident you can sell in one year. Otherwise, you have money tied up in inventory that would be better spent on marketing.

Using the recommended formula, here is a hypothetical example of how to price your book, based on a first run of two thousand copies. Adjust the figures to fit your actual cost factors.

$4,300	Three months' overhead expenses
0	Manuscript typing
	(you typed it, so your labor is included in overhead figure)
100	Editing
200	Design
600	Typesetting
2,800	Printing
$4,000	TOTAL

The $4,000 divided by two thousand books equals $2 per book. Multiplying by five yields a $10 suggested retail sales price. Take a tip from major retailers and set the price at $9.95.

We do want to reiterate that the five times formula is a guideline for establishing the *minimum* price at which you can make a profit. If your market research (bookstore browsing) proves that books of this type, length, and quality are all selling for $12.95, adjust the price upward. Surveys indicate that underpricing your product does not sell significantly more books. In fact, sometimes people are suspicious of a book that seems to be priced too low for its type and class. If you seek a sophisticated analysis, you might want to get a copy of John McHugh's publishing report, *How to Evaluate the Profit Potential, Measure Initial Investment and Figure the Break-Even Point of a Book.*

Of course, there is another point that must be considered. What if your market research indicates that the price is too high? The alternatives are: (1) Reduce costs by seeking better production bids. (2) Reduce the size or downgrade the specifications of the book. Perhaps you can eliminate photographs, have a less costly cover, or use cheaper paper stock. (Carefully study the chapters on production for other ways to cut costs.) (3) Price the book at five times anyway. This probably won't hurt sales drastically if it's only a dollar more than similar books. (4) Price your book at less than five times ratio. This will make a profit improbable, if not impossible. (5) Don't publish the book. As harsh as this sounds, it is probably best if your goal is to make money. If, however, you are more interested in seeing your work in print and leaving your literary mark on posterity, then move ahead. Some people and organizations have very valid motivations that have nothing to do with making a profit.

Your dollar breakdown

Where your book dollar goes on the first printing is demonstrated in the following breakdown:

50%	Marketing, promotion, and distribution costs. This includes complimentary copies, postage, discounts, promotional materials, and advertising.
20%	Production costs, including design, typesetting, printing, and binding
20%	Operating overhead
10%	Profit
100%	TOTAL

This breakdown of your dollars spent is critical to your success as a self-publisher. By the way, the "profit" percentage will be much heftier on subsequent printings when part of the production costs will disappear and the larger initial marketing expenses are over with. Moreover, if the book is going to be sold predominantly by mail order, there is no need to worry about discounting. If, however, your market includes bookstores, wholesalers, distributors, and schools, discounts will be necessary.

Discounts

Establishing discounts becomes simple if the experiences of those gone before are used. In a nutshell, bookstores must buy at 40 percent off the list or selling price to make a profit; wholesalers and distributors, which sell to libraries and bookstores, need 50-55 percent. Your discount schedule should get to 40 percent as soon as it is feasible; and to 50 percent on large quantities. While many publishers continue to give bookstores and wholesalers a discount on single title orders, the trend is *not* to do so. We totally concur.

After reviewing dozens of schedules and doing considerable cost analysis, we have arrived at the following suggested discount schedule:

Quantity of Order	Percent of Discount
1	0
2-4	20
5-99	40
100-up	50

Many publishers, including ourselves, do not discount to libraries unless they buy five or more books. We have sold a lot of books to them all across the United States and Canada using this approach. It doesn't seem to hurt sales as quantities are typically one or two copies at a time, and thus not profitable when discounts are allowed. Schools are happy with what is termed a "short discount," meaning 20 percent off the retail price. This applies to college bookstores as well.

There is another discount philosophy that is becoming increasingly popular. This is the "universal discount schedule." Discounts are based strictly on quantities regardless of whether the buyer is an individual, bookstore, wholesaler, library, or school. Of course, discounts are only offered if certain conditions are met.

T's and C's

Terms and conditions are the absolute, cast-in-bronze parameters under which your company sells its product. Think them over carefully. Feel comfortable with them and stick to your policies. Herewith are suggested T's and C's.

• Invoices are due and payable in thirty days from the first of the next month after the date of the invoice.

• Discounts will be forfeited if accounts are not paid with ninety days of due date.

• Interest of 2 percent per month will be charged on delinquent accounts.

• For orders of fifty dollars or more please supply the names of your three largest publisher accounts, plus one bank reference.

• Shipping charges will be added to all credit orders.

• Special-handling requests must be received in writing with the order.

• Special discounts or payment schedules are not available.

• Prices subject to change without notice. All costs slightly higher outside the United States.

Concerning the last item, note that the book's list price is higher outside the United States not just because of the increased shipping costs but because of the difference between the buying power of a dollar and that of foreign currency—what's called the exchange rate. Your banker can tell you the current exchange rate between dollars and particular foreign currency. These two factors—postage and the exchange rate—must be evaluated to figure out what to charge for books sent to customers outside the United States.

You may be tempted to make special deals with certain customers to increase sales. Don't! Be aware that the Federal Trade Commission (FTC) insists that any "deal" you make with one customer must be offered to all like customers. This means that if you sell fifty books at 50 percent discount to one bookstore, by law you must sell fifty books at the same discount to all bookstores. If net 120-day payment terms are allowed one, the FTC says they must be offered to all. Don't trap yourself.

You can legally increase discounts under certain circumstances, however, providing the buyer is willing to give up something in return. Tom has taken many orders for fewer than five books at a 40 percent discount. Contradictory? Not at all. Those sales were made at 40 percent off instead of 20 because of these modifications to the standard T's and C's: *Cash in advance* (books were hand delivered at time of sale, thus eliminating shipping and handling costs), and *no returns* were allowed. Tom had the money and they had the books in a one-stop sale. Ten percent was allowed for payment in advance with no handling and an additional 10 percent for waiver of return privileges. You are also at liberty to arrange special prices for such things as premium sales, which we'll discuss in Chapter 16.

Also be aware that distributors across the country will tell *you* what discount they require to carry your book. In this case, it's all right to go above the 50 percent discount you've established. The *average* discount given by publishers with annual sales of less than $100,000 is 38 percent, according to the 1987 Huenefeld Survey.

Return policy

Return policies are an absolute requirement if you intend to deal with bookstores and wholesalers. Industry return privileges range from 90 days (minimum acceptable to bookstores) to 365 days (far above the acceptable maximum for the self-publisher). After considerable research we arrived at 6 months. The following states a return policy that protects the publisher and satisfies the customer:

"All unblemished books may be returned for credit or refund if received within 6 months of the original invoice date. A copy of the original invoice must be included with return shipment. Shipments must be returned prepaid to [your publishing company address]. Unblemished books are not torn, mutilated, scuffed, or defaced in any way."

Standard terms and conditions of sale can be established by taking the components in this section and putting them together as your "Standard Terms and Conditions of Sale" sheet, which you will send to distributors, wholesalers, and bookstore chains.

Taxes and deductions

Of course, you'll be putting together a report for Uncle Sam annually.

The items listed below can usually be claimed as tax deductions. We suggest you consult a tax accountant or the IRS regarding your personal situation. A fine general guide is *Small Time Operator: How to Start Your Own Small Business, Keep Your Books, Pay Your Taxes, and Stay Out of Trouble,* by Bernard Kamoroff.

Working from your home. Although the reins on this law were tightened recently to eliminate tax breaks for an "office in the home" which is in addition to another office, some nice tax relief is still available. If you use one-half of your home solely for business purposes, you can deduct up to 50 percent of most of your home expenses. That includes such things as your mortgage or rent; gas and electric bills; water, sewer, or trash; and insurance. This amount of this deduction is restricted taxable income your business would have had if this deduction were not taken. As with all deductions, be sure to keep good records. Save those receipts.

Telephone. Whatever portion of your phone you use for business is deductible. (It is advisable, especially if you have teenagers, to have a separate business number.)

Office supplies. Be sure to get receipts for typewriter ribbons, pens, paper, file folders, and all other supplies you purchase. Also remember that stationery, business cards, printed forms, and promotional materials are deductible. And don't overlook the costs of duplicating. Those few copies every week add up to a chunk by the end of the year.

Postage. This will be a considerable amount. Train yourself to always get a receipt at the post office.

Books, magazines, newsletters, newspapers. Whenever you purchase a book for reference, a magazine for research, or subscribe to a newsletter (and virtually all printed matter you purchase falls into that category, right?), get a cash-register receipt so you can claim the expense. And don't forget to include your daily newspaper. No self-respecting writer-publisher could be effective without keeping his or her finger on the pulse of book reviews, not to mention possible local and national publicity tie-ins.

Educational expenses. Fees for seminars and classes related to your work are deductible, as are associated travel, meals, and lodging.

Dues. Dues for the professional organizations you join which relate to writing or publishing are deductible. And if you attend lunch or dinner meetings of these organizations, get a receipt. They're deductible, too.

Travel and mileage. Travel away from home for research, promotion, and speaking engagements is a legitimate expense. Travel for research must be capitalized, however, so you can't claim that expense until the research begins to pay off. Actually, this expense becomes part of the cost of your inventory and is expensed as you sell your books. (See "Major business purchases" below.) Of course, local travel is deductible, on the basis of either so much per mile or a percentage of the actual cost of operating your car. Keep speedometer readings and/or receipts. And don't overlook parking lot fees and the change gobbled up by meters and toll roads.

Entertainment. Be sure to claim any legitimate business meals. Note on the restaurant receipt the name of the person you're interviewing or the customer you're wooing. Don't abuse this category or you may be selected for an audit.

Contract labor. The fees paid any independent contractor are also deductible. If you have someone assist you with typing, editing, envelope stuffing, etc., be sure to keep records of how much you paid, to whom, and why.

Agent and consultant fees. If you use the services of an agent or our publishing consulting service, the fees paid are another deduction.

Major business purchases. There are two ways of handling purchased items. "Expensed" items are deducted totally as a current-year expense. The IRS may raise an eyebrow if the small business tried to expense any fixtures, equipment, or furnishings costing over $100. This will especially hold true if the business is showing a "paper loss."

Many times it is advantageous to you, as well as mandatory because of IRS rules, to "capitalize" larger purchases. Such items as a computer, typewriter, printer, modem, desk, chair, filing cabinet, tape recorder, and telephone answering machine would normally be capitalized and depreciated as "five-year property" (by IRS definition — property that has a useful life of more than four years and less than ten years). Here's an example of one advantage: If your current-year deductions reduce your taxable income to the point that you don't owe any tax, don't waste a valuable deduction by expensing it. By capitalizing the purchase, you will render it deductible as depreciation over several years. Usually it is not worth the paperwork to capitalize purchases under twenty dollars.

Although the 10 percent investment credit has been eliminated per se, the "Election to Expense Depreciable Assets" has more than replaced it. The amount of expense election is limited to $10,000. Except in your *start-up* year, common sense and good management might suggest limiting the expense election to the amount of taxable income before the election. For a profitable operation, doing this can allow a much larger deduction than the old 10 percent investment credit.

You may elect to expense depreciable assets for the current year regardless of the purchase date. (Example: On an IBM-compatible Turbo-XT computer complete with hard disk, printer, and software purchased for $2,995 on December 30, $995, assuming your taxable income before the election was $995, could be deducted as an expense that year.) The remaining cost of the capital investment would be depreciated over its useful life. Using the computer example and Accelerated Cost Recovery

System for a five-year property, you would deduct $300 the first full year, $440 for the second year, and $420 for years three through five. Of course, you may also elect a different depreciations schedule as long as it is longer than the IRS definition. In our example above, we could have elected a ten-year, straight-line depreciation schedule. Our deduction would have then been $200 per year over ten years.

One more thing to keep in mind: If you sell your fully depreciated computer (you have claimed the total cost as a business deduction), the price you sell it for must be reported as income. You may wish to avoid this by estimating the worth of your computer when it is fully depreciated. Suppose you estimate the depreciated value to $450—then your depreciation schedule would look like this: original cost $2,995, minus expensed amount of $995, minus depreciated value of $450, equals $1,550. Your depreciation deductions would then be $232.50 for the first year, $341 for the second year, and $241.50 for years three through five.

While the tips given above hold true in most cases, we do not purport to be tax experts. Consult the IRS office, a tax accountant, or a lawyer if you have questions about these guidelines as applied to your case.

Miscellaneous tips for a smooth-running business

Have you noticed how things get away from some people like a slippery bar of soap? These folks never seem to have a handle on what they're doing. While we know you don't fall in this category, there are a few suggestions we'd like to offer regarding daily business transactions.

Time is money to the self-publisher. Everything you can do to shortcut or save steps is important. When you get the mail, establish a habit of "batching" it for easy handling. You do this by dividing it into separate piles as you open it. Maybe setting up file folders labeled "orders," "payments," "inquiries," "correspondence," and "miscellaneous" would be useful. Another good idea is to create standard forms or checklists wherever possible. (Remember the one on page 67 that we used to solicit forgotten shipping charges?) These needn't be fancy—a typed form that is photocopied is sufficient. The idea is to save yourself from having to sit down and compose a personalized letter. Another timesaver, if you do a lot of phone work, is to keep a file folder of "quickie jobs" on your desk. This might include such things as checks to be signed and Zip codes to be looked up. When you're left hanging on "hold" during those calls, you can whip out these little random quickie jobs.

Speaking of telephones, did you know that if you live in the Rocky Mountain region or farther west, you can save a whopping 60 percent on long-distance phone calls to the East Coast by placing your calls before 8

A.M.? It will be two or three hours later on the eastern seaboard. The reverse works for easterners wanting to call the West Coast. Calls placed after 5 P.M. are typically 40 percent off the normal rate. Also be aware that many big companies have toll-free 800 numbers. To check, call (800)555-1212 and tell the operator the desired company name and location.

Using the telephone instead of writing letters often makes sense. Many calls are under a dollar when you use our money-saving tips — and much quicker than typing a letter. The telephone can also be a handy fig leaf for shy people. If you're timid and hate the thought of approaching local bookstores in person, consider selling to them by telephone.

Something else that will help you be more effective is a big wall calendar. We prefer the 24" by 36" Mylar plastic-laminated ones. You can write on them with colored felt-tip markers and erase at will. It's a great way to organize yourself to keep appointments, meet deadlines and production schedules, and keep track of needed sales follow-up.

As your publishing venture becomes more sophisticated, there are several "helpers" you may want to acquire. Such things as a postage scale, photocopier, postage machine, and computer can make life much easier. An additional benefit is that investment tax credits and depreciation are available on the more costly items. When this is taken into consideration, these laborsaving devices are exceptionally wise purchases.

We can't imagine trotting to the post office, buying an adequate supply of stamps, and licking all those dern things. A postage machine is quick and easy. True, you must pay a monthly rental fee or make some similar arrangement for this convenience, but it's well worth it. Check with your closest Pitney Bowes sales and leasing office for costs and details. Postage scales are available at most office supply stores or through mail order. Get one that goes up to twenty-five pounds plus a baby model for mailings in ounces.

Our photocopy machine is a blessing. We use it to produce sales literature as well as for normal office procedures. Another useful device is a speaker phone, which amplifies the conversation all over the room. With one of these gizmos you can do other things while talking on the phone, rather than being captive to the instrument. An answering machine on your telephone is also good business strategy.

A computer multiplies your results and divides your efforts. We'll be investigating in detail in the next chapter how this technological marvel can assist you.

As your publishing venture grows, if you find yourself in a bind and need some "people" help, an "intern" may be the answer. Interns are students who serve as temporary part-time employees. They perform a variety of jobs, usually for little or no pay. Their reward is the learning experience of working for an actual publisher and often course credit.

Unless you really have your act together, don't expect to acquire such services, as these folks deserve to have bona fide training. You can probably locate an intern through your local university or high school placement office. University English departments are another place to prospect.

We've been fortunate with the interns who worked for us. Bill was a delightful person who contributed a great deal during his internship with us. He remained a friend after the period had lapsed. Kathy was a bubbly young lady as enthralled with book publishing as a kid is with candy. After her intern stint we hired her as a regular employee. She later went on to become an editor with Harcourt Brace Jovanovich.

Our interns worked on specialized projects wherever possible. After being shown what to look for and given the proper reference materials, they did research for marketing plans. Another time they were responsible for proofreading manuscripts. Remember when you commit to using an intern that he or she will only be around a few months. You must find the proper balance between giving enough training and giving so much that you steal time from other important duties.

As we talk about business procedures, it is well to discuss one aspect that many self-publishers ignore. That is the area of revisions to your book. Most of us are so relieved finally to have that thing off the press and in print that we neglect to continue refining the product. As soon as you receive your printed book, you should set up a "revision" folder. Here's where you place updated material for future editions, new information you come across, or notes about obsolete material. It's also a good idea to take one book and designate it a "correction copy." Note any overlooked typos that friends tactfully point out to you or other errors you belatedly discover. By doing these two things, going back to press will be less effort and more fun.

One other aspect of your publishing business (which will *not* be fun) is handling complaints. From time to time people will call or write to say they never received their books. Check back through your sales log to verify that you received and filled their order. Then use a standard form to tell them when it was sent and remind them that book post is a slow mail procedure. Request that they check back again with you in a couple of weeks if they have not received the shipment. If that is the case, you have no alternative but to reship the books and swallow the loss. We've had the post office do tracers, which involved a lot of extra paperwork, to absolutely no avail.

The other form of complaint comes from someone who has received your book but is dissatisfied. If you've turned out a quality product, this will be a rarity. The secret to handling this type of complaint is to keep your cool, be especially gracious, and listen carefully. Find out exactly why the person is unhappy. For justified complaints (yes, you will have made a boo-boo sometimes) do what the person requests unless it's totally unreasonable. If you decide that the complaint is just sour grapes, explain your point of view in a professional way and why you don't agree. Perhaps some sort of compromise can be reached. Should you find the same customer complaining over and over again, refuse to be exploited by suggesting the customer discontinue doing business with you since he or she is so unhappy.

Now let's turn our attention to some different guidelines and explore how a computer could make your writing and publishing life ever so much easier.

CHAPTER 6

COMPUTERS IN PUBLISHING

In this chapter we'll be introducing you to the world of microcomputers, showing you five major ways you can save time and money with one, and offering some little-known tips for computer clout. And we'll be exploring the pros—and cons—of desktop publishing. We'll also tell you what to anticipate spending and make some helpful buying recommendations.

A brief introduction to microcomputers

Microcomputers have revolutionized the self-publishing industry. A recent issue of *Writer's Digest* stated, "Now you can produce, distribute, and market your own books as professionally as the large commercial publishers, by tapping the power of the personal computer." Because of this new technology—which makes everything easier, faster, and more efficient—many more authors are electing to accept the risks and rewards of publishing themselves. They are finding that by hiring a staff of one— a computer—they have new leverage to compete with trade publishers. The balance of power is definitely shifting; self-publishers are now able to achieve heights that were virtually unreachable before.

First, understand we're speaking here of the personal or professional computer (PC), also referred to as micros or microcomputers, not minis or mainframes used by multimillion-dollar corporations. And, in general, not so-called home computers—those chiefly designed to play games— although add-on capacities and peripherals can make even these usable if that's all your budget will allow.

Within the last decade microcomputer prices have plummeted. Today an IBM Compatible AT386 system complete with software (word processor, general accounting, spreadsheet, database, and desktop publisher) plus high resolution monitor, laser printer, and font library can be purchased for less than you'd pay for most new cars. Once adjusted to it (let's face it, the only person who likes change is a wet baby), most writers and publishers feel their computer would be a bargain at twice the price.

When we say "computer," we're actually referring to a whole computer system. This includes a computer — or the central processing unit, "CPU" as it's often called. It is the heart and brains of the system. But by itself it's useless, like an octopus without arms. The other "hardware" you need to make this creature do its thing includes an input device called a keyboard, which looks much like your regular typewriter keyboard. And for visual output you'll need a monitor or a video display which resembles a little sister to your TV set. Another must is a mass storage device, most commonly a disk drive — a unit that reads and writes data stored on a disk. Computers usually have two of these. All of the above constitute the "hardware" of your computer system.

But alas, just as the octopus needs crabs to feed upon, your computer must be nourished. Its food comes in the form of "software." There are two kinds of software: operating software and applications software. If you've heard such terms as "PC-DOS," "MS-DOS," "CP/M," or "UNIX," you heard people talking about operating systems. These systems are like traffic cops, controlling and coordinating all the internal functions. Applications software are the various program workhorses that do such things as word processing, preparing spreadsheets (which enter, edit, store, and do arithmetic calculations with rows of numbers), creating databases (electronic collections of information), and doing general ledger accounting.

The third group of items that round out your computer operation are called peripherals. To get all your data (which is computerese for information or material) from the screen to a tangible piece of paper, you need a printer. Printers are the most important peripherals and come in three versions: laser, dot matrix, and daisy wheel (more about them later). If you intend to use your computer for direct telephone communication, you'll also want a modem which connects to your phone (more about this later, too).

Five major ways a PC can save you time and money

Writing

A personal computer running a good word processing program is worth its weight in titanium. Electronic authoring will spoil you for ever going back to your typewriter. Although we have correcting typewriters, it feels like reverting to the Dark Ages to go from our IBM Compatible AT to the typewriter to produce something. Word processing is the number one use for PCs.

Using word processing has many advantages. It's much faster and neater. You can immediately spot a goof and, with the flick of a key, erase or correct it. Instead of three or four complete drafts, you'll probably have one you'll revise as you go, simply reworking the text right on the monitor screen. Electronic cutting and pasting are more efficient than traditional methods. Retyping is unnecessary. Change and revision become as effortless as breathing. Your personal productivity is multiplied manyfold, guaranteeing that you have a steady flow of new product. The critically acclaimed novelist Ernest Hebert, author of *Dogs of March*, estimates that his PC has quadrupled his writing speed. Your style will likely improve, too. Since you can do preliminary editing as you compose, it's easier to catch extra or redundant words, change sentence structure, and write for greater clarity. And your final drafts are masterpieces! One word of caution, however: Save your input often — about every half hour. Otherwise, a computer glitch can wipe out a whole day's work.

If you're not self-publishing, your editor will greatly appreciate receiving such a meticulously prepared manuscript, complete with subheads centered, chapter titles in boldface, and lists neatly tabulated. Be sure you provide a sharp, readable manuscript. Most trade houses are understandably unwilling to read poor quality dot matrix printouts.

Trade publishing houses also report that authors working on micros typically meet or beat their deadlines. A study launched by the Association of American Publishers found that authors are adopting electronic processing of manuscripts more quickly than are publishers. The association earmarked $250,000 to establish industrywide standards for preparing and processing electronic manuscripts. Since manuscripts prepared on a PC are cleaner and more error-free, they cut down on editing time and often save in composition costs. If you're dealing with a trade publisher, this might be a bargaining point for a larger advance.

Editing

Once your manuscript is in reasonably good shape, it's time to employ editing tricks and some special software programs. If you've chosen your basic word processing program carefully, you should be able to do all kinds of nifty things before the final manuscript is committed to paper.

By giving the computer a certain command, you can manipulate whole blocks of material. This can range from taking a sentence from the beginning of paragraph one and moving it to the end of paragraph six, to such massive reorganizing as altering your whole chapter arrangement. By just pushing a couple of buttons you can delete words, sentences, paragraphs, or whole sections. And the lovely thing is that the remaining text closes right up to form continuous copy.

With your word processing "search and replace" function (we certainly hope it has one!) you can do more neat things. Suppose you learn after you've finished writing the manuscript that you've misspelled the name of an authority who was cited several times. In the old days you'd have to go over every page looking for that name. With search and replace all you do is tell the computer to locate every reference to the expert's name and fix it. Should you decide to rename the protagonist of your novel, all it takes is a couple of commands and everywhere "Gertrude" appeared, the name of "Misty" will be written. Fixing the book will take all of ten minutes.

We've discovered another nice trick that S&R can accomplish. Suppose you're writing a book about Dolly Parton. Instead of spelling her name out every time, you might assign it some code like "DP." Then when you are finished writing, you tell the computer to go back to each place it finds DP and replace it with Dolly's name.

A good measure of how far software developers have upgraded word processing programs (in response to writers' and publishers' requirements) is the inclusion by all the top programs of such essential tools as spell checkers, thesauruses, indexers, and even footnoters.

Don't believe you needn't spell check all your documents—unless you are "Super Writer." The necessity for high quality spell checkers with big dictionaries has been reflected in software companies' new releases. These spell checkers keep getting bigger and better.

Also included in top word processing software is a thesaurus. A thesaurus can do wonders in helping you cut down on sloppy writing. If your vocabulary is getting repetitive this can be just the vehicle to encourage variety.

Indexing becomes a breeze with the programs resident in your word processor. If your word processing program does not include indexing capabilities, a program like IndexIt works well. It surely beats the old file card approach.

An additional tool which is not part of most word processing software is a style checker which examines grammar and punctuation. They can dramatically improve the "style" of your writing by pinpointing awkward sentences and incorrect grammar and giving you the option of changing them. Some programs go so far as to suggest alternative usages in writing style. Many catch repeated words such as "the the." Right Writer is one of the programs worth investigating.

The other dynamic advantage you'll have when using a computer to edit is that all duplicate proofreading and typing are eliminated. In conventional writing, where a fresh manuscript must be typed after the editing process, new errors creep in. Word processing eliminates these errors *and* the need to retype the whole book. See what we mean about a valuable tool?

Typesetting

In some cases you can save enough on your typesetting to almost pay for your whole computer system! Sound unbelievable? Let's examine the facts. Typesetting can be approached in a multitude of ways.

The most cost-effective ploy is for you to do the actual typesetting of the book on your own computer, thus saving $2,000 to $3,000 for conventional typesetting and paste-up. Many small publishers are choosing this approach. It is truly do-it-yourself publishing. Besides savings and speed, another advantage is complete control. Nothing leaves your office, and last-minute errors are simple to rectify.

If you've analyzed and chosen your word processing software and printer carefully, you can produce a book with justified margins (no ragged right side), proportionally spaced letters (the "m," for instance, is given more space than the "i"), larger and boldface chapter headings, italics for emphasis, and complete camera-ready type. Other ingredients needed will be the ability to paginate (number pages in consecutive order) and a laser printer or a plastic printwheel and single-strike ribbon on a letter-quality printer. If you use a daisy wheel printer you will also want to use a special clay-coated "repro" (as in "reproduction") paper to make paste-up easier. By manipulating your text typographically, you can produce an attractive book and save yourself thousands of dollars.

Another intriguing option is to code your manuscript electronically so a composing house's typesetting machines can interpret it. This is often referred to as the "captured keystroke." In addition to eliminating redundant keystroking (typing), it can cut your typesetting costs by over one-third! A study from the National Composition Association reports that computerized book text, with typesetting command codes inserted, reduces the cost of composition by 34 to 39 percent. You communicate with typesetters via magnetic tapes, diskettes, or telephone. (For this you'll need a "modem" and communications software that translates over phone lines.) Another plus with this method is that you trim your overall typesetting time considerably.

Many typesetters can use popular word processors as direct input. Our primary typesetting vendor converts WordStar 2000 diskettes (which have been formatted in-house in WordStar language) directly to Merganthaler photo typeset output. Using this approach we can provide our clients camera-ready pages at about half manuscript-to-photo typeset costs.

Our highly recommended word processors have basic typesetting and desktop publishing capabilities and can be used for many book type-setting projects.

Sophisticated desktop publishing is something now practical for many smaller publishers. According to the 1987 *Huenefeld Report*'s survey, 28.6 percent of those publishers with sales under $100,000 (which would include most self-publishers) use desktop publishing. A whopping 53.3 percent, however, are considering going to this technology.

Laser printers can be found for as low as $1,300, font libraries are available and affordable, and sophisticated desktop typesetting and lay-out can be produced by the use of Ventura Publisher or Aldus Pagemaker (the standard-bearers of desktop publishing software). Both programs are available for IBM compatibles. Pagemaker is the software used by the Apple Macintosh which provides a system many people consider to be easier to learn than PC versions of desktop publishing. PC advocates are quick to point out that the MAC with PostScript is much slower. So the choice would appear to be "easier" or "faster."

We do want to point out, however, that desktop publishing is not a cure-all. If you're only planning to do one book, the cost is too great; you're better off to pay for outside typesetting. Even if you're planning on doing several books, be aware that you'll have to learn a great deal about typography and layout before you can produce a satisfactory prod-uct. Of course, once you've mastered desktop publishing, you can create attractive promotional materials as well as books.

Although we won't be recommending laser printers as of this writing, we will be exploring and analyzing what is available.

Basically there are two disciplines in the laser printer world. Those are the Apple-introduced PostScript standard and the Hewlett-Packard LaserJet II standard.

The PostScript standard tends to be slower but does produce superior graphic density definition. So if shadings are important, a PostScript printer may be in order. An additional consideration before automatically settling on PostScript standard is the cost factor. PostScript printers range from $4,000 to $8,000. The super 600 × 600 dots per inch (DPI) resolution Varityper runs twice as much. The 600 x 600 resolution, however, gives quality that will pass for photo typesetting. The resolution standard for laser printers if 300 × 300 DPI. The HP LaserJet emulating printers start at $1,300 and range up to $6,500. They tend to be faster than PostScript printers with less density resolution in graphics mode.

If you are seriously in the market for a laser printer, get hold of a copy of *PC* Magazine, Volume 7, Number 18, October 31, 1988. This guide to laser printers is quite complete and an excellent reference.

If you are going to typeset with any printer—laser, daisy wheel, or dot matrix—make sure you have proportional spacing capability in both your printer and software. Some word processing programs are unable to justify margins when using proportional spacing. This is not acceptable for typesetting.

In choosing your laser printer, match the printer to your task. Make sure it will handle all your requirements. Carefully check formatting capabilities, as they vary widely.

So whether you decide that a Qume CrystalPrint WP at $1,299 will fill your need, or you determine only the Varityper VT600 at over ten times that amount will handle your project, there is a laser printer tailor-made for you.

Shop wisely, compare features and costs to make sure you get the best possible value.

Don't overlook the need for controllers and font libraries when harnessing a laser printer to a PC. It would be wise to get counsel from a larger computer dealer or a computer consultant before going too far.

General accounting procedures

Your computer will come in extremely handy for basic accounting. Most writers, being creative souls, find bookkeeping pesky at best and petrifying at worst. Although a computer won't teach you accounting, there are now many software programs designed to simplify the task. If you know basic small-business bookkeeping, it is easy to use a PC to record all income and expenses and keep a simple set of books. This consolidates bookkeeping headaches and dramatically reduces the time needed to deal with them.

Accounts Receivable (A/R) programs keep track of money your customers pay you. Such programs are faster, neater, and more accurate than they would be if you did the same function manually. They will prepare a personalized invoice, print a shipping label, issue a packing slip, and update your inventory totals—all in one operation. There is no time-consuming duplicate posting, as when you do bookkeeping by hand. Likewise, your payments are processed quickly and efficiently. And your computer can also be made to spew out monthly, quarterly, or annual summaries of your sales figures.

Accounts Payable (A/P) keeps tabs on the money going out. Your electronic genius can balance your checkbook in practically the blink of an eye. It will also provide you with detailed summary reports of exactly how much you spent on what, when the bill was paid, and to whom. This helps to highlight any area of spending that is becoming lopsided.

Two front runners in general small business bookkeeping that come highly recommended by reviewers and users are Peachtree and Dac Easy accounting programs.

For the rigors of A/R we have found it easier and more cost effective to create our own program using a SuperCalc 5 spreadsheet. We started with CPM SuperCalc in 1983 (it was bundled with our CompuPro 10) and have never found the subsequent upgrades (2, 3, and 5) wanting. Other top spreadsheet programs are Lotus 1, 2, 3 and Multiplan from Microsoft.

So whether it is general bookkeeping, order entry, inventory control, fulfillment, or accounts payable, your PC will be a tremendous aid and relieve you of many dull, routine jobs.

Marketing

Generating sales and promotional literature is a cinch when you're computerized. Word processing allows you to create a standard form letter, modify it slightly to fit the occasion or person, then have it typed personally to the individual.

Think what this can mean! When you want to sell serial rights to your book, for instance, you can send letters to various editors suggesting different individual chapters tailored to their readership. Perhaps you have a book on health. Want to put together a letter slanted to various segments of the medical profession? You can do a master letter, then tailor it to M.D.s, chiropractors, and dentists in a flash. And with a handy feature called "mail merge" you type in their addresses and each letter will be personally addressed. (Do be aware that for speed of operation on letters you'll probably want continuous-roll letterhead, not just single sheets.)

This same strategy works for news releases. Let's look at the health book again. While the same basic release would be used, you might change the opening for nutritional magazines, sports magazines, general interest magazines, and health publications. The possibilities are endless!

What may be a first is a thriller featuring—you guessed it—a computer detective. The author, Jaron Summers, posted the first chapter of *Safety Catch* on CompuServe and The Source, two of the largest electronic bulletin boards. What's more, he and his publisher offered $5 to anyone who posted the first chapter for thirty days on another bulletin board with a minimum of 1,000 regular users. Employing a unique twist to the old chain letter gimmick, anyone who could meet this criterion was invited to participate and earn a five spot. Said the publisher's editorial director, Jane Thornton, "This may well be the first ripple in the wave of the future when it comes to promoting books."

Another imaginative user of computers is Jeffrey Lant. He places articles about his books on GEnie, CompuServe, Delphi, and Boston Citinet. At the end of each article is full ordering information for the book it covers. This is truly direct response-oriented marketing and offers an intimate way to use computers for selling books.

A further important marketing function is list maintenance. By that we mean keeping an organized and updated listing of marketing sources. Take wholesalers as an example. You may want to get in front of them again when a particularly big review is about to break or a national media appearance is confirmed. With your computer it's a snap. Computerization allows you to do a lot of high-powered sales follow-up on the clerical level. By simply creating a sales follow-up letter and designating the time it should go out, you have a program for keeping in constant touch with your prime accounts. And as your customer base grows, you'll definitely want to log and control these names and addresses of prime prospects for future books.

The tool for maintaining your list is a *database management system* (DBMS). The more information you need about the entries on your list, the more sophisticated your database and the more powerful the database management software needed.

Our need for a heavy-duty database had us leaning toward the PC version of a mainframe database: Ingres for PC's, version 5. It's an extremely powerful Structural Query Language (SQL) database with lots of muscle.

However, we ultimately chose dBase III plus (to be upgraded shortly to dBase IV). Our decision was influenced by the fact that it is the standard and front-runner. The new dBase IV is comparable to any competitor as to speed and power and of being *the* database that most word processing and spreadsheets are compatible with.

FoxBase plus is a dBASE clone which is much faster and somewhat easier to use than dBASE. Novices will find FoxBase plus a treat to use. FoxBase is stripped of frills, bells, and whistles, and is a lean, powerful DBMS.

Two other strong contenders in the DBMS field are Paradox and R:base for DOS. Either program will fill most database management requirements for the small publishers. There are many other DBMS on the market but all are somewhat less powerful, speedy, and/or flexible than the leaders referenced above.

Before you buy a database—or any other software, hardware, or printer—it's wise to explore all your purchasing options. Computer stores are one obvious outlet, but don't overlook other retail stores and mail order dealers. You can often get great deals when buying through the mail. But do be aware that you're also buying service. If you're a rank novice, then perhaps paying more at a computer store makes sense. Then you have access to them for help when problems arise. One tip when making a purchase at computer stores is to shop the last couple of days of the month. Most of them have quotas. If they haven't made theirs, the price may well be shaved a bit, or more generous warranties included.

More little-known tips for computer clout

Your microcomputer can serve you in a multitude of other ways as well. It can be a research mechanism, an inventive way to market-test ideas, a method for publishing your work electronically, a filing system, a planning and cost projection tool, a secretary, an artist—and just plain fun.

If you need information not available in your own files and don't want to waste time researching in the library, you can turn to "data banks." You tap into these resources via a modem attached to your phone and a communications software program. Data banks, sometimes called databases, are stockpiles of computerized facts and information. They cover a vast array ranging from research abstracts to major news services to business information of all sorts. You can check on legislative records, get travel information, or gain access to obscure articles and reports on virtually any subject.

One of the primary advantages of this form of research is its speed. If you're researching on a timely topic, as Marilyn was recently, it can be invaluable. She read a couple of ads for computer rentals and decided this was the germ of an article—and perhaps a book. But traditional library resources revealed no information. An on-line data search, however, un-covered some very current material. Working from that, she was able to gather enough data to send out queries.

Not only are data banks faster, they can also unearth some rather obscure information. The Foundation Center (79 Fifth Avenue, New York, NY 10003) offers Comsearch, for instance, which is a computer printout of foundation grants for those seeking possible funding sources.

There's another way to use a computer that hadn't even occurred to us until Marilyn interviewed a stimulating telecommunications expert, David R. Hughes. Why not use your PC for market research? For instance, before you spend months writing a book on the life and habits of the duckbilled platypus, find out if anybody cares! We've used a far-fetched example, true. But the potential here is enormously exciting. It offers a practical, quick way to quantify your sales potential. By putting together a couple of punchy paragraphs and a table of contents, or a brief synopsis of your novel, then sending it out on a "bulletin board" (electronic rather than cork) to other computer users, you can get instant feedback on your idea. Time and space are annihilated. And you can use your computer to interact and communicate with each potential reader. You have the opportunity to question people and structure your manuscript accord-ingly. How much more practical than writing and publishing a book, only to learn that few people are interested, or that folks are especially hungry for information on an aspect of the subject you barely touched.

Another facet of telecommunications that Hughes brought up has us gripping the edge of our chairs. It is *electronic* self-publishing. This has all kinds of exciting ramifications. Instead of, or in addition to, producing a book, booklet, or newsletter in the old-fashioned print format, you put it out electronically via telecommunications. Other computer users—those who subscribe to a database such as NewsNet, Delphi, CompuServe, or The Source—pay a royalty for "reading" your information on their monitors. Subscriptions to these services may have no sign-up fees and a $20 monthly minimum charge; or they may have an enrollment fee up to $50 and monthly charges on a "use only" basis, whereby subscribers pay just for what they use.

Once a Member Publishing Agreement is reached, The Source provides space in its computers, and authors are solely responsible for the content and updating of their material. Prospective publishers should call or send a proposal. Since royalties are predicated on "usage," information must be timely and dynamic enough to get readers involved. Not all materials are appropriate for this medium. Electronic publishing will have the greatest impact on subjects where information is time-urgent. In these areas, computer-assisted technologies will bring about revolutionary changes in book printing within this decade.

By eliminating the printed page, you get timely information out immediately. Can you imagine what a benefit this is to technological fields where yesterday's facts are old stuff? We see this use of computers offering a fantastic competitive edge to small publishers.

Electronic filing is also possible for computer owners. Rather than having information scattered in manila folders stuffed in filing cabinets, why not condense it? Make it really easy to handle. Perhaps you want to catalog magazine articles on your book's topic or organize your interview notes by person or subject area. This can all be accomplished and you can command the computer to print out a neat listing by telling it a pre-assigned key-word code.

Production planning and cost projections are other valuable services your computer can perform. It is possible to study the economics of publishing and promoting your book before you ever invest a cent in the project. If you did your original P&L breakdowns on computer, you can run simulations: change one or another condition, setting up hypothetical situations, and see the effect. For example, you can compare unit costs for different quantities, look at the overall financial impact of going to a cheaper paper, and compute if a proposed advertising campaign is likely to pay off. This kind of advance planning, or forecasting, as it is often called, can spell the difference between a highly profitable publishing venture and one that just breaks even.

Your computer is also your secretary: never ill, never late, never grouchy (although it has been said in a moment of frustration that to err is human; to really foul up takes a computer). All sorts of general correspondence and standard forms can be generated on a PC. You can create standardized collection letters to dun slow-paying accounts and prepare forms for such purposes as requesting shipping costs when they are omitted from orders.

A computer can also serve as your staff artist. There are various graphics software programs, such as PC Paint or Dr. Halo III, that allow you to make pie charts and bar graphs. While these may not be of top-drawer commercial artist quality, they can serve well as interior illustrations and will certainly help you get correct proportions faster than by hand. With the right software and printer you can do anything from simple line drawings to three-dimensional effects that could be used for a futuristic-looking book cover.

And for those times when you're totally fed up with work, your computer provides an escape. You can use it to design a landscape plan for your yard or catalog all your recipes. Even more fun are many of the more than 200 games that have been invented. They range from such things as Space Wars, where you play against another person, to chess, where you are pitted against the computer itself.

Some buying recommendations

A well-equipped personal computer system, including software, will run you somewhere between $3,000 and $8,000. You really won't be spending that much, however. Sound like double-talk? Not so. You see, Uncle Sam will share the cost with you in the form of income tax breaks. While the procedure is complex, and you should consult your tax adviser, here's the gist of the 1984 Tax Reform Act: If you will be using your computer primarily for business purposes, you can write off—or expense—up to half your PC investment (up to $5,000) on your income taxes. Or you can use an accelerated depreciation schedule and whack off 15 percent the first year, 22 percent the second, and 21 percent over the remaining three years.

Strange as it may seem, you want to evaluate *software* before you purchase your hardware. The reason for this? Certain computers will not run certain software, and software is where it's at in the computer game. Educate yourself first by studying software reviews in computer magazines and reading appropriate books. Go comparison shopping at a few computer stores and ask salespeople to explain and demonstrate the software their particular system uses. But be careful not to be convinced too easily: What you need to find out is what's available and what you really need.

Let's look at the most popular word processing software. Nine top-of-the-line word processing programs were provided to us by their publishers for review, at our request. Our own evaluations and a review analysis from various trade publications have yielded the following:

WordPerfect has led the pack in word processing since the introduction of release 4.0. WordPerfect 5.0 continues the winning way with more improvements, power and user friendliness. WordPerfect 5.0 is a near desktop publisher with word processing facility. WordStar, because it is available for most systems, led the pack until the introduction of Word-Perfect. While those who mastered its complex 150 commands loved it, many were too frustrated to ever reach that level. But newer releases have eliminated this kind of frustration. In late 1984 the old WordStar was eclipsed by WordStar 2000, billed as "easy word processing you'll never outgrow." And in 1988 Release 3 made the old plug a racehorse. In addition, features were added to make WordStar a *personal publisher*. We use and like this version very much. A new user interface is intended to simplify use. This, plus other technical improvements, makes this powerful program a logical choice for self-publishers.

Nipping at their heels is Microsoft Word, WordStar Professional 50, and Xywrite Plus. Other possible candidates include Total Word, Office Writer, Multimate, and Samna Plus IV.

These programs are less popular and less powerful than the top five. Total Word is a new personal publishing/word processor from the makers of Volkswriter. Office Writer is tailored more toward the shorter documents of the business world. Multimate is a powerful program that has evolved from the Wang dedicated word processor. It will do a great job — but slowly. Samna Plus IV is powerful, complex, and rather slow as compared with our top five.

You must first find the features you need in software, then locate a PC that can accommodate that program. We have succumbed to the industry influence of IBM in the PC world. We use clones from various manufacturers. One caution: for clones, technical support is hard to find and warranties are scarce. We find the cost savings to justify the risk. If your budget is especially small, you might consider used or reconditioned hardware, available at about half the cost of new.

Next on your agenda will be an evaluation of printers. As we mentioned, there are three basic kinds: laser printers, daisy wheel printers, and dot matrix printers. Laser printers are the Cadillacs. They turn out near typeset quality at high speed, quietly! Daisy wheels turn out copies that look like letters you get from a regular typewriter, but have the disadvantage of being slow and expensive — typically, about ⅔ the cost of a low-end laser printer. (But then who said we could have everything, eh?) If you're going to typeset your own book, you want one or the other. Some dot matrix printers zip through your words at speeds up to four hundred characters (letters) per second. What the cheaper versions produce, however, threatens to turn 20-20 eyesight to 100-100 in a few months. Don't expect an editor to accept a dot matrix submission unless it's of good quality.

Some dot matrix printers (and some daisy wheels!) make as much racket as a demolition crew at work. There are three ways to mute a printer's noise: One is go into another room and shut the door. Two that are more practical are either to buy from your dealer a very expensive acrylic hood designed for your particular printer or else make a box out of Styrofoam (bought in sheets at a hardware store, cut with a knife, and glued with contact cement or white glue). The box should be high enough to cover the printer completely, and it should have a top and three sides. Leave the back open so the paper's movement won't be interfered with. Pop the box over the printer at printout time and a faint *clacketa-clacketa* will be all you'll hear. Such a box can be made for under $5 and works just as well as the fancy acrylic hood. Placing a felt pad under the printer will also muffle some noise.

We've discovered several machines that seem to offer a happy medium between dot matrix and daisy wheel or laser printers. They are basically dot matrix but have the ability to produce *correspondence*-quality printing. (Mind you, we did not say letter quality, though in some cases it is extremely close.) These machines—such as Epson's LQ1500 and Toshiba's P1351, or new versions—provide very nice-looking copies quickly and efficiently.

In making your purchasing decisions, be wary of much hype, little help. Many of today's computer salespeople were in other occupations six months ago, so they are learning right along with you. Check different computer stores until you find a salesperson who appears truly knowledgeable, then let him or her educate you. Another way to prepare for this important step is to read extensively. Become a sponge. Absorb helpful books on the subject. Pick up copies of computer magazines at newsstands. Some good ones are *Byte*, *Personal Computing*, and *PC Magazine*. By attending computer conferences you can get information about new state-of-the-art products, actually try out some systems, talk with vendors as well as users, and attend pertinent seminars. Another information-gathering tactic is to talk with other writers and small publishers to learn what they're using and how they like it.

Ernest Hebert suggests a writer first define both the minimum and the maximum system he or she needs. The minimum may actually suffice if you don't plan on doing your own typesetting. We'd suggest, however, that you buy the best you can afford. It's tragic to see people settle for a limited system, only to be faced soon with the predicament of buying all over again because they scrimped and their system won't do what is needed. Also investigate after-sale training and service. The best system around is useless if you don't know how to work it or can't get it repaired.

Whether you're computerized or not, there are various identifying numbers and early attention-getting strategies you'll want to employ. The next chapter, "Important Early Activities," tells what they are and shows how to implement them.

CHAPTER 7

IMPORTANT EARLY ACTIVITIES

We live in an age of numbers. Just as you had to get a Social Security number when you snagged your first job, your book also needs to be given some numbers as identification tags. It is wise to begin the process of acquiring these early in your prepublishing activities. You'll also want to determine approximately how big your book is going to be. Another important facet of getting started is establishing your publication date. And once you've done these things, a whole raft of advance attention-getting publicity avenues are open to you. These are the things we'll be discussing in this chapter.

Preparing a cast-off

No, we're not talking about setting out to go sailing. This strange-sounding technical term refers to estimating the length of your finished book. The estimate can be rough at this stage, but it is important for several reasons to determine approximately what length you are going to end up with. Obviously, if you have only enough money to publish a book of about 125 pages and your estimate adds up to a hefty 250 pages, you're in financial hot water before you even begin.

Another reason to begin getting a handle on how long your book will be is to have accurate information for typesetters and printers when you request bids. You will also need to state an approximate length on the sales and promotional literature you'll soon be developing. Now that you know all the reasons for doing this, let's proceed with the methods. (We'll show you specifics as we go along, so don't panic if it sounds like Greek at first.)

Let us take a look at some hypothetical examples. Suppose your typed manuscript is 285 pages long. You do a little preliminary scouting and decide on a page size, text image size, type style, and leading (all of which are explained in the next chapter), which, in this case, makes one finished book page equal to one and one-quarter pages of manuscript. Now computing the text pages in your book is a snap. Divide your total manuscript pages (285) by the 1.25 conversion ratio. The result tells you you will have 228 typeset text pages.

Now you must take into consideration several other elements that make up a complete book. Front matter in our example will consume eight pages. We will figure backmatter to consist only of an index (10 pages) and your order form (2 pages). Chapter and index headings will take up about one-third page each. For optimum design, you want each chapter to start on a "recto" (right-hand) page if you have the room. Figure half the chapters will fall wrong, so allow for a blank "verso" (left-hand) page for each and add that number of extra pages. Now consider interior artwork. Will there be any photographs, illustrations, charts, or graphs? Allow for them. Your book has definitely grown, hasn't it? Here's how our example breaks down.

Manuscript pages	228
Front matter	8
Chapter and index headings (12)	4
Chapters not starting on recto pages (estimate half)	6
Interior artwork (four charts at ½ page each)	2
Backmatter	12
TOTAL ESTIMATED PAGES	260

At this point, you have some decisions to make. It is much more economical to print books in what is known as even signatures. A "signature" is the number of pages a press can print on both sides of the paper in one pass. Most book manufacturers use presses with a 32-page signature capacity. If we divide our 260-page example by 32, it comes out 8.125. This is a definite No-No! You need to condense your book back to an even eight signatures.

In our example, this is easy. Our front matter includes a bastard title page, also known as the half-title page (two pages we can do without). Our backmatter includes ten pages of index, which by reducing the type size by two points, will likely shrink to eight pages. As you can see, you have just shortened your book to the ideal even-signature configuration. We could have dropped additional pages by allowing chapter title pages to start on verso pages, which we would certainly want to do if it means saving the cost of going into an additional signature.

Assume for a moment that our calculations had come out to a total of 252 pages. You now know this is not good. What should you do? Perhaps you could add a four-page preface or foreword. Our example allots the dedication and acknowledgment two pages—you could very easily start each on a recto page and use up two additional pages. Each page of the table of contents could be started on a recto page, using up two more of your blank pages. You could elect to simply leave two blank pages at the front and back of the book. If you do leave blank pages, it usually looks better to divide them, rather than leave them all in the back. In our opinion, eight blank pages would be maximum, and even that looks somewhat tacky. We feel there are much better uses for your dollar than to pay for blank pages. We'll bet if you really make an effort, you can come up with a way to add up to 16 useful and meaningful pages to your book.

Autocast, a great computer program that we evaluated for inclusion in this book, will make the exercise we just described a snap. It's easy to play "what if" with it and get instant results. If you plan to publish more than one book, you may want to check it out yourself.

The following figures show why we try so hard to stay in even signatures (sigs). Comparative costs are shown for 1,000 copies of even 32-page sigs as well as for additional 16-page, 8-page, and—worst of all—4-page sigs:

224 pages	$2,259	7 even sigs
228 pages	$2,385	7 even sigs + 1 4-pg sig
232 pages	$2,398	7 even sigs + 1 8-pg sig
236 pages	$2,433	7 even sigs + 1 8-pg sig + 1 4-pg sig
240 pages	$2,422	7 even sigs + 1 16-pg sig
244 pages	$2,428	7 even sigs + 1 16-pg + 1 4-pg sig
248 pages	$2,433	7 even sigs + 1 16-pg sig + 1 8-pg sig
252 pages	$2,453	7 even sigs + 1 16-pg sig + 1 8-pg sig + 1 4-pg sig
256 pages	$2,420	8 even sigs

Note that a full additional signature costs less than 12 extra pages (compare 236 pages with 256 pages). Compute the cost-per-page for the uneven signatures between 7 and 8. Amazing, isn't it, how more can cost less! It becomes very obvious how important your page count really is. Additional help on actual interior design is coming up in the next chapter.

Choosing the "right" publication date

There is an idiosyncrasy about publication dates you should be aware of. It stands to reason when you indicate a pub date that you would write down the first day you anticipate having finished books in hand, right? Wrong! In this industry, strategic reviewers prefer to pass judgment *before* the official publication date. Sometimes complete first editions are sold out prior to the pub date. So tack at least three months on to the actual anticipated delivery date to give reviewers a good chance to supply you with free publicity. (Example: If you will have books on January 1, set the publication date as April 1.) You will want to project the date at this early stage because you'll need it to complete an Advance Book Information (ABI) form, which is explained later in this chapter.

Some other considerations come into play when choosing a publication date. Bear in mind that trade advertising is concentrated during those times of year when the sales force is making its effort to sell the forthcoming major publisher lists. That is in January and February, and again in June and July. Also remember that the time from Labor Day until shortly before the December holidays is rather chaotic as publishers vie for Christmas gift dollars. Advertising and publicity (reviews especially) go hand in hand. If you can steer clear of these periods, you'll have a better chance of garnering publicity, as there simply won't be as much competition.

As we mentioned before, you might benefit by tying your pub date to some special event or day. A book on how to achieve success, wealth, and fame might well be launched on the birthday of Horatio Alger, Jr., January 13. Mae Day, in honor of the ultraliberated Mae West, is August 17. Got a book on how to attract men? This would make a heck of a link. You might even entice Suzy Mallery—president of Man Watchers Inc., which sponsors Mae Day—to include you in her promotions. How do we know about such kooky things? It's all in a book called *Chase's Annual Events*, compiled by William D. and Helen M. Chase.

The Bookland EAN scanning symbol

We're all familiar with the UPC symbol that over the last six or eight years has replaced good old-fashioned price tags in grocery stores across the country. The government uses a bar-code scanning symbol called LOGMARS. The health industry has adopted the HIBC symbol as its standard. The mass paperback industry began using the UPC/ISBN a few years ago.

So it was inevitable that the Book Industry Systems Advisory Committee (BISAC) would adopt the Bookland EAN code and symbol for the hardcover and trade paperback books of the U.S. publishing industry. In the spring of 1986, publishers were made aware of the Bookland EAN through the recommendations of BISAC and the International ISBN Agency.

Since bar-code technology has been proven in retail outlets throughout the world, publishers are being pressured to incorporate the Bookland EAN as soon as possible. Harry Hoffman, president of Waldenbooks, has been the prime mover behind Bookland EAN implementation in the United States. Waldenbooks is requesting that all suppliers include the

Bookland EAN bar code with the price add-on and the printed ISBN on all new publications before the end of 1988. And there have been rumors that Waldens may shun publishers who don't comply.

The symbol being adopted by Waldenbooks as a standard is the Bookland EAN with price add-on (Bookland EAN/5). It now appears, "as Waldens goes, so goes the publishing industry." We suggest you make it your standard, too.

The Bookland EAN size chart gives a pictorial presentation and dimensions for the three types of EAN symbols. The EAN/5 indicates price in U.S. dollars. A $16.95 book would be coded 51695.

APPLICATION FOR ISBN PUBLISHER PREFIX

ISbn

INTERNATIONAL STANDARD BOOK NUMBERING. UNITED STATES AGENCY.
*International Standard Numbering System for Books, Software, Mixed Media etc.
in Publishing, Distribution and Library Practices*
245 West 17th Street, New York, New York 10011 212-337-6971 FAX: 212-242-6987

International Standard ISO 2108   R.R. Bowker • The Information Reference Company • A Division of Reed Publishing U.S.A.

IN ORDER TO ASSIGN AN ISBN PUBLISHER PREFIX, WE REQUIRE THE FOLLOWING INFORMATION: (Print or Type)
NAME AND ADDRESS: (Complete if different from above)
WHAT IS YOUR PUBLISHING COMPANY NAME?_____
ADDRESS: _____CITY:_____ST:_____ZIP:_____
IF P.O. BOX, YOUR STREET ADDRESS IS REQUIRED_____

1. Year you started publishing .... _____
2. Number of titles published in 1986 .... _____   PLEASE INCLUDE YOUR PROMOTIONAL
3. Number of titles published in 1987 .... _____   MATERIAL AND CATALOG, IF AVAILABLE
4. Number of titles planned for 1988 .... _____
5. Number of titles you plan to do yearly ..... _____
6. Number of titles still available (backlist). _____
7. Are you a Sub./Div. of another company?_____Give name, address and ISBN Prefix:_____

8. Do you have other publishing subsidiaries/imprints in the U.S. or foreign country?_____
   Give name, address, ISBN Prefix:_____
9. Do you distribute for any U.S./foreign publisher?_____Give name(s), address(es) and
   ISBN Prefix:_____
10. Are you distributed or represented by another company in the U.S. or foreign country?_____
    Give name(s), address(es)_____
11. Return this application and the enclosed form(s) describing all of your titles. If more than
    one title, please make photocopies of the form. Please retain copies of the application and
    form(s) for your own records and for sending in your updated forms with the assigned ISBNs.
    The ISBN requested on the form will be reported by YOU upon receipt of your block of ISBNs.

12. Name of Company ISBN Coordinator:_____ Phone:(___)_____
    Toll Free Phone Number:(___)_____ FAX Number:(___)_____
13. Name of President/Director:_____ Date: _____

Emery Koltay, Director
ISBN/SAN Agency

Director: Emery I. Koltay • Coordinator: Beatrice Jacobson • Officers: Peter Simon, Ernest Lee

When ordering your Bookland EAN scanning symbol, the following film master parameters must be specified:

Magnification: we recommend 92%

Bar Width Reduction (BWR): .001 unless your book manufacturer requests otherwise

Positive or Negative film

Right reading with Emulsion Up or Emulsion Down

Indicate whether you want the OCR-A/ISBN above or below the EAN bar-code symbol.

Number of photoprints wanted: we recommend using these for position only in the cover design.

The current price from our vendor is twenty dollars for a film master and two dollars for a photoprint. They commit to shipment within twenty-four hours from receipt of order. They welcome questions; more important, they have the answers. With this quality of vendor, implementing EAN symbols is no big thing.

The only cautions to use when designing with the Bookland EAN are as follows:

Don't crowd the symbol—crop marks are provided to indicate necessary clearances. Crowding could result in a nonscannable symbol. The colors for the background, or spaces, can be white, yellow, or red. Don't try to overprint any shades of black, blue or cyan, as the scanner can't differentiate the bar codes from the backgrounds. Print the bar codes in dark inks only (preferably black or dark blue—reflex blue, process blue, and cyan are good). The bars must always be the darker color. Bar and space colors cannot be reversed.

Of course, incorporating the EAN into your cover design does present some new challenges, but since it's going to be around a long time, let's make the best of it. Certainly we don't want to lose book sales because an EAN wasn't included. A list of firms offering EANs is in the Appendix.

Securing your ISBN

One of those vital numbers we referred to at the beginning of this chapter is the ISBN, which stands for International Standard Book Number. This ten-digit numeral unmistakably identifies the title, edition, binding, and publisher of a given work. It is a mandatory sales tool, as it provides the basis for identifying books in all industrywide systems. Most bookstore chains, wholesalers, and distributors keep track of books solely by the ISBN.

So how do you go about getting this little goody? Just request the necessary forms from Standard Book Numbering Agency, R. R. Bowker Company, 249 West 17th Street, New York, NY 10011.

You will receive a letter of explanation and a Title Output Information Request Form, such as the one shown on the adjacent page. Complete the form. (One tip: Be sure to indicate that you expect to publish more than one book, since these numbers are a service to publishers, not authors.) You will then receive a computer printout containing numbers that serve as your registry log. Assign a number to each title you publish

---

ADVANCE BOOK INFORMATION

□ Please keep last copy for your files and return others when requested to: 61893

ABI DEPARTMENT; R. R. BOWKER COMPANY, 245 WEST 17th STREET, NEW YORK, NY 10011

TITLE:

PUBLISHER (Not Printer):
Address

SUBTITLE:

SERIES:

Foreign Language: Translation □, from what language:

Telephone

AUTHOR(S):

EDITOR(S):

DISTRIBUTOR, if other than publisher:
(If you distribute foreign books you must be their exclusive U.S. distributor. Please send us a copy of your documentation for exclusivity)

TRANSLATOR(S):

ILLUSTRATOR(S):

INTRO. BY; PREFACE BY; etc.

IMPRINT (If other than company name):

ILLUSTRATIONS   YES □ NO □

PAGES:

THIS WORK IS ESSENTIALLY (Check one):

□ FICTION   □ TEXTBOOK

AUDIENCE (Select Primary Audience):

College Text□   Young Adult □: Grade: □ POETRY   □ BIOGRAPHY

Elhi Text □: Grade: Juvenile □: Grade: □ DRAMA   □ OTHER _____
                                                                                                      Specify
Original Paperback □   □ CHILDREN'S FICTION

Revised □   Abridged □   2nd Ed. □   Other: □ ESSAYS

PUBLICATION DATE:
Reprint □: If reprint, name of orig. publisher & orig. pub. date:

ISBN NOTE: Put full 10 digit number in spaces below. The system requires a separate ISBN for each edition.

PRIMARY SUBJECT OF BOOK
(Be as specific as possible):

ENTER PRICE(S) BELOW: INT'L STANDARD BOOK NUMBER

On short discount (20% or less) □

HARDCOVER TRADE: _ _·_ _   ISBN _ _ _ _ _ _ _ _ _ _

If juv., is binding guaranteed?

LIBRARY BINDING: _ _·_ _   ISBN _ _ _ _ _ _ _ _ _ _

HARDCOVER TEXT: _ _·_ _   ISBN _ _ _ _ _ _ _ _ _ _

PAPER TRADE   _ _·_ _   ISBN _ _ _ _ _ _ _ _ _ _

PAPER TEXT: _ _·_ _   ISBN _ _ _ _ _ _ _ _ _ _

TCHRS. ED.:   _ _·_ _   ISBN _ _ _ _ _ _ _ _ _ _

WKBK: _ _·_ _   ISBN _ _ _ _ _ _ _ _ _ _

LAB MANUAL: _ _·_ _   ISBN _ _ _ _ _ _ _ _ _ _

OTHER: SPECIFY   _ _·_ _   ISBN _ _ _ _ _ _ _ _ _ _
LC#

Order # (optional):   Completed by: _____

---

and you're in business. The number must appear inside and outside your book. We'll discuss how to do that in the next chapter on design and production.

The all-important ABI form

Now that we've taken care of the ISBN, let's explore a way to generate orders before you even have a finished book in your hands. Bowker publishes a directory called *Forthcoming Books in Print* twice each year. It can be as helpful to you in generating orders as the yellow pages are to local businesses. And you can be included in it for nothing! Just write Bowker's Advance Book Information Department (see address above) and request ABI forms. You'll receive an instruction booklet that explains how to proceed.

Remember we warned that you would have to toot your own horn? The ABI form asks for a brief description of the book. Give it sizzle. Pizzazz. Make that book sound like a blockbuster. Your description should be persuasive, concise, and complete.

Cite your marketing plans. Expect to run mail-order classifieds? Then you're doing a "national advertising campaign." Going to travel a bit to promote the book? That's an "author tour." Are you sending out press releases and appearing on radio and TV? Then you will have "Promotion." To see how we've handled these things, read the adjacent ABI form example.

Before mailing the completed form, make several dozen copies. This is a concise presentation about your book which can be sent to select people as a prepublication attention-getter (more about that soon).

Since you're writing to Bowker regarding the ABI form, now would be a good time to ask the Customer Service Department for a copy of Bowker's free catalog. Because this company publishes so many of the reference books you'll be dealing with, having its catalog—which explains the scope of each of its titles—in your personal library will come in very handy.

Once you've gotten yourself started with Bowker, you'll get computer printouts about your book from time to time. It will automatically proceed from *Forthcoming Books in Print* to *Books in Print (BIP)*, which comes out in the fall each year and is referred to by everybody who is anybody in the book business. Additionally, you'll be listed in other Bowker specialized directories—such as paperback, business, or religious directories—as appropriate. The *BIP* data base is now also available online so that electronic subscribers throughout the country will have immediate access to the latest information on your title if you've done your part.

Cataloging In Publication data

Another important numbering key allows libraries to shelve your book more speedily. It is called the Cataloging in Publication Program (CIP). Without this data your book could sit in a library several months before personnel know how to log it or where to put it. By participating in CIP, you will be provided pertinent information that can be printed right on the copyright page of your book. To start the procedure rolling, write Cataloging in Publication, Thomas Jefferson Building 2034, Washington, DC 20540. (If, however, your material is in booklet form under fifty pages, light fiction, or an obviously privately published book of poems, don't bother. Librarians don't need CIP data for these.)

As a publisher, you will be expected to submit information on books several months prior to their publication, together with a special Library of Congress Cataloging Data Sheet. A word of caution here: CIP discriminates against self-publishers. If they realize you are one, they will deny you CIP. Use a contact name other than your own on the form. (You definitely want to do this before you get to the typesetting stage, as the information must be placed on the copyright page.)

They prefer receiving the whole manuscript, but we've always found that a copy of the copyright page, title page, table of contents, and introduction, plus any promotional material, gives them what they need to draw from. Within ten working days after they receive your material, the data will be on its way back to you for inclusion in the book.

Your Library of Congress catalog card number will be assigned at the same time. It, too, will appear on the copyright page of your book and in reviews and lists of leading book trade journals. This number allows subscribers to the Library of Congress catalog card service to order cards by number and eliminate a search fee. Approximately twenty thousand libraries belong. If you hope to sell to libraries—and it's a great market— you *must* have an LC number.

Other listing sources

There are several other places where you can list your title for added sales exposure. ANY BOOK is a bibliographic information microfiche service to which some bookstores and libraries subscribe. It will gladly list your publication in its file and products. ANY BOOK is published by The Library Corporation. To get the needed forms, call toll-free at (800)624-0559.

You can also get listed in the *ABA Book Buyers Handbook*. It is used by bookstores. To obtain an application, write the American Booksellers Association, 137 West 25th Street, New York, NY 10001. The ABA sponsors a program called STOP (that stands for Single Title Order Plan). By get-

THE LIBRARY OF CONGRESS	1. Date Form Completed
LC CATALOGING DATA SHEET No. 1-2 *	May 13, 1984
(Use with galley; if no galley available, answer item 17 in full.)	2. Form Completed by
	Marilyn Ross

3. Name of Publisher

Northern Trails Press

Phone: (303) 655-2504

4. Name of In-House Editor

Ann Markham

Phone: "

5. Authors' Names Appearing on the Title Page (last, first, middle)

	Birthdate
Tom Davis	5/15/48
as told to Marilyn Ross	11/3/39

6. Title

BE TOUGH OR BE GONE

7. If this is a _translation_ from a foreign language, give _original_ title:

no

8. Give title(s) of any _other_ English language edition(s) if _different_ from this title:

9. If this is a copublished book, give name of copublisher:

no

10. Projected date of Publication:

month Sept. year 1984

11. Check here if book has:

☐ bibliography   ☐ index

12. If title comprises more than one physical volume, the number of volumes planned is: n/a

This is the galley for volume number:

13. If title belongs to a series of monographs having a comprehensive title, and it will appear in the book, the series title is:

n/a

14. If the series is numbered, the number for this title is: n/a

15. Work is essentially a

☐ novel   ☐ biography   ☐ essays

☐ textbook   ☒ other   True adventure
· (specify)

16. Primary audience for whom book is intended.

☒ general   ☐ nurses   ☐ engineers   ☐ college students

☐ children _____ (age level)   ☒ other   young adults (specify)

17. Primary subject of the books OR Precis of the book in detail if galley is not available. (Be as specific as possible, continuing on a separate sheet if necessary.)

This book is based on the true adventure Tom Davis had taking a pack train from El Paso, Texas to Fairbanks, Alaska in less than six months.

18. The following information items are related for cataloging purposes. Use a single line for each ISBN involved, giving the rest of the information as fully as you can.

ISBN(s) and FORMAT OR VOLUME NUMBER	LC CARD NUMBER IF PREASSIGNED	PRICE (Specify if sold only as set)
0-914269-09-7		$6.95

19. Person and address to which CIP entry should be mailed

Marilyn Ross
About Books
P O Box 538, Saguache, CO 81149

607-6 (rev 10/73)   Use previous issues until exhausted.   * Use Cataloging Data Sheet No. 3 for photo offset reprints.

CIP application form.

ting listed, you make it easy for them to reach you. If you participate, however, expect to give a discount on individual copy orders, something we don't ordinarily recommend. Here's how it works: The bookstore sends you a specially designed order form and a check, typically restricted to a given maximum amount. You complete the check and fill the order; there's no further paperwork involved.

Dustbooks, at P.O. Box 100, Paradise, CA 95969, also offers a free listing service for both small publishers and individual titles. By contacting Len Fulton of Dustbooks, you can also get your book entered in his *Small Press Record of Books in Print*, a junior version of *BIP*.

Now that you've assigned your pub date, done a cast-off to determine the length of your book, pushed the right buttons to start the process for your ISBN, Cataloging in Publication, ABI, and other listings — what's next? A very intriguing set of maneuvers . . .

Prepublication attention-getters

Advance comments

Schedule your book so you have a little time between your completed, typewritten manuscript and the beginning of the typesetting phase. Why? Because with some imagination and a little research you can probably locate several noted people who might be interested in what you have to say. These might be generally recognized experts on the book's subject, people you notice either writing or being written about and quoted in the course of your research. Or they might be celebrities in *any* field, with a known interest in your subject that you'd discovered during your research for the book. Once you have their names, you can find out how to contact these people through listings either in *Who's Who* or in the specialized references organized by profession, available at your public library. Or, if they're writers, you might request their address from their publisher. And don't overlook asking friends or associates to refer you to someone they might have a connection with. Contacts are very useful in promoting your book, both now and in all future stages. Ask your friends to write or call the people they are referring you to, so your approach won't hit them cold.

Here, then, is how you proceed: Send them a photocopy of the manuscript, with a cover letter introducing yourself (and mentioning the friend who referred you, if this is the case). Explain why you feel they would find the material interesting and ask if they will read it and share their comments. These are busy folks — if you hope to wheedle them into cooperation, be direct. And it never hurts to stroke their ego a bit. To facilitate their reply, include a SASE for their convenience. Whenever you want someone to do something for you, make it as *easy* for them as possible.

If they're experts, and sometimes even if they're not, they well may comment in detail on the ways the book should be different. If these remarks seem useful to you and if there's still time to make changes, go ahead and rewrite. You've gotten a free expert reading! If it's too late for changes, reserve the suggestions for the revisions you'll do before another printing. But if the suggestions seem more of an annoyance than a help, thank the people very politely for all their interest and contributions, use their quotable favorable comments, and drop the rest in the trash. The fact that someone has an opinion doesn't require you to rewrite your whole book!

With the person's written permission these favorable quotes become "advance comments." They can be splashed across your promotional materials like paints across canvas. If the people are superstars in the field, their comments on your cover or dust jacket can send sales skyrocketing.

For instance, if you've done a book on money management, who could give a better endorsement than Sylvia Porter? Let's suppose you send Ms. Porter a copy of your manuscript, getting her address out of *Who's Who in America*. She writes back commending your book. Why not take it one step further and ask if she would consider doing a foreword? (In some cases it's easier to get cooperation if *you* volunteer to write it — subject to the endorser's approval, of course.)

Trade announcements

There are three major places where important fall and spring books of national interest may be listed. They are *Publishers Weekly, Library Journal,* and *Small Press.* It's wise to send them advance information about your book, as the more often people hear of it, the better. (This is not to say you'll be guaranteed a mention, as competition is fierce.) Here is where your duplicate ABI forms will come in handy. It's also a good idea to type out a brief "blurb" on your letterhead. It should include publisher, author, title, pub date, price, and binding information (hardback, paperback, or other). Also add about a ten-word description using a category such as fiction, how-to, or cookbook. In the case of *Small Press* magazine, you must provide information in a specific format, which is specified periodically in their publication.

It's easy to reach these three magazines. The first two are published by the R. R. Bowker Company. Address your information to Spring (or Fall) Announcement Editor. *Publishers Weekly* comes out fifty-one times a year and serves the entire book publishing trade. Among its approximately 40,000 subscribers are the people you particularly want to reach: wholesalers, subsidiary rights managers, booksellers, media personnel.

Library Journal is a full-service publication for librarians, predominantly those serving adult needs and interests in public and college libraries. It is published twenty times a year and has about 26,000 subscribers. *Small Press* is a bimonthly. It is now billed as "The Magazine of Independent Publishing." You can reach *Small Press* at Meckler Corporation, 11 Ferry Lane West, Westport, CT 06880. *PW* and *LJ* also put out special religious and children's book issues, so contact them for an announcement if you're publishing a title in either of those fields.

While you're at it, why not scatter a few more ABI forms around? Look in the Appendix under "Marketing Contacts." You will find a list of suggested galley recipients and another list called "Send Completed Books." The sources noted here are all honchos in the industry.

Baker & Taylor

Baker & Taylor is the largest wholesaler in the United States. It is education-oriented and concentrates on serving the library market plus some bookstores. And it can mean big bucks for you. The first step any new publisher wanting to do business with B&T should take is to send advance book information (ye ole ABI form will do nicely) to the Publisher Contact Section. In turn, you will receive a New Book Information questionnaire and a Vendor Profile Questionnaire requesting your terms, discounts, and returns policy. (See samples.)

Baker & Taylor maintains a master data base of publishers' names and addresses and will add you to it. This data base is used for placing special mail orders with publishers that the company doesn't regularly stock. To activate things with Baker & Taylor, write to the Publisher Contact Section, Baker & Taylor Company, P.O. Box 6920, Bridgewater, NJ 08807, and ask for their "Information Outline" for new publishers. (We'll be discussing this company in greater depth in Chapter 15 on Standard Channels of Distribution.)

Subsidiary rights

Although a whole chapter is devoted to this topic later on, we want to briefly introduce it here, as there are strategic early maneuvers you may want to make. Some subsidiary rights—such as book clubs and first serialization or excerpt rights—should be pounced on as soon as possible. The reason is very simple. Subsidiary rights offer a substantial opportunity to maximize your income. Let's take book clubs first. Two places to prospect for likely ones are *LMP* and *Book Marketing Opportunities: A Directory.* Your ideal goal is to click with one or more book clubs at this infant stage. Then you can produce the book club copies at the same time as those you plan to sell yourself, reducing the overall unit printing costs: The more books printed, the less cost to you per copy. If the arrangement is negotiated carefully, it can also yield you some "front money" to use for paying the printing bill.

Serial and excerpt rights apply to material appearing in magazines and newspapers. When they come out *before* the publication of a book, they're called "first" rights. That's what you're going after now. There is a list in the Appendix under "Marketing Sources" which will be helpful in your quest.

BAKER & TAYLOR
NEW BOOK INFORMATION FORM

TITLE:

SERIES:

AUTHOR: PUBLISHER:

                                 DISTRIBUTOR:

Binding	Price		LC Number:_____
Cloth	$_____		ISBN/ISSN Number:_____
Paper	$_____		Edition: First____Other (Specify)____
Spiral	$_____		Approximate number of pages:_____
Looseleaf	$_____		Reprint: yes_____no_____

Subscription service? yes__no__   If yes, give year of original
                                                publication_____

Unbound	$_____
Audio Cassette	$_____

Limited edition:
    Yes____No____Number____

Calendar	$_____

Is this a compilation of
previously published articles?

Software	$_____
Video	$_____

            yes____no____

Month (or season) and year of   Intended audience:
publication:

Description: Return <u>completed</u> form to:

                                        Publisher Services
                                        Baker & Taylor
                                        652 East Main Street
                                        P.O. Box 6920
                                        Bridgewater, New Jersey 08807

VENDOR PROFILE QUESTIONNAIRE
1. Publisher's Name and Address:
    (Please include orders/returns address if different)

    _____

    _____

    _____

    _____

2. Telephone:

3. Name and position of key contact:

4. ISBN Prefix:

5. Distributor (if other than publisher):
    (please indicate if this is an exclusive arrangement)

6. Will you sell to wholesalers such as Baker & Taylor?____yes____no
    if no, please indicate reason:

7. What are your wholesale business terms for the following:
    (please enclose printed schedule if available)

    Discount   Freight   Payment   Returns

8. How many titles do you publish annually:

9. What type of announcements do you issue?
    (please enclose copies)

10. What type of publications do you offer?

    BOOKS_____AUDIO_____SOFTWARE_____OTHERS (please specify)_____

11. What are your subject specialties?

12. What is your intended market(s)?

13. Do you publish serials or titles in series/sets?

14: Do you distribute English language books first published abroad____yes
    ____no. If yes, how many per year?

Prepared by:

Date:_____
Please return completed form to: Publisher Services
                                           Baker & Taylor
                                           652 East Main Street
                                           P.O. Box 6920
                                           Bridgewater, New Jersey 08807

To approach book clubs, magazine editors, and newspaper editors, your ABI form once again comes into play. All you need is that, a copy of the table of contents, and a cover letter in which you briefly describe the contents. If you have a computer, it's a simple task; if not, just create a typed form letter which you personalize with the name and address of your targeted source. Be sure to offer a free, no-obligation reading copy of your manuscript.

If you hear nothing within three weeks, send a brief letter saying you're just checking to make sure they received your original correspondence and asking whether they wish to consider the book. Wait a couple more weeks, then scan your list for the most promising. Now's the time to get on the phone and see if you can activate a spark of interest. Naturally, as time goes on, your book and promotional materials will be taking shape. If you get to the point where you have galleys, send them instead of a manuscript: It looks more "official." Likewise, use your news release and mock-up review after it is prepared. Remember, these editors are swamped with book proposals every day. If you want to be considered, stay in front of them by mail and phone until you've received a firm "no." This advice goes for any important sale or promotional opportunity you are pursuing.

Before leaving this important topic, realize that in major trade publishing houses, the subsidiary rights director would also be going after foreign sales and premium or sponsored editions at this point. We feel this is too sophisticated for self-publishers at this stage of their undertaking. These avenues are covered in later chapters.

Now let us move on to the actual creation of your book, the designing and printing phases.

CHAPTER 8

DESIGN AND PRODUCTION

Before embarking on the printing of your book, there are several points to consider. What kind of a cover design should it have? What types of cover blurbs are most effective? How vital is good interior design and how can it be achieved? What's the lowdown on typesetting and pasteup? Are there secrets to good proofreading? How do you create an index?

The importance of good cover design

Let's talk about the cover design. If you expect to market the majority of your books through bookstores, your cover is your billboard and it had better be good. Book browsers will only give a book a few seconds of consideration. It must wrench their attention away from thousands of other volumes nearby. Since most books are shelved spine out, this narrow strip is your first sales tool. Make it stand out with arresting color and compelling lettering. It should display the title, author, and publisher.

Next, book browsers look at the book's front. If it interests them, they'll turn to the back. If they're still intrigued, the front and back flaps— if there's a dust jacket—will receive their consideration.

The local bookstore offers a tremendous resource for cover analysis. Here you can look at the designs of best-sellers and books similar to yours. Do your homework well. Many self-published books turn out looking amateurish because of poor design.

Your cover must be distinctive! Make it capture the essence of the book. This can be accomplished through the use of lettering, dynamic copy, a photo, or an illustration. It should be consistent with the inside material and carefully slanted to the tastes of your potential reader. If you were doing a book of interest to attorneys, for instance, dignity rather than flamboyance would be the key. Don't confuse busyness with boldness. You want a dramatic cover, not one with meaningless clutter.

If you don't have genuine professional graphic arts experience, get in touch with professional graphic artists—ones who have done book covers or advertising layouts before—and talk concepts and prices. One place to look is in *LMP* under the "artists and art services" listings. Or try checking with nearby publishing houses. We located a couple of very talented local free-lancers by calling the Production Department at the San Diego branch of Harcourt Brace Jovanovich and explaining our dilemma.

John and Tom, who worked as a team, came out, read the table of contents and a couple of sample chapters, then talked with us about the "feel" of Marilyn's book *Creative Loafing*. They also asked about our budget allocations. A few days later, they came with rough sketches in hand. That gave us a whole new dilemma. We liked elements from each! Tom had designed logolike lettering for *Creative Loafing* that immediately captured our fancy. Yet John had come up with a pair of whimsical-looking people participating in activities mentioned in the book, and we liked the human interest they lent. Back to the drawing boards went John and Tom. They then incorporated the best elements of *both* roughs into a final drawing that had us nodding eagerly.

Our financial agreement, by the way, was to pay them only when they came up with an acceptable design. We ended up with a bill of around $700. This price included the more costly processes of hand lettering and a custom illustration. Of course this was a 1978 price—and as time goes by, we gain a deeper appreciation for the bargain we received even then. In today's market, you can get a basic cover design for anywhere from $300-$3,000, depending on the complexity and the custom work involved.

Usually you will be working with only one artist. After preliminary agreement on the flavor of the book, he or she will come back with a few roughs or thumbnail sketches. From these, the two of you should be able to pull together the final cover.

Cover considerations

Covers create different effects. To develop an aura of mystery and romance, the classic gothic novel sports a frightened young woman hurrying from a castle or an old house that has a solitary light burning in an upper window. To generate another feeling, the designers of the cover for *Chariots of the Gods* used large three-dimensional block letters. Check the following cover examples for *Buffalo Management and Marketing* and *Be Tough or Be Gone*. The type has a tough and rugged feeling. The photos used match the titles; they create the effect or mood that fits the book.

Type by itself, without illustrations, is often appropriate if the book is of a business or how-to nature. But even typefaces have different personalities and "feels," as we'll be explaining shortly, so be cautious to match your type choice to your subject. Note how the typeface and design for *Why Jenny Can't Lead* plays on the title implication. It actually seems to be *leading*! The cover for *How to Make Big Profits Publishing City and Regional Books* is bold and daring as an entrepreneurial publisher must be. Can you feel the turmoil in *Breaking the Stress Habit*? As different as these covers are, they have one thing in common: they all photograph extremely well. If you use just lettering, you may want to go to a hardcover book *without* a dust jacket and have the title stamped on the actual book cover itself. This technique was used for our original, self-published edition of *The Encyclopedia of Self-Publishing*. We chose a brown, leatherlike cover and stamped the type in gold. It was very rich-looking.

Color also plays a large role in book cover design. This is one place where one plus one does *not* equal two. It can equal three or even five or six! Why? Because a skilled designer uses one color of ink by itself, introduces another contrasting color by itself, then combines the two to create an additional color or two. Another color effect is created by reversing out the color and letting the white of the paper show.

The illusion of an additional color can be created by what is called a "screen tint," a tone created by a regular pattern of tiny dots—the denser the dots, the darker the tone. The eye sees the screened tone as a tint of color. Often, type appears over the tinted area. Screen tints are expressed as percentages—10 percent being very light, 50 percent much darker. If you want to print over the screen tint with the same color, don't use more than a 30 percent screen. Twenty percent is usually a safer specification for best contrast.

Screen tinting is an economical technique that will also give your promotional materials added appeal. If you count up the possibilities, you'll see you can get several colors while merely paying for a two-color job, and thereby reduce your cover printing costs by as much as 50 percent. If you are using a small, local printer and must be very cost-conscious, use their standard house inks, rather than special blend PMS (Pantone Matching System) colors.

Tom just completed the cover design for *Caring for Kids* (see the following). The base colors were yellow and magenta, two prime colors. From these two colors, he created bright red, orange, and yellow. White was created by reversing out all color. The result? A quick, four-color job for the price of two. In this case, he did add black for the small type and photograph. From just these three prime colors (yellow, magenta, and black), 197 PMS colors could have been created. Wow!

Be Tough or be Gone

Tom Davis
as told to Marilyn Ross

ANDREW G. GOLISZEK

BREAKING THE STRESS HABIT

BUFFALO MANAGEMENT & MARKETING

by Dana C. Jennings & Judi Hebbring

How-to-Make BIG PROFITS PUBLISHING City & Regional BOOKS

by the authors of the
Complete Guide to S

Marilyn & T

WHY JENNY CAN'T LEAD

UNDERSTANDING THE MALE DOMINANT SYSTEM

JINX MELIA & PAULINE LYTTLE

Another treatment that gets a lot of mileage out of two colors and a black-and-white photo is called a "duotone." In this process, two halftone negatives are made from one print. The darker and shadow tones usually are printed black, while the second color picks up the middle tones. Using black and brown is quite popular for producing expensive portrait prints.

As the competition for the buyer's attention intensifies, the use of metallic inks (gold, silver, and copper) on covers seems to be a growing trend. As you've probably noticed during your research, they are quite striking, especially if film laminated. However, you should consider a couple of things before specifying metallic ink.

First, the inks themselves are significantly more expensive than regular colored inks: just about double the cost. Second, and more cost significant, a metallic ink cannot be printed along with other colors in one pass through the press. Metallic ink is much slower drying than other type inks; therefore, the metallic ink must be run through the press by itself, then set aside to dry before the other colors can be printed on the same surface. Regular inks are usually laid on in one press pass. As you can surmise, your printer is going to charge for the additional press pass for the metallic inks. A recent book we did for a client had a three-color cover, one of which was gold metallic. The additional charge for using metallic gold instead of a regular PMS color was $260 for 5,000 copies.

Foil embossing is yet another option, but it is typically too expensive in the lower quantities that most self-publishers print.

When you choose a color photograph for your cover, you must use what is called a four-color process. This is sometimes called a *full*-color process because from the four "prime colors" (yellow, magenta, cyan, and black), every possible color is created.

This process is costly, and it probably should be avoided unless it will add substantially to buyer acceptance of your book. It could be warranted for something like a cookbook, a coffee-table book, or a travel guide where a lush photograph will be a major factor in capturing the attention of your audience. Perhaps a high adventure book, such as the *Be Tough or Be Gone* example, could be a case where a color photograph is necessary to capture the reader's curiosity. Again, if you're going to the luxury of a color photograph, make certain that it fits the tone of your book. Check the photo on *Be Tough or Be Gone*—we think you will agree it fits. Imagine the impact in full color. *The UNcook Book* is an example of showing the actual foods (in full color) to enhance a cookbook cover. It must be working, as this title just went into its fifth printing. The cover has garnered kudos from readers.

With full-color, costs, in addition to the photograph or illustration itself, are incurred for making color separations and printing. If you do elect to go this route, be aware that a photo will never gain sharpness in the printing process. As a matter of fact, subtle tones in a photograph do not reproduce well. Be sure the image you start with is as sharp as possible. Have your designer submit, if at all possible, negatives or slides, not

prints, for separations. If you must use a color print that is not the best quality, have your designer check into color correction. Even slight focus problems can be corrected by a good color separator. Talk to your designer or vendor about available services. Sometimes you can save money by accepting a *close* color match, rather than an exact one.

Covers usually include a photo of the author. On a dust-jacketed hardcover, we typically use the entire back for sales copy and put the author photo and bio on the back flap. Paperbacks typically have the sales copy and the author photo and bio all on the back cover. If you want to reserve the entire back cover for sales copy, you can include the author photo and bio on the last page of your book. You'll want a black-and-white glossy print (unless you're doing a full-color cover). Also, please realize that your author picture is for a different purpose than any photo you have ever had taken. It is to sell you as the expert.

We asked an experienced trade book editor to tell us what's wrong with most of the hundreds of author photos she's seen.

"What is usually wrong with the author's picture? Usually a snapshot is submitted instead of a thoughtfully and professionally composed photo, which means all the things wrong you'd expect—cluttered (even stunningly cluttered) background, out-of-focus shot of the author in a plaid blouse standing in front of the lilac bush in the driveway. A picture not only unflattering but uninteresting. This doesn't mean it must or should be a plastic, perfectly-groomed-but-lifeless grinning studio shot. Yes, it would be more appropriate for a writer to be in an unusual setting or an unusual pose doing something that is quintessentially them. It doesn't have to be sitting at the desk or in front of a typewriter—it's not only hard to get an uncluttered and interesting picture of same but that's pretty old-hat by now. It could be irreverent or quirky or even slightly bizarre—but it *should* give you a good sense of the persona of the author and most of all be close-up enough that you can actually *see* the face. It should be a well-composed and effective photograph of good reproduction quality—which means it should probably be taken by a professional or a really good amateur photo bug—which means most likely not your nephew or daughter-in-law."

For paperbacks choose a cover stock that is thick and has a glossy coating. Most publishers use a 10-point C1S (coated one side) stock. You can pay a little extra and get press varnish, Liquid (U.V. cured) Lamination or even film laminate which will give more durability and greater reflective quality. This is a good idea because it enhances the colors and protects the book from soil and scuffing. (Especially important with bookstore sales.) Film laminate also eliminates the need for shrink wrapping, which is a pain and costs extra. We find it is nearly a wash cost-wise to film laminate, and using this process provides convenience for the self-publisher and a sharper-looking cover for the consumer. To help gauge overall book or dust jacket dimensions, we've included visuals that identify proper sizing.

If you're doing a booklet, consider what's called a "self-cover." This simply means the cover stock will be the same as the interior pages and will be printed and saddle-stitched right along with them. In some cases it makes sense to upgrade to a heavier, perhaps colored, stock for more durability and a better appearance.

If your publication will be sold mainly through mail order, cover design takes on a different aspect. Color, a prime ingredient in bookstore sales, is not needed for mail order, for instance. What you want here is a cover that will photograph well so a picture of the book can be used in your advertisements (notice our previous samples). Choose large display type. If an illustration is included, make sure it uses strong lines that will photograph sharply and reduce well.

So now you've got a great design in mind. How do you determine the dimensions for the spine? In the cast-off you did in Chapter 7, you figured out a close approximation of the number of pages in your book. For many cover designs, this approximation will be close enough. For critical designs, however, you will need the final page count developed under "Working with Typesetting."

In either event, the dimensions needed are developed as follows: First we must determine the bulk. To do this, divide the page count by the pages per inch (PPI) of the paper you are using. (Get this PPI from your printer.) For a paperback, the bulk equals the spine width. That's all there is to it.

For a hardcover with a dust jacket, you must add the amount in the "plus column" of the Spine Width Chart on page 125 to allow the jacket to wrap around the extra thickness of the hardcover boards. Let's assume we have a 320-page book that we're printing on 320 PPI hi bulk paper. Obviously our bulk equals one inch. But we need to add $7/16''$ from the Spine Width Chart to give us a total spine of $1\ 7/16$ inches.

Whenever possible, Tom designs our covers or jackets so the manufacturer can make small, final adjustments on the spine width by adding or subtracting a fraction of "white space" on the spine. This procedure allows us to have our cover designs completed before books are totally typeset.

The other approach is to do the best possible job on your initial cast-off, perhaps by using an excellent computer program called Autocast. You determine your bulk at this point and adjust as necessary in typesetting to hold the bulk dimension. We use this technique for most full-color covers or covers with photos or illustrations that wrap around the spine—considered critical design.

DUST JACKET DIMENSIONS & COLORS

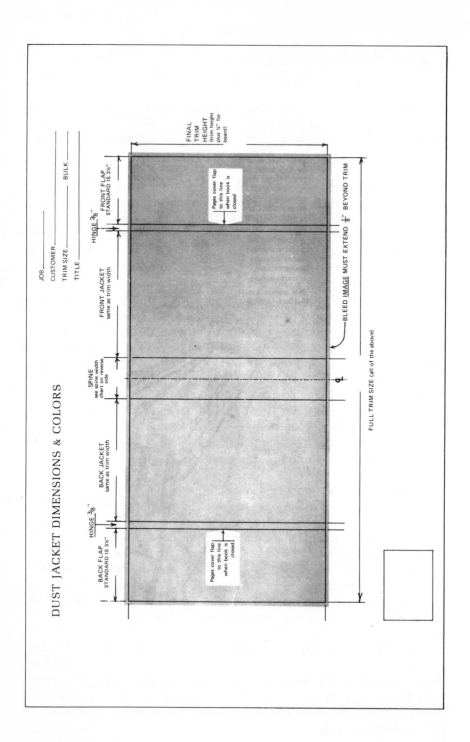

JOB

CUSTOMER

TRIM SIZE _____ BULK

TITLE

FINAL TRIM HEIGHT
(trim height plus ¼" for board)

FRONT FLAP
STANDARD IS 3½"

HINGE 3/8"

Pages cover flap to this line when book is closed

FRONT JACKET
same as trim width

SPINE
see spine width
chart on reverse
side

BACK JACKET
same as trim width

HINGE 3/8"

BACK FLAP
STANDARD IS 3½"

Pages cover flap to this line when book is closed

BLEED IMAGE MUST EXTEND 1/8" BEYOND TRIM

FULL TRIM SIZE (all of the above)

124

SPINE WIDTH CHART

THIS TABLE GIVES THE FINAL WIDTH OF THE SPINE (INCLUDING THE ROUNDING) OF NORMAL CASE-BOUND BOOKS MADE BY LITHOCRAFTERS.

Adjustments will have to be made in the case of extra-heavy binders' boards, a change of paper, or extra rounding.

(Not applicable to flat-back bindings.)

bulk	plus	total width
$\frac{3}{16}$	$\frac{1}{4}$	$\frac{7}{16}$
$\frac{1}{4}$	$\frac{1}{4}$	$\frac{1}{2}$
$\frac{5}{16}$	$\frac{1}{4}$	$\frac{9}{16}$
$\frac{3}{8}$	$\frac{1}{4}$	$\frac{5}{8}$
$\frac{7}{16}$	$\frac{1}{4}$	$\frac{11}{16}$
$\frac{1}{2}$	$\frac{1}{4}$	$\frac{3}{4}$
$\frac{9}{16}$	$\frac{5}{16}$	$\frac{7}{8}$
$\frac{5}{8}$	$\frac{5}{16}$	$\frac{15}{16}$
$\frac{11}{16}$	$\frac{5}{16}$	$1''$
$\frac{3}{4}$	$\frac{3}{8}$	$1\frac{1}{8}$
$\frac{13}{16}$	$\frac{3}{8}$	$1\frac{3}{16}$
$\frac{7}{8}$	$\frac{3}{8}$	$1\frac{1}{4}$
$\frac{15}{16}$	$\frac{3}{8}$	$1\frac{5}{16}$
$1''$	$\frac{7}{16}$	$1\frac{7}{16}$
$1\frac{1}{16}$	$\frac{7}{16}$	$1\frac{1}{2}$
$1\frac{1}{8}$	$\frac{7}{16}$	$1\frac{9}{16}$
$1\frac{3}{16}$	$\frac{7}{16}$	$1\frac{5}{8}$
$1\frac{1}{4}$	$\frac{7}{16}$	$1\frac{11}{16}$
$1\frac{5}{16}$	$\frac{7}{16}$	$1\frac{3}{4}$
$1\frac{3}{8}$	$\frac{7}{16}$	$1\frac{13}{16}$
$1\frac{7}{16}$	$\frac{7}{16}$	$1\frac{7}{8}$
$1\frac{1}{2}$	$\frac{1}{2}$	$2''$
$1\frac{9}{16}$	$\frac{1}{2}$	$2\frac{1}{16}$
$1\frac{5}{8}$	$\frac{1}{2}$	$2\frac{1}{8}$
$1\frac{11}{16}$	$\frac{1}{2}$	$2\frac{3}{16}$
$1\frac{3}{4}$	$\frac{1}{2}$	$2\frac{1}{4}$
$1\frac{13}{16}$	$\frac{1}{2}$	$2\frac{5}{16}$
$1\frac{7}{8}$	$\frac{1}{2}$	$2\frac{3}{8}$
$1\frac{15}{16}$	$\frac{1}{2}$	$2\frac{7}{16}$
$2''$	$\frac{1}{2}$	$2\frac{1}{2}$

$2''$ to $2\frac{1}{2}$: add $\frac{9}{16}$
$2\frac{1}{2}$ to $3''$: add $\frac{5}{8}$

Spine width chart.

Next, let's look at the overall cover width. The front and back jacket width, or cover width, always equals the trim width. If your book is 5¼" wide, you'd multiply that by two and add it to the spine width. For you folks who are doing hardcovers, there is another step. Your dust jacket has flaps. Allow about 3½" each for the front and back flaps, plus ⅜" for each flap hinge, where the jacket will wrap around the edges of your book.

As to height, for a paperback, the final trim height equals the trim height. So if your book is 8½" high, that's the cover height. On hardcovers, however, you must add ¼" to the dust jacket dimensions so it will extend over the boards on the top and bottom.

A final caution: If your book has bleeds (where the color goes clear to the edge of the paper) extend ⅛" beyond your trimmed cover dimension on both the height and the width.

Cover copy

Now that we've talked about the visual impact of your cover, let's discuss the copy that will appear on it. "Cover blurbs" are the sales message. To get an idea of what to say, study Avon and Bantam publications. These two publishers employ some of the nation's top copywriters. Read 'em. Study 'em. Imitate 'em.

Usually about twelve words work well on the front and about seventy-five on the back. They must have wallop! Zip! Punch! We find it amusing that many reviewers parrot the message that appears on the back and/or flaps of a book, sometimes without even changing a word. (Study the chapters on Advertising and Direct Marketing for tips on powerful advertising copywriting.) Of course, you won't want to make any false claims in this, or any other, sales literature.

If you've garnered a foreword by an authority or celebrity, don't forget to splash the person's name on the front. This will give your book greater respectability and sales appeal. Some self-publishers have also put sneaky things such as a dramatic label-like graphic proclaiming "destined for #1 BEST-SELLER" on the cover, with "destined for" in very tiny print. An often-seen technique for the back cover is to print the table of contents. Another possibility is to use any powerful advance comments you've received from notables in the field or prominent book critics.

Along with these cover blurbs you will want to develop material for the jacket flaps if you're doing a hardcover. The front flap should tantalize the prospective reader with more nice things about the book. If you're going to list the price, this is a good place to put it. (For paperbacks place the price on the bottom of the back cover.)

There rages a controversy over whether or not to print the price on the book. On the "yea" side, bookstores in the United States much prefer that books be priced; otherwise, they must sticker each one. Those who say "nay" contend that pricing poses two problems: Canadian booksellers, who must charge more for you to make the same profit, resent having to up the printed price of the book. And if *you* decide to raise the price, this limits you considerably. (People *do* tear off those stickers and peer at what's underneath.)

The back flap is best devoted to information about the author. Here's where your photo and bio appear. Toss away your humility. This must be an ego-puff piece. Study what is written about other authors and mold yours around them. As an exercise, it's helpful to make a list of your accomplishments, honors, awards, degrees, experience, past writings, and organization memberships. This list will yield many ideas for developing your biography. Remember to slant your copy to the subject at hand. Make the information establish you as an authority on your subject.

To make ordering easy, include your publisher's name and address on the back flap of hardcovers or the back cover of paperbacks. If you're not using a Bookland EAN Scanning Symbol, by all means include the ISBN number on the right foot (bottom corner) of the outside paperback cover. For hardcovers, it should be on the outside back cover and the back of the jacket.

At this point you've got a smashing-looking—and -reading—cover. What about the interior text? Are there design questions here, too? You bet there are!

Interior book design

Trim size

For economic reasons relating to the size of paper and printing presses, most books fall into the 5³⁄₁₆" by 8¼" to 6" by 9" size. A new size in the general range of 7" by 9" to 7" by 10" is also emerging. Think about the use for your book. If you want to include business letters or forms, 8½" by 11" might be more practical. If you choose to use an odd and unconventional trim size, be prepared to pay more and work closely with your printer.

You may wonder why we seem to avoid the 4" by 7" mass market paperback size. Wouldn't that be cheaper yet, sez you? No, sez us, and we'll give you some good reasons why: Because of the high number of words-per-page, the high page count, and the low prices (usually four or five bucks), print quantities must be very high. Print runs for mass market paperbacks often run around 100,000 copies. But even more intimidating, let us share with you what the Spring/Summer 1988 *Author's Guild Bulletin* stated: "In returning mass market books for credit, retailers ordinarily mail back *only the covers* (italics ours). They are supposed to destroy the rest of the books, but often they are sold instead. The practice is said to cost publishers some $20 million annually." We certainly can't afford such practices. Can you?

Paper

Another thing to think about is the paper used. While this is a design consideration, it also affects cover design because of spine width, and it has great bearing on your overall printing costs. Depending on the number of pages and the quantity of books printed, paper costs from 28 to 50 percent of the total printing bill! In the early seventies when a paper shortage existed, paper companies raised their prices every few weeks until they had almost doubled them in two years. Unfortunately, they're on another roll. Paper prices have skyrocketed. We've just experienced a 13 percent increase in two months. The real culprits are catalogs and newspaper supplements, which have proliferated in recent years. Since they use coated paper—and paper merchants can charge more for coated paper stock—many have stopped making book paper and switched to coated stock. The few merchants left who make book paper keep raising their prices à la the old supply-and-demand rationale. To get a better grasp of the cost factors, study the visual "Text Paper Comparative Cost Finder."

Paper is chosen for its weight, opaqueness, and color. Let's say you have a skinny book. Use a "high bulk" paper and it will appear fatter. You'll pay a little more for high bulk stock, but if it makes your book appear to be a better value and allows you to charge more for it, it's a wise investment. Paper is measured by PPI (pages per inch). You'll usually be working with those in the 330 to 480 range. This is standard text paper for books with 120-400 pages. Most books are done on 50-, 55-, or 60-pound paper. Ask your printer for samples. If you will be using photographs or artwork with heavy ink coverage, be sure the stock has good opacity so the material from the other side of the page doesn't show through. To test it, place your art under the sample and observe how much you can see.

Unless you specify otherwise, your book will be printed on stark (blue white) white. Yet books on a natural or off-white stock that is easier on the eye are often favored by schools and libraries. If you're publishing a long-term reference book, scholarly publication, or high-priced literary work, you may want to use a special acid-free paper. Though it costs more, it means your book will still be in good shape half a century from now. If you're producing a special deluxe edition—perhaps one that is numbered and hand-sewn—you may also want to upgrade to a more

TEXT PAPER COMPARATIVE COST FINDER

Many of our customers are interested in cost comparisons of the various weights and shades of text papers. The reasons for this are varied; weight savings, bulking, shade preferences and others. The cost trade-offs involved are often significant in reaching a decision. This Text Paper Comparative Cost Finder will help in these decisions.

The use of this chart is very easy. Using 50# Delta White offset book rolled stock as the base, or 100%, compare the other shades and stocking to calculate the comparative prices.

For example, if you have an estimate based on 10,000 copies of a book printed on 60# White sheets and want to calculate the approximate savings if printed on 50# White rolls, compare the 50# rolls listed below to the 60# sheets, or 100 vs. 130. Paper savings on the job would be 30%.

Text paper costs run between 28% and 50% of the total printing costs, depending on total pages in the book and the quantity of books produced. Therefore, in the example given, the overall cost savings would probably be about 15% (50% of 30%).

These figures cannot be used to calculate exact figures. They are only intended to give you a guide in figuring the comparative costs and specifications for your book.

STOCK	AVAILABLE IN	COMPARABLE PERCENT
50# Delta	Rolls	100
50# Delta	Sheets	112
60# Delta	Rolls	115
60# Delta	Sheets	130
45# Delta	Rolls	92
45# Delta	Sheets	105
70# Delta	Sheets	185
30# Omega Book	Rolls	78
35# Alpha Workbook	Rolls	65
50# Theta Natural Text	Rolls	115
50# Theta Natural Text	Sheets	130
50# Litecoat Beta Book	Rolls	110
60# Pica Matte	Sheets	215
60# Kappa Coated Book	Sheets	195

PAPER BULK CHART

Bulk	1 16"	1 8"	3 16"	1 4"	5 16"	3 8"	7 16"	1 2"	9 16"	5 8"	11 16"	3 4"	13 16"	7 8"	15 16"
312 ppi	20	39	59	78	98	117	137	156	176	195	215	234	254	273	293
320 ppi	20	40	60	80	100	120	140	160	180	200	220	240	260	280	300
330 ppi	21	41	62	83	103	124	144	165	186	206	227	248	268	289	309
336 ppi	21	42	63	84	105	126	147	168	189	210	231	252	273	294	315
352 ppi	22	44	66	88	110	132	154	176	198	220	242	264	286	308	330
364 ppi	23	46	68	91	114	137	159	182	205	228	250	273	296	319	341
368 ppi	23	46	69	92	115	138	161	184	207	230	253	276	299	322	345
384 ppi	24	48	72	96	120	144	168	192	216	240	264	288	312	336	360
392 ppi	25	49	74	98	123	147	172	196	221	245	270	294	319	343	368
396 ppi	25	50	74	99	124	149	173	198	223	248	272	297	322	347	371
434 ppi	27	54	81	109	136	163	190	217	244	271	298	326	353	380	407
436 ppi	27	55	82	109	136	164	191	218	245	273	300	327	354	382	409
440 ppi	28	55	83	110	138	165	193	220	248	275	303	330	358	385	413
444 ppi	28	56	83	111	139	167	194	222	250	278	305	333	361	389	416
448 ppi	28	56	84	112	140	168	196	224	252	280	308	336	364	392	420
476 ppi	30	60	89	119	149	179	208	238	268	298	327	357	387	417	446
480 ppi	30	60	90	120	150	180	210	240	270	300	330	360	390	420	450

Bulking chart.

expensive paper stock. One other thing to remember about paper is that it has a definite grain, or direction, to it. Be sure your printer prints your book *with* the grain—meaning the grain runs parallel to the spine. Otherwise, the book will snap shut like a mousetrap.

Photographs

When using photographs inside a book, for best results work from 8" by 10" black-and-white glossies. However, 5" by 7" glossies will save some developing costs, are a little easier to work with, and will give results almost as good. You can crop (omit from the printed photograph) edges of the picture to do away with unneeded or unwanted details or background. The best way to do this is to lightly mark the edges of the photo with a grease pencil indicating which parts of the photos are not to be used. Be aware that it is easy to have your photograph reduced or enlarged to fit the allocated space. This is called scaling. A photograph gets snappier when it's reduced; it can lose quality when it is enlarged. From a glossy photograph the printer makes a "halftone" by a process that converts the picture into a pattern of tiny dots, which the printer's camera can then read. One tip for ending up with quality photographs is to take instant pictures first. This helps you determine proper lighting, balance, etc. Another tip is to place your photographs so they will have some white space around them, rather than running them clear to the edge of the page. When you do run them to the edges it's called a "bleed," and will add extra cost to your printing bill, because a larger size of paper will be needed.

Of course, a good printer will be able to produce an adequate job from less than perfect photographs. We've done client books on city histories, for instance, where many of the photographs were priceless old gems of the horse and buggy era. Many were faded and had a matte rather than a glossy finish, and some were scratched. Nonetheless, the printed photographs turned out well. So don't despair if the photos you have to work from are less than ideal. We've also worked from color slides, having them converted into black-and-white glossies. When using photographs, key them to your manuscript by using the page number as the photo number. (If there's more than one to a page, go to a 91a, 91b, 91c tactic.) When numbering photos, do so *very lightly* on the back with a soft pencil.

Photographs, and often illustrations and charts, require an explanation. This is called a "cutline." It should be brief but clear. Decide how you're going to approach this task, then be consistent. We find that making an "artwork log" is helpful. We list the number of the photo or art, then type the cutline beside it. This helps the typesetter and gives us a quick and complete reference list. It also gives you a ready reference when preparing the list of illustrations for front matter.

As was mentioned earlier, using color photographs boosts the printing costs very quickly. There are ways, however, to minimize the costs. With careful planning by someone who knows what he's doing and can design the color between signatures, it might be economically feasible for a self-publisher.

Illustrations

Photographs are only one option for interior art design. You may be an artist yourself, or want to include illustrations to amplify certain points. Professional artists are listed by fields of activity in *LMP*. Look over their portfolios before you commission one. Illustrations help people understand better. Many of us comprehend pictures more easily than words. These needn't be works of art per se; a simple sketch showing how to do something you're explaining can be a real aid to the reader. If you're an amateur artist, don't cheapen your book with poor art. Otherwise, use black India ink for any drawings and avoid large blocks of ink, such as an all-black dog. (Why do you think old Spot is so popular?) When large expanses of ink are used, there's apt to be bleed-through to the reverse side of the page, with paper of average quality. The alternative is to go to a heavier, higher-quality, and more expensive grade of paper through-out the text.

A cardinal rule for interior art design is always to place the piece of art *after* your discussion of it. Have you ever tried to read a book where a diagram or illustration precedes the text that explains it? Confusing, at best.

And try not to bunch your art all in one place. Artwork breaks up the page after page of text and gives your book texture and a sense of liveli-ness. If you want to add this touch by spending practically nothing, con-sider "clip art." Various publishers issue books of illustrations that you simply clip out and paste into position wherever desired. You can find books on such subjects as cartoons, animals, religion, business, sports, old-time subjects, and so forth. There is a list of clip art sources in the Appendix.

Clip art is also a wonderful way to enliven your sales materials. And it's a cheap way to give a book of poetry fresh interest. Also don't overlook illustrations in government publications, most of which can be freely re-used. You may even find something in your local newspaper or the "junk mail" pile (assuming it isn't copyrighted). When using such materials, however, keep in mind that black and red reproduce well but that many light colors, especially blue, don't.

Are there any special diagrams, charts, graphs, questionnaires, or ex-ercises that could enhance your book? Be sure to consider an attractive approach for displaying them. If you're presenting technical information, be sure it's accurate. Nothing is more frustrating than to follow a plan for a woodworking project only to learn that the measurements are off.

Chapter title pages

Depending on your subject matter, a decorative touch on the chapter title pages might be nice. You could use clip art to suggest the chapter theme. Another frequently used visual device is a relevant quotation. A bold vertical line might work.

Your text for each new chapter typically begins about a third of the way down the page. Above it you have the chapter number, title, or both. Start each chapter on a recto page unless you're condensing to fit into even signatures. If you're also dividing your book into parts, each part-title will ideally have a page to itself.

Here again you have an opportunity to put typography to good use. For contrast you can use larger bold, italics, or a combination of both. Many book designers also add a second typeface for chapters, subheads, or sub-subheads as long as it coordinates well with the text type.

Subheads

What about subheads? If you're doing a nonfiction book, these are not only helpful but for some subjects almost mandatory. Subheads allow the reader to scan and quickly find a topic. Think about how much less useful this book would be if there were only the main chapter titles without any subdivisions. In many cases sub-subheads are also helpful. We're using that technique right now. This will increase your typesetting costs a bit, but it will make your book more marketable, and easier to use.

Image size

Think about how much of the interior page you want covered with type. In a 5½" by 8½" book you might want an image size of 4" by 7". Be sure to leave plenty of blank room in the "gutter"—the space where facing pages come together. Don't have margins that are too skimpy. If you've ever picked up a mass-market paperback with barely a quarter inch of margin, you'll know what we mean. On the other hand, if your margins are too big, readers will feel you tried to stretch the book. The best test is to look at several volumes. You'll quickly gain a feel for what is pleasing. You'll want a dab more room at the bottom of the page than at the top for good visual balance. Following is a sample page identifying where elements should go, and a *bad* example as well (one of those cases where a visual is worth a thousand words).

Remember, here is a place to expand or shrink the page count of your book. You can shrink the image size by deleting one pica or adding one line per page—either will result in the few pages' difference you might need to fit in even signatures.

Ink color

Most books are done in black ink. There is no set rule for this, however. A book of poetry or a cookbook might be more interesting if printed in brown, a lively green, or a rich blue, for instance. The increased cost is insignificant. But if your design requires that you use two (or more!) ink colors, and if you believe that the increased cost will be justified, either aesthetically or by increased sales, then go ahead. Just be sure you calculate the higher cost in working out when, if ever, your book can be expected to break even (earn enough to cover expenses) and start making a profit.

6″ × 9″ DUMMY PAGE

*Running Head

*Page No.

27 picas × 45 picas

4½″ × 7½″

Image Area

¾″ Gutter

¾″ Margin

Bleed

*Recto page shown. Reverse position of running head and page no.
for Verso page.

An example of page design.

8
DESIGN AND PRODUCTION

*Before embarking on the printing of
your book, there are several points to
consider. What kind of a cover design should it have? What types of
cover blurbs are most effective? How
vital is good interior design and how
can it be achieved? What's the lowdown on typesetting and pasteup?
Are there secrets to good proofreading? How do you create an index?*

The importance of good cover design

Let's talk about the cover design. If you expect to market the majority
of your books through bookstores, your cover is your billboard and it
had better be good. Book browsers will only give a book a few seconds
of consideration. It must wrench their attention away from the hundreds or thousands of other volumes nearby. Since most books are
shelved spine out, this narrow strip is your first sales tool. Make it
stand out with arresting color and compelling lettering. It should display the title, author, and publisher.

Next, book browsers look at the book's front. If it interests them,
they'll turn to the back. If they're still intrigued, the front and back
flaps—if there's a dust jacket—will receive their consideration.

The local bookstore offers a tremendous resource for cover analysis. Here you can look at the designs of best-sellers and books similar
to yours. Do your homework well. Many self-published books turn out
looking amateurish because of poor design.

Your cover must be distinctive! Make it capture the essence of the
book. This can be accomplished through the use of lettering, dynamic
copy, a photo, or an illustration. It should be consistent with the inside
material and carefully slanted to the tastes of your potential reader. If
you were doing a book of interest to attorneys, for instance, dignity
rather than flamboyance would be the key. Don't confuse busyness
with boldness. You want a dramatic cover, not one with meaningless
clutter.

An example of bad page design.

Footnotes

Unless you are producing a scholarly work or a textbook, it is best to avoid footnotes. They distract the reader and up the typesetting costs. When you must use them, place an asterisk after the material to be annotated and give the explanation at the bottom of the same page. When there are a lot of footnotes, it is best to number them in the text, then type a consecutive list at the end of the chapter or book.

Front and back matter

Just as a sandwich has a piece of bread on the top and bottom to hold the ingredients inside, a book has pages of front and back matter that sandwich the main text. While in most books front matter is either not numbered or numbered with roman numerals, we suggest using letters of the alphabet on your manuscript copy of the front matter for the sake of simplicity and clarity. If you want roman numerals on the finished book, the typesetter (who will know the difference between XVI and XIV) can put them in for you. If you want to mark either numbers or letters on the galleys, use a pencil with light, nonrepro blue lead which won't photograph. It is our opinion that front matter should be designed to fill up all available pages without going over, thus keeping down printing and paper costs.

Let's elaborate on that for a minute. Offset books are printed on large flat sheets or continuous roll paper with four, eight, sixteen, or thirty-two pages to a side. Since these sheets are printed on both sides, books are ultimately made up of "signatures" that are twice these increments. Signatures most commonly consist of thirty-two pages. It is important that you be aware of these multiples and plan for them in your book. Ask your printer what size signatures his or her press provides.

If you envision a sixty-four-page book, but find it is going to run into sixty-five pages, you will be charged for another whole signature or for the manual labor required to cut out the unnecessary pages. So it makes sense and saves dollars to use all available space or to look for ways to trim your manuscript to avoid going into an additional signature. Perhaps you can change the size of the type image on the page, delete or reduce a photograph, or tighten chapter beginnings.

Page 1. The half-title (also known as the bastard title) page consists only of the main title. The subtitle is omitted, as is the author's name.

Page 2. The back (verso) of the half-title page is usually blank.

Page 3. Your second page on the right (recto) will be the title page. It should include — you guessed it — the title, subtitle if any, the author's full name, plus your publishing house name and address. Also include the illustrator's, editor's, photographer's, and foreword writer's name if any

First printing 1979
Second Edition printing 1979

Library of Congress Cataloging in Publication Data

Ross, Marilyn Heimberg.
    The encyclopedia of self-publishing.

    Bibliograpy: p.
    Includes index.
    1.   Publishers and publishing — Handbooks, manuals, etc.
I.   Ross, Tom, 1933 —   joint author   II.   Title.
Z285.5.R67   658.8'09'070573   79-4054
ISBN   0-918880-05-X

Printed in the United States of America

A sample copyright page.

of these people are well known or otherwise important to the book.

Page 4. The copyright page (title page verso) is the back of the title page. (*Verso* means a left-hand page.) It contains much vital information. See the adjacent sample. There is the © symbol (which secures world rights), the year, and your name as the copyright holder. Speaking of copyright, here's a trade secret that was told to us by a top executive of a major New York publisher: when a book will roll off the press anytime after September first, they automatically assign it the *next year's* copyright date. Thus a book published September 15, 1989, would carry a 1990 copyright date. This prevents the "yearling effect" that is so prevalent in horse breeding—that on the first of January everything is a year older! We suggest all small publishers follow their example and give themselves sixteen months to promote the work as a new book instead of just four. Of course, this applies to books published in October, November, and December as well. (We also checked with the copyright office and found that this is an acceptable practice and that you don't forfeit any protection.) Also be sure to include the terms "All Rights Reserved," and "Printed in the United States of America," plus "First Printing" and the date. You can secure copyright merely by publishing your book with a valid copyright notice. Registration with the copyright office just registers a copyright that already exists; this can be done at any reasonable time after the book has been published—even years later. The self-publisher must be very sure to print the copyright notice in the proper form. If this isn't done, the copyright may not be valid.

This is also where you will list your Cataloging in Publication Data, which includes your Library of Congress Catalog Number, and your ISBN. If you want to place a disclaimer in the book, this is an appropriate spot. Here is a disclaimer we used for a client's book on a health subject:

> Although the authors and publisher have exhaustively researched all sources to ensure the accuracy and completeness of the information contained in this book, we assume no responsibility for errors, inaccuracies, omissions, or any inconsistency herein. Any slights of people or organizations are unintentional. Readers should use their own judgment or consult a holistic medical expert or their personal physicians for specific applications to their individual problems.

Page 5. Here is a good location for your dedication and acknowledgment. You may also want to list any previous books you've written either here or on a separate page.

Page 6. At this point you can put in the foreword, "Note to the Reader," or preface. Note that the author's preface should follow any of the above. While many would also tuck the introduction in here, we suggest it be placed as the first item following the table of contents. It's much more likely to be read there.

Page 7 (or later if your previous entries run longer than our example). Now comes the table of contents. Begin on a recto page. Take pains in writing your table of contents. Many people make buying decisions by scanning this recap of a book's contents. Give it sizzle. Make sure it presents a thorough, enticing overview of the ingredients. You might study the table of contents of this book as a model. (Also be alert to leaving space for the appropriate page numbers, which must be added after the whole book is typeset and numbered.) If your book contains many illustrations, diagrams, or charts, you should create a list of illustrations. It typically falls on the back of the table of contents page.

This concludes front matter. You may choose to spread things out a bit to have key elements on recto pages for easier reading. Just be aware that such luxurious designing may cause you to run over into another signature and boost the cost of the book considerably. Of course, you can use this technique as an expander, filling out a few pages and thereby getting to an even signature. On the contrary, you can shrink your book by eliminating the half-title page and flipping some of the recto starts to verso starts—such as moving the table of contents from page XII to page XI—to prevent running over even signatures.

Now on to back matter. You may choose not to have all the things we'll be talking about, so just skip over what doesn't apply. First there is the appendix. If you have long lists of items or names and addresses, these are best saved for an appendix. This has two advantages: It makes the material easy to locate for quick reference, and it doesn't interfere with the flow of the book itself. Next comes the bibliography. A glossary, if included, follows. Then the index. Its purpose is to help the reader find information quickly and easily. In some manuals you also see an afterword, which is a personal message in which the author wishes the reader success and sometimes requests feedback for improving subsequent editions. Occasionally a "colophon" will appear at the end of the book. A colophon details the production facts about the book, such as the computer and word processing system used, the type style, designer, typesetter, printer, kind of paper, binding, and so forth. It's a good idea to include a final page with an order-form coupon for obtaining additional books. Try to place the coupon so readers will not be snipping away part of the book when they cut out the order form.

Turning your raw manuscript into an attractive book is a challenging and satisfying process. There is really no reason you can't do the interior design yourself if you adhere to the tips we've offered so far and pay attention to the next section. While it would be nice to hire a professional graphic designer to do the whole thing, if you have only so much cash, we feel a pro can better serve you by creating the cover.

If you've decided to handle all the design functions yourself, there are two books we recommend you get: *How to Understand and Use Design and Layout*, by Alan Swann, works wonders for the novice trying to wade through technical details. And the *Business Guide to Print Promotion*, by Marlene Miller, is helpful not only with book design, but also for brochures, direct-mail packages, and other promotional pieces.

Working with typesetting

Now let's look at the actual typesetting phase of publishing. When getting your book ready for printing, you can take one of many approaches. You can prepare the text yourself, hire a typesetter, or do a combination of both. While hiring a typesetter may seem expensive, it can be a lot less so than charging out and buying additional computer equipment to do the job yourself. If you suspect you are a one-book person, it probably isn't prudent to spend several thousand dollars on a laser printer, font interface, and publishing software. If, on the other hand, you foresee a continuum of books on the horizon, the money would likely be well spent.

If you read Chapter 6 carefully, you know that you can professionally typeset your book yourself if you have the right equipment and software. If you are computerized—and we certainly hope you are, or soon will be—several typesetting options are available. We're assuming in this exercise that you have one of the word processing programs we've recommended.

1. If you have a good daisy wheel printer with proportional spacing, you can do a reasonable job of setting text. You will need to use "transfer letters" or "press type" for chapter titles. Following is a sample of a page set this way.

2. Assume you have a top-of-the-line, 24-wire print head, dox-matrix printer. You can accomplish at least the quality of the following Epson LQ1500 sample page.

3. And of course, there's the laser printer, font interface, and desktop publishing software. Take a look at the sample page set with Ventura Publisher, Lasermaster font interface, and a Cordata laser printer.

4. Or you can format your book using one of the powerful word processing programs and provide the keyboarded, edited, spell-checked, and formatted copy directly to a phototypesetter who is set up to translate your compatible diskette or modem input into typesetting codes for his phototypesetting system. (There is probably less chance for error using a diskette transfer of data.) This book was produced in this manner.

We still tend to prefer phototypesetting for most jobs because it is much easier to work with. There is also less chance of damaging your camera-ready boards by smudging, smearing, or abrasion. All of the methods depicted in one through three above involve creating an image by transferring ink to paper. Ink tends to smear easily when handled. You must be very careful doing any pasteup. Wax will almost certainly create a smear, so you're relegated to using rubber cement for tedious stripping of corrections or any embellishments you want. If you're doing the setting yourself, we recommend that you reprint the entire page rather than attempt to make corrections by pasteup. In short, if you have the time and already have the equipment, it's cheaper—although it's a lot harder to handle than phototypeset material.

We use a PC and word processing program to write, edit, and format our clients' books, then contract phototypesetting through our outside vendors. Using this procedure, we can provide our clients complete design and top-quality, phototypeset, camera-ready copy for under ten dollars per page for most books.

Although we don't recommend it in most cases, your book can still be do-it-yourself set without the help of any computer tools (shudder, shudder). If you absolutely can't afford a truly professional product, you can still use an ordinary typewriter. If you're selling specialized information via direct marketing, your readers may not mind a typewritten book. And many poetry collections and family histories are done this way. On the other hand, you will hurt your chances immeasurably if you're trying to make a hit with reviewers, libraries, bookstore buyers, and educational institutions.

Let's evaluate what is involved in this process. Find as good a typewriter as is available to you; we believe a correcting Selectric to be the minimum. A typewriter with changeable fonts is best. This way you can at least italicize and make chapter headings bigger where needed. If possible, use one that has proportional spacing and right justification (even right margins). Make sure the typewriter is well adjusted and cleaned before you start. Use a pica type that will give twelve characters per inch. You might want to try special "repro" paper, available from a typesetter or printer's supply source; it gives a crisper impression.

Again, you will need to use transfer letters to create your chapter titles. With some practice, you can create headlines that appear almost professional. Find some clip art or uncopyrighted drawings, and presto! your book is illustrated.

But suppose you prefer to go the professional route all the way. Be sure to have a manuscript that's as clean as possible, free from excessive corrections, misspellings, and coffee spills. It should be typed or printed double-spaced on 8½" by 11" white paper—*one side of the paper only.* Number all pages and keep a copy yourself.

Step two is to shop. Compare. Negotiate. Find a typesetter you personally like and can work with, someone who is willing to take the time

Working with typesetting

Now let's look at the actual typesetting phase of publishing. There are many approaches to getting your book ready for printing. You can prepare the text yourself, hire a typesetter, or do a combination of both. While hiring a typesetter may seem expensive, it can be a lot less so than charging out and buying additional computer equipment to do the job yourself. If you suspect you are a one-book person, it probably isn't prudent to spend several thousand dollars on a laser printer, font interface, and publishing software. If, on the other hand, you foresee a continuum of books on the horizon the money would likely be well spent.

If you read chapter six carefully, you know that you can professionally typeset your book yourself if you have the right equipment and software. If you are computerized -- and we certainly hope you are, or soon will be -- several typesetting options are available. We're assuming in this exercise that you have one of the word processing programs we've recommended.

1. If you have a good daisy wheel printer with proportional spacing you can do a reasonable job of setting text. You will need to use "transfer letters" or "press type" for chapter titles. Following is a sample of a page "set" this way.

2. Assume you have a top of the line 24-wire print head dot matrix printer. You can accomplish at least the quality of the following Epson LQ1500 sample page.

3. And of course there's the laser printer, font interface, and desktop publishing software. Take a look a the sample page set with Ventura Publisher, Lasermaster font interface and a Cordata laser printer.

4. Or you can format your book using one of the powerful word processing programs and provide the keyboarded, edited, spell checked, and formatted copy directly to a phototypesetter who is set up to translate your compatible diskette or modem input into typesetting codes for his phototypesetting system. (There is probably less chance for error using a diskette transfer of data.) This book was produced in this manner.

Working with typesetting

Working with typesetting

Working with typesetting

Working with typesetting

Now let's look at the actual typesetting phase of publishing. There are many approaches to getting your book ready for printing. You can prepare the text yourself, hire a typesetter, or do a combination of both. While hiring a typesetter may seem expensive, it can be a lot less so than charging out and buying additional computer equipment to do the job yourself. If you suspect you are a one-book person, it probably isn't prudent to spend several thousand dollars on a laser printer, font interface, and publishing software. If, on the other hand, you foresee a continuum of books on the horizon the money would likely be well spent.

If you read chapter six carefully, you know that you can professionally typeset your book yourself if you have the right equipment and software. If you are computerized -- and we certainly hope you are, or soon will be -- several typesetting options are available. We're assuming in this exercise that you have one of the word processing programs we've recommended.

1. If you have a good daisy wheel printer with proportional spacing you can do a reasonable job of setting text. You will need to use "transfer letters" or "press type" for chapter titles. Following is a sample of a page "set" this way.
2. Assume you have a top of the line 24-wire print head dot matrix printer. You can accomplish at least the quality of the following Epson LQ1500 sample page.
3. And of course there's the laser printer, font interface, and desktop publishing software. Take a look a the sample page set with Ventura Publisher, Lasermaster font interface and a Cordata laser printer.

ing there's a chance of failing, such as when we play the slot machines or have children. I'm speaking instead of those moments of naïve innocence when we honestly believe we've figured things out, only to end up worse off than when we started. When we least expect it, the Whoops! Factor transforms our noblest intentions into their opposite.

The Whoops! Factor in Medicine

Nowhere is this principle more common than in medicine. Take, for example, the "war on cancer." Congress declared war on cancer in 1971 when it passed the National Cancer Act. Since then, we've spent more than $25 billion on cancer research.

In 1985, a prominent cancer researcher named Robert T. Schimke made a startling admission about our progress in that war. Chemotherapy, he declared, tends to make cancer worse. The problem, he explained, is that cancer cells *resist* chemotherapy, and that resistance mimics the very processes of cancer itself. Dr. Schimke drew his conclusion from research sponsored by the American Cancer Society. He reported it in a lecture he gave at the National Institutes of Health in Bethesda, Maryland, where he was being honored for receiving the Alfred P. Sloan, Jr. Prize for his research. *Chemotherapy tends to make cancer worse*, this esteemed scientist said. This is serious Whoops! Factor territory.

No less sobering is what antibiotics do to bacteria. Scientists began searching for antibiotics during the late 1800's after Louis Pasteur formulated the germ theory of disease, and Robert Koch developed ways to isolate and identify varieties of bacteria. Today we've got more than sixty different antibiotics, all designed to kill bacteria.

But they also make the bacteria stronger. Today we face bacteria that didn't exist in Pasteur's and Koch's day, ones that even our best antibiotics won't touch. These bacteria have come to *resist* antibiotics. One study showed that, when an antibiotic was added to chicken feed, virtually all of the chicken's bacteria developed resistance to it within one week. Within six months, 80 percent of the farm family's bacteria were resistant as well, just from having to explain things and to advise. Ask for, and study, samples of his or her work. If errors are found in the samples, beware. If this is the *best* work, think what the normal work must be like!

Prices for typesetting fluctuate wildly. While one company will turn out work for eight dollars a page, the next wants twenty-five. Of course, the condition of the manuscript you provide will have some bearing on your costs. Clean double-spaced copy—with correct proofreader's marks in red indicating what you want—goes a long way toward getting a good deal. Make sure you are comparing apples to apples, not apples to oranges, when getting bids. Every bid should be for the identical product. Do all include typesetting of running copy plus chapter heads and pasteup? If "A" bids twelve dollars a page but doesn't include heads or pasteup, and "B" bids sixteen dollars a page but *does* include them, "B" may actually be more economical.

One tip for trimming costs is to schedule your work during "downtime." Although "downtime" is often used to refer to the period when equipment isn't usable because it's broken or being fixed, we're using it here to mean time when the typesetter's business is very slow. Equipment is idle, but there's still a payroll to meet. Often a typesetter will settle for a smaller margin of profit under these circumstances. Unfortunately, the best competitive book typesetters seldom have a lull. Our suppliers all seem to keep a healthy backlog. And of course, this could cause your job to take longer, since you will be last priority. Discuss this with your typesetter.

Another possibility for shaving costs is to coordinate with your typesetter before preparing the final draft of your manuscript. Some companies have computers that "read" certain IBM typewriter fonts, thereby cutting manual labor and slicing typesetting costs significantly. (Refer to Chapter 6, "Computers in Publishing," for additional savings.)

The decisions to be made about the type itself include style, size, and the white space around it.

When designing fliers or ads, you can be daring with typefaces. In book design, however, the hallmark of good typography is *legibility*. It gets the job done without calling attention to itself. There are two major families of type: serifs and sans serifs. Serifs are much easier to read because they have little hooks on them which serve to hold the eye on the line. Readers have been trained to read body copy in serifs from the time they enter kindergarten. Schoolbooks, newspapers, and most magazines are done in this family. Some common easy-to-read styles are Century, Times Roman, Bodoni, Garamond, and Bookman. When you find a style that pleases you, stick with it rather than mixing faces. The place to introduce something different, such as a sans serif typeface, is in the chapter heads or subheads.

Calligraphy, which is hand lettering, is another option. It is used to create intimacy with the reader for poetry and children's books and certain booklets. It can also give a feeling of tradition. Many cookbooks are done this way. If your subject matter lends itself, you could take a class in calligraphy and letter your book yourself. But be sure, whether the work is yours or someone else's, that it is neat, straight, and easily read.

What about size? "Point" is one of the standard units of measurement used in typesetting. A point is approximately $\frac{1}{72}$ of one inch. In other words, there are seventy-two points to an inch. The other standard unit of measurement is the "pica." One pica equals twelve points, or (approximately) $\frac{1}{6}$ of one inch. Line lengths for typeset copy are specified in picas. For instance, a line that measures four inches wide would be designated as twenty-four picas. Picas appear on the accompanying type comparison gauge on page 149.

The white space between lines is called "leading." It is typically the type size plus two. For example, "10/12" indicates 10-point type with 12-point leading. Its purpose is to make the lines of type spread apart enough that they do not strain the eye.

Most newspapers and magazines are done in 9- or 10-point type. The higher the number, the larger the size. On the type comparison gauge you will see that 11 point is a nice, readable size (though it can vary from one style to another). The kind of book often dictates a size range. A children's book, for instance, will want larger type. And for goodness' sake, if you have a long book with few illustrations for relief, don't force the reader to plow through the whole thing in 9-point type! How condensed the typeface is will also have a bearing on how much you can get on a page. Some really pack in the copy. If your book is running a bit too long, you can use a more condensed type that is still highly legible, and you'll save going into a new signature for just a page or two. For instance, Garamond is more condensed (has more characters to the inch) than Bodoni.

Now is a good time to refer back to your initial cast-off. Will the typeface, point size, and leading you selected give the characters or words-per-page you calculated? If not, it is easy enough to adjust things to expand or shrink your book to size. If you are using Autocast or the more refined and precise Autospec computer book-design programs, the task is very easy. If you plan to do only one book, these programs are too expensive; but should you figure on a publishing career, they can be an excellent investment.

There are certain things you may want highlighted by the use of boldface or italics. Chapter headings and other important divisions might be done in boldface, though the larger the point size, the denser, or heavier, the type in "lightface." Ask for samples.

When you've selected the style, size, and leading and have narrowed

The Author's Guide to

UPPERCASE CHARACTER · LOWERCASE CHARACTER · COUNTER · SERIF · ASCENDER · X-HEIGHT · BASELINE · DESCENDER

The words are yours and type is the medium used to convey these words to the reader. The right typeface can enhance your concepts and embellish the appearance of your book. It is the job of the designer to make those choices that would most effectively convey your meaning. To give you a sense of what the designer deals with, the following is a general description of the most used typographic terms:

Melior

Optima

Palatino

Serif
Gothic

Bodoni

Caslon

Bauhaus
Demi

Benquiat

Baskerville

Caledonia

Ascender—The part of a lowercase letter above the x-height

Baseline—The line on which the characters appear to stand

Characters—Individual letters, figures and punctuation marks

Counter—The enclosed or hollow part of a letter

Descender—The part of a lowercase letter that falls below the baseline

Em—A printer's unit of width measurement which is equal to the body size of the type in question. An 8-point em is 8 points; a 14-point em is 14 points, etc. It takes its name from the widest letter in any typeface: M.

Font—A complete alphabet: one typeface in one size

Italic—A type in which the forms slant to the right

Justify—To set a line to a desired measure

Leading—The spacing between lines (measured in points)

Letterspacing—The space between the letters in a word

Lowercase letters (l.c.)—The small letters

Pica—A unit used to measure the length of a line of type. One pica (0.166") consists of 12 points and six picas (72 pt.) equal one inch

Point—Used to measure the typesize—from the top of the ascender to the bottom of the descender plus space above and below to prevent the lines of type from touching. The point (0.1383") is the basic unit of printer's measurement.

Typography chart. From *The Children's Picture Book: How to Write It, How to Sell It* by Ellen E.M. Roberts, designed by Hal Siegel. Reprinted courtesy of Writer's Digest Books.

Ragged right , ragged left—Unjustifed type that is allowed to run to various line lengths

Roman—A type in which all the letters are upright.

Sans serif—A typeface without serifs

Serif—The short strokes that project from the ends of the main body strokes of a typeface

Typeface—A specific design for a type alphabet

Type family—All the styles and sizes of a given type

Word spacing—The spacing between words in a line

Uppercase letters (u.c. or c.)—The capital letters or caps

x-height—The height of the lowercase x in a given typeface

Three commonly used faces shown in various sizes.

Baskerville	Times Roman	Univers
9/10	9/10	9/10
Once upon a time once upon a time once upon a time once upon a time once upon a time once upon a time once upon	Once upon a time once upon a time once upon a time once upon a time once upon a time once upon a time once upon	Once upon a time on ce upon a time once upon a time once up on a time once upon a time once upon a time once upon a t
10/11	10/11	10/11
Once upon a time once upon a time once upon a time once upon a time once upon a time	Once upon a time on ce upon a time once upon a time once up on a time once upon a time once upon a	Once upon a time once upon a time once upon a time once upon a time once upon a time
11/12	11/12	11/12
Once upon a time once upon a time once upon a time once upon a time once upon a time once upon a time	Once upon a time o nce upon a time on ce upon a time onc e upon a time once upon a time once u pon a time once up	Once upon a time once upon a time once upon a time once upon a time once upon a time once upon a time

A showing of 18 pt. Souvenir Roman (the face used for this book).

abcdefghijklmnopqrstuvwxyz1234567890
ABCDEFGHIJKLMNOPQRSTUVWXYZ$

Trade
Gothic

Garamond

Century

**Cooper
Black**

Univers

Korinna

Gill Sans

Helvetica

Tiffany

Times Roman

Futura

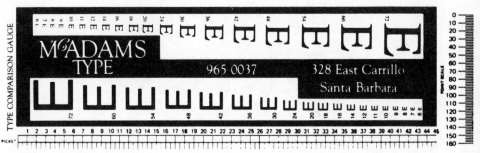

Type comparison gauge.

the field to two or three typesetters, ask for a couple of sample pages. Some vendors will supply samples free of charge when they know you are seriously considering them for the job. Be sure to provide pages from your manuscript, as you want to find out how many of *your own* words fit on a typical page . . . it won't help a bit to know that the Declaration of Independence will go on it six times. In addition to specifying typeface, point size, leading, and column width, tell them the paragraph style you wish: Indented or block? Extra space between paragraphs? The vast majority of books are done with what is called "justified" margins. This means everything ends up aligned, as opposed to ragged. Clue your vendor in on what you want here, too.

Your sample pages can be quite an eye-opener. Some years ago we gave two vendors pages from one of our titles. Working from the same manuscript, both using Century Medium 11 point, leaded 3, our pages turned out amazingly different! With one typesetter we got 332 words per page. The other produced 367 words on a page. What a shock! We always figured that machines given the same specifications would produce the same amount of copy per page. Not always so. In one case the individual letters were separated by more white space than the other, thus the variance.

Armed with a couple of sample pages, you can now do a final cast-off. There are approximately 400 words on an average typeset book page if you use 10-point type. Say you get 395 words per page, and your manuscript is 70,400 words long. Simple division shows that equals just over 178 pages of text. Remember to add extra room for chapter heads, for starting all chapters on a recto page, and for space taken up by subheads, if any. And don't forget interior art and the pages of front and back matter. Be sure to count all blank pages, too; your printer surely will. You'll recall we detailed how to compute this cast-off at the beginning of the previous chapter. It's time to massage your data, make any necessary adjustments, and create your final typesetting specifications. See the example on page 150.

Drop running heads 36 pts

First line of text drop 60 pts

offset gutter by ½ pica

Bold
36 pt

Flush Right

Drop 180 pts Chapter Title

First line of New Chapter text Drop 216 pts

Set 11/12 Garamond
Image size is 24 pica line
X 39 lines of text
468 pts Depth

Bottom line of text 468 pts

Chapter title page # X X 540 pts

Typesetting Specification Sheet

One final tip: If you are doing the pasteup, ask your typesetter to run you *two* sets of numbers for your book. One set you will obviously use to identify each page when you paste up the book. From the second set you can draw the appropriate numbers to complete your table of contents. By ordering extra numbers now, you don't have to waste time going back to the typesetter for them later.

Proofreading procedures

When you get back the "galleys" (long sheets of typeset copy), read with the eye of an eagle. Make any corrections you want clearly, using accepted proofreader's marks (see page 156) and a red pen. Watch especially for things like transposed letters and omitted or duplicated words. When you find such a mistake, correct it and write "PE" in the margin, signifying printer's error (if, indeed, it was a printer's error). This way, *you* will not be charged for correcting the error. Should you find oodles of errors or a serious blunder, always request a corrected set of proofs to be sure the problems are rectified.

If there is something *you* want to change, make the change and mark it "AA," which stands for author's alteration. From here on, changes become expensive; this is *not* the time to do extensive rewriting. Each line you alter will cost from 50¢ to $1.50 a line. Although that doesn't seem like much, some changes require retypesetting a whole paragraph or even the entire page! Costs can escalate quickly when this happens.

It's a good idea to ask a friend, relative, or associate to cross-check the manuscript against the typeset copy with you. Typesetters have been known to omit whole paragraphs or repeat words. Far better to take some extra time now than suffer the heartbreak of catching major errors when the *book* is in your hands. Errors in your finished book will flash like neon signs. To accomplish this double check, one person reads aloud while the other follows the text. Trade off occasionally so neither of you loses your voice.

Or, you may want to have a professional proofreader do the job for you. This will help weed out any spelling or grammatical errors resulting from your own blind spots, errors the typesetter has reproduced. Proofreading will cost you but chances are your book will be the better for it. Your printer or typesetter may be able to give you a name.

However you do your proofreading, close scrutiny at this point will prepare a quality product for moving into the pasteup stage. One of the greatest advantages of using your computer diskette as input to your typesetter is that the proofreading has already been done. The chance for error has been greatly reduced. We still recommend, however, you spot check it in case any computer gremlins have taken up residence in your project.

Tips for easier pasteup

Next comes pasteup, where you put all elements together on the page—well spaced, even, and ready for the printer. (Of course, you can pay to have your typesetter do this, but it is something any self-respecting publisher should be able to accomplish, time permitting.) What you might want to do to give yourself added confidence and catch problems before you begin messing with the actual repro is to prepare a "dummy"—not the Edgar Bergen kind, the publishing kind. A dummy is a complete physical representation of the entire book. Page for page, it shows where photos or charts fall, replicates chapter heads, etc. (At least do a dummy for the front and back matter so you see exactly how those pages lay out.)

To make a dummy, you'll need photocopies of the galleys which you can cut up, mark, and put sticky fingerprints on without damaging the originals. These copies you'll cut up and attach to sheets of paper the same dimensions as two facing pages of the finished book, leaving room for any tables or illustrations which interrupt the text and for the "cut-lines" (captions) belonging to the artwork. You'll allow for consistent white space at chapter beginnings and uniform gutters (margins) down the middle, between the pages. Note on what pages all artwork will appear and make the calculations for reducing or expanding the size of the originals to fit the spaces you've given them.

Review your dummy with the following in mind: Is the book thoughtfully presented? Are the subject areas and subareas clearly marked? How about "arty" touches that make reading a pleasure? Do graphics provide a visual rest as well as being helpful and stimulating?

Watch for "widows" and "orphans." No, we don't mean women who have lost their husbands or parentless children. A widow is the last line of a paragraph that appears alone at the top of a new page while the rest of the paragraph is on the bottom of the previous page. An orphan is the first line of a paragraph that appears alone at the bottom of a page while the rest of the paragraph is on the next page. You display a cleaner design if you let the page fall short or run long rather than allowing widows or orphans.

When you have a finished dummy, you'll be ready to begin pasteup. For pasteup, you'll need a few basic tools. Ahead of time, get some heavy stock for using as pasteup "boards." The paper should have a smooth finish and not be heavy enough to opaque your light table when you've put two sheets of paper—your backing sheet (explained on page 154) and your boards with strips of galley attached to them—on top of the light table's glass. You can experiment by holding two sheets up to a window and seeing if the light still shines through.

We purchase ones with light blue guidelines already printed on them from Nolo Press in Seattle. Some printers also offer them free to their customers, so ask. The other materials you'll need include a T-square, triangle, metal ruler, and an X-acto knife plus extra blades. Get a good technical drawing pen that will lay down smooth, firm lines if you'll be drawing any boxes or rules. An alternative is to use strips of charting and graphic art tape for rule lines. You'll also need a couple of light blue nonreproducing pencils for corrections and instructions to the printer (the camera doesn't see light blue) and a little wooden or plastic gizmo called a burnisher—to smooth and attach the edges of the galleys firmly to the pasted-up pages. Some white correction fluid to opaque goofs might not be a bad idea either. Top this off with a jar of rubber cement, some Bestine (or other, similar solvent), and cotton pads to clean your boards, and you're in business! All these supplies can be bought at an art store. If you can afford a little more elaborate setup, we'd strongly suggest replacing the rubber cement with an electric waxer. It's faster and cleaner.

Do *not* use wax for other than phototypeset pages unless you're a masochist. Wax causes ink to smear badly, so it should be avoided by desktop publishers who produce their finished copy on laser printers.

Another marvelous though not absolutely essential tool is a handy little device called a "light table." It has a smooth translucent surface with a light underneath so you can readily line up elements and type. If you're like Marilyn with her first book, you just don't have any friends who carry light tables in their hip pockets, nor the cash to buy one. So you improvise. You can make a perfectly good light table out of a large picture frame with glass. Turn the frame on its face and put one of the stick-on type of fluorescent tubes underneath. And an ironing board makes a good, adjustable base.

Here's how to proceed:

• Number all your boards with the blue pencil.

• Trim the excess from the tops and right sides of the typeset galleys.

• Draw guidelines (which are set according to your original design) on a backing sheet for all items (margins, page number position, heading, text length, etc.) that will be uniform from one page to the next. Tape this sheet to the glass of your light table and line up each working sheet exactly on top of it. If you can't manage even a makeshift light table, use a ruler and a T-square to make sure all measurements are the same from page to page.

• As you pasteup, double-check each typeset correction for accuracy. Some typesetters will deliver all corrections on one or more sheets you'll have to cut up, inserting each tiny corrected line exactly over the incorrect original. Other typesetters are kind enough to redo completely either the paragraph or the whole page in which an error appears. In either case,

PASTE-UP SHEET

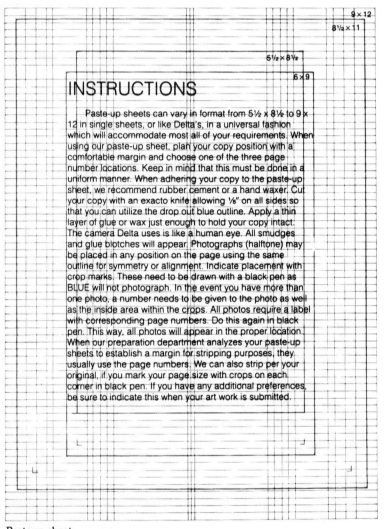

INSTRUCTIONS

    Paste-up sheets can vary in format from 5½ x 8½ to 9 x 12 in single sheets, or like Delta's, in a universal fashion which will accommodate most all of your requirements. When using our paste-up sheet, plan your copy position with a comfortable margin and choose one of the three page number locations. Keep in mind that this must be done in a uniform manner. When adhering your copy to the paste-up sheet, we recommend rubber cement or a hand waxer. Cut your copy with an exacto knife allowing ⅛" on all sides so that you can utilize the drop out blue outline. Apply a thin layer of glue or wax just enough to hold your copy intact. The camera Delta uses is like a human eye. All smudges and glue blotches will appear. Photographs (halftone) may be placed in any position on the page using the same outline for symmetry or alignment. Indicate placement with crop marks. These need to be drawn with a black pen as BLUE will not photograph. In the event you have more than one photo, a number needs to be given to the photo as well as the inside area within the crops. All photos require a label with corresponding page numbers. Do this again in black pen. This way, all photos will appear in the proper location. When our preparation department analyzes your paste-up sheets to establish a margin for stripping purposes, they usually use the page numbers. We can also strip per your original, if you mark your page size with crops on each corner in black pen. If you have any additional preferences, be sure to indicate this when your art work is submitted.

9 × 12
8½ × 11
5½ × 8½
6 × 9

Pasteup sheet.

Rules available from hairline through 24 point.

Hairline

½ Point rule

1 Point rule

1½ Point rule

2 Point rule

3 Point rule

4 Point rule

be sure that the inserted corrections are precisely straight, cover the whole error, and are pasted and burnished down especially tightly to be sure they won't be rubbed off as you shift and handle the boards. Use a sheet of paper between your burnisher and the text to avoid catching an edge and pulling off a strip of the galley or, even worse, tearing it!

• When you put together different sections of the galley, be sure the lines make sense as you read from one to the other.

• Check the bottom of each page against the beginning of the next page to be sure you didn't accidentally leave something out.

• Add any artwork at appropriate places.

• Be particularly careful to put everything on *straight*. Remember, what you see is what you get.

• Remember to leave blank pages if necessary so that chapters will start on a recto page (if you have enough pages for this lavish format!).

• Number all pages with a nonrepro blue pencil so that any necessary adjustments can be easily made.

• After your final check, affix typeset page numbers beginning after the table of contents. (You count, but do *not* actually number, chapter title pages and full pages of illustrations.)

• Clean all boards with Bestine, watching carefully for any smudges or spills. (Rubber cement leavings resemble fly droppings on the printed page.)

• If you're using transfer letters or clip art, treat the completed camera-ready artwork with a few swats of aerosol hair spray or fixative to "set" the type. Otherwise, they are apt to rub off or come loose.

Proofreader's Marks
Compliments of **Writer's Digest School**

WDS

MARK	EXPLANATION	(In margin.) **EXAMPLE** (In text.)
e	Take out character indicated.	*e* Your manuscript *e*
stet	Let it stay.	*stet* ~~Your~~ manuscript.
#	Put in space.	# Your manuscript.
⌒	Close up completely.	Writer's Di gest School.
tr	Transpose; change places.	*tr* Yuor manuscript.
caps or ≡	Use capital letters.	*caps* writer's digest school. writer's digest school.
lc	Use lower case letters.	*lc* Your Manuscript.
bf or ﹏	Use bold face type.	*bf* Writer's Digest School. Writer's Digest School.
ital or ___	Use italic type.	*ital* Writer's Digest Writer's Digest.
⌄'	Put in apostrophe.	⌄' Writers Digest School.
⊙	Put in period.	⊙ Your manuscript ⌃
?/	Put in comma.	?/ Your manuscript ⌃
:/	Put in colon.	:/ Your manuscript ⌃
;/	Put in semicolon.	;/ Writer's Digest School ⌃
⌄ ⌄	Put in quotation marks.	⌄ ⌄ He said, Yes.
(?)	Question to author.	(?) No hyphen OK Free lance writer.
=/	Put in hyphen.	=/ Free lance writer.
!	Put in exclamation.	! This is great ⌃
?	Put in question mark.	? Are you starting ⌃
c/⊃	Put in parenthesis.	c/⊃ Your first rough draft.
¶	Start paragraph.	¶ a writer. Learn to sell
‖	Even out lines.	‖ ⌐Writer's Digest and Writer's Digest School.
⊏	Move the line left.	⌐ Your manuscript.
⊐	Move the line right.	Your manuscript.
NO ¶	No paragraph; run together.	*NO* ¶ a writer. There are more needed
out, sc	Something missing. see copy.	*out, sc* Writer's School.
spell out	Spell it out.	*spell out* Your ms.

Proofreading symbols. From *The Writer's Encyclopedia,* edited by Kirk Polking. Reprinted courtesy of Writer's Digest Books.

• Flip the boards over and burnish them down tight with your burnisher.

• Double-check that they are in the correct order.

• Add the typeset numbers to your table of contents.

• Be sure all photos are numbered, have cutlines (captions), and are in the proper order.

• Photocopy your pasteup boards before sending them off to the printer (always keep at least one set for your own reference).

• Now is the time to create your index. (See below.)

• Package for mailing in a sturdy box. And don't forget to insure it!

By the time you've done a dozen pages, you'll be zipping right along. And the nice thing about learning pasteup is you can use these same skills to produce all kinds of promotional pieces.

How to create an index

An index increases a book's usefulness and salability. Dolores Simon, manager of Harper & Row's trade copyediting department, calls indexes "a very important part of the package for the nonfiction book." Libraries definitely favor books with indexes.

But how do you go about giving this mass of information shape and form? Indexing can be reasonably simple when approached logically. It is basically a series of decisions. And no one is more familiar with the material—or better equipped to make these decisions—than you. (Ironically, many trade publishing houses delegate this function to a free-lance indexer, who earns eight to twelve dollars an hour, typically paid out of the author's royalties!)

In creating your index, work from a photocopy of the final book so you don't mess up your pasted up boards. First, think through the book ... review your outline or the table of contents for a mind jog. You wouldn't want to slight any primary idea or philosophy. This is an intellectual, as well as clerical, task. Decide on the main concepts of your book. Consider how readers will use it. What questions they will have? What material may they wish to locate again? Look at the indexes in several books from your personal library to get a feel for format.

Regardless of whether you're indexing by computer or manually, you get to read your book again. As you read, highlight the items to be indexed. (If you are indexing manually, arm yourself with a horde of 3" by 5" cards and a file box with A-Z alphabetical file dividers.) Begin scanning on page one. Identify and mark—write each on a *separate* file card if you're doing it manually—subjects, proper names, charts, etc., and their page numbers. (No adjectives, folks; just the facts, please.) As you make a notation on a file card, place it behind the appropriate A-Z divider, then if you find the same subject on a later page, it will be easy to locate the card and add the new reference. Alphabetize entries strictly by the first word, disregarding "the," "an," "of," and "a."

Try to hit a happy medium: neither too general nor so nit-picky that the index ends up almost as long as the book. The American Society of Indexers contends there should be five pages of index for every hundred pages of text, though this may be a bit ambitious for self-publishers. The length can also be drastically influenced by type size and leading.

Don't overlook cross-indexing. Suppose you have a cookbook with a recipe titled "Marinated Fish Supreme." It should be listed under the "M's" and the "F's" ("Fish, recipes for"). Use subentries generously. When there are several references to a general topic, it's convenient to enter the reference to general discussion first, then the specific features in alphabetical order, as:

> Formal writing, 123-235
> mixed with informal, 132-33
> sentence structure of, 128
> when appropriate, 126-27

If you are using a new, powerful word processing program that has an indexing feature, you have some make-ready to do. Go back through the book on your computer and repaginate it to match exactly your type-set boards. (Of course, if you typeset the book yourself, this is already done.) Now you simply follow the instructions for your index program. Happily, alphabetizing is done automatically.

Let's suppose you have a computer but no index program. You can still do an index on your computer more easily than by hand. First, set up an A-Z format. Then enter all the highlighted data alphabetically. If you goof and put something in the wrong place, it's easy to electronically move it around with a computer. Of course, there are many computerized index programs—such as Indexit—on the market. While most of them require that you keyboard in the words to be indexed, they rescrabulate all the data and provide you with an alphabetized printout—a big time saver.

When you've finished categorizing the entire book, review each file card or your computer screen to make sure you haven't added fluff or meaningless words that shouldn't be indexed. Are the most obvious and helpful key words used? Remember to think like a reader who's using the book. Further, to see if you've accomplished your aim, take a few random pages and look up the subjects they relate to in the index. Are they covered? Any cross-references missed the first time around? Are all the cards properly alphabetized? If so, all that remains is to type the 3" by 5" cards into page form and you have an index ready to fire off to the typesetter.

If you're computerized, print out your index in double columns calculated to match your typesetter's "characters per pica" or "characters per inch." Use the index in this book as a guideline; design and format yours accordingly. Proofread it thoroughly.

Virtually all the new word processing programs have powerful built-in indexing capabilities. While with some you have to mark appropriate words in preexisting text, when you print the index it automatically adds the page numbers and creates an alphabetical list. This is a tremendous boon and saves laborious hours for frustrated authors.

Of course, if your book is fiction, you can omit the indexing process and move right on to the book manufacturing, which is covered in the next chapter.

CHAPTER 9

BOOK MANUFACTURING

Book manufacturing, also known as printing, will be your largest expense. But paper stock can make a big difference in overall production cost. And the size and binding you choose affect it dramatically. So do many other variables. With all this, even an intelligent person can feel like a dummy when it comes to book manufacturing. By studying the following tips, however, you will find it a heck of a lot easier.

The manufacturing process: printing your book

One of the first things you want to do is to seek out full-service book *manufacturers,* as opposed to regular printers who do offset lithography. Why a book manufacturer? Because typical printers earn a living churning out forms, fliers, and stationery, whereas book manufacturers specialize in books. That means they have technical know-how for you to lean on, they buy paper by the carload, their prices are more competitive, and they handle binding as well as printing so you don't have to find a bindery as well. It is better to deal with one company, rather than subcontracting jobs to a lot of different ones who will never be able to agree who was at fault if something goes wrong. A selected list of book manufacturers is included in the Appendix.

Another reason to go to a book manufacturer is that they will have a range of equipment and can choose the most efficient and cost-effective method to print your book. There are a number of variables that affect this choice. Some general guidelines are:

sheet fed press: These are efficient for a run of 1,000-5,000 copies of a book with illustrations.

web presses: Mini-webs are efficient for 5,000-7,500 copies, webs for 10,000 and up of illustrated books. These are particularly good for books with high page counts.

A manufacturer with a Cameron Belt Press can also slice a chunk off your printing bill — as much as 20 percent — if you're printing 2,000-50,000 copies or more. Although this would *not* be a good choice if your book contains photographs, because this particular press can't reproduce the sharp edges and contrasts that the printing of photographs requires, it is good for black-and-white line drawings, graphs, etc. The Cameron Belt Press saves money because it integrates many functions into one immense machine. While standard book manufacturing requires separate printing, folding, binding, and trimming operations, all performed at separate work stations, such is not the case with a Cameron. These are extremely expensive babies and only a few manufacturers have them. Some of these are: the Banta Company, R. R. Donnelley & Sons, BookCrafters, Inc., The Book Press, Inc., and Arcata (who worked with Mr. Cameron to develop the first one). Another thing to be aware of with a Cameron Belt Press is that the thirty-two-page signature rules no longer apply. Each trim size has a unique signature.

Something to keep in mind is that in the printing business more is less, meaning the more books you print, the less each one costs. That's because much of the expense revolves around the time it takes to set up the presses — called "make ready" time. It requires just as long to prepare to print five hundred copies as it does ten thousand.

As the quantity escalates, the unit price shrinks dramatically. Makes it seem tempting to print the ten thousand, doesn't it? Don't. That's a whopping order. As a rule of thumb, never print more than you know you can use in the first year. Do a one-to-five-thousand-copy run first. You can always reprint after the book proves itself. In fact, poets and others may want to print a thousand or less initially. This reduces the risks and capital outlay required.

It's a good idea to get estimates first. That's just a rough figure of what the book would cost to produce. It will help you determine expenses, set the book's retail price, etc. A very helpful publication is the *Directory of Book, Catalog and Magazine Printers*, edited by John Kremer. Another great book to help you better understand all the intricacies of the printing process is *Getting It Printed* by Mark Beach, Steve Shepro, and Ken Russon. In addition, Delta Lithography Company puts out a free publication called *Planning Guide*, a nifty aid for first-time publishers. And both Griffin Printing and Thomson-Shore offer complimentary newsletters that are helpful to publishers.

When you've found two or three vendors whom you like working with, and who seem in line cost-wise, ask for a price *quote*. Unlike the estimate, a quote is a firm commitment to print your book at the stated

---

REQUEST FOR BOOK PRINTING PRICE QUOTE

Please quote your best price and fastest delivery on printing and binding the following book:

BOOK TITLE: [Complete Guide to Self-Publishing]

TOTAL PAGES INCLUDING FRONT AND BACK MATTER: [416]

TRIM SIZE: 5½ x 8½   [6 x 9]   8½ x 11

PAPER: [60# bluewhite; 400-440 ppi offset furnished by printer]

TEXT PRINT: [Offset; black ink; no bleeds]

ARTWORK: [10 halftones, 50 pieces line art]

BINDING: [Hard] Soft

COVER: 1 color   2 color   [3 color]   4 color   [Customer will provide
                                                           camera-ready mechanical]

COVER MATERIAL: [Rainbow 2 linen]

COVER STAMP: [Approximately 12 sq. inches foil; dies furnished by printer]

BOARDS: [.088 pasted oak]

ENDLEAVES: [80# bluewhite]

HEADBANDS AND FOOTBANDS: [Yes]

PRINT QUANTITY: 1,000   2,000   3,000   4,000   5,000   [10,000]

TEXT PROOF: [One set blues for o.k.]

PACK: [5,000 loose onto 4-way banded pallets]

                [5,000 bulk carton onto 4-way banded pallets]

DELIVERY DATE: ____ weeks from receipt of camera ready copy

SHIP: [FOB point of manufacture. Provide estimated freight costs to
                Cincinnati]

TERMS:

Additional Stipulations

NEED ____ COPIES OF FOLDED & GATHERED SHEETS

OVER/UNDERRUN NOT TO EXCEED 10%

FINISHED PRODUCTION MUST CONFORM TO APPROVED BLUE-LINES

THIS QUOTATION GOOD UNTIL 90 DAYS FROM DATE INDICATED BELOW

Please also provide a separate bid for dust jacket overruns in the following quantities:

   [1,000]   2,000   [5,000]   10,000

VENDOR'S REMARKS OR SUGGESTIONS FOR ADDITIONAL COST EFFECTIVENESS:

_____

_____

SIGNED _____ DATE _____

Request for printing price quote.

price. It is guaranteed for a given length of time, usually thirty or sixty days (although you should push for ninety). Our Request for Printing Price Quote Form is shown.

We recently conducted an interesting experiment. We contacted three dozen of the top book manufacturers for a price quote. To make a long story short, the results were quite amazing. The price ranged from a low of $3,532 to a high of $6,914—almost twice as much. We had not been dealing with the vendor who offered the lowest price, but since the company had a good reputation, we decided to try it for the next book we published. What a mistake! That one printing job entailed more problems than we've had for all our other jobs combined. Moral of the story: Don't automatically choose the cheapest.

Consider quality, too. Request a couple of samples of similar jobs. Examine these carefully. Look at the paper, ink, and binding planned for your job. One self-publisher suggests you interview the high bidders simply to get in practice for working with those on the low end to whom you'll finally give your business. If you have any reason to doubt the company, check it out with the Better Business Bureau and have your bank run a Dun & Bradstreet rating on it. Also ask for referrals from other jobs the company has done—and check them out. Unless you live in the relatively few areas where manufacturers are clustered, you'll probably get better prices and service from an out-of-town firm. However, being personally involved with the job would make communication easier, perhaps help you avoid mistakes, and teach you more, so that is another consideration.

Here, too, ask about down time to shave costs. But beware. Even under normal conditions, getting your book printed happens about as fast as getting your teeth straightened. To wait for down time may delay the process beyond a hint of practicality. It's always a good idea to pad a vendor's promised delivery date anyway: They're notorious for running late.

It is important to get your book manufacturing agreement in writing. Printing and binding costs can loom like the national debt to a self-publisher, yet the beginner hesitates to identify specifications, tending to operate with vague verbal agreements.

Always insist on approving proofs, which are sometimes called "bluelines." Mischievous printer's gremlins have a way of sneaking into your perfect work somewhere between the typesetting phase and the time when the pages roll off the press. Check for errors in pagination, meaning the pages are out of order or missing (as page 33 was in *Creative Loafing*). Also watch for misplacement of illustrations, the wrong captions under photographs, crooked pages, blurry type or illustrations, and any missing elements. This is the last stage you can check before the presses roll. Be aware that changes are expensive at this point!

While we're talking about printing, let us make a suggestion that can save you a lot of money on promotional materials. While the book manufacturer is printing your book, have him or her do what is called an "overrun"—an additional quantity—of the cover or dust jacket. Because the press is already set up and running, all you actually pay for is the paper. We just ordered a five-hundred-piece overrun on a four-color cover and paid a paltry $52. What a bargain for full-color sales literature! And for a few bucks more you can have the flaps trimmed off (assuming it's a dust jacket) and you have a dynamic brochure. To get added mileage, print your table of contents and ordering information on the reverse side. *Olé!* You're ready to do business. In some cases you can even negotiate with your printer to do the covers early—and thus your overrun of sales materials—so you have very professional-looking advance promotional materials. If you're doing a paperback, have your overrun done on 80# enamel paper rather than the stiff cover stock.

And if you didn't get extra galleys from the typesetter or photocopy your pages before sending them for manufacturing, let your printer know that you'll want extra sets of "folded and gathered" pages, usually referred to as F&Gs. These are loose-leaf pages of the book, minus binding, which you will send to prime book reviewers who appreciate having an advance opportunity to screen new titles. (More about that in Chapter 13, "Publicity.")

Talking about covers, there is an optional thing called "shrink wrapping" that you may want to get on your books, if you haven't followed our advice and your cover isn't film laminated. It's a clear plastic protective covering. If your cover has heavy ink coverage in a dark tone, chances are the books will be scuffed during shipping to your buyers if they aren't shrink-wrapped. This can be done individually or in lots of three or five and will only cost a few pennies per book. A good investment, considering no one wants to buy a book with a beat-up cover. We favor the film lamination protection and convenience.

Another detail you may want to work out is to have your printer drop ship case lots of books directly to your major customers. This saves you having to pay for the books being shipped to you, then reshipping to them. One other point some folks negotiate is that the negatives and halftones for their job be considered their property and returned to them when the work is completed. (Some manufacturers are testy about this.) Be sure to specify that materials for printing the cover or dust jacket, as well as the dies for stamping the hardcover boards, be included. In some cases, the text printing and the cover printing and binding are done by different vendors, so don't assume your requirement for negatives and halftones will automatically include all the cover printing materials.

Something else you have to work out with your printer is what form the books will arrive in. Larger publishers often take their books banded on skids which result in a stack of books almost five feet tall. You want to have your printer ship your books cartoned (how many to a box depends on how big your books are) and shipped on skids.

By the way, when you get your printing bill, don't be surprised if there is an entry for *x* number of additional books at *x* price. There is an industry standard that says a printer may print "overs" and "unders," meaning a 10 percent variance either way. Inevitably, it's always over, so be prepared to come up with a little more on your printing bill. (Sometimes 10 percent over or under can be negotiated in the printing agreement. Ask your printer.) Oh, and don't forget to figure in shipping costs, which will be extra. Printers will give you a general estimate of freight costs, so be sure to ask for this when you request a price quote. It often runs into several hundred dollars.

Before we leave the area of printing, there is one other option we want to mention. There are those who do their color separation and four-color printing in Asia, primarily Singapore, Taiwan, and Hong Kong. The advantage of this arrangement is simple: No American manufacturer can compete with Asian labor prices. The disadvantages are three: Communication can be a real bugaboo, manufacturing can take six months and you have to add 37 days ocean shipping to that and—because of a special U.S. "manufacturing clause"—American residents can't import more than two thousand copies of a book manufactured overseas. This limitation does not apply, however, if any part of the manufacturing process (such as typesetting or binding) is done in the United States. (Art books with more illustrations than printed text are exempt from this clause altogether.) One other publishing aspect that is causing a lot of international concern is piracy, especially in Taiwan, which is becoming famous for copyright infringement. If overseas printing seems like a worthwhile option for you, you should read section 601 of the "new" copyright law which can be found in *Law & the Writer*, listed in our bibliography.

And lest we forget the poet or booklet publisher who wants to start out with only a couple hundred copies, here is something to think about. You could make arrangements with someone with a letterpress who will let you print the books yourself. Another thought would be to simply use a duplicating machine and fold them yourself. There are also printers who specialize in these short runs. They advertise in *Writer's Digest* and several are listed in the Appendix. For monographs on very specialized subjects, photocopying is often the best approach.

Binding options

One of the major decisions in book production is the binding. Should it be a hard or soft cover? Are the traditional sewn or glued spines the best, or will stapling or "comb binding" be more suitable? There are many factors that will help you make this decision.

Think about how the book will be used. If it is a source book that readers will be in and out of many times, hardcover (frequently referred to as cloth or casebound) is more durable. A collection of photographs designed as a coffee-table book would definitely be hardcover.

The Cadillac of bindings is Smythe sewn. In this technique thread is used to stitch the signatures before they are glued into the cover. While the most expensive, it is the sturdiest and also allows the book to be opened flat, which is a definite plus. For a top-quality book spend a little extra and get "headbands" and "footbands." They are little reinforcing strips of cloth added to the top and bottom of the book which help it to stay together through rough use.

"Perfect" or adhesive binding is another method—and currently the most popular. In this process the signatures are collated, run through hot adhesive, and the cover affixed. It is frequently used because it gives a spine surface and is the least expensive of quality bindings. Your local phone directory, many hardcover books, paperbacks, and some magazines are bound this way.

With book prices escalating so rapidly, softcover (often called paperback) books are accepted most places today. While libraries have traditionally preferred hardcovers, they are becoming more accepting of paperbacks all the time. So, too, has the educational field come around. In fact, many prefer softcovers to keep prices down. They can cost between $1 and $1.50 a book less to manufacture than their fancier sisters—plus they weigh less, and will save postage and freight costs.

But unfortunately, many reviewers still tag paperbacks with a stigma that goes back to the days when they were all reprints. Many of today's paperbacks are still shunned in spite of the fact that they are originals. So if book reviewers play a large role in your plans, you may want to stick with hardcovers. They are simply taken more seriously by these critics.

Happily, you don't have to go strictly one way or the other. What some people do is to bind three-fourths of their books in paperback and do the remaining fourth in hardcover. This is called a "split run." How do you avoid guessing wrong and running out of the softcover edition while still having oodles of hardcovers left—or vice versa? Some smart publishers elect to bind only half of the split run and leave the other half as flat sheets stored on pallets at the manufacturer's or the bindery until they determine which version book buyers want. Or you may want to come out in hardcover first, with the idea of launching a paperback edition the following year after sales for the more costly version have peaked.

Since 1982 there has also been another option. It's called Flexibook and is midway between hardbound and paperback. Developed by the bookbinder A. Horowitz & Sons, it allows a publisher to couple economy with quality. With Flexibooks the cover materials are sturdier than those used in the average paperback and extend slightly over the text pages, protecting them. This added strength and durability make such books more attractive to libraries and other purchasers. Although Flexibooks are typically merchandised as paperbacks, the costs are from seventeen to thirty cents more per book than paperback but significantly less than doing a hardcover. Books of any size and thickness can be bound this way, and normal cover art can be used. As of this writing, the Flexibook process is available only from A. Horowitz & Sons, Box 1308, Fairfield, NJ 07006.

By the way, when we refer to paperbacks, we are talking about the larger "quality" or "trade" paperback, not the small 4" by 7" mass-market paperback. To be profitable, the latter has to be printed in quantities of 100,000 or more. Mass-market paperbacks also involve a very impractical distribution system for a small publisher, which we discussed earlier.

While we're talking about bindings, be aware that you have further options. The least expensive method, which will work for monographs and booklets, is to use staples. You can staple one corner of a report or through the fold on a small booklet. A more ideal method is to "saddle-stitch" them. This horsey-sounding term simply means to staple where the fold is located. It requires a special machine.

If your work is a manual to which readers may want to add pages or if you are starting a series of some sort, a three-ring binder with a silk-screened cover might be best. Many office supply sources sell plain binders with clear plastic fronts under which can be slipped a printed title page. (Libraries hate material presented in notebooks, however, because patrons "appropriate" favorite pages.) A cookbook might be most usable with a spiral comb binding that allows it to be laid flat or folded back to the chosen recipe.

Hand-sewn binding might be your choice if you have a special literary work. You will need access to a binder or a letterpress and someone to show you the ropes—pardon us, the threads. With a little practice you should be able to turn out a couple of dozen books in an hour's time.

There are a few things you should do when you get your books from the printer. First count the cartons, multiply that by the number of books per carton, and make sure your total figure matches that on the freight company's paperwork. Next sample random cartons to determine the books are not damaged or bound wrong—like upside down. Now celebrate! It's been a long time coming. Right?

Don't forget to recover all your original artwork, cover art (plus all materials and dies, if a hardcover), pasted-up boards, and if possible, the negatives and halftones for your job. Store all of these in a safe, dry place.

Copyright registration

The function of copyright is to protect your writing so that others may not use your work for their purposes. It does for the printed word what a patent does for an object. There are many who would contend that a copyright gives far better protection than does a patent. To be valid, your copyright notice must contain three elements: the symbol © or the word "copyright"; the year of first publication; and the name of the owner of the copyright, for example, copyright 1989 John Jones.

On January 1, 1978, new statutes went into effect. The copyright term now lasts for the life of the author, plus fifty years after his or her death. Another important change is that manuscripts are now protected by copyright *before* they are published. Form TX, which covers "nondramatic literary work," is used for fiction, nonfiction, poetry, periodicals, textbooks, reference works, directories, catalogs, compilations of information, and advertising copy.

The Form TX application for copyright registration can be obtained from the United States Copyright Office, Library of Congress, Washington, DC 20559. It comes replete with line-by-line instructions, so we won't duplicate them here. To register an unpublished work, you deposit one complete copy, the filled-in form, and a check or money order for ten dollars made payable to the Register of Copyrights. To register a published work, send two copies of your book, plus the other items. We suggest to clients that they wait to register a book until it is actually printed. The copyright office is touting a new "hot line" number which you can call to get application forms day or night. It is (202)287-9100. Good luck. We had a technical question while researching this book and called about a dozen times before giving up and writing.

A couple of words of caution are in order here. Don't ever distribute copies of your material — for instance as handouts to a class — without the copyright notice appearing on them. If you leave out the notice, the work is considered "in the public domain" and no longer your sole property. Also be wary of trade publishers that insist on copyrighting your book in *their* name. This is not standard practice and should normally be avoided.

While we're on the subject, any copyrights (and all royalties due you from contracts with trade publishers) should be provided for in your will. Ownership of a copyright can be passed on to your heirs just like a piece of real estate. If your book is selling well, these funds can be a meaningful part of your estate. Be sure to spell out how proceeds are to be divided among the beneficiaries.

Now that you've taken the steps to produce a first-class book, let's move ahead into the chapter on advertising and find out how to give it a fitting send-off.

FORM TX
UNITED STATES COPYRIGHT OFFICE

REGISTRATION NUMBER

_____

| TX | TXU |

EFFECTIVE DATE OF REGISTRATION

_____

| Month | Day | Year |

DO NOT WRITE ABOVE THIS LINE. IF YOU NEED MORE SPACE, USE A SEPARATE CONTINUATION SHEET.

1

TITLE OF THIS WORK ▼

BANDWAGON TO HEALTH: The All-Natural Way to Eat, Think, and Exercise

PREVIOUS OR ALTERNATIVE TITLES ▼

PUBLICATION AS A CONTRIBUTION If this work was published as a contribution to a periodical, serial, or collection, give information about the collective work in which the contribution appeared. **Title of Collective Work ▼**

If published in a periodical or serial give: **Volume ▼**   **Number ▼**   **Issue Date ▼**   **On Pages ▼**

2

NAME OF AUTHOR ▼

a   Elizabeth Baker

DATES OF BIRTH AND DEATH
Year Born ▼ 1913   Year Died ▼

Was this contribution to the work a "work made for hire"?
☐ Yes
☒ No

AUTHOR'S NATIONALITY OR DOMICILE
Name of Country
OR { Citizen of ▶ United States
{ Domiciled in ▶ _____

WAS THIS AUTHOR'S CONTRIBUTION TO THE WORK
Anonymous? ☐ Yes ☒ No
Pseudonymous? ☐ Yes ☒ No
If the answer to either of these questions is Yes, see detailed instructions

NATURE OF AUTHORSHIP Briefly describe nature of the material created by this author in which copyright is claimed. ▼
co-author

NOTE
Under the law, the "author" of a work made for hire" is generally the employer, not the employee (see instructions). For any part of this work that was made for hire" check Yes" in the space provided, give the employer (or other person for whom the work was prepared) as "Author" of that part, and leave the space for dates of birth and death blank

NAME OF AUTHOR ▼

b   Dr. Elton Baker

DATES OF BIRTH AND DEATH
Year Born ▼ 1911   Year Died ▼

Was this contribution to the work a "work made for hire"?
☐ Yes
☒ No

AUTHOR'S NATIONALITY OR DOMICILE
Name of country
OR { Citizen of ▶ United States
{ Domiciled in ▶ _____

WAS THIS AUTHOR'S CONTRIBUTION TO THE WORK
Anonymous? ☐ Yes ☒ No
Pseudonymous? ☐ Yes ☒ No
If the answer to either of these questions is Yes, see detailed instructions

NATURE OF AUTHORSHIP Briefly describe nature of the material created by this author in which copyright is claimed. ▼
co-author

NAME OF AUTHOR ▼

c

DATES OF BIRTH AND DEATH
Year Born ▼   Year Died ▼

Was this contribution to the work a "work made for hire"?
☐ Yes
☐ No

AUTHOR'S NATIONALITY OR DOMICILE
Name of Country
OR { Citizen of ▶ _____
{ Domiciled in ▶ _____

WAS THIS AUTHOR'S CONTRIBUTION TO THE WORK
Anonymous? ☐ Yes ☐ No
Pseudonymous? ☐ Yes ☐ No
If the answer to either of these questions is Yes, see detailed instructions

NATURE OF AUTHORSHIP Briefly describe nature of the material created by this author in which copyright is claimed. ▼

3

YEAR IN WHICH CREATION OF THIS WORK WAS COMPLETED This information must be given in all cases.
1984 ◀ Year

DATE AND NATION OF FIRST PUBLICATION OF THIS PARTICULAR WORK
Complete this information ONLY if this work has been published.
Month ▶ March   Day ▶ 22   Year ▶ 1984
USA ◀ Nation

4

See instructions before completing this space

COPYRIGHT CLAIMANT(S) Name and address must be given even if the claimant is the same as the author given in space 2. ▼

Elizabeth and Elton Baker
P O Box 149
Indianola, WA 98342

APPLICATION RECEIVED
ONE DEPOSIT RECEIVED
TWO DEPOSITS RECEIVED
REMITTANCE NUMBER AND DATE

DO NOT WRITE HERE OFFICE USE ONLY

TRANSFER If the claimant(s) named here in space 4 are different from the author(s) named in space 2, give a brief statement of how the claimant(s) obtained ownership of the copyright. ▼

MORE ON BACK ▶ • Complete all applicable spaces (numbers 5-11) on the reverse side of this page.
• See detailed instructions.   • Sign the form at line 10.

DO NOT WRITE HERE
Page 1 of _____ pages

Copyright registration form.

170

DO NOT WRITE ABOVE THIS LINE. IF YOU NEED MORE SPACE, USE A SEPARATE CONTINUATION SHEET.

PREVIOUS REGISTRATION Has registration for this work, or for an earlier version of this work, already been made in the Copyright Office?
□ **Yes** ☒ **No** If your answer is "Yes," why is another registration being sought? (Check appropriate box) ▼
□ This is the first published edition of a work previously registered in unpublished form.
□ This is the first application submitted by this author as copyright claimant.
□ This is a changed version of the work, as shown by space 6 on this application.
If your answer is "Yes," give: **Previous Registration Number** ▼   **Year of Registration** ▼

5

DERIVATIVE WORK OR COMPILATION Complete both space 6a & 6b for a derivative work; complete only 6b for a compilation.
a. **Preexisting Material** Identify any preexisting work or works that this work is based on or incorporates. ▼

b. **Material Added to This Work** Give a brief, general statement of the material that has been added to this work and in which copyright is claimed. ▼

6

See instructions before completing this space.

MANUFACTURERS AND LOCATIONS If this is a published work consisting preponderantly of nondramatic literary material in English, the law may require that the copies be manufactured in the United States or Canada for full protection. If so, the names of the manufacturers who performed certain processes, and the places where these processes were performed **must** be given. See instructions for details.
Names of Manufacturers ▼   **Places of Manufacture** ▼

Bookcrafters   Chelsea, MI

7

REPRODUCTION FOR USE OF BLIND OR PHYSICALLY HANDICAPPED INDIVIDUALS A signature on this form at space 10, and a check in one of the boxes here in space 8, constitutes a non-exclusive grant of permission to the Library of Congress to reproduce and distribute solely for the blind and physically handicapped and under the conditions and limitations prescribed by the regulations of the Copyright Office: (1) copies of the work identified in space 1 of this application in Braille (or similar tactile symbols); or (2) phonorecords embodying a fixation of a reading of that work; or (3) both.
a □ Copies and Phonorecords   b □ Copies Only   c □ Phonorecords Only

8

See instructions.

DEPOSIT ACCOUNT If the registration fee is to be charged to a Deposit Account established in the Copyright Office, give name and number of Account.
Name ▼   **Account Number** ▼

CORRESPONDENCE Give name and address to which correspondence about this application should be sent. Name/Address/Apt/City/State/Zip ▼

Marilyn Ross
P O Box 538
Saquache, CO 91149
Area Code & Telephone Number ▶ 303-655-2504

9

Be sure to give your daytime phone number

CERTIFICATION* I, the undersigned, hereby certify that I am the
Check one ▶
□ author
□ other copyright claimant
□ owner of exclusive right(s)
☒ authorized agent of
of the work identified in this application and that the statements made   Name of author or other copyright claimant, or owner of exclusive right(s) ▲
by me in this application are correct to the best of my knowledge.

Typed or printed name and date ▼ If this is a published work, this date must be the same as or later than the date of publication given in space 3.
Marilyn Ross   date ▶ 4/26/84

Handwritten signature (X) ▼   _Marilyn Ross_

10

MAIL CERTIFICATE TO

Name ▼
Elizabeth and Dr. Elton Baker
Number-Street-Apartment Number ▼
P. O. Box 149
City/State-ZIP ▼
Indianola, WA 98342

Have you:
• Completed all necessary spaces?
• Signed your application in space 10?
• Enclosed check or money order for $10 payable to Register of Copyrights?
• Enclosed your deposit material with the application and fee?
MAIL TO: Register of Copyrights, Library of Congress, Washington, D.C. 20559

11

Certificate will be mailed in window envelope

CHAPTER 10

GENERAL ADVERTISING POINTERS

You could have one of the greatest book ideas of the century, but if only "the Shadow knows," you're not likely to sell many books. So how do you remove the cloak of secrecy? Advertising, of course! Advertising can indeed be a mystical business which sometimes seems to border on the supernatural. How else can we explain why a one-word change in a classified ad can resurrect it from the graveyard and make it a winner? Or conversely, an ad can die because of a wee change. None of us will ever know all of the answers all of the time. The marketing genius John Wanamaker summed it up when he stated, "I know that half the money I spend on advertising is wasted. I just don't know *which* half." By understanding and applying some fundamental rules, however, you will be able to solve many of the mysteries of this vital key to your publishing success.

The trade publishers' approach

In an article in the Spring 1984 issue of the *Authors Guild Bulletin* Robert A. Carter explains why trade publishers advertise books:
1. To help sell an individual title to the trade
2. To help sell an individual title to consumers
3. To help sell subsidiary rights
4. To impress authors and agents
5. To establish an image for the house

After studying these reasons, it soon becomes obvious why self-publishers must take a different approach. Even though numbers 1 and

3 above are of concern to self-publishing, the only item that really counts for us is number 2. But let's probe deeper into the advertising practices of trade publishers, as there are lessons to be learned. Fact: Their overall advertising and promotion budget is typically placed at 10 percent of the expected sales income of the first printing. Unless you've got a blockbuster book, 'tain't much. (This is the major reason it is so important for trade-published authors to be aggressive in promoting their own books.)

And even then, advertising is often ineffectual. Some trade publishers admit it doesn't get people out to buy a book. One publishing executive quipped, "A lot of advertisements are for the author, his mother, and his agent."

When publishers are pushing a book to "the trade," that means booksellers, wholesalers, and libraries. The medium they use most often is *Publishers Weekly*. When you realize that a single page in *PW* goes for over $2,600, it becomes apparent that the average budget will quickly be wiped out at that rate. An intensive sales campaign might also include *American Bookseller*, a monthly journal of the American Booksellers Association, plus *Library Journal*, *Booklist*, *Choice*, and selected wholesalers' publications.

But the big guns come out when Publishers' Row wants to convince the general reading public they should buy a book. The medium most frequently used for that is the *New York Times Book Review*. Would you believe one page on Sunday costs $13,675? Other favored publications are the *New York Review of Books* (especially if it's a scholarly work), the *New Yorker*, the *Washington Post*, *Wall Street Journal*, the *Los Angeles Times*, the *Christian Science Monitor*, *Time*, and *Newsweek*.

But if a book is a flop, not even a fortune can turn it into a best-seller. Wealthy businessman Jack Dreyfus spent about $2 million of his own money promoting his book with full-page ads in newspapers and magazines around the country. In spite of his outlandish spending spree, *A Remarkable Medicine Has Been Overlooked* was itself overlooked by millions. Another businessman's crusade, *The Trimtab Factor*, died a similar death in spite of the $1 million spent by the author to boost it to stardom.

Needless to say, that kind of ad program is simply out of the league of most self-publishers. But that doesn't mean you can't have effective advertising. Quite the contrary. Much of the success of any advertising effort depends on the basics: the development of sales materials with pizzazz, an effective means to determine who should receive these materials, and a repetitive campaign.

Developing sales materials with punch

A punch is quick and to the point, right? Start noticing ads that grab your attention. Betcha it isn't just the full-page spread or the full-minute spot on radio or TV. It doesn't take a full-course meal to whet the appetite. A short well-done ad pulls much better than a long ineffective one. The key is not length, but rather quality and repetition. You'll get more for your money by investing in twelve identical small ads than from one large, full-page spread. Most people only give you a few seconds to set the hook. Boiled down to basics, it becomes: Stay in front of your prospects. If you keep in front of them with punchy sales material, you will make sales. We've included several examples on the following pages.

Some of your sales material can be created in parallel with the jacket or cover by printing an overrun as we discussed previously. Note the adjacent catalog sheet, which is simply a one-page flier telling about our book. It's straightforward, low-key, and to the point; it quickly communicates the message. The title and subtitle are used as headlines, while the text and photographs give substance to the piece. Notice how the table of contents is presented as a bulleted list for a quick, catchy summary of the book. The catalog sheet plays an important role in promoting to libraries, bookstores, wholesalers, and educational systems. This piece has withstood the test of time. Although it is in its third printing, it remains identical to the first run. Take heed: If it's working, don't change it. This trade-oriented catalog sheet is different, however, from a flier directed to *consumers*. The consumer promo piece is much more salesy, has a "you" approach expressed in a benefit way, and contains an order form (see following sample).

Use your imagination and those beautiful third-party accolades that drift in from reviewers, columnists, educators, and media personalities. We sought and received permission to reprint a nationally syndicated column by Jack Smith that lauded one of our books. A lot of extra mileage can be gained from use of this type of material in your sales kit. We paid fifty dollars for permission to reprint this copyrighted material, and it was money well spent. How about the letter from Claude Pepper, chairman of the House of Representatives Select Committee on Aging? We rest our case for third-party testimonials.

Examine the *Creative Loafing* "Dear Friend" letter. It, too, is short and to the point. Using the italic font on our Selectric typewriter and artwork from the book cover made it simple to create in-house.

Also take a look at our correspondence announcing a "How to Get Successfully Published" conference. It demonstrated the use of all the elements we've touched upon. Again, short and to the point, it uses third-party support to land its punch.

Now let's review some basic rules about effective sales material.

• Keep your budget pared as low as feasible to start. Lean toward the less expensive options for creating your material. Start off with a flier with one color of ink. Use standard colors of plain bond paper. To save on

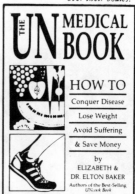
postage, print on the lightest weight paper that won't bleed through.

• Increase your odds by offering prospects several choices. Use the piggyback principle. Team up with another self-publisher or two (locate them by checking with librarians, bookstores, and/or writers' groups) and include materials about their books, while they do the same for yours.

 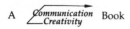

Catalog sheet.

• Sell the sizzle, not the steak! If you've been around salespeople at all, surely you've heard this well-worn phrase. Tell folks what the book does for them. Will it make them healthy, wealthy, safe, wise? People don't buy books to make this a better world or to support your family. They buy books to make their own lives easier, to make them more successful or sexier or to give them an edge in this competitive world.

• Stress *benefits* rather than features. Here is an example of what we mean: A feature of a book is that it "shows how to go job hunting in Chicago." But expressing this as a benefit, we could say "discover how to find high-paying, hidden jobs in Chicago." See how much more powerful the second statement is? It relates to the specific needs of the potential book buyer. Always give your sales material the "Benefits Test": Are you highlighting the specific advantages the reader will derive from buying your book?

• Don't assume that "more is better." Many times we have the urge to keep hammering away, lapsing into verbosity trying to make the point. Your prospective buyer loses interest quickly. Like a crop duster, you need to swoop in, deliver your payload, and pull up before you hit the trees.

• The organization of the material should make your message obvious. The way you use folds, layout, type, artwork, and color can all bring your message into sharp focus. Make it easy to understand what's going on. Compel the reader to feel this was written just for him or her. That's effective communication.

If you adhere to these rules, many of the eerie mists shrouding advertising will be lifted. Don't forget that repetition is more important than length, but that quality is the first consideration. Shoddy sales material will make potential customers assume that your book will be shoddy, too—and pass it by. An excellent reference is Nat G. Bodian's *Copywriter's Handbook: A Practical Guide for Advertising and Promotion of Specialized and Scholarly Books and Journals.*

How to launch an in-house ad agency

Do you recall the discussion of "hats" in an earlier chapter? Guess what? You don't actually have to become the Mad Hatter to delight in the Wonderland of self-publishing (although there are those who claim that it's an advantage). As you probably have gleaned by now, the shrewdness of a Cheshire cat is an attribute that helps the little person remain in the big race for the book buyer's dollar.

By switching hats a few more times, you can save yourself fifteen cents out of every advertisement dollar. How's that? Most media offer a 15 percent discount to approved ad agencies. As you have read, it's not difficult to set up a business. An agency is certainly no exception. The

CLAUDE PEPPER, FLA.
CHAIRMAN

EDWARD R. ROYBAL, CALIF.
FRED B. ROONEY, PA.
MARIO BIAGGI, N.Y.
WALTER FLOWERS, ALA.
IKE F. ANDREWS, N.C.
JOHN L. BURTON, CALIF.
EDWARD P. BEARD, R.I.
MICHAEL T. BLOUIN, IOWA
DON BONKER, WASH.
THOMAS J. DOWNEY, N.Y.
JAMES J. FLORIO, N.J.
HAROLD E. FORD, TENN.
WILLIAM J. HUGHES, N.J.
MARILYN LLOYD, TENN.
JIM SANTINI, NEV.
TED RISENHOOVER, OKLA.
ROBERT F. DRINAN, MASS.
DAVID W. EVANS, IND.
HELEN S. MEYNER, N.J.
MARTY RUSSO, ILL.
STANLEY N. LUNDINE, N.Y.
MARY ROSE OAKAR, OHIO

WILLIAM C. WAMPLER, VA.
RANKING MINORITY MEMBER

JOHN PAUL HAMMERSCHMIDT, ARK.
WILLIAM S. COHEN, MAINE
RONALD A. SARASIN, CONN.
WILLIAM F. WALSH, N.Y.
CHARLES E. GRASSLEY, IOWA
JAMES ABDNOR, S. DAK.
THAD COCHRAN, MISS.
MATTHEW J. RINALDO, N.J.
MARC L. MARKS, PA.
RALPH S. REGULA, OHIO

ROBERT S. WEINER
STAFF DIRECTOR

JAMES A. BRENNAN
ASST. TO THE CHAIRMAN

WALTER A. GUNTHARP, PH. D.
MINORITY STAFF DIRECTOR

U.S. House of Representatives
Select Committee on Aging
Washington, D.C. 20515
TELEPHONE: (202) 225-9375

December 19, 1978

Ms. Anna Klepper
Communication Creativity
1340 Tourmaline Street
San Diego, California 92109

Dear Ms. Klepper:

Thank you for forwarding me a copy of "Creative Loafing"
by Marilyn Ross.

As Chairman of the House of Representatives Select Committee
on Aging, I realize the great impact that increased leisure time
and decreased budgets have on the lifestyles of our retired citizens.
The importance of remaining active during retirement years cannot
be underestimated. Many believe it has a direct bearing on the
total well being of seniors.

"Creative Loafing" serves as a delightful guide of activities
and projects available at low costs and would certainly be a
valuable resource for anyone, old or young. I was especially pleased
to discover that the book highlights developing and exercising one's
talents through projects, community service, and hobbies.

I wholeheartedly endorse "Creative Loafing" as a positive
addition to any senior citizen's bookshelf or to any organization
interested in activities for seniors.

With best wishes, I am

Sincerely,

Claude Pepper
Chairman

CP:ks

Publicity letters.

Dear Friend:

Discover how you can enjoy hundreds of free fun activities. Save money while you explore new and unusual leisure ideas. CREATIVE LOAFING, our exciting new book, shows you how!

This unique shoestring guide to leisure tells how to meet people and have more fun. Now you can experience the excitement of auction hunting, gate crashing, courtwatching, volunteering, contesting, frolicking at feasts and festivals, or watching famous athletes...all for free! The subjects range all the way from active outdoor adventures to fulfilling indoor pastimes.

But that's not all. CREATIVE LOAFING is written in a light, informal style. There are oodles of suggestions on how to awaken the "child" within you. You'll also find ways to rediscover the world around you. Printed in larger-than-usual type for easy reading, this handy source book is also indexed. You'll love the revealing quizzes and exercises. They will help you decide which activities will be most personally enriching.

What's more, you can own this exciting new book for less than 3¢ a day! That's right. The price is only $9.95. If you divide that over a year of fun, it amounts to less than 3¢ a day. And there is absolutely no risk to you. This offer carries a 10-day money-back guarantee. If you should decide for any reason you don't want to keep the book, we'll cheerfully refund the purchase price.

SPECIAL BONUS FOR ORDERING EARLY: Send for your book today and we'll give you a free "I Practice Creative Loafing" button to wear.

Very truly yours,

Tom Mulvane

Tom Mulvane

TM:am

P.S.   A book is a loving gift. CREATIVE LOAFING makes an ideal birthday present...or a pick-me-up for anyone feeling low...or a great Christmas gift! Why not buy a copy for someone special?

P.O. Box 9512   San Diego, CA 92109   (714)/459-3386

Dear Author:

You can get your book successfully published!

Are you disillusioned with vanity press schemes? Tired of trying to break into the mere 1% who are accepted by trade publishers?

I don't blame you. Nothing is more frustrating than to have a good book and not see it in print. Discover the third alternative! As reported in the Los Angeles Times on November 21, 1978, "self-publishing has become respectable and even fun" (not to mention a money maker for those who approach it properly).

> A few of the success stories about authors who have earned big money through the vehicle of self-publishing include How to Be Your Own Best Friend by Mildred Newman and Bernard Berkowitz, the novel Ecotopio by Ernest Callenbach (165,000 copies in print) and How to Keep Your Volkswagen Alive by John Muir (1,000,000 copies sold).

Copy Concepts, Inc. is dedicated to helping writers make money on their books. Our consultants have shown hundreds of writers "How to Get Successfully Published." The conference program was developed to provide you easy access to proven methods on how to launch your book.

If you're tired of being in the dark about publishing options, industry trends and why many authors are acquiring fame and prosperity with books no better than yours, you owe it to yourself to capitalize on this opportunity. Discover how to get results and make good money from your book.

Read the enclosed brochure, learn what other authors are saying about our service, and take the first step toward getting successfully published — today!

Sincerely,

Alana M. Klepper
Alana M. Klepper
Vice President
Educational Services

AMK:pl
Enclosure

P.S. The August, 1978, issue of Writer's Digest called self-publishing "The Do-It-Yourself Way to Success." AMK trick is getting "approved" status. By advance planning and learning to become a "quick hat-change artist" you can usually qualify. Let's look at the process for setting up an advertising agency to optimize your approval ratio.

First, establish a new business entity for your agency. You might choose a name such as Creative Impressions, The Ad Group, Copy Concepts, or Images International. To check name availability, call your city or county fictitious names department. Register your agency name and get any required licenses and permits. Use another post office box to give the agency an address different from either your personal one or your publishing company. If possible, set up a different telephone number, too. That should really set the agency and the publishing company apart. Right? Well, almost.

Some media will not give a discount to an "in-house" agency. (An agency that is part of the client company is considered in-house.) That being the case, it makes sense to take all possible precautions to avoid announcing this fact. We believe honesty is still the best policy, however; so if they ask, 'fess up. But how in the world would they tie your two companies together?

Once there was a self-publisher who had followed all of the rules you've learned to this point. Her advertising agency was properly established. She enjoyed the 15 percent discount on all media ads—that is,

---

Ad order form.

until she inserted an ad in the *National Enquirer*. They require that a sample of the item you intend to advertise be submitted for approval.

The book, written under the name of our heroine, was shipped off to the *Enquirer*, along with an official insertion order and the agency's check for the ad. A few days later the advertising agency phone rang. Our hat-change artist reacted superbly and answered the phone using the agency name. "This is the *National Enquirer* calling," she was told. "Are you an in-house agency for . . . ?" She answered that this was so. She was then informed that the *Enquirer* does *not* give discounts to in-house agencies. Our bewildered entrepreneur hung up the phone, wrote a check for the difference, then reflected on the call.

How in the world had they figured out that the agency was in-house? Suddenly she knew. Do you? An alert employee had noticed that the author's name, which appeared on the book jacket, and the signature on the check were the same. Thus our lady had to shell out an additional 15 percent.

How do you prevent that happening to you? Just as you can register a fictitious name DBA (doing business as) for your company, you can set up a fictitious AKA (also known as) for yourself. Register both with your bank when you open your agency checking account. Simply sign your agency checks with your AKA signature, and go about your business. Thus you save some 15 percent on your advertising costs, and with rates for a 6" by 9" ad tallying $9,256 in the *Enquirer*, that amounts to well over a thousand bucks! To further solidify your official status, submit all ads on an "insertion order" such as the following sample.

Using another name is also very useful when promoting your own book. It seems a bit pushy when John Jones calls or writes someone lauding this great book by John Jones. We send out news releases, sales letters, and do all publicity for our own books under the name of Ann Markham. (Ann is Marilyn's middle name; Markham her maiden name.)

Before you ship off any ads, use your letterhead to write and ask for sample copies of publications you are considering, demographics (particulars about their readers as to age, sex, socioeconomic status, etc.), and a rate card. Study these materials. The *Enquirer*, for example, requires that you guarantee satisfaction or state a money-back guarantee in the body copy of your ad.

If you prefer not to embark on your own agency, you can attempt to hire a commercial ad agency. You won't be welcomed with open arms, however, because of your small ad budget. One alternative might be to hire these creative services on a flat fee retainer basis rather than the customary 15 percent commission on ad placements, if you can find an agency willing to work with you on that basis.

There is yet another way to get exposure and, lo and behold, it's a "freebie."

INSERTION ORDER

AGENCY: TO:

PRODUCT: DATE:

ADVERTISER: THIS ORDER APPLIES TO OUR CONTRACT NO.

dates of insertion	number of times	caption to read	key or code	space ordered

COPY TO READ:

SPECIAL INSTRUCTIONS & REQUESTS:

RATE:

_____times at $_____   Less____% frequency discount $_____
= $_____   Less____% agency commission $_____
Check #_____   Less____% cash discount $_____
By:_____   Net amount of this order $_____

Insertion order.

Getting free "PI" and "PO" ads

Many smaller magazines and newspapers will cooperate with you on what is called PI (per inquiry) or PO (per order) advertising. This is a win-win situation wherein the publication lets you have unsold ad space in

a colorado corporation

Dear Advertising Sales Manager:

Please send us full details regarding display advertising in your publication. I especially need the following circled items:

Demographics of Readers

Next Closing Date

Current Rate Card

Audited Circulation Figures

Three Recent Sample Copies

Promotional Subscription

We would also appreciate your placing our agency on file to be notified of any future rate or policy changes.

Thank you for your prompt response.

Sincerely,

Ann Markham

Ann Markham,
Space Buyer
Communication Creativity

AM:sdw

415 Fourth Street, P.O. Box 213, Saguache, Colorado 81149-0213   303-655-2504

Agency rate letter.

exchange for a percentage on all book sales that result from the ad.

To make such an arrangement, have your ad typeset camera-ready. (In fact, you may be smart to do a couple of standard sizes—say, a one-fourth page and a one-third page—to give you flexibility in fitting into their available space.) Adjacent are two sample PI ads; one was designed to resemble editorial copy. Contact the advertising sales manager indicating you'd like to discuss an opportunity for generating additional revenue on unsold space. Expect to give the publication somewhere between 30 and 50 percent.

So as to keep tabs on each other, have people make their checks or money orders payable to your company but mail them to the publication. This is an excellent "no risk" way to try out publications and to develop added sales. It isn't necessarily wise, though, to do this with a magazine or newspaper that would normally be an outstanding market for you. You could give away more by sharing a percentage of sales than you would by purchasing the ad space outright.

PI ad.

By the way, a few radio stations also participate in this PI concept. In this case, you would need to give them a thirty- or sixty-second written commercial to plug the book. In writing your commercial be sure to start off with an intriguing question or statement to capture the attention of the listening audience immediately. Give order information twice in a thirty-second commercial and three times in a sixty-second one. Why not contact appropriate media and see if you can get access to some free print space and airtime?

Promoting to target audiences

If you, as a small publisher, try to compete with the biggies in overall advertising, you will look like a mouse in the shadow of a lion. If, however, you identify a specialized core audience who would be interested in your book, you can come on with a mighty roar of your own. That's why it's so important to promote to target audiences. Because your sphere of influence is much smaller, you can afford to *dominate* it.

This is often done on a geographical basis. Perhaps you have a regional history or a guidebook to restaurants. By pounding away just in San Francisco or exclusively in Houston, for instance, you can develop high visibility and reap dramatic results.

Advertising in a specialized trade journal can be a good way to reach a given target market. This works well when trying to sell specific professional groups, such as accountants, attorneys, and educators. We contacted health professionals for one client who had a book appropriate for this audience. Now *The UnCook Book* is carried in the offices of many physicians, chiropractors, dentists, and nutritionists. You, too, can find a niche of highly susceptible buyers. Whenever you can influence one person to influence many, your sales figures take quantum leaps.

Point-of-purchase sales aids

This strange-sounding term refers to things you can make available to bookstores or other retail outlets to help promote your book to consumers. They earn you extra display space. One of the best received — and cheapest — we've discovered is bookmarks. You'll notice by examining our samples that we use them as subtle sales tools, but we also make sure they have a double purpose by putting temperature scales on the back. The advantageous thing about bookmarks is that they perch right next to the cash register, thus reminding people about your book and stimulating impulse buying.

One enterprising author got himself top billing right next to the cash register with a poster on an easel. How did he manage that? On the reverse side of his poster, visible to the cashiers, was a description of how to identify a counterfeit bill. It was to the store manager's advantage to keep that information handy. When doing posters, it's a good idea to have them printed on *both* sides. When they are placed in a window, you get double exposure.

One other possibility for point-of-purchase (POP) aids is to provide free display stands — or "dumps" as they are called — with quantity pur-

Selling Knowledge Nets Big Payoffs

by Marilyn & Tom Ross

The authors of *The Lazy Man's Way to Riches, How to Keep Your Volkswagen Alive* and *Wake Up the Financial Genius Inside You* have never been on a bestseller list. Yet their books are all bestsellers that have made each of them millionaires. Karbo, Muir and Haroldsen have something else in common. They literally "cashed in" on their personal know-how. So can you!

We've written a book showing how to publish, promote and sell your own knowledge. And we've taken all the mystery out of it. Thousands of people have already used the techniques we describe. Having self-published and sold several books ourselves, given nationwide seminars on the topic, and consulted with hundreds of people who realized the value of do-it-yourself publishing—we know of what we speak.

Of course, people write books for different reasons. The profit motive is certainly a valid one. But as a businessperson, writing a book can have dramatic impact, offering new recognition and personal rewards. As an author you're an expert—with even greater visibility and credibility than before. TV, radio and print media open up to you. If you've written on a topic related to your business, new avenues of promotion are created that will generate a wider customer base. You may find yourself in demand as a speaker (an excellent way to sell books since you have a captive audience).

Our reference guide covers every facet of writing, producing and marketing a book. You'll learn about titles that "hook" readers, book pricing formulas, ways to select a typesetter and printer, an easy method for organizing your book, the ten best ways to generate working capital and copyright law.

Realizing that promotion and sales is the real bottom line, we devote much time to discussing such topics as mail order techniques, how to get free "P.I." advertising and capturing the lucrative library and educational markets. The 14 most powerful selling words, getting listings in free directories, creating promotional tie-ins, saving 15% on ad costs, using your book to generate new business is also covered.

But don't take our word for it. Here's what others are saying about our book: "Complete information on all aspects of successfully publishing your own book ...and a reference section that is worth its weight in gold bullion. I've read a lot of books on this subject. This is the most comprehensive, practical guide I've ever seen," observes businessman Dan S. Kennedy.

"*The Encyclopedia of Self-Publishing* is a steal. It can save you thousands of dollars and be the difference between having a successful book or a flop," comments nationally syndicated columnist Sid Ascher. *The Entrepreneurial Manager's Newsletter* calls it "A very well done 210-page volume" and the National Mail Order Association dubs it "The one book you'll need...in 75 fact-filled sections it covers every phase of self-publishing."

Of course, not every book should be self-published. We're talking about writing and selling information. Teaching people how to do something...or to do it better. Americans are especially hungry to make or save more money—be more attractive—be healthier. This country is in the middle of an information explosion ...and you can fan the flames with your own know-how!

We wrote *The Encyclopedia of Self-Publishing* because we felt there was a need for more people to be exposed to and understand this exciting alternative. Self-publishing is not like dealing with a trade commercial publisher such as Simon and Schuster, Doubleday or Macmillan. It also differs widely from subsidy (vanity) publishers where you sign a restrictive contract, then pay them to print your book. We're talking about true entrepreneurialism. Having control. Using your creativity. Enjoying a potential profit margin of 25% or 30% or more.

Our book gives you all the facts and figures you need to successfully launch your own publishing business. It also includes sample sales letters and promotional pieces, plus names and addresses of buyers. It's all here for only $29.95...everything you need to know to turn your knowledge into a new revenue base. And there's no risk on your part. We personally guarantee that if you are dissatisfied for any reason, we will promptly refund the full purchase price if you return the book within 10 days. You have everything to gain and nothing to lose.

As a special bonus for acting immediately, we'll also include a complimentary copy of our idea-packed newsletter, the *Communique*. So get your order off today!

© 1980 Tom and Marilyn Ross, 1340 Tourmaline Street, San Diego, CA 92109

Mail to: FLYING COLORS/SKY, Dept. CC
8701 Collins Avenue
Miami Beach, Florida 33154

Yes, I want to invest $29.95 to reap greater profitability, credibility and visibility. Please rush _____ copies of *The Encyclopedia of Self-Publishing* so I can get started. I enclose $29.95 per book, plus $1 for postage & handling. (CA residents add $1.80 sales tax.)

Name _____

Address _____

City/Zip _____

My check (payable to Communication Creativity) in the amount of $_____ is enclosed.

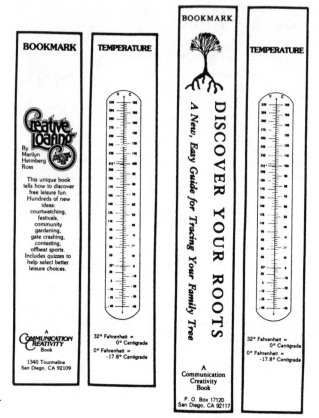

Sales aids.

chases of ten or more books. These cartons help prevent a book's being shelved spine out with other titles and getting lost in the shuffle. This is a smart move if you plan on placing your book in specialty stores and other retail outlets (an especially lucrative sales approach we'll explore in detail in Chapter 16, "Additional Money-making Strategies"). While in theory providing a dump will help keep your book well positioned, it could end up being used for someone else's title unless the stand is identified with a header card advertising *your* book. To locate suppliers who can provide these stands, look in the Appendix for a helpful list ... , "Point-of-Purchase (POP) Suppliers." A field trip to local bookstores may be in order first to determine who will use such displays.

Co-op advertising

Now let us take a minute to explain what is known as "co-op" advertising. This is an arrangement whereby the publisher and a bookstore divide the cost of a newspaper or magazine ad, with the publisher picking up the biggest part. The ad appears under the sponsorship of the bookstore and lists its name and address. While on the surface that may sound appealing, it can be deadly. You see, FTC regulations say that if you honor such an arrangement with even one bookstore, you are mandated to do so with *any other store that wants to participate.* Such a practice could break a self-publisher in no time. That is why we suggest you leave this to the biggies. Co-op ads certainly have their place in the industry, but they are not good ammunition for the small publisher to use. Besides, your ad budget will do you a lot more good spent in other ways where you don't have to split the profits.

Exhibiting at conventions and book fairs

A form of advertising that may make sense is to exhibit your book at strategic specialized conventions and book fairs. The two biggest general conventions of interest to book publishers are the American Booksellers Association, affectionately dubbed the ABA, and the American Library Association (ALA).

The ABA, which was organized in 1900, has the largest English-language book show in the world. In addition to featuring some fifteen hundred exhibits, there are daily book and author breakfasts and many informal luncheons and parties.

While in the past, the ABA convention has always been held over Memorial Day weekend, beginning in 1989 it will be in early June. *Where* it is held has a great bearing on your potential success. We discovered by painful personal experience that "party" cities such as New Orleans do not mean good business in the exhibit hall. No doubt the convention scheduled for Las Vegas in 1990 will suffer the same plight. Washington, DC, and Anaheim, California, on the other hand, had upbeat moods and lots of registered attendees.

Some major changes are planned by the ABA for 1989; as we go to press, they're still under wraps. We're told, however, that booth prices are projected to cost from $750 to $10,000; smaller 6' × 8' booths in the small press section are going for $350. The term "booth" can be a misnomer. Some of the conglomerates span whole aisles, becoming mini-halls within the larger ABA universe. And the cost of the booth is only the beginning. What do you put inside? (In 1988, Warner Books hired the same people who did the set for the movie "Dirty Dancing" to create their extravaganza.) Shelving, tables, and draping material are very expensive. So is professional design. Add to this travel, accommodations, and meals, and you're looking at an expenditure beyond all but the most well-heeled self-publisher.

But let us suppose you decide to spring for a booth. Take full advantage of your presence at this Goliath of book events. Plan ahead and review afterwards.

Publishers Weekly puts out a pre-ABA issue listing all those who have rented booths. It amazes us that each year many publishers never bother to submit anything for this free listing. Here is a sales opportunity. Use it. Also write to wholesalers, bookstore accounts, rights agents, etc., you've been wanting to connect with, giving them your booth number and asking them to stop by. If you have a particularly newsworthy book or angle, contact the ABA about setting up a press conference. And you might even be able to get yourself in one of the author-autographing sessions—assuming you're willing to give away a lot of books.

Now it's set-up day at the convention. Get an extra copy of the program, hole up in your hotel room that night, and study that bugger for contacts. Make yourself an itinerary—plan your coverage by booth number, or you'll be exhausted from criss-crossing the convention floor. One of the greatest mistakes you could make is to constantly stay captive to your own booth during the convention.

Get out and meet people. (And the following advice applies whether you rent a booth or simply attend.) Baker and Taylor always has a couple of representatives there to talk with new publishers. Make yourself an appointment. Find out where Quality Books is and go over and get acquainted with Tom Drewes and his crew. Early in the show, stop by all the booths of distributors who carry your book and be sure they have a copy prominently displayed. (If they don't, provide one!) Place some flyers in the Press Room in case a reporter's fancy might be caught by your story. Take full advantage of this unique opportunity to get face to face with those who might buy your book or be interested in subsidiary rights.

If you don't want the expense and the commitment of having a booth, you can learn a great deal just by going as a spectator. Nowhere can you put your finger any closer to the pulse of book publishing. Nor are there many places where you can come home with such a haul! Books, to be sure. But also catalogs, buttons, tote bags, pens, food, drink, and any number of invitations to unusual promotional events (such as a private showing of *Superman III* or a free exercise class with Victoria Principal). It's a wild, giddy whirl—but also a place to make some valuable contacts. Editors come out from behind their closed doors for the ABA; so do key marketing people. Using patience and persistence, a self-publisher with a track record could well snag a reprint sale here. And an unpublished author with a manuscript may just corner a trade publisher that is willing to take on his or her work.

There is an alternative to spending the time and money to personally attend the ABA and other important conferences and conventions to hawk your own book. Many exhibit services will do it for you. These companies offer displays wherein you pay them so much per title and they include your book in their booth. Watch to see whether they will display your book spine out or face out. Face out is preferable, as it gives you better exposure. Included in their fee is listing in a catalog that conference attendees may keep for reference.

COSMEP has an exhibit service that displays a single title at both the ABA and the ALA for a very reasonable rate. PMA (Publishers Marketing Association) also exhibits books. The Publishers Book Exhibit (86 Millwood Road, Millwood, NY 10546) exhibits at major North American conferences. They will promote your book at professional meetings in the areas of medicine, science, education, and at regional library meetings.

We've participated in many different exhibits at the ABA and ALA over the years. In all honesty, our results have been nonexistent; we hear others occasionally have more favorable experiences.

It might be wise to attend or exhibit at conventions directly related to your product. This is called "vertical marketing" and can be extremely effective. There are trade associations to match your book subject matter, and most of them sponsor at least one big meeting a year. To find out whom to contact, consult *National Trade & Professional Associations*. If you have a book on computers, for instance, COMDEX is one of the big trade shows for that industry. Book sales can be brisk when you're in the heart of a large gathering attuned to your subject. Your new title on underground houses might go very well at the annual convention of the Associated Builders and Contractors. The connections are endless.

If you want to go into this in a big way, you might get the exhibits directory put out by the American Association of Publishers. It is touted as "the most comprehensive, definitive annual guide to exhibiting possibilities."

Before we leave this subject, let's chat a bit about book fairs. They are less structured, regional events that give you a reasonably priced opportunity to sell books. Here you can also get to know other nearby authors and publishers, compare notes on the small-press industry, and hear a diverse group of guest authors talking about their craft and giving readings.

There's the annual New York Is Book Country fair, where Fifth Avenue is closed to traffic to allow exhibitors to create a generous pedestrian mall. It features a storytelling area and an auction for such things as book memorabilia and cooking lessons from a cookbook author. (Some great ideas here for a self-publishing organization to work with.)

Book fairs are not the sole province of New York, however; many flourish in other locales. The annual Small Press Book Fair in San Francisco lets participants reach thousands of people for a paltry sum. And the Great Midwestern Bookshow convenes on the University of Minnesota, Minneapolis, campus. The atmosphere there is usually charged with controversial literary dialogue and debate, sparked by guest writers, publishers, and speakers from all over the country.

The Miami Book Fair International has emerged as a world-class literary gathering. For eight days in November it brings together readers, authors, and publishers for a celebration of all things literary. A virtual city of books takes residence in downtown Miami. In 1988, more than 130 authors and 250 publishers participated. Around the country, festivals are raising the visibility of books. Book fairs have sprung up in Boston, New Orleans, and Milwaukee over the years. So when you are deciding how to allocate your advertising budget, don't overlook exhibits and book fairs. They could be an interesting merchandising tool. *Book Fairs, An Exhibiting Guide for Publishers* covers the subject well.

Innovative advertising

There are many other imaginative advertising pursuits you can use to enhance your sales position.

Prepublication

Selling prepublication copies of your book—taking orders before the books are printed—has several advantages. One obvious plus is that it helps generate cash to pay your printing bill. Another is that you get a feel for how receptive the public is to your book. Of course, it gives you a head start on your full advertising campaign and gets people talking about your title before it is even released. If you're promoting through the mail, be sure to state clearly that people are purchasing the book for future delivery. About four months ahead is the longest realistic lead time. And indicate the delivery date, to avoid hassles with postal regulations. We did this very successfully when we first brought out the *Encyclopedia of Self-Publishing,* and you can, too!

Gimmicks

It never hurts to dream up some odd little thing to draw attention to your book. One way to beef up awareness is to have buttons made. Ours say, "I practice Creative Loafing." They're great attention-getters and conversation pieces. They also make nice giveaways to bookstore personnel and others who help promote the title. You can even carry it a step further and have a personalized T-shirt silk-screened, which you—or others—can wear to promote the book. There are many companies that manufacture specialty items like personalized notepads or pens. One way to see that your book stays in a buyer's mind is to have notepads printed up sporting the title. Give or send them to prime accounts and use 'em to woo large prospective buyers.

Order blank

Don't overlook the order blank at the end of your book as an ad medium. It can be one of your best salespeople. Readers often want another copy for a friend or relative; or people borrow the book, then want a copy themselves. The order form makes it easy. In fact, the designers of the *1984 Microcomputer Market Place* were really thinking. Their order blank is headlined: "Did You Borrow This Copy?" It goes on to say that if so, now is the time to order your own personal copy so you'll have a directory to refer to day after day.

Here are a few tips regarding the order form: Always compute the tax yourself for sales within your state and express it as an exact amount, rather than a percentage the customer must figure out. Be sure to include adequate postage and shipping. We find $2.00 suffices for most books. Remember, you have not only postage but also a mailing container and your time involved. It's a good idea to say something like "Bulk purchase inquiries invited." This lets people know they can buy quantities of books at a reduced cost and may trigger them to start carrying the book if they own a retail outlet.

If your title sells for over ten dollars, it may be worth your while to also offer VISA and MasterCard options on the order form (and on your other sales literature, of course). We're hearing lately that banks are much more reluctant to give small publishers credit card privileges. You may have to shop around a lot to find a cooperative banker, although our new bank in Buena Vista, Colorado, was immediately cooperative.

But suppose you've already printed your book and didn't include an order form? Don't despair. Have some labels printed as an order form and slap them on the inside back cover. Mission accomplished.

Bounce-backs

Another possible advertising approach is called "bounce-back promotions." It works best when you have more than one book or are working with another writer-publisher. This is a merchandising trick used by virtually every retailer who ships products to customers. When an order is filled, a flier or catalog sheet is included offering an additional item—in your case another book. Thus, a bounce-back is an order received as a direct result of a promotional offer enclosed with a product shipment. The welcome windfalls from this kind of merchandising are typically 5 to 15 percent. For a "free ride," you can have a big impact on overall sales by using this strategy.

Telemarketing

What about using your telephone for advertising? Telephone solicitations to select markets can be very effective. If you want to reach feed stores, marinas, or florists, for instance, you can first prospect in the yellow pages for a list, then cover a lot of territory in a few hours on the phone. As in print advertising, think through what benefits your book offers. It's a good idea to jot down a few notes or develop a script until you become relaxed at this type of sale. Using the phone is also wise to follow up on accounts you've already opened face to face. If you start doing much long-distance calling, you may want to trim costs by looking into Sprint, MCI, or one of the other private long-distance phone companies.

As you begin to propel your book into national attention, you may have another use for the telephone. What about a toll-free 800 number? There are companies that will rent you a portion of an 800 number, accept orders over the phone, even write up credit card sales. With this kind of coverage you can widely advertise your 800 phone number. Once again, you've made it *easy* to buy.

Card packs

Merchandising through direct-response card packs is another possibility if you have a high-ticket, professionally oriented book. Titles geared to engineers, accountants, and executives, for instance, are all prospects. Card packs are packages of anywhere from ten to fifty business reply post cards stacked and polysealed, then mailed to a carefully targeted list. When asked about card packs, a librarian at Syracuse University remarked to one book marketer, "They are wonderful. The professors bring in the cards and say, 'Please order this book.'"

For those who are serious about wanting more information on this method of reaching prospective buyers, we've made arrangements with Larry Bauer at Solar Press to send readers of *The Complete Guide to Self-Publishing* complimentary copies of their report, *Beyond Lead Generation: Merchandising Through Card Packs*. Mention our names when you write him at 1120 Frontenac Road, Naperville, IL 60566.

Christmas catalogs

In some cases—for a certain type book that is already doing well—a Christmas catalog can be the best place to put your advertising dollar. First, you must have a title suited for this kind of advertising—a gift book or what's called a "perennial" (something of popular appeal that sells in all seasons and is as good today as it was last year or will be next year). You must also have a fat budget. While you may find a catalog that will accept a one-unit ad (about one-tenth of a page) for $400 or $500, it's more likely the price tag will be in the thousands. Of those who have tried it, however, at least one reports a gross dollar return of six to one.

Recently, B. Dalton's forty-page Christmas catalog appeared in *People* magazine, and the American Booksellers Association ran its first catalog as an insert in *Time*. Waldenbooks elected to distribute its catalog in its stores and via direct mail, continuing a practice begun over a century ago when Aaron Montgomery Ward sent a one-page list of 163 general merchandise items — such things as bonnets, boots, and blankets — to Midwest farmers and their families. Mail-order catalogs have been big business ever since.

If you're tempted to try and crack this medium, you need to start about February by writing to catalog companies and requesting their deadline, costs, and circulation figures. Some have a circulation of 300,000; others go as high as 5 million. Naturally, ad space is more costly for the latter. Be prepared to meet some resistance. They're used to dealing only with trade publishers and may fear you won't be able to supply the demand their catalog may generate. Such a problem!!! Seriously, though, you must have the cash resources to print a lot of books in a hurry if things click.

Next, let's investigate something where you can click for a lot less money: the world of mail order.

CHAPTER 11

PREPARING MAIL-ORDER ADS

Trying to start an advertising program without employing mail order could be likened to becoming a gourmet Italian chef without using oregano or basil. Unlike those herbs, however, mail order can either stand on its own merit or be used to enhance a direct-mail program (more on this in Chapter 12). Let's sample this wonder ingredient and see what makes it so popular.

What is mail order? It involves products which are advertised in newspapers, magazines, and catalogs and which are ordered by customers and shipped via mail.

From the publisher's vantage point there are five important keys to succeeding in this marketplace: product suitability, reader profile identification (demographics), media analysis, the ad itself, and timing. Let's examine these points.

Product suitability

Not every book is suitable for a one-title mail-order campaign. Bookstore shoppers go browsing with the idea that they'll buy a book when they find the right one. The mail-order buyer typically has no thought of buying until motivated by your ad. Whereas the browser may shop for several minutes, the mail-order counterpart is usually won or lost in seconds.

What triggers this almost instantaneous urge to own? Usually it's an offer that promises to improve the quality or pleasure of life. Remember, we talked about people wanting to be safer, healthier, more attractive, sexier, more loved, smarter, and richer? Does your book tell readers how to get a job, find a mate, or make more money? In other words, does it solve a problem or offer something most people need or want?

If your title fits into one of these slots, mail-order sales could be a natural. Notice, we qualified our statement with "could be." That's because one other factor is crucial to success in single-title mail-order campaigns: price. Although not in itself a limiting factor, the price must be considered. Books must be at least twenty dollars, say most experts, to be viable for mail order. Ask yourself this question: Is the book priced so that the sale will yield a return of 2.2 times the cost of advertising? As we discussed earlier, this is the formula.

Certainly it's impossible to know for sure, especially when placing your first ad, what the volume of response is likely to be. Look at other, similar books and arrive at what you think is a reasonable and competitive price, taking the 2.2 guideline into account. Then round that price to the next higher dollar. Mail order experience in advertising is just the opposite of that in retail sales: even-figure prices do better than the ninety-five or ninety-eight cent price endings which retail stores post. Try to hit the best balance possible between pricing your book out of the market and making it such a bargain that you end up making little, if any, profit.

Pinpointing your potential customers

Okay, you've determined that your book is ideal for mail order. Now analyze it from a reader-appeal standpoint. In this hypothetical exercise it is imperative that you describe your reader as precisely as possible. One way to do this is to create a "reader profile sheet." Establish categories of people. Within each category, list as many characteristics as possible. Rank each one on a scale as a percentage of potential readers. Example: After street-corner surveys, asking relatives and friends, and considerable soul-searching, you have concluded that only 20 percent of your readers will be men. It therefore follows that 80 percent will be women. Such deduction!

So forget men and follow your female profile. Your research has determined that 90 percent of your readers are single women between the ages of eighteen and forty and that 80 percent of these work. Therefore, your prime customers are single working women between eighteen and forty. You have just charted the demographics of your readers!

As you can see, armed with this information, you know whom you are trying to reach. Now it must be determined which medium is the most likely vehicle for your message. Be observant and talk to people (especially eighteen-to-forty-year-old female workers). Find out what they read. Go to the library for additional research.

Media analysis

In the main branch you will find several volumes from Standard Rate and Data Services, Inc. (SRDS). The volume we need for this analysis is called *Consumer Magazine and Agri-Media Rates and Data*. Here a wealth of information about magazine publications will be unveiled — rates, editorial slant, and so forth.

When you are analyzing in which publication to buy space, try to stick with those that have *audited* circulation figures. This means the figures have been checked and that x number of people do indeed subscribe to the magazine. If there is reference to just "circulation," a magazine often includes not only the primary recipient of the magazine but also the two, three, or four other family members who might also look through it. While it appears that this publication may be a better place for your ad, it actually represents a smaller overall readership.

SRDS is a valued reference. Spend some time with this gem. In addition to perusing the rates and data, look for ads. Really study them. They offer much "inside" information about reader demographics. After all, magazines are advertising for advertisers, just like you! They know what information you need. Referring back to our example, it would appear from our research that *New Woman, Cosmopolitan, Working Woman,* and *Today's Secretary* would be prime targets for your ad.

If you plan on putting ads in newspapers, *Newspaper Rates and Data* is your source. And if you have published a technical or professional book, look in *Business Publication Rates and Data*.

After perusing SRDS for likely candidates, write to those on your list, asking for classified ad rates, a media kit, and three recent sample issues. Once the prospective publications have sent you their literature, you're ready to select the most suitable media.

Having identified the audience for your book and the media vehicle to reach that audience, it is now time to create an ad. We subscribe to the philosophy of "start small and test, *test, TEST!*" Not every idea will work. You run an idea up the flagpole and wait to see if people salute it. If nobody does, you haul it down pronto. Even Joe Karbo's full-page newspaper extravaganzas plugging *Lazy Man's Way to Riches* didn't start full-blown. He followed the rules and began small.

The ad

Most experts agree that a modest-sized classified ad is usually the best way to begin. An ad is a sales tool. It must be designed to sell. In spite of this, two out of three classified advertisers use copy that is watered down and ineffective. A word, the turn of a phrase, or a benefit properly described makes all the difference in the number of inquiries or sales your ad pulls.

Don't try to shorten your copy so much that it loses its punch. Agreed, longer ads cost more. But will a ten-word ad that costs forty dollars and sells three books be cheaper than a twenty-word eighty-dollar ad that sells a hundred books? Give yourself enough room to use persuasive words and action verbs in the ad. According to Yale University researchers, the twelve most persuasive words in the English language are:

save	health	love	proven
discover	you	easy	results
safety	guarantee	money	new

In addition to these, here are some more winning words from a list of one hundred famous headlines that were profitable: "your," "who," "now," "people," "want," and "why." We also find that "how to" and "free" pull well. Integrating these words with action verbs helps create compelling, selling copy.

Let's dissect a few ads which appeared in the *Globe*. How about the following headline: "Seaweed recipes, $3.00." Would that move you to action? Hardly. Why not embellish it as one advertiser does: "Delicious seaweed recipes! Nutritional, economical! $3.00." Notice the implied health and money-saving benefits?

Don't expect an ad like the following to make profits: "Pound cake recipe, $1.00." Instead, sell it with "Absolutely delicious pound cake. You will beam with pride when they ask who made the cake. Send $1.00." This ad is personalized for the reader and uses an action verb to create involvement: "You will beam with pride."

How about this for selling the sizzle: "Want money? Hate work? Lazy ways to big money explained in full. Send $2.00." This has pulled a whale of a lot of two-dollar responses. The "you" in the ad is very evident. Do *you* want money? Do *you* hate work? It could possibly be improved further by substituting "easy" for "lazy."

Someone with little knowledge of advertising principles might put together nursery item headlines like these: "Plum Trees," "Strawberry Plants," "XX-6 Plant Food." The advertising pro senses the dullness of these heads and brings them to life. "Pick delicious plums from your own trees." "Plump luscious strawberries that grow bigger than hen's eggs." "Now—watch your plants grow healthier, faster, without danger of fertilizer burn. Use XX-6!"

Need we say more? Classified ads can work only if the copy is crisp and clear. Sell the *benefits* of your book. Describe its qualities in terms of the reader's desires and needs. The greatest secret in advertising is to keep it human. Remember that your potential buyer isn't just a statistic.

He or she is a person with hopes and emotions, ideas and prejudices. Get that person involved.

Timing

If you were selling skis, you'd want your ads to appear just before the first snowflakes come down. Your book may have a less obvious seasonal tie-in, but there probably is one. You'll want to time your ads to take the most advantage of a reader's increased interest either in the subject of your book, or in books in general. For instance, summers are generally a bad time: your potential customers are outdoors or even on vacation, not reading magazines or thinking about ordering books. If the subject of your book has to do with summer activities — salad recipes, for instance, or vacation guides — run your ads in the spring when readers are just beginning to think about such things. Interestingly enough, gardening books, like seed and plant catalogs, do better in the wintertime, when people are stuck indoors and like to poke through bright, summery photographs of flowers, anticipating winter's end and making plans for warmer weather.

If your book is a cold weather item — a cookbook on baked goods, knitting, or ways to winterize one's house to save energy, for instance — then fall is a good time to advertise it. If the book is about making gift items, or if it's a likely candidate itself for being given as a gift, plan to place ads enough in advance of Christmas to allow time for orders to come in and for the book to be shipped and received by the beginning of December, or even the middle of November. Remember, your customer may, in turn, want to mail it someplace else, so leave time for this to happen, too. Early October might be a good time for such an ad to begin running.

Or your book may be related to some other specific date — a holiday or an upcoming or annual event likely to be in the news. As in the case of Christmas, keep this event in mind in planning when your ad should appear.

Always think from the customer's point of view: time your ad to run at the time when there's likely to be the most interest in your book and its subject. This will help you get the best response for your advertising dollar.

Tracking results

Recognize that you will be testing for two major things: which wording is most effective and which publication generates the most inquiries. A well-worded ad may pull beautifully in *Popular Mechanics*, yet fail dismally in the *Star*. If you want to be even more definitive, you can try running under different classifications, such as "personals," "books," or "of interest to all."

We recommend starting with a single insertion of your ad. Don't respond to the urges from media salespeople to save money by running several consecutive ads. Sure you will save due to a "frequency discount," but what good is that if your ad is not pulling the required 2.2 times cost?

To track results you must code each ad. Include a different department number for each variable you use. *Go slow . . . TEST.* Measure effectiveness, then build up in frequency and/or size. Here is an ad for *Creative Loafing* that did well. "DISCOVER CREATIVE LOAFING! . . . New book shares hundreds of money-saving ideas for having fun and meeting people . . . Free details . . . Leisure MW88D, 5644 La Jolla Boulevard, La Jolla, CA 92037." Note the "Leisure MW88D." The MW88D is a code to indicate where and when the ad was run and which of several ads it was. The "MW88D" tells us it appeared in *Moneysworth,* August 1978. The "D" shows it started with "Discover." If you use a P.O. Box, consider affixing a code to it. Our Box 538 could become Box 538B. The "B" would represent a specific ad in a specific publication.

Notice also that our ad offers "free details" instead of asking for the sale. Most mail-order experts agree that a small classified will not usually be effective for items costing more than five dollars if you ask directly for money. So offer to send more details. When these inquiries are received, you shift to the direct-mail selling approach (covered in the next chapter). However, let's not be hasty about leaving this discussion on testing and tracking your results.

The question that needs to be answered as soon as possible is "How many sales will this ad pull?" If you are advertising in a monthly periodical, it could take six months to get 96 percent of the final results.

Obviously, you could hardly organize a mail-order campaign if forced to wait that long before the next ad could be placed. On the other hand, it would be foolhardy to repeat a dud. It becomes apparent that some method of predicting results must be used to allow an ad to be repeated or changed long before all results are in. To partially solve this problem, mail-order merchants have developed a system for forecasting advertising responses.

Industry experts warn that prediction charts provide only rough estimates and not accurate projections. Responses fluctuate widely depending on price, type of product, timing, ad medium, ad size, and other factors. Most of these experts also agree that the longer you can hold off before predicting, the more accurate the prediction will be. As soon as possible, you should create a chart for your own product based on actual results. However, since we must have a forecast before results can be tallied, let's use this chart. The one below serves as a guide for predicting sales. Elapsed times are calculated from the date of the receipt of your first order—not the day the ad appears. Percentage figures indicate the proportion of the total response.

Elapsed Time	Dailies	Weeklies	Monthlies	Direct Mail
1 week	50-70%	35-40%	7-10%	33-52%
2 weeks	78-95%	60-65%	18-33%	60-65%
4 weeks	93-99%	79-81%	25-65%	89-90%
2 months	97-100%	89-90%	57-83%	96%
6 months	—	99%	90-96%	99%

Using this table, an advertiser receiving 20 orders during the first week of response from an ad in a monthly publication would estimate his total to be 140-200 orders. At the end of the second week 15 more orders are received. Be sure to revise the forecast to 106-194. At the end of the fourth week 75 orders had been received. Forecast is now 108-300. Two months yielded 95 total orders. Note the forecast is now 114-167. As can be seen by looking at this example, the chart allows a tremendous range which could be forecast at the end of the fourth week. We favor the conservative approach. Using the example above, we would have used 140 as our projection at the end of week one, revised it to 110 at the end of week two, and then done our forecasting to determine if it will pay off.

Let's assume that our ad cost $100 and we are selling a book for $3.95. If we add $100 for postage and processing, we compute our return as 110 × $3.95 ÷ $200 = 2.17 times cost. That's close enough to the 2.2 factor to have us insert the ad a second time.

Graduating to display ads

Once we have proven the suitability of our book for mail order, pin-pointed appropriate media, and developed an approach theme in classi-fieds—we are prepared to increase our ad size and/or frequency. Let's assume we have outgrown classifieds and are ready for display advertis-ing. Again exercise caution. Start small, code, test, and measure. It wouldn't be prudent (to say the least) to jump from classified to half-page ads.

You may want to start out with "hemorrhoid ads." These are little scatter ads—perhaps only $1/12$ of a page. They got their less-than-decorous name because someone once advertised:

> # HEMORRHOIDS?
> ## Cured in 15 days
> ## or your money back!
> ## free details:
> ## box XXX, Somewhere, USA

It was a to-the-point, effective ad. If you were plagued by these pesky things, your attention was riveted to the ad. Naturally, this kind of brief ad will work only for certain subjects. But if you can tell your story in a one-, two-, or three-word grabbing headline, it could lead to identifying thousands of potential buyers.

On a more conventional level, one thing you can do is go with publications that have "split runs." That means they publish regional editions, and you can test different ads in the same magazine or newspaper in different regions to see which one pulls best. The *Wall Street Journal*, for example, publishes a Western Edition, a Southwestern Edition, and so forth. Rather than biting the bullet and paying the high costs to run an ad for your business-oriented book in the entire newspaper, you might test it in one of the regional editions.

There is also a possibility of picking up what is known as "remnant" space (same thing as leftover pieces of fabric). This happens when another advertiser takes some, but not all, regions. The oddball leftover space can be bought for 25 to 50 percent below rate card price. Ask advertising sales representatives if they offer remnant space.

Let's take a look at some ground rules for creating effective display copy. Perhaps you will simply want to include an illustration and an order coupon with expanded copy from your classified. Four elements are essential for effective display ads. They are strategy, media selection, design, and copy. Media selection has been covered previously. The strategy as defined here is to sell direct to the consumer. For the self-publisher it probably doesn't make sense to run ads directing people to bookstores; the majority of them won't stock your book. This, then, brings us to design.

Designing winning display ads

The physical layout and visual effect of your ad is the tool for getting the attention of the reader. There are a couple of ways to stand out on a busy page of competing ads. One is by using what is called a "reverse."

That means the background of your ad is black, with white lettering, instead of the usual black lettering on a white background. Another ploy is to use a heavy or decorative border around your ad to separate it from the others. Don't get too busy. Lots of "white space," that area where there is no printing, gives a freer, more attractive appearance.

Your layout should also help the reader understand as quickly as possible by guiding the eye through the ad. Another school of thought suggests that ads shouldn't look like ads. Advocates of this approach use straight copy to simulate editorial matter. (A sample of this type of ad appeared earlier.)

Choice of type is also important. While headlines should not focus attention on the design itself, they must command attention. For them, choose a display type that is punchy and bold enough to stand out on the page. As we said earlier, typefaces have personalities just like people. Ask your typesetter to show you some display typefaces. Some are fun, some sophisticated, some old-fashioned, some dramatic. Windsor Outline is as different from Hollywood as Blippo Bold is from Computer. Look at a display type chart and you'll see what we mean. The order coupon and body copy of the ad should be easy to read. Avoid condensed faces and don't use a type size so tiny readers must examine it with a magnifying glass. It's best to not intermingle a lot of different fonts. Use variations of one "family" instead, such as Garamond bold, Garamond italic, and Garamond roman to give variety and emphasis. (Never use large amounts of italic, however; it's hard on the eye in big doses.)

Copywriting gives room for creative expression. Crisp copy which straightforwardly describes the benefits of a product is hard to beat. The trick remains to use persuasive, compelling words that move the reader quickly to action. Coy indirectness is apt to confuse the reader.

You may also want to tailor your ads to different audiences. This is considered market segmentation and can often be done by simply changing the headline. This is an underused but powerful concept. Let's say you have a book on how to set up an appliance repair shop in your home. One market is the entrepreneur-type magazines; a second is the trade journals for the appliance field, such as *Appliance Service News*. For the prospective entrepreneur you might use a headline such as "Make Thousands Every Month Without Ever Leaving Your Home." In the appliance trade journal, which is read by people who possess some technical skill, you could try "Become Your Own Boss: Turn Your Talents into Big Dollars." By creating ads with a different appeal, you will incur slightly larger production costs, but you can double your responses . . . and it's the bottom line that counts.

Design and copy must be coordinated so they complement each other. You can't put together a good ad by closeting the designer and the copywriter separately, then pasting together the results. Many successful book ads consist of visuals of the book (either photographs or illustrations) supported by copy about the contents and an order coupon. Don't forget your jacket copy for ideas. As the ad size grows, copy can be expanded to offer author's credentials, reviews, reader testimonials, and additional supportive material about the book.

We suggest that students and clients become pack rats. Get copies of as many magazines as possible. Start reading mail-order ads for books. Study them. Clip, emulate, paraphrase. Soon you will have a solid feel for an effective presentation. Of course, you may decide to get assistance in this process. You can locate advertising consultants in *LMP* who specialize in working with the book trade, or contact a reputable local ad agency through the yellow pages. A fascinating book on the subject is *Which Ad Pulled Best*, by Phillip Ward Burton and Scott C. Purvis. It details fifty case histories on how to write ads that work. Regardless of how your ad is created, to be profitable it should pass the following tests:

• Can you conservatively project a return of 2.2 times the cost?

• Does the ad offer some grabber to get the reader's attention — or will it be lost in the fifteen-hundred-odd promotional appeals the reader is bombarded with daily?

• Will the ad clear the split-second interest test? Once you've caught readers' eyes, you have only six or seven seconds to get them to nibble. The majority whose eyes you catch will be lost here. They are still subconsciously resisting the urge to read your ad. The most compelling reason people should be interested in what you are selling must be stated in very few words. The words must be immediately obvious to the reader whose eye your ad momentarily caught.

• Even after the ad passes this test, your catch is still a long way from the boat. The ad must be organized to lead the reader smoothly through your message. Any confusion will try the reader's patience and cause his or her attention to wander. Layout, typography, and illustrations help avoid breaking reader attention.

• Once readers have nibbled, is the product presented forcefully enough to cause them to want to strike? Here copywriting takes over. It should give the reader the clearest, crispest, most appealing concept of the book you're trying to sell. Flamboyant adjectives or cute copy seldom help — and may even detract from credibility. A straightforward overview, or even the table of contents if space permits, is a good backbone for your message. As we've said before, stress the benefits to the readers. Solve their problems. Make your point strongly and as quickly as you can. Remember, you must still be concerned about losing the reader's attention.

• Do you adequately overcome suspicions and objections? Unfortunately, this is a snag that brings many trollers up short. Let's face it: People are suspicious of sales pitches and will use this as their final objection against buying. One of the quickest ways to dispel suspicion is by using testimonials, particularly those from people who are well known or who are in positions of trust. Of course, excerpting select reviews is a powerful persuader, too. If you can't come up with quotes or reviews, describe reassuring author credentials. Offering a money-back guarantee will further crumble resistance to buying.

• Is it easy for the reader to respond? Have you called for action? Are you clear as to exactly what's to be done? Including an order coupon simplifies the reader's response. Make sure instructions are complete. Consider offering the option of putting the purchase on a credit card. Now the hook is set!

When you enter into the world of display advertising, you should capitalize on the cumulative impact of repetitive insertions. All things being equal, it will yield better results to run four one-quarter pages repeated in the same media than to pop for a one-shot full-page spread.

Let's examine positioning for a moment. This refers to where the ad appears. If you're willing to spring for a big ad, the back cover and the inside front cover get a lot of reader attention. Whenever possible, try to have ads placed on a right-hand page in the top half of the page—they will be easier to notice there. If you're using a coupon, stipulate that it must not back up to another coupon. (Otherwise, people can ruin your ad while cutting up the other one.)

And while you're negotiating with the space sales representative, ask whether you can get editorial coverage as well. This means the publication would write up a little feature story on you or your book. Some magazines have a policy against such practices; others will gladly comply, especially if you provide suggested copy for the piece.

For logging results we recommend the Mail Order Sales Record form available from the National Mail Order Association, 5818 Venice Boulevard, Los Angeles, CA 90019. It provides an easy method to record activities, evaluate ad effectiveness, and do a cost analysis.

Once you've developed a selling ad and have pinpointed magazines and newspapers that pull well, it's time to set up a contract. If you run in a magazine three, six, or twelve times, you'll get a reduced rate over single insertions. With newspapers you do this on a bulk-rate basis, committing to use so many lines of display space over a year's time. Opt for the *least* space available. If you go over that, the lesser rate is automatically granted. But if you don't use up enough space, at the end of the year you'll be "short-rated." That means you will be billed for the difference between your contract rate and the regular price. And remember that successful advertising is saying it again. And again. And again.

CHAPTER 12

DIRECT-MARKETING KNOW-HOW

Often the best approach is the direct approach . . . direct mail, that is. As the name implies, this is a strategy wherein you mail sales literature to the prospective buyer. According to recently published statistics, 19.6 percent—or almost one-fifth—of everything sold is now sold by direct marketing. During the last ten years this method of selling has been growing at *double* the rate of retail store sales.

An American tradition

Direct mail has turned starry-eyed entrepreneurs into retail giants. Consider Sears, Roebuck & Co., for example. That's right. Mr. Sears and Mr. Roebuck decided to expand their distribution into distant rural areas through catalog sales. They certainly succeeded! Although Sears now has retail outlets in cities throughout the United States, catalog sales are still an important part of their business. Tom, who was raised in the rural Midwest, was twenty before he discovered that a Sears store wasn't an 8½" by 11" catalog two inches thick. He's still a mail-order buyer.

There are now, always have been, and always will be consumers (yep, book buyers) who buy through the mail whenever possible. No, these aren't necessarily country folk; many live in the hearts of major cities. They just prefer to shop from the comfort of their armchairs. We would therefore be quite remiss if we didn't suggest ways you can take advantage of this lucrative opportunity. In fact, the 1987 Huenefeld Survey reported that the publishers with the briskest growth rates—a hefty 20 percent increase—were those using direct marketing for professional, vocational, and scholarly books.

A direct-mail campaign has three crucial areas: the offer, the package, and the list.

The offer

The offer has to do with what you're selling. Of course, for you it will be a book or books. Pricing has a lot to do with your offer. Will you give a discount? Is there a time limit? How about a money-back guarantee? Will a free gift be included? Is there a deluxe alternative—such as a limited, numbered, and autographed edition? Can buyers use their credit cards? These are all offer considerations.

The package

Direct-mail packages usually consist of an outer envelope, sales letter, brochure, order form, and business reply envelope (BRE). Begin saving the so-called junk mail you receive. Study it. There are marvelous lessons to be learned here.

Your outer envelope

Your first challenge is to get recipients to open the envelope. If you fail here, it doesn't matter what's inside. There are different schools of thought on which strategy works best.

Many experts say you should use a "teaser message." We just received a package that said "Inside—Valuable TIME & MONEY-SAVERS for the Overworked, Understaffed Editor!" It was obviously what some people call junk mail, but it did an effective job of appealing to a need, offering a benefit, and arousing our curiosity. We opened it.

Some experts feel that impressing people is most effective. They go for elegant simplicity, using expensive envelope-paper stock and appearing dignified and businesslike. Mail that looks important or official will often get opened.

Still others contend you're better off with a blind envelope that gives no clue as to the contents. With this approach, you either leave off the return address entirely, or just use a street address or post office box with a person's name rather than any business identification.

Developing effective sales letters and brochures

This is one place where more is better. A two-page letter will out-pull a one pager; often four pages is even stronger. Make it open and airy. Start off with a benefit-laden headline. Do your very best writing here—

or hire a professional copywriter. This is an important document and must be carefully honed.

To create an effective sales letter, you need a plan. To develop this plan, assemble information. This doesn't need to be reams of information, but it is an important step. There are three main things you need to keep in mind when writing your sales letter: the exact objective of the letter, who your prospect is, and the important characteristics, features, and benefits of your book.

Use the following checklist for developing your sales letter.

• Does the headline or first sentence attract attention by promising the most important benefit of your book?

• Is interest built quickly by enlarging on the promise?

• Have you appealed to the emotions to arouse a desire to possess?

• Have you emphasized the unique features of your offer? (Maybe this is the only way the book is available, or you're offering it at a reduced price, or adding a little gift as an incentive to buy, or personally autographing copies.)

• Is one central idea emphasized so strongly that it avoids confusion?

• Have you included believable testimonials?

• Do you offer a guarantee?

• Is your letter organized so that it is easy to read? Paragraphs should not be too long, especially the first two.

• Have you closed with a final bid for action indicating exactly what you're offering, the price, how it will be shipped, and why the prospect should respond now?

• Have you included a postscript? This is one of the most read portions of any letter. Even if you lose the prospect after the first couple of sentences, the eyes will probably turn to the P.S. Repeat your main sales feature in brief, make a special offer, or drop in a personal line to support the reader's decision. "If Brand X isn't everything we say it is, just return it and we'll cheerfully refund your money!"

If possible, run your letter in two colors; this helps personalize it. Use colored ink for the letterhead, your personal signature, and to underline main points.

While some direct-mail packages contain giant four-color brochures, such elaborateness is not necessary to sell books. Yours can be a small, two-color affair. An overrun of your cover can even be used. The important element is the selling job. As in your letter, creative copywriting is vitally important here. Be sure it is targeted to the market you're trying to reach. Dramatize and expand upon your book. Cite reviews or testimonials. If it is packed with sizzle, you might reproduce the table of contents. Be sure you tell a complete story and move the reader to action.

The order form

It has been said that the order form is "the moment of truth." Many prospects make a final decision on whether to buy after reading it. Therein lies a message: Don't forget to continue selling on the order form! It should begin with a benefit headline such as: SECRETS OF HOW TO LIVE LONGER REVEALED IN NEW BOOK.

The order form offers another controversy among experts. One school says neat, specific, nonconfusing ones are best. The other side claims busy, cluttered, important-looking forms do better.

We feel the order form should make it clear to the customer exactly what needs to be done to get the desired books. Surprisingly, many buyers will go straight from the headline that hits their "buy button" to the order form. If you get your prospect to the order blank, you surely don't want to confuse and lose the sale now. State the exact amount of state sales tax to be included, not a percentage the buyer must compute. (You may also want to use your order form for market research.) A money-back guarantee is especially reassuring to a potential buyer. It assures there is no risk. If your book is good, seldom will the guarantee be invoked, but the very fact that this option exists will make some sales for you.

Clearly state the terms. If you're selling to individuals, we recommend that it be cash with order or a credit card sale. For a small charge, the bank will make arrangements to accept VISA and Master Charge. Especially if you're handling a high-ticket book, this is a good idea. It makes it easy to buy . . . and easier for you to sell.

When selling to stores, schools, or libraries, you won't make many cash sales. State your standard terms, which were covered in Chapter 5. If this offer is multititle (for more than one book) and includes low-dollar items, you may need to specify a minimum order. If you feel that would hurt sales, at least make sure you cannot lose money on any single-copy order.

The business reply envelope (BRE)

A reply envelope will definitely increase response to your direct-mail offer. We do not feel that postage-free business reply envelopes (BRE) are worth the extra money. However, as with many of the variables in direct marketing, this can only be determined by testing your offer. The post office requires that the business reply envelope be imprinted per their specifications. There is a nominal annual fee and charge of twenty-five cents for each return. Your main post office can supply you with full details.

Finding your market

Mailing lists consist of the names of people interested in a given subject. They are often compiled from subscribers to special interest magazines, buyers of particular types of products, and so on. With such a list, you have a ready source of potential buyers whom you can contact by mail.

To begin trying to find a suitable list for your book, consult SRDS's volume entitled *Direct Mail List Rates & Data*. Here you'll discover detailed information on who rents what lists. You'll also find firms that will be happy to help. These "list brokers" can provide names for almost any category imaginable. While researching, it would also be eye-opening to take a look at the *Direct Marketing Market Place*. Updated every year, it lists leading direct-marketing companies, major service firms and suppliers, and creative individuals and organizations. And Target Marketing has *Who's Who in Direct Marketing*, which is reported to be the largest and most comprehensive directory of all. *LMP* also has a related section, "Mailing List Brokers & Services."

In the educational field you can pinpoint decision-makers in science, vocational education, computer-assisted instruction, music, and every other curriculum area. Within the business community you can rent a list of 1,261 steamship companies, 14,946 appraisers, 21,141 psychologists, 39,176 CPAs, 3,679 dairy farmers, or 2,923 communication consultants, just to mention a few.

COSMEP rents lists to members for below the prevailing industry rates. From them you can get a host of book-related lists. The R. R. Bowker Company is into renting lists in a big way. Because they have data bases to rely on, their information is updated monthly and thus very current. Here you can get lists for such specific library groups as religious libraries by religious affiliation, government libraries, law libraries, and many others. And if you have a business book, they have 582 bookstores that specialize in business books, not to mention 634 bookstores that sell cookbooks and 347 that carry primarily law books, to name a few. You can reach Bowker's mailing list department by calling (212) 337-7164 -7165, or 7166.

The fine points of mailing lists

Getting the right list is so important! Mailing lists come in three types. There is the "occupant" list, which includes every household in a given geographic area. Then there is the "compiled" list, which is derived from phone books and other directories. Finally there is the "response" list, which is made up of people who have already bought related products. For your purposes a response list is probably the best. It will also be more costly, as it targets your potential buyers most precisely.

List rental fees range from fifty to ninety dollars per thousand names. Give the list dealer your reader profile and all the information you can about your book, so he or she can match it with the best list for maximum results. The broker will work with you. Most list owners require prior approval of your material before they will rent their lists. It is understood that a list is rented for *one*-time use only and may not be photocopied. Notice we are saying *rent*. Seldom do you buy a list.

Be wary of ordering mailing lists at prices that seem *too* low. There are fly-by-night outfits offering cheap lists that tend to be rather "dirty" (you will get a lot of returns because the addresses are no longer good—or because the list contains duplicates). In the long run it'll cost you more to use a cheap list and have a lot of mail come back than to pay more to begin with for a relatively "clean" list of correct and current names and addresses.

Again the message: *Go slow . . . test.* Rent a list of 2,000 to 5,000 names. Your broker can supply these by what is called nth name selection. For example, if the list you are interested in has 300,000 names and you want 3,000 names, you would request that your test order be made up of every 100th name from the list. This gives you a good random sample and avoids misleading results. Don't ever fall into the trap of expecting a list that is terrific for Los Angeles to give the same results in New York. It may, but again it may not. In this case New York may only be half as good as Los Angeles. (We know, folks—it happened to us.)

Do a careful analysis of any planned mailing to make sure it will give you a minimum return of 2.2 times the money you spend. (Include costs of design, printing, mailing list rental, postage, and mail processing.) If your mailing pulls 1 to 2 percent of the list, will the return equal 2.2 times the cost? If not, reconsider your program.

More strategy

Timing also plays an important role in your direct-response success. Some months are much better than others. January and February are the all-stars; June, July, and August are bad months for mailing because people go on vacation. If you're promoting a Christmas item, October or early November is when your literature should hit the mailboxes. It's also a good idea to avoid having your mailing reach the customer on Monday or just after a holiday. There's too much other mail competing for attention then.

For large mailings you will want to cut postage costs to the minimum (if you can call the 25 percent increase in bulk mail costs sprung on us by the postal service in 1988 a minimum). To do this, use third-class bulk-rate mail. A bulk mailing permit costs sixty dollars for a one-time application fee, plus sixty dollars per year. Getting one will save you considerable dollars if you anticipate doing much mailing. Present bulk rates are 16.7 or 13.2 cents per piece for profit organizations, depending on how finely they're sorted.The post office requires special ZIP code sorting and bundling. Minimum quantity per mailing is two hundred identical units. If you plan on using the mails a lot, the U.S. Postal Service publishes a free monthly newsletter. You can subscribe by writing *Memo to Mailers*, c/o U.S. Postal Service, Box 999, Springfield, VA 22150-0999. Another idea is to ask your local postmaster or postmistress for last year's ZIP code directory when the new one comes out. You'll need one for the office, and this is an easy way to get a freebie if you have established good relations with that person.

After thinking about the hassle of sticking on labels, stuffing, sorting and trips to the post office, you will probably decide to use a mail fulfillment house (listed in your local yellow pages) to take care of the whole thing for you. We decided early that it was poor pay to do large mailings ourselves.

When renting mailing lists, you will need to make a decision about the type of labels available. If you intend to use a mail fulfillment house to do the actual mailing for you, consult them about what they need. Your labeling choices will include such options as gummed, four-up, three-up, pressure-sensitive, heat-sensitive, and Cheshire. The mail fulfillment house will explain which of these they need.

Now your mailing is out. Figure all your costs and get ready to track results. It is important to remember that you are testing two things: the mailing piece and the list. If your returns are at least 2.2 times the cost, expand your program. Test other lists. Try improved mailing pieces. Keep testing and keep tracking. If you proceed as suggested, you will risk little and gain much.

Another way to create a mailing list is from the inquiries drawn by an ad like the *Creative Loafing* example used earlier. The names of people who've inquired become your own mailing list. Keep it updated and add the names of customers you get from your direct-mail program. Although you can only use a rented list once, when someone responds, that name is then yours to use forever. Keep a permanent record of customers and potential customers. Companies that do a lot of direct marketing soon find that a computer is their most treasured tool. According to a recent survey in *Target Marketing*, 72 percent of DM firms use a computer for list maintenance. It's a snap when it's computerized.

By the way, if you're involved in direct marketing, you can get a complimentary subscription to the magazine *Target Marketing* by writing 332 Eighth Avenue, 18th Floor, New York, NY 10001. The sophisticated publisher using this method of moving books can also get a free subscription to *DM News* by writing on company letterhead to: Circulation Department, *DM News*, 19 West 21st Street, New York, NY 10010. And Ad Lib Publications has put together *FormAids for Direct Response Marketing*, a collection of forms to end hassles and save time and money.

As the months and years go by, you will find your list of names is a viable source for additional income. In turn, it can be rented to others. Clean the list periodically by adding "forwarding and address correction requested" to the outer envelope.

Then for a quarter or so, any undeliverable mail will be returned and you can update your names and addresses accordingly. It's also a good idea to "seed" your own list with an address of your own so you'll know immediately if someone uses it in an unauthorized way.

Direct mail and mail order are marketing techniques that can be tailored to nearly any budget. Their success depends primarily on imagination, common sense, and diligence in following the rules. Many fortunes have been made starting with minimal investments in the direct-marketing field.

An excellent reference for those especially serious about this subject is *Successful Direct Marketing Methods*, by Bob Stone. It just came out in an all-new, fourth edition.

Direct-marketing success stories

Joe Karbo, who was teetering on the brink of personal bankruptcy when he did his *Lazy Man's Way to Riches*, was certified to have a net worth of more than $1 million before his death at age fifty-five. Karbo would receive most people's vote as the top mail-order self-publisher of the twentieth century.

He had an innate knowledge of human behavior and a unique talent as a wordsmith. His full-page ads were — and are — splashed across newspapers and magazines from coast to coast.

Len Fulton, head of Dustbooks, which began in 1963 as a literary magazine, has amassed quite a string of titles. Based in the mountains of Northern California, Fulton presides over a mail-order-based company that produces such reference works as *The International Directory of Little Magazines and Small Presses* and the *Small Press Record of Books in Print*.

Under his guidance Dustbooks also publishes a monthly magazine called *Small Press Review*, runs the Small Press Book Club, and publishes or distributes novels, poetry, nonfiction, anthologies, and how-to books on publishing.

Bud Weckesser, whom you may remember from *Dollars in Your Mailbox*, has expanded his Green Tree Press to promote and sell the works of other writers as well. His full-page spreads are found in many national magazines.

From these examples of mail-order success, it's obvious that your book can be made a best-seller — without its ever seeing a bookstore shelf.

CHAPTER 13

PUBLICITY

Publicity and promotion are very nearly the same. Both are the exposure which a product or service receives and for which there is no payment. But a rough way of distinguishing between them might be that promotion is what you, the author, do; publicity is what, if you're shrewd at promoting, you'll get from the media as a result. Promotion is giving the book a push from behind; publicity is a pull from the front, from the world you're trying to reach.

Facts of life

It is a fact in the publishing industry that books perceived as strong by reviewers, booksellers, readers, and publishers will command the necessary resources and space to make them strong. This axiom is every bit as important to self-published authors as it is to those who are trade-published. It is the policy in major trade publishing houses to allot a minuscule amount of publicity and advertising budget to most books. After that tiny allotment — and only then — will the ones that show promise command greater energy and money commitments. Consequently, every author should realize it's a "publicize or perish" game.

Publicity and promotion are the great equalizers for the little publisher or the unheralded writer. By knowing what buttons to push, you can generate thousands of dollars' worth of free publicity. A couple of excellent basic titles on generating publicity are *The Publicity Manual*, by Kate Kelly, and *The Unabashed Self-Promoter's Guide*, by Jeffrey Lant.

Getting reviewed

Every day millions of potential book buyers turn to the book review page of their local newspaper to see what interests them. Thousands of people in the book industry also study reviews and book listings in newspapers and magazines.

Thus book reviewers have a tremendous impact on publishers and writers. They decide which few of the some 135 titles published in any given day will be reviewed. Book reviews are often regarded as the most persuasive book-buying influence of all. Much of the available review space gets gobbled up by celebrities with virtually guaranteed best-sellers and the huge trade publishers who woo the most important reviewers and editors and spend thousands of dollars in advertising each month.

In spite of these facts, it isn't hard to get a fair share of publicity from book reviewers if you astutely organize your promotional efforts. You will probably be very frustrated if you concentrate all efforts on the *New York Times, Publishers Weekly, Library Journal,* the *Christian Science Monitor, Time,* or other prestigious mass-circulation review media. Go after less-in-demand sources.

Of course, you shouldn't automatically eliminate these choice plums either. *Publishers Weekly* does capsule forecast reviews of about 5,500 of the approximately 53,000 books published each year. The biggies hover around their editorial and book review staff like seagulls around a garbage scow. Yet *Creative Loafing* was reviewed. Need we say more?

Self-publishers who have followed the points in this guide and who are willing to search for the review media whose editorial interest most closely matches their book will get reviews and a resulting boost in sales. The secret is to romance your prime media with a planned and persistent campaign.

Best of all, this valuable review space or electronic media time doesn't cost you a cent. In print media, however, the ad sales department may attempt to convince you to place advertising. Be aware that any review medium with credibility does not decide which titles it will critique on the basis of advertising commitment. Resist the overzealous salesperson who implies that an ad will influence editorial decisions — and gushes about how wonderful your book is. We've stopped working with one prominent West Coast book publication because of its pushiness in this area.

Perhaps a word should be said here about the fine art of "review pruning." Just as you cut away the dead wood of trees and bushes so that new growth can flourish, so, too, you will excerpt quotable bits of praise from longer reviews. The sheer limitations of space require that material be condensed. Naturally as you do this encapsulation, you want to throw out the less desirable phrases while preserving the especially complimentary gems. Realize as you do this, however, that to change the actual intention of a review by taking words out of context is flagrantly wrong.

Brigitte Weeks, former editor of the *Washington Post Book World*, tells a story about the manipulation of one of their reviews: They ran a disgruntled review of a Paul Theroux book, which said *"The Fire Arsenal*, as explosive as a firecracker and sometimes as dazzling, is ultimately as chilling as dry ice."* And what did the publisher splash across the cover of the book? "Dazzling—William McPherson, *The Washington Post.*" The reports of such abuse are legion among book reviewers. In case you're wondering, by their very nature, reviews are quotable, in whole or in part, without permission.

But don't think that a magazine or newspaper is unsuitable just because they don't run formal book reviews. Many have sections that tell of newsy items or new products of interest to their readers. These mentions can be golden. Think what would happen if your book were plugged on the cover of the "Life" or "Money" section of *USA Today!* We got a nice plug in *Writer's Digest* Magazine this way. (See sample.)

Developing a nationwide marketing plan

The way to secure reviews, get your book mentioned in nonreviewing publications, and generally light a fire that will ignite word-of-mouth recommendations is to create a nationwide marketing plan. This will include national book reviewers, syndicated columnists, newsletter editors, book club editors, and excerpt rights buyers. It will also pinpoint selected distributors, wholesalers, bookstores, and libraries. And if you're smart, you'll add to your list selected radio and TV programs, associations who may buy in bulk, special retail outlets, and various innovative ideas for moving books.

Don't overlook regional magazines and newspapers. Some publications serve specific areas, for instance, that target to business-persons or women. If you have a book slanted to either of these audiences—and you ignore the regional media—you're cheating yourself. Also consider alternative newspapers around the country if you have a controversial or exposé title. And what about civic, social, fraternal, and alumni associations to which you belong? They like to highlight the accomplishments of members. When you prepare a nationwide marketing plan, you pull together every conceivable source—both general and specialized—that may talk about or buy your book.

Developing a mailing list of the reviewers you want to court is one of your first priorities. Tailor your list to potential contacts whose editorial slant matches your type of book. This will save significantly on promotional material and postage costs. It will also avoid tempting a lot of folks, who wouldn't seriously consider reviewing your book, to request a free copy anyway.

TIP SHEET

ried, divorced or what. Are there children? Does the spouse work?

√If there are battles going on within the business and they're known to the public, you can't ignore them. But, you can deal with them in a positive way:

Fazlin's first attempt at starting his own company was a joint venture with another larger firm, which has since gone out of business, and "philosophical differences" forced him to leave after less than two years.

Usually, investigative reporting is not expected in writing business profiles. Most of the editors for whom I've done these profiles wanted very little in the way of controversy and prefer "chamber of commerce" journalism; affirmative and upbeat with the problems getting little space.

The beauty of business profiles is that they are easy to resell to other magazines. In 1983, I wrote about a 25-year-old Venice, Florida, millionaire who sold his chain of six computer stores to start his own software company. In the last four years, I've sold the story to 11 different magazines. Net pay; $3,650 for two interviews and several phone call updates.

—*Lary Crews*

8 CITY/REGIONAL BOOK IDEAS AND 1 SOURCE OF INFORMATION

Include city and regional books—those aimed at a specific geographic area—among the beneficiaries of the computer revolution. In *How-to-Make Big Profits Publishing City and Regional Books* (Communication Creativity, Box 213, Saguache, Colorado 81149-0213; $14.95 paperback), authors Marilyn and Tom Ross explain how even a small personal computer puts these books into the individual writer's reach. They also analyze the market often overlooked by large publishers, and suggest these eight types of city/regional books:

√*Travel and tourist guides* introduce visitors to an area.

√*Consumer books* serve as shopping guides for residents.

√*Activity guides* detail recreational opportunities.

√*Nature field guides* explore a region's flora and fauna.

√*Special-interest titles*, such as *The Greatest Honky-Tonks in Texas* or *Single in Portland*, appeal to specific segments of the population.

√*Historical books.*

√*Regional cookbooks.*

√*Photography books.*

There are other possible regional subjects that defy categorization, say the authors—everything from trivia books to anthologies collecting works of regional writers.

6 BEST BETS FOR INTERVIEWS

The #1 trick of the trade in writing local newspaper features centers on searching out personalities within the publication's circulation range. Articles with local and regional subjects, as are those suggested here, ring the bell with feature editors, who like eye-catching and/or provocative leads as well as plenty of anecdotes and quotes. You might adapt some of the stories for regional and national magazines. Here are six topics to get you started—with a few interview points for each.

√*A woman pilot for an airline that serves your area.* Number of years she has spent in aviation; airport jobs she has filled. How did she start? Her closest calls as a pilot. Farthest travels; her favorite cities and states. Members of her family (husband, father) who are fliers.

√*The county probation officer.* The effectiveness of probation as a correctional method. How the officer keeps close supervision of those granted paroles. Do most parolees do well with their jobs in the rehabilitation program? Helping with personal and family problems.

√*The leading teenage model in your region.* A pretty face and charming smile as her secrets of

success. When she began her career, and her highest paid assignments so far. Her kinds of work: posing for newspaper and magazine ads, TV commercials, fashion shows and catalog modeling. Do her ambitions include acting? Her modeling agency's predictions about her future. Or is the leading model a young man?

√*The baby veterinarian at a local or a nearby zoo.* His or her services for the newborn animals. Feeding the babies with spoons or bottles; solving animal tots' problems and pulling the creatures through sickness. The most difficult animals as patients. The vet's extensive knowledge of animal diseases.

√*The youngest mayor in your county and, in contrast, the oldest.* Their common bonds and their spirit of cooperation for the county's progress. How the two mayors represent the enthusiasm of youth and the wisdom of age. Compare their towns' most pressing problems and their proposals for solutions.

√*Queen of the local bowling alleys.* The skill and confidence that brought her the championship. Her rating among the state's bowlers. Trophies and cash prizes she's won in league and tournament plays; her best scores. Is she a trick-shot expert? Tours.

—*Frank A. Dickson*

Building your list

If you publish a general-interest book, you should at least contact the Selected Book Review Sources listed in the Appendix. An additional list can be harvested in *LMP* or *Book Marketing Opportunities: A Directory*. Here you can locate magazine and newspaper review editors, plus radio and TV review sources. For your convenience we've included a list of Selected Syndicated Columnists in the Appendix.

If your work is of specialized or regional interest, include review sources that have parallel concerns. Build by researching thoroughly and selectively. In the main library you will find several directories that provide marvelous aids for developing specifically targeted rosters. The *Standard Periodical Directory* is an essential reference work. It lists nearly 67,000 U.S. and Canadian periodicals. *Ulrich's International Periodicals Directory* offers an excellent source of magazines of the entire world. This directory is broken down by subject and cross-referenced, allowing you to be quite selective. It also notes in which periodicals book reviews are regularly used. One other source you might want to consult is *Ayer's Directory of Publishing*. It includes key names for both newspapers and magazines.

You may want to purchase a personal copy of the *All-In-One Directory*. It lists more than 21,000 PR outlets in a single volume. You'll find all daily and weekly newspapers here as well as consumer magazines, the business press, and radio and TV. *Working Press of the Nation*, published by the National Research Bureau, Inc., offers a comprehensive rundown of names and addresses. This four-volume directory covers newspapers, magazines, radio, television, and syndicated columnists. Research here will net a list covering the important reviewers in both print and electronic media who would typically be interested in your title. Volume 1, the *Newspaper Directory of WPN*, not only lists reviewers' names for all daily papers but also gives special-interest papers, religious newspapers, and ethnic papers. This is also an ideal place to prospect for syndicated columnists, as they are cross-referenced by subject area. In addition, you might want to consult *Gebbie's All-in-One Directory*, and many PR professionals swear by *Bacon's Publicity Checker*.

There is another work that is most helpful: the *Encyclopedia of Associations* is a fat and expensive reference set listing almost eighteen thousand organizations covering thousands of subjects.

To reach newsletter editors, there's nothing better than *Hudson's Newsletter Directory*. It offers current information on subscription newsletters worldwide.

Several specialized directories can lead you to radio and TV producers in your area and of national prominence, as well. There is *TV Publicity Outlets Nationwide, Cable TV Publicity Outlets Nationwide, New York Publicity Outlets, Metro California Media*, and the *National Radio Publicity Directory*. Larimi Communications also publishes many practical and comprehensive media guides. They offer *Cable Contacts Yearbook, Radio Contacts, Television Contacts*, and *TV News*. And if your book has spiritual overtones, a copy of the *Directory of Religious Broadcasting* will provide contact names and addresses for more religious programs than you'd ever have time to appear on.

For your convenience we've gathered together many of the above-mentioned books—plus most of the others recommended throughout this guide—into the Maverick Mail Order Bookstore. To get a catalog, simply send a #10 SASE with 45¢ postage to P.O. Box 1500-MOB, Buena Vista, CO 81211.

Advance activities

After you've developed your nationwide marketing plan, study the list of sources and determine which are more apt to give your book the best boost. These are your prime contacts. As we discussed earlier, these people should receive a copy of the ABI form as soon as it is prepared. The main point of this mailing is to get the name of the book and the author in key people's minds. (Notice the "Important Fall Books" announcement on page 224 clipped from *Publishers Weekly*. This came as a result of such early promotional activity.)

Galleys or folded and gathered pages should be sent to your list of prime reviewers as soon as you have the material in hand. We recommend that galley review packages be shipped by first-class mail, not fourth-class. You might even consider one of the special delivery services or UPS to set you apart. If yours is a general-interest book with nationwide appeal, use the list "Where to Send Galleys or Page Proofs" we provide in the Appendix. If it is a specialized or regional book, select prime review sources based on the publications you have culled from research. Invest in a phone call to get the correct editor's name.

Some publishers go to great lengths to make their galleys stand out from the crowd. For *Butcher's Theater*, a novel by Jonathan Kellerman, Bantam had a letter opener (aka knife) piercing the cover of the bound galley. Said marketing director Matthew Shear, "Buyers receive a tremendous number of advance bound galleys of upcoming books, and a key marketing challenge is to get them to pay attention to our book and hopefully to read it." Give you any ideas?

Sending actual review copies is more than just mailing galleys, folded and gathered sheets, or a book. Remember, this is a *promotional effort*. Make it good.

In addition to the book itself, each review shipment should include at least a news release (the hows and whys of which we'll be explaining shortly) and an acknowledgment card. A sample card is pictured on page 225. It tells us when reviews will appear. While the return rate is not fantastic, we find it worthwhile. It also seems to encourage people to send back books which they choose not to critique. Since a galley has no cover, include a photocopy of your cover art if available. Be sure to include a galley title page containing all the important facts about the book. To help you construct this, we've included a sample.

We're amazed at how many trade publishers neglect to ship any promotional material with their review books. Most complimentary copies we receive at Communication Creativity have no promotional literature with them whatsoever. Half the time we don't even know how much the book sells for. Also share with the reviewer any advertising or publicity campaigns that are planned. If you've set up an author tour, don't keep it a secret.

Always follow up on prime review copies. This can be done by letter or telephone. Some editors of major publications reportedly are so busy that phone calls from publishers are annoying. We haven't found this to be typical. If approached in a sincere and businesslike manner, most reviewers are quite congenial. The best way to jog them without being offensive is to inquire if they received the review copy. Remember, as we pointed out earlier, using your telephone before 8 A.M. and after 5 P.M. saves you much, so look where reviewers are located, then try to schedule your call to catch them during the cheaper rate time.

But what of all the other sources left on the nationwide marketing plan that were not deemed as "prime"? You should contact all of them about a month before you have the finished book in house. For *Creative Loafing* we developed the promotional package shown on the following pages. It included trimmed dust jackets (be sure to clue the printer into getting your overrun of jackets or covers out as quickly as possible), the cut-off flaps, an introductory letter, the news release, and a business reply card.

The letter should be brief and enticing. Tell reviewers what the book is about, when the publication date is, and why it will be of interest to their audiences (fills an immediate need or solves a current problem). Explain your promotional and advertising plans and any special qualifications of the author. The business reply card requires no postage, thus making it easy for them to order. (Since creating this package, however, we've done away with postage-paid business reply cards and don't find our results being hampered.) We've also added something new: a mock-up book review. This is simply a review which *you* write. We have ours typeset so it appears to have been clipped from a newspaper or magazine. This strategy has one big advantage. Many reviewers are too busy—and some are too lazy—to read your book carefully. A mock-up review makes it easy for them. They can simply print the review intact or pull passages from it.

Of course, reviewers aren't your only targets. Why not offer a special early sales inducement to wholesalers, distributors, and bookstores? Major publishers use this ploy all the time. You could offer one book free with every five ordered before the official publication date, for instance.

Requests for review copies are filled just like standard book orders. When you receive the request card, it is a good idea to create a 3" by 5" "control card" noting the person's name, publication or media, address, phone, and date the book was sent for easy reference and future follow-up.

Include promotional materials with the review copy. If it's for a prime reviewer, the sources listed in the Appendix under the title "Send Finished Books," send the package fast: either first-class or UPS. If it's *not* for a prime reviewer, ship fourth-class (book post). About now, you're recalling how slow book post is. But if you followed our advice, the publication date is still three months away, so there is time enough to take advantage of the special fourth-class rate.

Regardless of how thorough your investigation has been, you will probably wind up getting requests from unknown people asking for review copies. Log these in and send them a book—pronto.

Some reviewers tell us they appreciate good black-and-white photographs of the book or the author. You can get extra impact this way. Sometimes they will be used to dress dull review pages. They are even occasionally used with just a caption when a review is not forthcoming. Of course, if you plan to merchandise your book via direct marketing, a photo of the book is a must. To make your product stand out, use a contrasting background and don't go in for a lot of busyness. A simple shot is all that's required. If you are going to supply photos, it's a good idea to have them made in the 3" by 4" size, as these will fit in a #10 envelope. Here's a tip that will more than save you the cost of this book: Contact Ornall Glossies, Inc., in New York at (800) 826-6312, and get 100 4" by 5" glossies from them for only $18 plus shipping.

Of course, editors of specialized media are not as deluged with attention from publishers. A phone call or a lunch, if it is convenient for you, can make your name and written material mean a great deal to such folks. And if your book is highly specialized, they could do you more good than the mass media.

Like all promotion, communication with reviewers is playing the odds. It reduces to a matter of percentages. But if you proceed in a planned, persistent, friendly manner, the amount of free publicity it yields can have a substantial impact on your book sales. And it can go on for years and years as new review sources emerge, or editors change at existing publications.

Special literary publicity opportunities

The person with a book of poetry or fiction or an avant-garde literary

Publishers Weekly excerpt.

work faces a unique challenge. While most nonfiction lends itself to publicity quite readily, the novelist and poet must be more creative. Often this is doubly difficult, as these talented people are not the assertive, business-minded type with few qualms about self-promotion.

To make this campaign less painful, we've entered two lists in the Appendix. One is titled "Literary Review Sources"; the other "Libraries with Small-Press Collections." If you use them as the foundation for your promotional efforts, you'll be off to a good start.

Another place to prospect is the *1984 Directory of Literary Magazines*. Prepared by the Coordinating Council of Literary Magazines, it can be ordered from 2 Park Avenue, New York, NY 10016. You should also subscribe to Dustbooks' *Small Press Review* to keep abreast of happenings in the field. Other newsletters of significance include *Literary Markets* and *Alps Monthly*. (See the bibliography of newsletters for the addresses of these and others.)

One of the most beneficial organizations you could get in touch with is Poets & Writer's, Inc., an information center for the U.S. literary community. It publishes *Poets and Writers Magazine*, puts out several reference

★★★**Here Is Your Pre-Publication Review Copy**★★★

of

BANDWAGON TO HEALTH
The All Natural Way To
Eat, Think, & Exercixe

Publication date: May, 1984
Price $6.95
Softcover edition
210 pages   5½ x 8¼
ISBN-0-937766-08-9

DRELWOOD PUBLICATIONS

Distributed by
Communication Creativity
P.O. Box 213, Saguache, CO 81149
(303) 655-2504

PLEASE ACKNOWLEDGE!
_ _ _ _ _ _ _ _ _ _ _ _ _ _ _ _

☐   We expect to review this book in _____

_____

on approximately _____

☐   We are seriously considering stocking this title.

☐   We are seriously considering the following subsidiary
     rights on this title.

_____

☐   Sorry, we did not find **BANDWAGON TO HEALTH**
     suitable for us. The copy you sent is returned herewith.
_ _ _ _ _ _ _ _ _ _ _ _ _ _ _ _

Signed _____

Title _____

Affiliation _____

Address _____

City_____State_____Zip_____

Phone (_____) _____

Send to: COMMUNICATION CREATIVITY
P.O. Box 213
Saguache, Colorado 81149
We will appreciate two tear sheets of any printed reviews or
features and advance notice of electronic media mentions.

Review-copy form.

GALLEY TITLE PAGE

```
TITLE:      Marketing Your Book: A Collection of Profit-Making Ideas
            for Authors and Publishers
AUTHORS:  Marilyn and Tom Ross
PUBLISHER: Communication Creativity
CLASSIFICATION: writing, publishing, marketing
PRICE:     $9.95
BINDING:   Paper
NUMBER OF PAGES: 128
ISBN:  0-918880-21-1
PUBLICATION DATE: August, 1989
FINISHED SIZE: 5 1/4 x 8 1/4
BACK MATTER: index

Reviewers are reminded that this is an uncorrected copy of
Marketing Your Book: A Collection of Profit-Making Ideas for
Authors and Publishers

For additional information contact: Ann Markham
                                    (719) 395-8659
```

Galley title page.

and source books, helps to sponsor workshops and readings by poets and fiction writers, and serves as a general information resource. You'll definitely want a copy of the organization's *Literary Bookstores in the U.S.*, which notes store specializations.

Suppose you have a book for a culturally elite audience or a work of interest primarily to a specialized or minority group. One of the most important things you can do is substantiate why you wrote the book. A tome decrying nuclear buildup will be more widely received if the world knows it was written by a nuclear physicist. A political novel, written by a political scientist, carries more weight than the same book written by a biology teacher. So if you have specific qualifications that bear on your book, for heaven's sake *don't keep them a secret.*

Also don't keep the general subject matter of your novel a secret. Often this can be tapped for a promotional tie-in to a current event, local angle, or human-interest aspect. If you've written fiction with a heroine who aspires to this nation's highest office, for instance, you could have hooked on to Geraldine Ferraro's campaign and sent your book to new heights. (By the way, don't feel you can only do this when your book first comes out. Always be on the lookout for newsworthy angles.) Suppose you've done a novel with detailed background information on hunting. The National Rifle Association might review it in their publications and

Date

Dear Reviewer:

       The work week shrinks. Companies grant earlier retirement. Our life span increases. Most people reel from the one-two punch of lots of spare time . . . and too little money. Unfortunately, Americans have never been shown how to constructively cope with leisure. <u>Creative</u> <u>Loafing</u> fills that void! In addition to being a lively trade book, it is a suggested text for leisure, retirement and gerontology studies.

       This exciting newcomer offers a shoestring guide to new leisure fun that contains hundreds of ideas for free spare time activities. An unusual source book, it includes special quizzes and exercises designed to steer the reader towards pastimes that will be personally enriching.

       The publication date for <u>Creative</u> <u>Loafing</u> is October 1, 1978. The book will be launched by "Creative Loafing Days", a gala Leisure Fair. Held in San Diego, the author's home town, this event will feature many of the unique activities discussed in the book. This title has been allocated a generous advertising budget. A nationwide author tour is scheduled to begin in September.

       After you've enjoyed looking over the enclosed material, simply complete and return the reply card. We will see that you promptly receive a copy of <u>Creative</u> <u>Loafing</u> to read for yourself!

                              Yours truly,

                              Tom Mulvane

                              Tom Mulvane

                              Marketing Director

TM:et

Enclosures

Letter to reviewer.

promote it to their membership. Similarly, if immigrants' experiences at Ellis Island are featured in your novel, there might have been some potential tie-in with the renovation of the Statue of Liberty.

Poets can also slant their work to certain target audiences. Just as Chaucer's bawdy stories in verse entertain many literate people, and the folksy verse of James Whitcomb Riley appeals to midwestern farmers and rural people, so too might your poetry find a home with a specific segment of the populace. If crass commercialism doesn't grate against your creativity too much, see if there is a segment of the market that your material will particularly interest.

Any award you may have won, along with literary merit, is a good way to promote fiction and poetry. If you live in Arizona, Colorado, Idaho, Montana, Nevada, New Mexico, Oregon, Utah, Washington, or Wyoming, another possibility awaits you. The new Western States Book Awards are presented biennially to outstanding authors and publishers of fiction, creative nonfiction, and poetry working in the West. Among other things, the awards are designed to increase sales and critical attention nationally for fine literary works from the West. For information contact the Western States Arts Foundation, 141 East Palace Avenue, Santa Fe, NM 87501. Information on general book awards can be found in *LMP*.

There is another interesting award program that has no geographic limitations. It's the Editors' Book Award, founded by Bill Henderson. In 1984 it was won by David Bosworth, who wrote a novella titled *From My Father, Singing.* His was one of sixty-four manuscripts nominated by editors from thirty-three publishing houses. It had been rejected by nine publishers. The Editors' Book Award honors an important manuscript overlooked by commercial publishers. If you're publishing a collection of poetry, you should get listed in Dustbooks' *Directory of Poetry Publishers.*

These are some ideas to help you develop your own specialized nationwide marketing plan. Literary works *can* be financially, as well as creatively, rewarding if you're willing to take the steps to make that happen.

Writing effective news releases

A major step toward generating free publicity is effective and timely news releases. They are relatively simple yet enormously productive. Jack Erbe, publisher of the *Fifty Billion Dollar Directory,* told us of generating 1,350 requests for information about his book from a news release. And 245 of those free leads were converted into firm orders for his high-ticket marketing guide.

By the way, we refer to them as "news" releases rather than "press" releases for a very good reason: electronic media do not necessarily consider themselves press, so why run the risk of offending them?

A news release is essentially a short news piece. It should tell the story *behind* the book, not just the story *of* the book. These brief news stories that publicists churn out by the thousands are often the lifeblood of harried newspaper and magazine editors who want to keep their readers abreast of what's new but don't have the editorial staff to cover such things themselves. It is estimated that fully three-fourths of what you see in print is a result of news releases.

News releases present a challenge. One never knows how much of the planted text will be used. Editors cut releases to fit available space. Since this is the case, it is prudent to get the five W's—who, what, where, when, and why—solidly covered in the first paragraph. Although some editors rewrite the release, most will not. But they will keep cutting material from the bottom until it fits the space. If the point is strewn over three pages, they'll probably just throw the entire release in the trash.

This medium demands tight, snappy copy to be effective. Start out with a provocative statement, startling statistic, or question to arrest attention. After covering the five W's in the first paragraph, add supportive information in order of importance. The overall goal remains to get the message across, no matter how much falls off the bottom.

Of course, as in all promotional writing, it is most effective if you can state a problem or concern with which the editor and readers can identify. Your book offers the solution. In the case of fiction an intriguing synopsis can be the attention-getter, or tie into current events if possible.

Include the author's credentials for writing this book. These should be condensed into one power-packed paragraph. You should be able to adapt or use the author bio that you wrote for your cover. Don't be alarmed if your name is not a household word. A little imagination and brainstorming will soon disclose supportive information about your qualifications. Certainly you are qualified—you wrote the book!

Last comes information as to where your book may be acquired. Include the name and address of the publishing company, the retail price, and any shipping charges. While many editors feel this is too salesy and will cut it, others will let it ride. Look over the adjacent sample news release. A release should never be more than two double-spaced typed pages. One page is even better (and we often "cheat" and do it 1½ spaces to make it fit on one page). Be sure to include *all* pertinent information—the title, author, price, ISBN, LC number, pub date, pages, size, binding, illustrations, and any back matter—in a little blurb at the beginning or end of the written text. Always include a contact person and a phone number (day and evening if they are different).

The presentation is important. Type your release on your publishing

FOR IMMEDIATE RELEASE
CONTACT: Tom Mulvane
          (714) 276-7171

"CREATIVE LOAFING" IS TOPIC OF UNIQUE NEW BOOK

SAN DIEGO, CALIFORNIA, AUG. 17 - As the work week shrinks, companies
grant earlier retirement and our life span increases, Americans find
themselves with more spare time. A new book, CREATIVE LOAFING, tells
how to constructively cope with this avalanche of leisure. Its major
theme is banishing boredom and overcoming loneliness. Written by
Marilyn Heimberg Ross, this shoestring guide describes hundreds of
free or very low cost leisure pursuits. Communication Creativity, a
San Diego-based publishing company, has just released this unusual
source book.

CREATIVE LOAFING explores such experiences as auction hunting,
gate crashing, court watching, volunteering, frolicking at feasts and
festivals or watching famous athletes . . . all for free! There are
suggestions on how to awaken the "child" within you and rediscover the
world around you.

This book embraces all types of leisure activities from the
innocence of sand castle building — to the Museum of Erotic Art.
Readers can find the excitement of orienteering - or the peacefulness
of birdwatching. Then there is the comic romp of clownology - or the
intensity of political activism. Those who read CREATIVE LOAFING
are invited to see an elaborate Chinese New Year celebration - or stay

————more————

News release.

230

at home and create winning contest entries.

The book concludes with a chapter of quizzes and intriguing exercises designed to help the reader decide which activities will be most personally enriching. Written in a refreshingly casual style, it is printed in larger-than-usual type for easy reading.

Over the past three years, Marilyn Ross has done extensive research for numerous articles on leisure, and ultimately this book. As a result, she has become a recognized expert in the field. Her classes and seminars on leisure have been extremely popular in the San Diego Community Colleges. A prize-winning author and teacher of writing, she has two previous books to her credit. Mrs. Ross states, "Everyone can have a rich, full life if they look for creative ways to have fun. The amount of joy a person gets from leisure activities need not have any relation to his or her income."

CREATIVE LOAFING can be purchased for $9.95 in area bookstores, or ordered directly from the publisher, Communication Creativity, at 1340 Tourmaline Street, San Diego, CA 92109

CREATIVE LOAFING: A SHOESTRING GUIDE TO NEW LEISURE FUN
by Marilyn Heimberg Ross
5½ x 8½ casebound
ISBN 0-918880-01-7
L of C# 78-59410
Quizzes, Appendix, Bibliography, Index
publication date: Nov. 14, 1978
$9.95

Aug. 17, 1978

-30-

Marilyn Heimberg Ross

Creative Loafing

A SHOESTRING GUIDE TO NEW LEISURE FUN

Ross **CREATIVE LOAFING** A Shoestring Guide to New Leisure Fun

Communication Creativity
0-918880-01-7

ISBN 0-918880-01-7

"Mankind has admirably organised one part of his life—work—but has forgotten to organise the other part—leisure."

—George Bernard Shaw

Creative Loafing shows you how to have more fun for less money.

Do you find yourself "killing" time instead of enjoying it?
Are you bored because activities cost too much?
Do you want to further enrich your life?

Creative Loafing is your answer!

Written in a sprightly and conversational style, it is a practical Shoestring Guide to New Leisure Fun. Hundreds of innovative ideas for free entertainment are contained in the source book. The author also includes easy exercises to help you decide which activities will bring you the most joy.

Creative Loafing . . . .

- Shows retirees how to pioneer new spare time fun and find companionships to enrich their lives
- Offers fresh alternatives for middle-aged marrieds whose days have become tinged with dull banker's gray
- Tells the divorced or widowed how to cultivate friendships and seek new adventures
- Is chockful of cheap thrills for young singles and growing families on tight budgets

A **COMMUNICATION CREATIVITY** Book

About the Author

Marilyn Ross has done extensive research for numerous articles on leisure and ultimately this book, over the past three years. As a result of this research, she has become a recognized expert in her field.

Marilyn is president of Creative Loafing, a leisure association and counseling service. Her classes and seminars on leisure are extremely popular and in heavy demand in the San Diego community colleges.

A prize-winning author and teacher of writing, she has two previous books, a newspaper column and many articles to her credit. Her recent book, *Discover Your Roots—A New, Easy Guide for Tracing Your Family Tree* (written under the name of Marilyn Heimberg) is used in libraries and classrooms throughout the U.S. She belongs to the Author's Guild, the National Federation of Press Women, California Press Women and the World Leisure and Recreation Association.

Marilyn and her husband, Tom, are parents of four teenagers. For fun she and her family practice Creative Loafing.

ISBN 0-918880-01-7

A Communication Creativity Book
1340 Tourmaline Street
San Diego, California 92109

From the time we enter kindergarten and people ask, "What do you want to be when you grow up?" we are methodically instructed to work for a living. But rarely does anyone attempt to teach us how to have fun . . . or help us explore new and unusual leisure time . . .

. . . fills that gap! Through it you will discover how to work on living, not just for a living. This is a book about having fun. It's also about saving money. There are literally hundreds of unique adventures—or mellow meanderings—to help conquer boredom or further enrich your life.

Creative Loafing explores such experiences as auction hunting, court-watching, gate crashing, volunteering, frolicking at lakes and festivals or watching famous athletes at no fees! There are suggestions on how to awaken the "child" within you and rediscover the world around you.

This new source book embraces all types of leisure activities from the innocence of sand castle building—to the Museum of Erotic Art. You can find the excitement of orienteering—or the peacefulness of birdwatching. Then there is the comic romp of clowning—or the intensity of political activism. You might go to see an elaborate Chinese New Year celebration—or stay at home and create winning contest entries.

Creative Loafing concludes with a chapter of easy quizzes and intriguing exercises designed to help you analyze which activities will be the most enriching.

Dust jacket.

TABLE OF CONTENTS

© 1978 T.M. & Marilyn Ross

Table of contents.

☐ Yes, I would like a Review/Examination copy of

(please print)

Name _____

Affiliation_____

Address _____

City _____

State/Zip_____ Phone (   ) _____

FIRST CLASS
Permit #10795
San Diego, Calif.

BUSINESS REPLY MAIL
No Postage Necessary if Mailed in the United States

POSTAGE WILL BE PAID BY

MARILYN HEIMBERG

1340 Tourmaline St.
San Diego, CA 92109

Mailing samples.

company letterhead or on plain paper so it can be duplicated on letterhead. Then have it reproduced at your neighborhood print shop. Send news releases to magazines, newspapers, radio and television stations, and newsletters that reach groups which would have a natural interest in your book. Always be sure to cover your hometown thoroughly.

Some clever PR people also include a clip sheet of reproduceable artwork—such as illustrations from the book, book covers, logos, or other camera-ready art. By providing the media with easily reproduced art to illustrate their news story, you heighten your chances of getting coverage.

Submitting news releases should be a saturation campaign. The more that go out, the better your chances. Do be aware that a release is not automatically run. In fact, most will wind up in the round file. But those that are used are like a third-party endorsement of your book. If a large metropolitan daily newspaper publishes your release, hundreds of thousands of people are reached. A few such victories will outweigh the cost of paper and postage manyfold. Remember, exposure for you and your book is the goal. The more often people hear or see the name, the more apt they are to buy the book.

Where to obtain free listings

Another way to take advantage of sales-boosting free publicity is to avail your book, your company, and yourself of the various listings in the industry. These listings fall into three basic categories: book, author, and publishing company.

The top-line listing is, of course, *Books in Print*. Assuming that you processed the Advanced Book Information (ABI) form as indicated in Chapter 7, your book will automatically progress from *Forthcoming Books in Print* into *Books in Print*. This comprehensive index catalogs by author, by title, and (if nonfiction) by subject. If your book is for children, grade levels K through 12, you'll also be listed in *Children's Books in Print*. There are additional supplements such as *Business Books and Serials in Print*, *Religious Books and Serials in Print*, and *Paperbound Books in Print*.

Cumulative Book Index (CBI) is an international bibliography of new publications in the English language. Subscribers include many major libraries and booksellers throughout the world. *CBI* has both a printed and an online data base version. Although *CBI* reportedly will not consider books having less than one hundred pages, or of which fewer than five hundred copies are printed, we suggest you ignore these limitations. Our seventy-two page *Discover Your Roots* is listed in *CBI*. To have your title included in this index, send a copy of their completed form (see example for *Be Tough or Be Gone*), and the book if you wish to *Cumulative Book Index*, The H. W. Wilson Company, 950 University Avenue, Bronx, NY 10452.

Please return THIS SLIP with information

Description of new book for FREE record in Cumulative Book Index, published by
The H. W. Wilson Company, 950 University Ave., Bronx, N.Y. 10452

The Cumulative Book Index is published monthly.

A copy of the book or descriptive material will be appreciated.

Author Tom Davis as told to Marilyn Ross
(Full Name) (Please print)

Title BE TOUGH OR BE GONE
(Verbatim)

Subject The adventures of a modern day cowboy, Americana, history

Series and Number

Edition 1 No. of vols 5,000 Size 5½x8½ No. of pages 210 Illustrations photos

Binding paperback Retail price $6.95 Date of publication 7/24/84
(In your currency) (Exact)

Name and Address of Publisher Northern Trails Press
(From whom the book may be obtained) PO Box 964, Alamosa, CO 81101

For IMPORTATIONS the following additional information is REQUIRED: (a) Are you the sole U.S. agent for the book? .... (b) What is the U.S. publication date? .... (c) How many copies will be on hand in this country on the U.S. publication date? (or are on hand now)? ....

30M   T.E.S.   PLEASE COMPLETE

CBI form.

You will also want to send copies of the ABI form and books as soon as possible to the following places: The Library of Congress, Cataloging in Publication Division, Washington, DC 20541, and the Weekly Record Department, c/o R.R. Bowker, 245 West 17th Street, New York, NY 10011. These serve as a means of getting your title on public record in the *National Union Catalog, Weekly Record,* and *American Book Publishing Record.*

Additionally, send information to the "Books Published Today" column of the *New York Times,* 229 West 43rd Street, New York, NY 10036. Be sure to include the specific publication date so they know when to list it.

That should cover everything, you say? Not quite. We certainly wouldn't want to overlook the annual *Small Press Record of Books in Print.* The twelfth edition listed some sixteen thousand individual books, pamphlets, broadsides, posters, and poem-cards. To have your book included here, send a copy of the ABI form to Dustbooks, Box 100, Paradise, CA 95969. Another place to get listed is in *Alternatives in Print.* Contact Elliott Shore, Contemporary Culture Collection, Temple University Library, Philadelphia, PA 19122.

Another copy of this form, along with a catalog sheet and your Standard Terms and Conditions of Sales, should go to the American Booksellers Association, 137 West 25th Street, New York, NY 10001. This is the major trade association of retail and wholesale middlemen, so it's advantageous to be listed in their *Book Buyer's Handbook.*

The above represent the major listings for your book. We do recommend you study the Bowker catalog which we suggested should be in your library. Are there other specialized publications in which you might be listed?

Author listings are a good way to boost credibility and increase prestige. These are also important to you for future writing assignments and speaking engagements. Certainly they are worth more than the slight effort required to fill out the necessary questionnaires.

Contemporary Authors (Gale Research Company, The Book Tower, Detroit, MI 48226) is published twice a year and contains over 42,000 sketches. In addition to biographies of major living literary figures, it lists the first-time novelist, the provocative essayist, the new poet, and other writers beginning their careers. The prerequisites for inclusion are that a person be published by a recognized house (not a vanity press) and that the subject be on the popular, not scientific or technical, level. Both adult and juvenile writers are covered. Drop them a line on your company letterhead and request author entry forms. And December Press publishes *Who's Who in U.S. Writers, Editors and Poets*. Contact them at Box 302, Highland Park, IL 60035.

Are you a poet or novelist? Then you will want to be included in *A Directory of American Poets and Fiction Writers*. For information write Poets and Writers, Inc., 72 Spring Street, New York, NY 10012. There are many other specialized directories. To get a feel for others in which you might appear, ask your reference librarian to steer you to where such volumes are kept.

Company listings help to establish the credibility and image of a publisher. Dustbooks' *International Directory of Little Magazines and Small Presses* will be glad to know of your existence. Write Len Fulton, the editor-publisher, at P.O. Box 100, Paradise, CA 95969. Another place to get a free listing for your publishing house is in the *Publishers Directory*. This reference is put out by Gale Research Company, 150 East 50th Street, New York, NY 10022.

And when you are up to three or more titles annually, your company can be included in *LMP* and *Writer's Market*. If you grow to the point where you have an official catalog describing all your titles, get a free listing in *Publishers' Catalogs Annual* by contacting Chadwyck-Healey, Inc., 623 Martense Avenue, Teaneck, NJ 07666.

It should be obvious at this point that there is a multitude of free publicity opportunities available to the small publisher with the initiative to seek them out. Now let us investigate promotion, a close sister to publicity.

CHAPTER 14

PROMOTION

Promotional activities open even greater vistas. In this chapter we'll be exploring how to get more newspaper coverage. And we'll investigate the world of radio and TV, telling how to generate interviews and what to do when you're a guest. Various creative and low-budget promotional vehicles will also be examined.

Getting more newspaper coverage

Print media offer the enterprising writer-publisher a bumper crop of opportunities for promotion.

Of course, as we mentioned in the last chapter, copies of your book announcement and press releases should be directed to all local newspapers. If your main daily features book reviews, a set of galleys or folded and gathered sheets are a good investment. And don't overlook regional magazines for your area, such as *Los Angeles* magazine, *Palm Beach Life,* and *New York* magazine. Some carry book reviews, but even better, many give special feature consideration to local authors.

Just because the small independent newspapers don't publish reviews, don't think you can afford to ignore this potential harvest. They, too, can be of assistance to your campaign. Alert them to newsworthy activities. And don't overlook the college press. These bright young reporters may give you valuable space. Press releases to hometown papers about author tours filter into coverage in columns or feature stories. You might even consider contacting the media in any town where you've previously lived.

One of the best ways to get into the news is to hitchhike with another item of current interest. Perhaps your book solves a problem that has just hit the headlines. Such was the case of one clever author who had written a book on how to stop snoring. One day his newspaper vigil uncovered an obscure two-liner about a pending divorce. It seems the poor harried wife could no longer tolerate her snoring spouse. The dispatch, to the presiding judge, of a long-distance call, a couple of bottles of booze, and an airmailed book resulted in a front-page spread with pictures. The judge was said to feel that this book could save the marriage. Picked up by the wire services, the word spread swiftly and the book went into four editions. This is one story of many that confirm the value of a "news peg" and the hitchhiking principle.

Don't forget the wire services. Should you be fortunate enough to lock into one of them, your book could skyrocket to stardom virtually overnight. If you live in a major city, check the phone book for local editorial offices. Otherwise, write the Associated Press (AP) at 50 Rockefeller Plaza, New York, NY 10020; United Press International (UPI) at 16th Floor, 5 Penn Plaza, New York, NY 10001; and Reuters at 1700 Broadway, New York, NY 10019.

To add verve and flair to your promotional campaign, you might again consult *Chase's Annual Events* to see if there is a special day, week, or month you can hitchhike with. Got a book on raising turkeys? Don't overlook April 9. That's the date of a Wild Turkey Drive in Kirksville, Missouri—and that's just the sort of kooky thing the wire services pick up. Have you written a novel with a protagonist who is addicted to scuba diving? Perhaps you can tie in with National Scuba Diving Week, August 12 to 18.

Interviews

Another way to increase your newspaper coverage is the author interview feature story. The book review pages are only one place to gain exposure.

Such areas as the "Life-style" or "Trends" sections, known in the old days as the "women's pages," is another good bet. Other more specialized sections (Business, Religion, Sports) may also welcome you, depending on the subject of your book. Notice the reprint of an article which appeared in the *San Diego Union*. We appealed to the film critic on behalf of our client, Charles Shows, who had written a book called *Walt: Backstage Adventures with Walt Disney*. Frankly, you're usually better off in special sections if you have a general consumer title. It takes a true book-lover to digest the book review pages, but all kinds of folks read the other sections. Gardeners, for instance, will have their noses buried (no pun intended) in the gardening section, but would seldom discover your book on organic gardening if it were only promoted in the book section.

Surely you have looked with awe and maybe envy at full-page

The San Diego Union

SAN DIEGO, CALIFORNIA, WEDNESDAY MORNING, FEBRUARY 6, 1980

Writer Recalls His 'True Side'

Life With Walt Disney: An Uncanny Touch

By CAROL OLTEN
Film Critic, The San Diego Union

When Charles Shows first went to work at Disney Studios in 1954 he was dispatched to Tomorrowland, an assignment by the late Walt Disney that still baffles him. Shows was a comedy writer, a gourmet of the gag. Did Disney think the future was going to be funny? Why an assignment in Tomorrowland instead of Frontierland or Fantasyland or Adventureland — other areas of big, new development in Disney's planned ABC network television show called "Disneyland"?

But, Shows recalled the other day, there he was, in a nirvana inside the studio's animation building, an elaborate suite of offices proudly labeled "Tomorrowland." Disney and about two dozen animators, writers and production chiefs were gathered with story boards enthusiastically discussing their first project for the futuristic world. But the subject was not space, robots or intergalactic travel. It was of man's future with the wheel.

"Disney asked me what I thought of the idea," Shows said. "I told him it was lousy, that any idiot could see the future was space. But as soon as I said that I thought, boy, this is it. I'll be fired the first day. Disney said, 'Well, what's your idea?' For some reason I had a Life magazine under my arm and the cover was a drawing of Wernher von Braun's moon rocket. Disney read the whole article while everybody waited. When he finished, he was like a child who had found a wonderful new toy."

Shows was assigned to write and illustrate three stories for Tomorrowland based on man's space explorations — a project that was to include von Braun in-residence at the studios as a technical adviser. It proved the first of many projects he was to work on during the decade that came to be known as the Golden Age of Disney. He recounts those experiences in a new book, "Walt: Backstage Adventures With Walt Disney," being distributed locally by Communication Creativity of La Jolla.

"I didn't set out to do a hatchet job on Walt," Shows said, "but I believe there is an actual, true side of Disney for the world to know. Two previous books on Disney both were slanted by the studio and neither writer really knew the man. My book may get a little silly but I think it still has Disney coming through."

Shows discusses Disney's penchant for spur-of-the-moment hiring and firing of animators and directors, his prudish production standards as well as a dogged dedication to perfection, his distrust of unions, and his insistence on frugal operation even though he casually would toss a million dollars out the door to reshoot a scene for no seeming reason. He also talks about Disney's lifetime infatuation with his first and foremost invention — Mickey Mouse. The mouse, for instance, not only was emblazoned on every studio truck, stationary, memo pad, calendar and clock. But it also was imprinted on every employee paycheck.

"I think," Shows said, "the reason Walt was always so concerned about Mickey is that he lost Oswald the Rabbit. He created the rabbit character before Mickey and didn't know very much about copyrights. A distributor stole the rabbit and it was like Walt had lost one of his children. He was bitter and wanted to make sure nothing like that happened to the mouse. It represented his success and I believe he honestly thought that if he lost the mouse, everything he had created would bomb.

"Disney liked to have absolute control over everything going on in the studios. He would look in wastebaskets to see what kinds of ideas the writers threw out to be sure the wrong ideas were not being tossed away. He couldn't really write or draw himself, but he had an uncanny sense of story. He could look at the Bible and tell you where the flaws were. The Disney touch was that he couldn't have a rabbit chasing a squirrel without a little limp on the rabbit and, honest to God, it was these details that made everything come to life."

CHARLES SHOWS
. . . tells of
'absolute control'

Shows worked as a writer and, later, in areas of directing and producing when Disney's focus was on features such as "20,000 Leagues Under the Sea." The era also saw heavy Disney involvement in true-life adventures, an entry into the fledgling medium of television and the birth of the first child of the empire — Disneyland.

Shows refers to the period as "Christmas morning, Mardi Gras, Alice in Wonderland, a three-ring circus and open house at an insane asylum — all at the same time."

"It was Disney's idea that everybody was at the studio to make pictures, not money," Shows said. "If you were talented, Walt liked you and in some cases tolerated bad habits. But he liked yes men around him, too, that never challenged him. He kept control by two things. First, everybody was afraid of him and afraid of being fired. Second, he seemed like everybody's father and kept personal relationships with his employees even though there were about 3,000 at the time. He'd call you a dumb bastard one day and, maybe, the next meet you in the hall and want to go to lunch."

When Shows' Tomorrowland project met with success, he was quickly pigeonholed, he said, as the resident expert on the scientific future. "The next thing I got put on . . . was atomic energy," he said. "I wrestled with atoms for a full year and began to wonder what's a guy who used to write about seasick sea serpents doing here. Finally, I wrote an outline for a story — 104 pages. Walt sent it back and said he wouldn't read anything over two pages. He was the kind of guy who would have insisted 'Gone With the Wind' be written on a postcard."

Shows was hired by the Disney Studios after "Time for Beany," the early television series which he wrote and directed, skyrocketed in the ratings. He had developed "Beany" on a lark and a bet that the show wouldn't last two days.

"I had been writing a television show called 'Speaking of Animals,'" he recalled. "Another fellow came to me with this character named Beany. He wanted funny stuff and Beany talking back and forth with other characters

like 'Kukla, Fran and Ollie.' I started writing real smart aleck stuff and ended up with a complete, 15-minute story every night with little cliffhanger endings. It swept the town."

"Beany" also won an Emmy Award but Shows didn't make any money. In the razzle-dazzle days of early television, he said, "I was always signing my stupid name in the wrong places." Shows also wrote and made a pilot called "Don't Be a Sucker." Later, he said, it was swiped out from under him and became the immensely popular "Racket Squad." Similar circumstances developed with "Bozo the Clown." "I wrote 104 of those things and was so stupid I gave them away," he said.

Shows has no real vengeance, however. He is now at work on a book about the wonderful days of early television. It was a time, he said, of much promise. "I'm not a snob or an intellectual, but right now," he concluded, "it's all plain garbage. The game shows are so stupid that a man guesses his wife's correct birthday and the audience screams like we've just won World War III. Watching clothes tumbling in a dryer is better entertainment than the soap operas and the newsmen are all in show business.

"But, you know, I came out here from El Paso in a 1934 Ford, broke, determined (television) was the greatest invention of all and that I'd make a million. I never made the million but I still think that it's the greatest invention. Disney must have thought so, too, because he used it and made Disneyland a household word around the whole nation."

5644 La Jolla Boulevard,
La Jolla, California 92037

Sample book review.

spreads about authors and their books, complete with numerous photographs. Worth a lot? Bet your sweet bippy it is! Don't buy into the idea that only famous best-selling authors get that kind of coverage. 'Tain't so.

William Zimmerman would testify to that. He's had spreads in the *Washington Post, Business Week,* and the *New York Times.* Zimmerman, founder of Guarionex Press, which published his *How to Tape Instant Biographies,* comments, "I've shown how you can leverage no money and gain a lot of national attention and sales." The *Times* feature about him prompted two thousand inquiries replete with countless orders for his book.

Plan your publicity for the print media to coincide with the publication date of your book. Let the press know you will be available for interviews during this period of time. Oh yes, there is definitely a technique for letting the press know! Here is one that has proven extremely successful for us. Create an "Available for Interview" announcement. This needs to be a power-packed fact sheet about the book and the author. Ideally, this package should go out under a name other than your own, such as your ad agency pseudonym. This makes it more credible when the book and author are lauded.

Take a look at the example. Now start brainstorming. Focus clearly on your book's premise. Think of as many short punchy zingers about the book as possible. Cover the "what" and "why" thoroughly. Boil down your ideas, combining and eliminating, until you have five or six strong points. Don't forget the material on your book cover as a resource.

Now let's work on promoting the author. You're an expert . . . you wrote the book . . . so let's establish that fact beyond doubt. As you can see, half of the grabbers about the author feature subject and writing qualifications and credits. Give a strong logical reason why the author wrote this book. Go through the same exercise for pruning your "about the author" comments into their most productive form as you did for the book. Brainstorm, write a bunch, cut, condense, improve—until five or six emerge as the pick of the crop.

This kind of media kit, which included a news release and the dust jacket promotion piece and flaps, produced as many as seven interviews in one day during our *Creative Loafing* tour. That was almost too much, even for Marilyn. We suggest that four or five per day produce less stress and better interviews.

Be sure to get the Available for Interview material to editors in plenty of time to accommodate their scheduling. (And be sure to indicate specific dates you are available even if it's only going to your hometown paper.) For newspapers and weekly magazines allow four to six weeks minimum. Three to four months is a normal lead time for monthly periodicals. Allow a couple of weeks for your information to filter down to the proper desk, then follow up by phone. Find out if the package was received and the reaction. In the case of newspapers, if the recipient doesn't exhibit much enthusiasm, ask if he or she could suggest a reporter in another department who might find the information more appropriate. Then you can contact the new person, say that so-and-so suggested you call, and go into your spiel. Interested editors will request a copy of your book.

With some imaginative PR and a little persistence you should fill your interview calendar nicely. Keep control cards on which you record all pertinent information. In particular, note if a book is sent. That way you will be able to anticipate what depth the interview may take. Don't be surprised, however, if the interviewer hasn't read your book. Such is the case about half the time. And don't overlook the possible advantage of inviting an editor to be your guest at breakfast or lunch. This may be just the touch that convinces him or her to interview you. Besides, if you keep a detailed calendar and keep all receipts, such lunches are deductible. There may be, as the proverb says, no such thing as a free lunch, but a profitable lunch you don't even end up paying for comes pretty close!

We can't emphasize enough the value of media exposure. You get a twofold benefit from print features: First, you get space that would cost thousands of dollars if you had to buy it. Second, most of what is printed becomes quotable support material which can be used as sales aids and promotional literature. Reprints of uncopyrighted articles can be used to develop direct-mail promotion and to convince radio or TV producers that yours is a dynamite story.

Generating radio and television interviews

You are unique indeed if, at some time in your life, you have not visualized yourself as an idol of the silver screen or its smaller sister, TV. Some of you may have even accompanied Captain Midnight or the Lone Ranger in their daring capers across the radio waves. Well, your time has arrived. Come along now and let's make you a star!

Putting together a radio and television promotion campaign is much the same as dealing with print media. In fact, we can use the identical "Available for Interview" promo package. Be aware of one difference, however. In electronic media, formats and personnel change like bed linen. It's a pressure-cooker world, making radio and TV mobile career fields. As personalities move on, often the shows they chaired change with them.

Timing can also have bearing on your success. Television networks conduct regular rating sweeps in February, April, and November. These are *bad* times for you. The local program producers will be seeking blockbuster guests to pull in greater viewing audiences and boost their ratings.

Television, being the most prestigious of promotional media, many times presents the largest challenge to your imaginative publicity cam-

COMMUNICATION
CREATIVITY
a colorado corporation

Lisa Wells
Contact: (303)655-2504

AVAILABLE FOR INTERVIEW   T O M & M A R I L Y N R O S S
Publishing consultants and authors of The Encyclopedia of Self-Publishing

ABOUT THE PUBLISHING INDUSTRY:
. "Me-ism" gives way to "we-ism"...the 80's bring new trends in what people will
  be reading.
. Conglomerate takeovers and mergers are squeezing out talented but unknown
  writers and threatening the very quality of American literature.
. Blockbuster books like Judith Kranz's Princess Daisy scoop up $3.2 million for
  paperback reprint rights...typically enough to purchase about 60 novels.
. Subsidy "no-win publishing" traps exposed...the leading subsidy (vanity)
  publisher admits only a fraction of the money authors hand over to print their
  books is ever recovered.
. More and more people are deciding to capitalize on their special knowledge by
  writing a book; then doning the entrepreneur's hat and publishing it themselves.
. Exploring behind-the-scenes in self-publishing. Some current, privately
  published success stories include:

    How to Flatten Your Stomach--1,000,000 copies in print; it's been on the best
    seller list for almost a year.
    Carla Emery's Old Fashioned Recipe Book--After selling 70,000 copies herself,
    Carla auctioned the paperback rights to Bantam for a cool $115,000.
    The Lazy Man's Way to Riches--Over 700,000 copies sold through mail order at
    $10 each--and it costs Joe Karbo a mere 50¢ each to print them.

ABOUT THE ROSSES:
. Nationally recognized contemporary leaders in the self-publishing movement.
. Pioneers in offering help to others, they are the founders of About Books,
  Inc., a writing, publishing, and consulting firm located in Saguache, Colorado.
. Professional speakers who also present "How to Successfully Self-Publish Your
  Book" seminars nationwide. They have appeared on radio and TV shows across the
  country and been featured in major newspapers and national magazines.
. Authors of The Encyclopedia of Self-Publishing. Its 75 sections cover all
  aspects of how to write, publish, promote, and sell your own work. After being
  out for only six months, this book has already gone into a second printing and
  been awarded the top prize for non-fiction books by the California Press Women.
. MARILYN ROSS is a prize-winning author of four books, as well as a dynamic
  lecturer. She heads her own publishing company--an outgrowth of her self-
  publishing accomplishments. Marilyn is a member of the Author's Guild, the
  National Federation of Press Women and the National Speakers Association and is
  listed in Contemporary Authors and the World Who's Who of Women. She offers
  articulate, enthusiastic and knowledgeable comments for the media.
. TOM ROSS is president of About Books, Inc., a writing and publishing consulting
  service that also specializes in book and author publicity. He is an editor,
  an author, and has masterminded nationwide promotional and sales campaigns.
  Tom is a member of the National Speakers Association and the International
  Platform Association and is listed in Who's Who in the West. He shares
  interesting, revealing and authoritative observations on all phases of the
  publishing industry.

415 Fourth Street, P.O. Box 213, Saguache, Colorado 81149-0213   303-655-2504

Interview form.

paign. Always contact TV stations in main metropolitan areas at least eight weeks before your availability date. Major network shows will require even longer lead times. Call the producer's office to find out how far ahead their guests are booked, and ask the name of the producer or guest coordinator. Again the same Available for Interview package will serve nicely as a door opener. Add copies of any good press you have received. We recommend both the front- and back-door approaches to television in the big cities, meaning you send one package to the general program director and another to the producer of any specific show that you wish to be on. Of course, both should be followed up if you haven't heard anything in a couple of weeks. As with all promotion, tenacity and repetition often turn the key.

Radio programming is not normally scheduled as far in advance as television, so your mailings can go out as little as four weeks in advance. We found results were better, however, with six to eight weeks advance mailings. Your material should be addressed to the producer of an individual show or, if you're in doubt which show would be best, the station program director. After a couple of weeks follow up by phone. Be politely persistent.

As soon as you've made contact with the proper person, start keeping notes on your Media Control Card (see sample). This will be of immense help in preparing for the interview. Think about the subject matter of your book and how it could be made interesting to television audiences. Offer any suggestions to vary the normal interview format. One author we represented, who had done a book on nutrition, prepared a food demonstration on the air. If you've written a book about camping and hiking, you might give a demo on how to pack a backpack. Written a how-to book on flower arranging? It's a natural for a demonstration.

After the interview is scheduled, ask questions. Find out what they want to cover. Suggest areas that "your author" wants to touch on. You may get insights into the personality of the host or hostess and some hint as to the slant needed to put yourself and your book in the best light. A comprehensive book on the subject is *Getting Your Message Out*, by Michael M. Klepper. It tells how to get, use, and survive radio and television airtime.

If the thought of being grilled by a TV interviewer scares your socks off, don't be dismayed. This is common with many of the authors we've worked with. The world of television — studios behind closed doors, cameras, bright lights, people rushing everywhere — is foreign to most people. (One way to become more at ease is to muster up your bravado and join Toastmasters.) Watching the shows you'll be on gives you a higher comfort level, as you know more what to expect. Role-playing with friends and family is also excellent training.

By having in mind a clearly defined agenda you wish to explore, you'll cut through apprehension like a hot knife through butter. Make specific notes of the points you want to cover. Some people even go so far as to type out a list of questions to provide interviewers. Anticipate in advance the questions you're likely to get, and don't dodge the difficult ones. Then you won't be surprised when you're thrown a "zinger." Train yourself to expect the unexpected. Remember, you're the expert. You know your subject backward and forward. Rehearse your answers and comments to build your self-confidence. The key to successful interviewing is organization; it's what keeps you focused. Want to know exactly how you'll look and sound? Use a VCR or a mirror and tape recorder.

City _____   Date _____

MEDIA CONTROL CARD

Name of show _____

Interview day/date _____ Arrival time _____

Station/publication _____

Phone ( ) _____

Mailing Address _____

City/state/zip _____

Studio address (if different) _____

Producer/guest coordinator _____

Host/hostess _____

Live or taped? _____ Air date/time _____

Format _____ Length _____

Interview confirmation date _____

Visuals/props needed _____

Comments:

Date thank you sent: _____

Media control card.

When dressing for TV, avoid distracting plaids and busy stripes. Keep it simple. Women shouldn't wear glittering or jangly jewelry. Take your notes, any visuals you plan to use, two copies of the book, and a duplicate promo package along. Plan to arrive about a half hour early. Ask someone for a glass of water if you feel tense. Take several big breaths. Before airtime study your notes, psyche out probable questions, and rehearse your answers. Most times, you will be the better prepared of the two of you.

With this kind of preparation you're bound to have a good interviewing "presence." This is the quality every TV person wants: someone who is relaxed but not sloppy; informed but not overbearing; vivacious but not silly. During the actual interview ignore the camera and crew. Concentrate your attention on the person interviewing you. Resist the urge to fiddle with the mike, a handkerchief, or any other object. Keep your voice lively and assured. Smile, be friendly and enthusiastic.

Be sure to speak in human terms; don't get mired in a bunch of statistics. Brief, clipped, precise answers are better than rambling replies. Suppose you get a question that requires you to pause and gather your thoughts? Don't panic. A good trick we've used to stall for think time is either to repeat the query or to say, "That's a good question." Reply positively to negative questions. Explain what your book is—not what it is not. Mention the title instead of referring to your work as "it" or "the book." And be ready to plug your book if the host or hostess happens to forget. If you're doing a seminar or appearing to autograph books, mention this. "Show and tell" goes on in broadcasting as well as in kindergarten.

Some stations will flash information on the screen if you've made prior arrangements for your address or phone number to be shown. The words trail along the bottom of the screen and reinforce what you say.

After the interview there's still one vital detail to handle. If you made a good impression, the audience is going to want to know where to buy your book and how to contact you. Be sure you've brought several cards telling all ordering information about the book—including which local stores stock it, as well as mail-order particulars—and how to reach you. One of these cards should be left with the host or hostess, one with the talent coordinator or producer, and one with the station's switchboard operator. Some broadcasters have information centers that handle inquiries. Ask if this station has such a thing, and be sure they know where your book can be purchased. It is a nice touch to send a thank-you note to the producer and the interviewer. You may want their cooperation again soon and this will help them remember you.

And we hasten to add that the things we're discussing here are not the sole domain of the self-publisher. Every author can—and should—

become involved in the promotion of his or her book. It can make all the difference.

Take Callan Pinckney, for instance. In 1984, her *Callanetics* was launched by Morrow. It sold a respectable 10,000 copies, then went back to press for another 5,000. But interest waned and books went unsold. Not one to give up easily, Pinckney arranged media visits to southern cities, then wangled her way onto a Chicago television show. Within an hour of her appearance, Kroch's & Brentano's received some 400 orders. That was the firing pin that catapulted her book into best-seller status. Recently, with 182,000 copies in print, the paperback rights were sold to Avon for a reported $187,000 guarantee—all because an author took an interest in her own book.

Radio

Radio shows come in several types, and hosts come in various degrees of preparedness. Some interviewers will not have bothered to read the book and will depend strictly on you and the cover blurbs. Others pride themselves on being up on their subject and will chat at length about specific passages in the book. Most of the same tips we offered earlier work for radio. The one thing to remember is that your voice must do all the work. A smile is important; it *does* carry over a microphone.

Several cases come to mind where the host or hostess was so high on *Creative Loafing* that the whole program became a fantastic third-party endorsement of the book—just one long commercial from an enthusiastic radio personality. Imagine for a moment what a *thirty-minute* commercial is worth. But it didn't cost one red cent! The beauty of publicity demonstrated again.

The most effective radio programs are interview shows and news features. Early morning and late afternoon drive times—when folks are traveling to and from work—are probably the first choice, with midday programs being good for some audiences. Of course, a lot depends on the host. Some have tremendous listening audiences even during bad hours because they are talented, dynamic people.

While we're talking about radio, there is another option available if you shudder at trotting from station to station to "do your thing." Many radio programs will interview you via long-distance phone call. This is a great way to get national exposure for literally pennies. Most of the media directories previously mentioned state whether specific shows do phone interviews. We cover this subject extensively in our new title, *Marketing Your Book: A Collection of Profit-Making Ideas for Authors and Publishers*.

Many newsletters have come into being since the first edition of this guide. For a fee they advertise authors for telephone interviews. Yes, they can get you some interviews—but they're usually in very obscure places with tiny listening audiences. In our opinion, these ads are generally not worth your investment.

One other aspect of radio that could be very meaningful to some of you is public service announcements, better known as PSAs. If you are a nonprofit organization—via structure, not happenstance—you are eligible for *free* airtime. This is a terrific boon to churches with cookbooks to peddle and nonprofit associations that have produced books about their aims. The Federal Communications Commission says that all stations must allocate a certain portion of their time to these PSAs. What they usually amount to is unpaid commercials. This free time goes to those bold enough to seek it. So if you qualify, get in there and get your share!

Getting on the news

One thing in television that should not be underestimated is the power of a short news spot. Today there are more outlets for broadcast news than ever before. News seems to fall into two types: "hard," which covers matters of local, national, and international consequence; and "soft," the kinds of human-interest features that people find fascinating. An author is more likely to capture the latter. As we discussed earlier, you can also "use news to make news" by packaging your subject matter with something else of current note. Perhaps you can create some news. Can you do a survey or study on a topic of timely interest that relates to your book? Are you a featured speaker at a convention or trade show? Have you received an award? All of these things can be catapulted into news stories for the media.

News time is precious time. Learn to zero in on the essence of your story quickly. You may only have seventy-five to ninety seconds in which to pack your punch. But think of all the thirty- and sixty-second commercials that sell millions of dollars' worth of products and services each year. (And the sponsors have to pay for those.)

We were once booked for a taped news slot on a popular station in Phoenix. Because we were usually well on our way to the next stop, or because the programs were live, we typically missed seeing them. So imagine our surprise when we walked into our hotel room, flipped on the TV, and heard the anchorman say that they would be talking about *Creative Loafing* later. Then a full-screen shot of the book appeared. Needless to say, we were glued to the set, afraid to blink for fear we would miss the anticipated few-seconds spot.

What transpired left us a little breathless. A thirty-second clip from the prerecorded fifteen-minute interview had Marilyn introduce the subject and the book. Then for five minutes we were entranced by film clips from the station's news file showing people participating in many of the activities suggested as pastimes in the book. These were interspersed with narrated close-ups of the front cover. Another thirty seconds of Marilyn's prerecorded interview closed the segment.

Six minutes of prime TV time, including a long plug by a local news celebrity. Who could have guessed that such a gem would be aired on the six o'clock news on the most popular network TV station in town? Do you have any idea of the value of such exposure? We don't know of many publishers who could afford to buy that kind of coverage. The great equalizer struck! And it can strike for you, too.

Our point, of course, is that a minute or two of prime-time news coverage can have greater impact than a half-hour midmorning talk show. We believe, however, that any TV coverage can have significant impact on bookstore managers' purchasing decisions. We book 'em all. Since TV is so influential, competition for available time is fierce — especially with all the celebrity authors out stumping these days. With imagination, a creative approach, and tenacity, you should be able to land some shows.

Going national

Television guest coordinators and producers of large national shows are understandably particular about the interviewees they schedule. TV producers are responsible for the show's ratings and will only book people they are convinced will be interesting to viewers. Not willing to take as big a gamble as the smaller shows, they will be extremely interested in your past appearances on radio and television. Sharing your experience with them will be necessary if you hope to land any bookings. One of the best ways to do this is to buy a videotape of previous good performances. This can be arranged with the production staff at the close of an interview.

As you work with major media in the large markets, another dimension may be added. You may be asked for an exclusive. That means you will appear on that television show, that radio station, or in that paper *only*. Don't take exclusivity lightly. Be sure what you're getting is worth the concession. Look at such things as audience size or circulation, prime-time exposure, the prestige of the program or paper, and the enthusiasm of the people involved. Then be grateful they feel you are important enough to warrant such a request.

Don't expect to start out with *Oprah* or *Donahue*. You must prove yourself first.

Get several important local interviews under your belt before tackling a major network show. You will find that once you have booked a major program, the rest are much easier. Here again, start at home and fan out according to the appeal of your book and the availability of travel funds. Use the news peg idea to open doors. If you piggyback on a hot news item, you will find tight schedules can get shifted to make way for airing timely items quickly.

Of course, the other ingredient needed for any successful media campaign is to get books into the stores. Beverly Nye, whom you met in Chapter 1, was being interviewed on *Morning Exchange* where she showed a copy of her book. Before the program was aired, she scanned the yellow pages under "Book Dealers—Retail" to gather a list of sales outlets. She organized them by area, called to learn the names of buyers, then hit the streets. She and her son peddled a lot of books—in threes and fives and sometimes tens. The day after she hit the airwaves, Cleveland, Ohio, was in a turmoil. Walden's on the West Side sold a thousand books. Customers kept coming in and requesting *A Family Raised on Sunshine* for weeks afterward.

Beverly Nye took to the media—and they to her—like the proverbial duck to water. A year later she had her own syndicated radio series on which she gave homemaking tips. Radio stations across the country carried her sixty-five-show package, paid her royalties, and plugged her books. By now she had written *A Family Raised on Rainbows*. Of course, not all of us feel about a camera and a microphone as Beverly does.

Fortunately there is a service dubbed Book Call that offers nationwide distribution to support author interviews and tours. They maintain an 800 number customers can call for ordering. You simply give that number during the interview; Book Call does the rest. For details, write them at 59 Elm Street, New Canaan, CT 06840.

Creative promotional vehicles

For self-publishers with budgets tighter than shrink-to-fit jeans, there are several intriguing ways to stir the publicity pot. None of these cost more than money for postage or gasoline, yet they can yield dramatic results.

One idea is to provide magazines with "freebie" chapters (although you should be aware that this could detract from subsidiary rights revenue). Editors are always interested in receiving well-written pieces relevant to their publication's audience—especially if they don't have to pay for them. Be sure to study the magazine or newsletter format. Look for such things as the length of pieces, whether they use an anecdotal approach and whether their style is casual or formal, elementary or sophisticated. In your cover letter indicate that you have written a book and are willing to provide selected chapters without any cost to them. Include some of your promotional materials so they can taste the flavor of your message. Also state that at the end of the excerpt you would like a reference to the book and a mention of where it can be purchased.

If your book is on a computer, you can go one better. Take a chapter, alter it slightly, toss in an introduction, plop on a little conclusion—and you have a fresh article.

If you don't want to turn over actual parts of your book, why not write a short piece on the subject in general? We did this about self-publishing for *Southwest Airlines Magazine, Toastmaster Magazine,* the Women in Communication trade journal, and several others. Of course, we always insisted on an editor's note that gave specific ordering information for our book.

We've had good luck using Letters to the Editor in strategic publications. (You do subscribe to the trade journals relevant to your publishing subject area, don't you?) When *PW* columnist Lisa See talked about reissues of regional titles in her "West Watch" of April 24, 1987, we took this as an invitation to promote our *How to Make Big Profits Publishing City & Regional Books.* Marilyn's Letter to the Editor ran a full column and talked about doing *new* area books, of course mentioning our title in the process. We were able to directly trace several orders to this source.

Developing a support system of your peers also makes sense. Networking with other authors and small publishers provides mental stimulation and emotional comfort. Find a club or association in your area or organize one if none exists. The collective promotional ideas will amaze you. You may also find someone willing to serve as an informal mentor, guiding you toward greater heights in this exciting venture.

Capitalizing on contacts is a surefire way to expand awareness of your book. Be sure to alert all friends, relatives, acquaintances, and business associates about your "new baby." They may know someone who produces a local TV show or be able to put you in touch with an organization that would be interested in making bulk purchases. But don't stop there. Tell the main newspaper in the city of your birth that a native son or daughter made good. If your parents, children, or brothers and sisters have influence in their hometown, see if you can ride on their names to get mention in a newspaper column or maybe even a feature story by telephone.

Anything you can do to get people talking about your book is like money in the bank. The most baffling and elusive element in a book's success is word-of-mouth. Statistics form a Gallup poll bring this point quickly into focus: When asked why they bought fiction, 4 percent of the respondents said it was because of ads in magazines and newspapers; book reviews fared only slightly better. By contrast, 27 percent bought because they were familiar with the author and 26 percent because a friend or relative recommended the book. Powerful testimony to word-of-mouth. Said the former president of B. Dalton in an interview in the *New York Times*, "I would probably rate the most effective techniques for selling books as being the individual telling a friend, reviews, and the author's ability to appear on talk shows."

Sometimes you can turn adversity into opportunity. When the Wall Street crash struck in October of 1987, the financial community mourned the loss of a fortune. Meanwhile, the publishing community dreamed of a fortune to be made. Publishers across the land reached into their back-lists and dusted off titles having to do with the stock market and investing. Headlines capitalized on the crash. Simon & Schuster's new ad campaign shouted, "Brilliantly plausible . . . Horrendously disturbing . . . and starting to come true." It's the old story: if life gives you a lemon, make lemonade!

There's yet another way you can creatively merchandise your book. How about trading it for things you want? Many small publishers barter with each other. Perhaps someone has published a book, newsletter, or magazine you would enjoy. Offer to exchange a copy of your book for theirs. This can even be carried further to bartering for small items or services.

Look around for other possibilities. If you or your spouse is employed in a large company, it may have a newsletter that mentions employee happenings. (If you have written your book while working for someone else, be sure the boss knows of this accomplishment and that mention of it lands in your personnel file.) Your college alumni newspaper is another place for publicity. And don't overlook any associations or organizations to which you belong. The more times your name and the name of your book get in print, the better.

There is another way to use the printed word. How about testimonials? These are fan letters you receive or comments that people make about your book. Letters from readers will become one of your most priceless treasures. There is nothing like knowing that your book significantly contributed to the life of another person. These devoted fans are usually delighted you would want to use their letters. When we asked Gabrielle Maynis for permission to reprint her letter, she was very pleased, as was Terri Pare.

We felt good recently to get a note from Charles Shows, for whom we did a book in 1979. He wrote to tell us he's had literally hundreds of letters from folks saying his book was the most enjoyable and fun to read book ever. Charles told us of selling copies in Helsinki, Finland, and being interviewed by phone on BBC London and Australia.

Of course, you don't have to meekly wait for such lovely accolades. You can solicit them! Whenever someone tells you he or she enjoyed your book, or pens a brief note, capitalize on it. Make up a form similar to the following example, explaining that you are interested in using comments from satisfied readers to tell others about this new book. To encourage a high return, include a SASE. We have used this system with great success, gaining "quotable quotes" from television personalities, legislators, doctors, journalists, and educators.

To corral even more exposure, launch your book with a special publication date splash. One way to do this is to create an event that is newsworthy. For instance, if your book is about photography, schedule an exhibition to coincide with the publication date and invite cultural editors from the local press.

Or you might team up with a local worthy cause as we did. We introduced *Creative Loafing* by putting on a fund-raiser for the Aerospace Museum and Hall of Fame Recovery Fund in San Diego. It was called (appropriately enough) "Creative Loafing Days." This gala event was a weekend in Balboa Park during which activities in the book were depicted. We had jousting matches, magic shows, a frog-jumping jamboree, poetry readings, fiddlers, archery demonstrations, fencing, puppet shows, and more.

Since we were working with a nonprofit organization, free radio public service announcements were available to us and we got coverage in many local newspapers — not to mention landing on the evening news of all three network TV stations! It was a tremendous amount of work, but the net result was a $5,000 donation to the Aerospace Museum and good, local name identification for our book.

Poets and novelists can create their own artistic events. Be aware of local anniversaries and special celebrations with themes around which you can plan something. The trick is to work far in advance. Talk with your Chamber of Commerce or visitors' and convention bureau to keep abreast of upcoming things that might offer a showcase for your talents. Do not, however, let the effort involved in coordinating such activities consume you.

Another way to draw attention to yourself is to sponsor an award that ties in with your title. You get free publicity when you announce the contest and again when you declare the winner(s). In addition, it's a fun and legitimate way to educate people about your subject.

A few years ago, we decided to sponsor an annual award to encourage quality and acknowledge excellence in the field of self-publishing. Entries are judged on overall design, content, and performance in the marketplace. We're pleased to report that the books look better and better each year. If you'd like an official entry form for The Most Outstanding Self-Published Book Award, write us at About Books, Inc., "Award," Box 1500, Buena Vista, CO 81211.

Major trade publishers occasionally use gimmicks to draw attention to their wares. Here are two recent — and unique — examples. Maybe these

August 7, 1978

Dear Marilyn Ross:

Since I read your book ''Creative Loafing'' when I was typesetting
it, I told myself I had to find time to write to you with congratu-
lations and appreciation for writing such a great book.
It is wonderful and is certainly going to bring much joy to
a lot of people. Thank you for caring so much!
Your book is full of enthusiasm and hope foreverybody, young
and not-so-young. I want to buy a copy as soon as the books
are available to the public. We want to go to all the
marvelous places that you described in your book and do
so many enjoyable things. It opens so many horizons!
 I already started our garden with all kinds of vegetables
and m seven-year-old is after me all the time so I'd take
him to the museum in San Diego ''where they have clouds
on a room.'' We certainly are going to go to the Reuben
H. Fleet Space Theater and Science Ctr. before the summer
is over.
I think that your book is the best gift than anybody
can ever receive and I'm planning to give it to my
friends for their birthdays, as many of them are
housewives who have even more free time than I.
Thank you again for alll the time, love and care
that you put on those pages; much happiness will
come from it to so many people!

                         Respectfully yours,

                         Gabrielle Maymir

Fan letters.

STATE OF RHODE ISLAND AND PROVIDENCE PLANTATIONS

DEPARTMENT OF ELDERLY AFFAIRS
150 Washington Street
Providence, R. I. 02903
(401) 277-2858

October 3, 1978

Ms. Elizabeth Thurlow
Communication Creativity
1340 Tourmaline Street
San Diego, Ca. 92109

Dear Ms. Thurlow,

I have just finished reading a review/examination copy of
"Creative Loafing, A Shoestring Guide to New Leisure Fun"
and I can't tell you how much I enjoyed it! Our Legislative
Liaison, Jackie Wolf, shared it with me and am I glad she did!

Since I'm the Retirement Planner for the Department of Elderly
Affairs I feel the book can be a terrific resource in our
Pre-Retirement Planning Programs, especially in the session
concerning meaningful use of time.

Additionally, we are planning our biennial Governor's Conference
and we are considering having a workshop on creative loafing.
Nothing like this has been done before and I'm sure it will
stimulate a great deal of interest.

Thank you so much for sending such a unique book to us. Ms.
Ross really has a winner!

Sincerely,

Terri Pare'

Terri Pare'
Retirement Planner

TP/adr

Dear Reader:

Thank you for your kind words about _____
We are interested in using comments from satisfied readers to tell others
about this exciting new book. May we share your views as excerpted below
with others?...Or feel free to write anything additional!

_____

_____

_____

_____

Yes, I agree that my comments may be used for national publicity and
advertising. I understand that I will not receive any payment or compensation
for this permission. My name or initials (circle your preference), as well as
the city and state in which I reside, and my occupation may also be used.

_____   NAME _____
SIGNATURE

                          ADDRESS _____

_____ _____   CITY _____
DATE   OCCUPATION

Thank you! Please return this form in   STATE/ZIP _____
the enclosed self-addressed and stamped
envelope.

NOTE: BE SURE TO INCLUDE A SASE!

Comment card.

stories will ignite a fiery idea for you. Warner Books, which put out *The Pasta Diet* in late 1984, is proving it isn't just another diet book. How? Using a "belly band," they're touting an unheard-of offer: a money-back guarantee! If book buyers don't lose ten pounds in fourteen days, Warner will refund the full purchase price.

And M. Evans, publisher of *The I-Like-My-Beer Diet* (written by a physician, yet!), gave retailers a liquid enticement. Interested booksellers were offered galleys of the book and a *free case of beer* if they were willing to test the diet. One bookseller was quick to commend Evans on this "civilized method of bribery."

These are just some ideas for developing creative promotion. No doubt you can dream up others, or adapt some of the above strategies, to give your own promotional campaign zest. In addition, there are "tried and true" methods for selling books. These are covered in the following chapter.

CHAPTER 15

STANDARD CHANNELS OF DISTRIBUTION

There are several proven methods for moving books. In the following pages we'll be investigating selling to bookstores and reaching wholesalers and distributors. We'll also explore tapping into the lucrative library market, going after educational opportunities, using sales reps, and remaindering. If your main aim in life is to see your book emblazoned on best-seller lists, then this chapter holds valuable information. These lists are compiled from sales figures reported by individual bookstores, bookstore chains, wholesalers, and distributors.

But be aware that many books which never see a best-seller list are immensely profitable. In fact, only 54 percent of book sales go through traditional bookstore channels! We'll explore the other lucrative options in Chapter 16.

Getting your books into bookstores

Bookstores base their decision on whether or not to carry a book on one question: "Will it sell?" They couldn't care less if it has great literary merit, deals with significant subject matter, or is beautifully illustrated. Of course, you've done your homework as we suggested in Chapter 2 and made sure you've chosen a salable subject and that the manuscript is well written and produced, so this shouldn't present an insurmountable obstacle. Be aware, however, they are very hesitant to deal with a one book publisher. Too much paperwork, they say.

While there are bookstores in most small towns, the major markets are New York and Southern California. Lucky you, if either of these locales is your home. Book sales are dominated by the two big chains, Waldenbooks and B. Dalton Bookseller, with more than 1,500 stores between them.

It was very distressing to learn in the May 6, 1988, issue of *PW* that Dalton has stopped buying direct from smaller publishers. The number-two chain informed some small publishing companies that if their annual volume is less than $100,000, they would have to piggyback onto a larger publisher's distribution or work through a wholesaler. The National Association of Independent Publishers reported in their newsletter that Dalton's excuse for this unprecedented freeze out is, "We're just eating away all our margin in freight." They contend that if a book gets hot, they'll order through Baker & Taylor, Ingram, or other wholesalers.

Leonard Riggio, Dalton's president and CEO, said in a letter of clarification that the change in policy was intended "to increase the opportunities for small publishers to sell our chain—not diminish them." If you can figure that one out, please let us know!

Waldenbooks, on the other hand, recently stated "We are very committed to smaller publishers and have just established a smaller publishers merchandising group to give them more attention." This group includes all but Walden's top 50 vendors, publishers like Random House and Bantam.

Although these two chains are the biggest, they are far from alone. In fact, a recent *American Book Trade Directory* lists 437 multistore bookselling chains. Some of the other large ones are Cokesbury, Little Professor, Doubleday Book Shops, and Crown. Crown is a discounter. They offer books below the normal retail price. In 1983 Crown spent more than $2.3 million to advertise "If you paid the full price you didn't buy it from Crown."

Naturally, it's the independent bookstore—usually owned and staffed by true book lovers—that feels the brunt of these cut-rate practices. But because they often cater to certain segments of book buyers—and give the kind of caring, personalized service long absent from chains—it is our hope independents will continue to thrive.

They are really the counterpart to the small-press movement—entrepreneurs who want to control their own operation and who love books. We find Denver's Tattered Cover Bookstore a delightful place. One of the three largest independents in the country, its buyers are warm and receptive to our books.

And David Unowsky of Hungry Mind in St. Paul, Minnesota, feels it's "good business to sell small-press books. I can build a market in my store for these books," he said in a *PW* article of June 24, 1988. He often holds well-publicized small-press readings and signings. Bravo for the independent booksellers!

Many of the smaller chains operate in specific geographic areas. This can be ideal for you, because their main office will be close by. We learned of one that wasn't at all close, however, and ended up selling them a quantity of a client's book, *Be Tough or Be Gone.* We discovered Alaska's Book Cache chain by reading *Publishers Weekly.* (See what gems you can pick up there.) A long-distance introductory phone call and a sample book, plus promo materials, had them hooked. You see, part of the book takes place in Alaska, so there was a definite geographic tie-in that caught the attention of Book Cache buyers.

There are two methods to catch the attention of local bookstores. The first is setting up an appointment. That way you don't arrive to find the person you must see has the day off. If, however, you prefer "cold calling" (going unannounced), plan your visit just after opening or around 3:30 P.M. These are the least busy times, and the buyer won't likely be out to lunch or dinner. Be sure to determine whom you should be talking with. Ask for the store manager or the hardcover or paperback buyer. It is useless to spend ten minutes giving your pitch to a friendly salesperson, only to learn he or she has no authority to make purchasing decisions.

You will quickly meet the comment "Oh, we can only take your books on consignment." Very tempting. We suggest you usually resist. Why? For several reasons. Put yourself in the management's position. If you have two books to sell—one of which you've already paid out hard cash to acquire, and the other you have on consignment—which one will you push? Exactly. If your books don't move, the burden to go back and pick them up is all on you. In addition, as a small-business person, you can hardly afford to have large blocks of inventory tied up unproductively. By holding a hard line on consignment we had stores end up handing over cash to purchase books. Of course, you will be expected to offer a 40 percent discount and give return privileges as noted in Chapter 5.

Another dodge you will frequently encounter when you call on a branch of one of the larger chains, such as Waldenbooks, is that individual stores aren't allowed to make purchases. "Everything must go through the central office," you'll be told. Don't necessarily believe it. Often the local manager has complete authority to purchase books independently. But it's up to you to convince the manager to exercise that authority.

How do you do this? Be prepared! One good method for developing a presentation is to put together a loose-leaf binder with such things as a copy of the dust jacket or cover, prepublication announcement, newspaper interviews, advance comments, reviews, Standard Terms and Conditions, and discount information. You might also wish to make a list of the highlights, the chief points which you think will be most effective in capturing the sale and which you want to be sure you don't forget to mention. Be sure to take along purchase order forms. The kind that comes in sets is good for this purpose because you can leave one and still have copies for your records and future billing. Go armed with extra sales literature and an adequate supply of books.

If you aren't used to selling, it's a good idea to role-play with a friend before confronting a potential buyer. Get comfortable with your sales presentation and the use of your sales aids. Buyers are especially interested in your advertising and promotional plans, since this is what will motivate people to come in and ask for the book. They are also interested in author affiliations or qualifications, if the author is a native son or daughter, and any regional or local references in the text. Experience has shown us that it works better to make your sales presentation and then offer a copy of the book. If you hand over the book as soon as you walk in, the buyer will be so busy thumbing through it, he or she won't hear what you say.

Now ask for the order. But give your prospective buyer a choice. The best choice is between something and something rather than between something and nothing. You could say, "Would you prefer to order five copies or would ten meet your needs better?" Be sure to get the purchase order number or collect the cash. If you have any point-of-purchase sales items leave them. With certain titles it also makes sense to discuss with the store manager where he or she intends to place the book. A title that principally deals with nutrition, for instance, could inadvertently be shelved with diet books, where many of those most concerned with its contents might never think to look. Better to place it in "health."

Bookstore contact card.

Follow-up is an important part of building business relationships. Make up a card similar to the adjacent sample of our Bookstore Contact Card on which pertinent information can be recorded. Do this for unsuccessful sales calls as well and remember to note the manager's reason for not buying or any other remarks. You may figure out how to overcome these objections later.

Stay in touch. Drop a note with a copy of any favorable reviews. Check back to see if the store's inventory needs replenishing. If the book is hard to find in the store, suggest how it might be displayed to better advantage.

You may want to suggest an autograph party . . . then again, if you value your time, you may not. For an unknown author, autograph sessions, at best, do little more than give an ego boost. They are a cherished idea—about as effective as hubcaps on computers—which seldom sell books. But like everything, there are exceptions. We placed a nice front-page newspaper story about one of our clients which noted he would be available to autograph copies of his book at a local bookstore. Before the session was over, the author had signed eighty books! A more normal scene is long leisurely talks with bookstore personnel, complete with embarrassed, apologetic comments about where everybody was.

Then there's the true story of a Texan who heard Jeanne Horn, author of *Hidden Treasure*, mention on the *Today* show that she would be autographing books that same afternoon at Brentano's in New York. One Dallas tycoon jumped in his private plane, flew to New York, rushed into Brentano's, and bought an autographed copy to present to his wife as a Valentine's Day gift. (On a more realistic level—for the rest of us—you might consider setting up a fund-raiser with an organization and doing a special autograph party.)

We have another idea to share with you regarding autographed copies, however. Why not personally sign several copies you leave with the store and request they put a sticker on them that says "autographed copy"? If a customer is debating between two books, they're sure to choose the autographed one. And they make nice gift items.

When working with bookstores, Lady Luck is more apt to be on your side if your contacts are made before the summer season and again in early fall. Timing is important. In the fall buyers stock up anticipating the holiday barrage of customers. June is their second busiest period, with graduation gifts, Father's Day, and summer vacation reading accounting for extra business. Is the college bookstore your target? Remember, they replenish stock just before each new term starts.

If your book is highly specialized—on becoming a born-again Christian, for example, or marble sculpting—it might be wise to look into renting a mailing list of specific stores which handle that kind of reading matter. Bowker rents lists of religious bookstores, museum and art book-stores, and outlets that specialize in metaphysics or black studies, to name a few.

Now let's weigh the advantages of going after the major bookstore chains. Once you've cracked the resistance of a chain, it's open sesame for getting books into virtually all their stores. Naturally, you can't afford the staff of salespeople that biggies like Harper & Row and Doubleday put into the field. Nor can you pay for full-page ads in *Publishers Weekly*. But you don't have to sneak into bookstores under the cover of darkness, either. You can sell to this strategic market by mail and by phone. In a recent study of a dozen chain buyers 38 percent said they learned about new titles from publishers' direct-mail promotions—certainly a vehicle available to SP-ers.

If you want to have an impact on these chains with their centralized buying power, get in front of them and stay there! Use the list of major bookstore chains we provide in the Appendix, or look in the *American Book Trade Directory* to create your own list. Send them prepublication announcements, press releases, a copy of the dust jacket (or cover), and copies of reviews or letters from strategic people. Offer a complimentary copy of the book upon request. Some small publishers have generously scattered reading copies of their books to store personnel, who got so excited about the book they became walking, talking advertisements—another example of the power of word-of-mouth. Not a bad idea for certain kinds of books.

Periodically follow up with a phone call. This is the procedure we used to court Waldenbooks. After an initial mailing we called. When that didn't do the trick, we continued to pelt them with promotional mailings. It took time, but we succeeded in getting on the microfiche, and then any store in the chain could order *Creative Loafing* simply by requesting the ISBN.

We do have some reservations about dealing with the big chains, however. Let's take a hypothetical situation. Suppose you produce a timely good-quality book and do an exceptional job of convincing a buyer from a major chain to take it on. The chain may buy several thousand copies. You're elated! You've sold all your first-print run, so you scurry back to the manufacturer and order another five or ten thousand copies. Then the world crashes in around you. The chain says the book is not moving and wants to return it. Meanwhile, they've paid you—but now expect a refund. And there is the printing bill for the second run to cope with. Get the picture? To survive in this business, the small-business person must be leery of putting all his or her eggs in one basket, especially when the basket can be upended any minute.

Today, various small publishers and associations tout mailings to bookstores. Their fees range from a couple of hundred dollars to five or six hundred (plus the cost to prepare and print your flyer or ad). The problem with such mailings is you get lost in the crowd. It's been our experience—and that of most with whom we've talked—that paying to be part of such a mailing program isn't cost-effective.

Reaching wholesalers and distributors

If you want wide distribution, wholesalers and distributors (sometimes called jobbers) must be romanced. While the terms "wholesaler" and "distributor" are frequently used interchangeably, there is a difference. Wholesalers are bigger, seldom do promotion on their own, and actually buy your book outright. Distributors work on a consignment basis, paying you for sales ninety days after they have been made. Because distributors represent fewer books, they sometimes try to influence stores and libraries on your behalf. You woo both of these groups much as you do the chain buyer. For your convenience we've included a selected list in the Appendix.

But before you seek outlets clear across the country, make sure your own backyard is tended. Check the yellow pages or call a local bookstore to find out who the local wholesaler is. Set up an appointment and do a good selling job. But don't feel you are all done when they accept your book. That doesn't mean they will push it, it simply means they will stock it. Fortunately, you can influence how well it moves.

Find out who services local accounts and stocks bookstore shelves. Then climb on your campaign wagon and let them know about your book. In our case we learned that the truck drivers for San Diego Periodical Distributors held weekly meetings at 7:30 A.M. All it took was a request and we were invited to be present at the next session. Guess who went armed with promotional materials, a convincing spiel, books, and some freebies to pass out? It's very important to PR these people, who wield much more clout than normal truck drivers. Many bookstores place great weight on their opinions and give them carte blanche to stock shelves as they see fit.

Wholesalers will want to see your Standard Terms and Conditions as well as your book. There is no sense in their getting excited about a title if you have structured your business in such a way as to make it impossible for them to do business with you. Most will expect discounts in the 40 to 50 percent range. If you live near any of them or plan to travel in the vicinity, a visit might be worthwhile. Go armed with color graphics, your complete nationwide marketing plan, your credentials as an author, your publishing company business plan, and a willingness to commit to advertising in their catalogs or other media.

Baker & Taylor

Baker & Taylor is to book sales what Colonel Sanders is to chicken. The country's oldest and largest library wholesaler, they have branches in Reno, Nevada; Momence, Illinois; Commerce, Georgia; and Somerville, New Jersey. Over the last few years they have also dramatically increased their bookstore sales. They maintain an inventory of nearly 10 million books in these four distribution centers to readily serve their vast customer base. An earlier chapter detailed how to get started working with B&T's Publisher Contact Section.

They aggressively court small publishers, sending an information kit and asking for a catalog and other background information. Also, at the ABA, they have several people who interview new publishers, and they've just added a small-press page to their *Book Alert* publication.

Creative Loafing was stocked in three of the centers and on computer in the fourth. That didn't happen by accident. First, we found out who had authority for buying hardcover nonfiction books. You can do this by writing or calling and asking the name of the appropriate buyer for your type of book. It's the same treatment again — stay in front of your contact. Keep sharing good reviews, letters, important media appearances, and so forth. Be aware, however, that B&T is "order driven." That means they won't start ordering from you on a stocking basis until they see a swell of orders from libraries and bookstores. They've recently begun a new payment practice that allows publishers to receive payment when they get a purchase order, which is a trouble saver for all concerned. Before you can be included in their new draft system, however, they require that some paperwork be completed, so contact publisher services for details.

There is another form of leverage you can use to encourage B&T to stock your book. the different centers will automatically trickle in mail orders for one, two, three books. These special orders are in response to requests from their customers. It's an expensive proposition for them because, if you've established your discount schedule as we suggested, you don't give any discount on one book and darn little on two or three. Audit these orders. When a center begins to place frequent tiny orders, you have marvelous ammunition to suggest that B&T select you for its Final Approval Program. The reason you want this is so that your book will be included in its cataloging data base, become part of its bibliographic journal, *Directions*, and be afforded valuable exposure to the thousands of accounts the company serves. The initial order will be from zero to one hundred copies — but bigger things are just around the corner. If you do it right, the prepublication stocking order is typically five hundred copies.

Once Baker & Taylor carries your title, there are several things you can do to stimulate sales. It has three publications that accept advertising: *Forecast, Directions,* and *Book Alert. Forecast* goes to 17,000 public libraries in the United States and Canada. Prices for a half page begin around $600. For slightly more than half of that you can buy ad space in *Directions,* which hones in on academic, university research, and special libraries. *Book Alert* goes to 4,500 retailers and 4,000 public libraries. It only offers full pages—at a hefty $1,365. If your title meets B&T's buyer approval, there are more options. You could do a special microfiche promotion, use the company's telephone solicitors to plug your book, or participate in its continuation services memorandums, which send out fliers. Details on all of the above can be gotten by contacting B&T's advertising space sales department.

A point of interest: B&T will carry your books even if you choose not to help push them by buying special advertising. (It will expect you to demonstrate some sort of sound plan for achieving promotional impact, however.) The next two wholesalers we'll be discussing are less open on this point. They are rather insistent that you commit yourself to advertising in their media before they will stock a given title.

Ingram

Just as Colonel Sanders' success has attracted Picnic 'n Chicken and other contenders, there are more large book wholesalers. Headquartered in Nashville, Tennessee, with regional warehouses in the City of Industry, California, and Jessup, Maryland, Ingram is the next biggest wholesaler. Its forte is fast delivery of popular books to bookstores. It also offers a lot of computerized assistance to stores, including actual stock selection and inventory control.

Ingram is an intriguing outlet for the small publisher who desires national distribution. And word has it that Ingram's strategic plan includes "aggressively" expanding the number of titles it carries from small and medium-sized publishers. Getting on its microfiche system is a prize accomplishment. Ingram, as well as B&T and Bookpeople, ships a weekly negative 4" by 6" fiche inventory listing to stores. When a bookseller receives a request for a book not in his inventory, he simply looks it up on the fiche to verify that it's available, places a toll-free call, and has the book in stock in a matter of days. Microfiche ordering offers retailers a fast way to supply the needs of their customers without tying up large sums in inventory. It offers you an opportunity to make your book available to thousands of bookstores.

In a recent discussion Ingram's Fran Howell expressed a desire to see a completed book rather than galleys or F&Gs. Howell commented that "ninety-seven percent are rejected because of a poor printing job." If that passes muster, then the subject matter is given a close scrutiny. When he does find an interesting book—and determines it is receiving support promotion—the initial order is usually fifty or one hundred copies.

Howell has some understandable reservations about dealing with self-publishers. He explains it this way: If Ingram buys a book, gets it into the inventory system, and sells it, all is well. That is, until it starts coming back, which can take place over a whole year. When dealing with trade publishers, Howell explains he can return these books for credit on other titles. But with an SP-er there are no other titles. That means getting the cash back, something the self-publisher may find difficult to do after such a long time. In this case the return becomes his problem and any profit is quickly eroded. If you hope to convince him to carry your title, be prepared to counteract this negative possibility.

Ingram's telephone promotion has proven valuable for many books. When customers call in with an order, they are asked if they would like to hear about interesting new titles. Those who say yes are treated to a twenty-to-thirty-second spiel on three or four different titles.

Not every book is appropriate for this sales pitch. First, it must be of wide general appeal. Second, you must have about four thousand books on hand and be able to come up with another five thousand within three weeks if things really take off. Third, you must have about $1,000 to have your book plugged by the forty people on Ingram's order desk for one week. Does it work? We know of one instance where a book was selling at the rate of three hundred copies per week before doing a phone promotion. When the order desk plugged it, orders zoomed to nineteen hundred copies that week, seven hundred the next.

Like B&T, Ingram also sells advertising in its *Advance* magazine, a monthly that goes to about nine thousand bookstores. A quarter page starts at $420. (It also puts out *Paperback Advance*.) And for about a grand you can include an 8½" by 11" flier in its microfiche or statements.

Brodart

Another wholesaler you may want to PR is Brodart. Sandra Rose is currently its book acquisitions manager. From its Williamsport, Pennsylvania, headquarters it serves the library market with one-stop shopping. Rose wants to be convinced your book will get reviews and have an aggressive publicity campaign behind it. Like the foregoing wholesalers, Brodart publishes monthlies in which your participation is expected. Brodart puts out *Tartan Book Sales* and *Prime Magazine*.

Quality Books Inc.

Quality Books can be a tremendous asset to self-publishers whose books pass their high standards. They are a jobber and direct-sales company dealing strictly with schools and libraries. President Tom Drewes told us, "I can use all the good books I can get." We feel so strongly about the value of this distributor for self-publishers that we have included, below, their description of the "ideal book." Use it as a checklist when developing your product.

1) Adult nonfiction
2) Timely subject
3) New—copyright date is the current year
4) Well organized
   a. Includes an index and table of contents
   b. Title is the same on cover, spine, and title page
   c. Information is readily accessible
   d. No "fill in the blanks"
5) We receive sample copy or galley proofs prior to official publication date
6) Book has not been exposed to the library market
7) Publisher's primary market is outside of the library market
8) Subject coverage "fills a gap"—book is clearly differentiated from others in its field
9) The cover and title effectively and clearly convey the book's purpose *at a glance*
10) Book is bound durably and functionally

QBI's sales efforts include twenty-five salespeople; contracts, bids, standing orders, and approval plans with most of the largest library systems in the United States; and exhibits at some fifty state, regional, and national library conventions. They also add suitable books to the on-line information system ALANET, the information network of the American Library Association. With a customer base of over six thousand active accounts, QBI specializes in working with small presses that do fewer than ten new titles a year. To be considered, you should write for general information and the New Book Consideration form.

For books that are selected, Quality Books offers two consignment stocking arrangements: a 55 percent discount, payable net 90; or 60 percent off, payable net 60. You can ship in even cartons, the company is nice to work with, and they pay promptly. They will want twenty-five sales aids in the form of news releases, covers, or damaged copies of books to use for promotion.

There are hundreds of other wholesalers in addition to those mentioned here, some reputable and fast-paying, others not. You will begin to recognize them as you receive special orders. As we suggested with B&T, if any one of them sends repeat orders and pays promptly, you may want to contact its buyer about carrying your book in regular stock.

We've had brushes with many distributors, some less than pleasant. One outfit didn't pay us, wouldn't return the unsold books upon request, and had the gall—*six months* after the order was delivered—to say we had short-shipped. It was only after a letter threatening to write the American Booksellers Association, COSMEP, and the Better Business Bureau that we got paid and our unsold inventory was returned.

Such dealings are child's play compared to the agreement one of our seminar students passed on for our evaluation. She had been contacted by a company that wanted exclusive distribution rights to her book, not only in the United States but all over the world! Now, that sounds like heavy stuff, right? But as we analyzed the contract, here are some of the zingers we discovered. While the company was tying her to an exclusive contract for an entire year—thus prohibiting her from selling any books herself—it was taking only five hundred copies itself. Up to fifty of these would be non-revenue-producing review copies. The agreement gave the company permission to grant discounts of up to 55 percent. The author would be required to pay a 25 percent commission on all moneys collected, plus nine cents per book to help defray handling costs. And— believe it or not—she would have to pay a nonrefundable fee of $250 to cover computer setup, inventory processing, and promotional material.

Let's assume all five hundred books were sold. She would end up receiving the grand total of $202.81, or 40.6 cents per book. If we use the formula for pricing a book of five times manufacturing costs, she could *lose* as much as 18.4 cents on each book sold! We are happy to report that this company has gone out of business.

It should now be obvious that you must evaluate every distributor before entering into any agreement. One of the first things you want to know is their discount requirements. While most will buy at 50 percent discount, there are exceptions.

Bookpeople

Bookpeople, headquartered in Berkeley, California, insists on a 52 percent discount. Most self-publishers, however, find this is a wise investment. Bookpeople caters to small publishers and specialty stores, carrying primarily mass-market and trade books. Many of its accounts are outlets for titles on health and fitness, spiritual awareness, alternative life-styles, women's issues, gay and lesbian subjects, plus literature and poetry. Contrary to popular belief, it is not just a regional distributor. Fifteen percent of its business comes from foreign booksellers.

The giant of the distributors, Bookpeople recently doubled its size by moving into a new 31,000-square-foot facility. More changes are taking shape. Bookpeople want to become more service-oriented, telling booksellers, "This is what we can do for you." The company is exploring a voluntary approval program for retailers in which Bookpeople would automatically ship a selection of appropriate titles to certain stores. BP has redesigned its semiannual catalog to list books by subject area, not just by title and publisher. It also puts out a monthly review called *Bookpapers.*

Inland Book Company

Inland Book Company is totally dedicated to small presses and sells the titles of about 450 independent publishers through thematic catalogs. President David Wilk comments, "We carry many titles simply because we feel good about them." Many literary books find a home here. Decisions on which publishers and titles to accept are made via a blend of intuition, idealism, and business savvy. Discounts run from 52 to 55 percent.

Specialty jobbers

If you publish literary works, you should contact Bookslinger in St. Paul, Minnesota. Religious titles might be placed with Cicero Bible Press, which distributes the books of seventy-five publishers.

Got a story for preschoolers? Gryphon House is your entry into the world of the younger set. It is the sole American distributor and wholesaler of children's books exclusively for early childhood programs. Currently carrying eighty imprints and about eight hundred different titles, Gryphon looks for multiethnic, nonsexist books that deal with real problems and make kids feel better about themselves.

New Leaf Distributing Company was started in 1975 with a lot of idealism, a strong vision, and little else. It has experienced great growth since then. Its specialized subject areas are holistic health, self-reliant lifestyle, and new-age spirituality and metaphysics. Discounts here are 55 percent. We especially enjoy working with this outfit, as there is never a wait or a hassle for payment. Along with the monthly sales report, New Leaf sends a postdated check for the money owed. You simply wait until the appropriate time rolls around, then cash your check.

"Waiting for the appropriate time" brings a story to mind. About ten years ago we took on a client who wrote and published a title called *The UNcook Book.* Our marketing research turned up a wholesaler called Nutri-Books Corp., which specialized in health-related titles. Since our book dealt with eating raw food, this company seemed a natural. Its buyer didn't agree. We were sent a polite letter declining the book and saying the company was already carrying several volumes on raw foods and sales were soft. But since we knew Nutri-Books was our open sesame to the lucrative health food store market, we didn't give up. It was a case of the old 80/20 rule, which says 80 percent of your business will come from 20 percent of your customers. Every time we got a favorable review or someone wrote a letter commending the book, a copy was fired off to Dan Nidess, who decides which titles Nutri-Books will handle. This went on for several months. (See copy of one letter on page 271.) Finally—in desperation to shut us up, perhaps—a purchase order arrived for two cases. Pretty soon another purchase order arrived. Then another.

Today *The UNcook Book* is one of Nutri-Books' biggest sellers. Thousands of copies have been merchandised through this one source and it has gone into five printings. The moral of the story is if you have a gut feeling that a book is really right for certain outfits, but they say no, don't give up. Polite persistence does pay off. The other thing that paid off for us was designing and printing fifteen thousand fliers (see sample) which were provided to this wholesaler free of charge. Nutri-Books in turn enclosed them with every mailing that went out. This helped keep the book in front of potential buyers and reminded them it was a strong seller.

Should you have a health-related book, here are some of the factors Dan takes into consideration: content, appearance, price, originality, readability, and market trends. He receives some three hundred books each month and can only accept fifteen to twenty.

Another kind of specialized wholesaler is the one that deals regionally. These are usually small firms with a sales rep or two who beat the bushes aggressively.

We deal with Gordons Books in Denver (which is by no means small). When we chatted with Robert Hobson, he commented how few authors or publishers keep them abreast of breaking reviews or other noteworthy publicity. Take a tip from this good advice: Keep your wholesalers and distributors informed. That way they can do a better job of stocking stores and making sales for you.

Then there's Beyda and Associates, a Los Angeles jobber of children's books; and Small Press Distributors in Berkeley, California, which represents fiction, poetry, and essays. There are surely one or two in your area. Look for them in the yellow pages.

A different version of this is newsstand distribution. These jobbers serve grocery stores and other nonbook outlets. While they typically deal only with mass-market paperbacks, sometimes you can make inroads here. Tom Davis had his *Be Tough or Be Gone* in all the local Safeway stores. It sold so well that newsstand distributors in other parts of Colorado and Wyoming took it on, too. If you do connect here, be sure they understand that any returned books must be *intact and resalable*. (They are used to simply ripping the covers off mass-market paperbacks and returning just

COMMUNICATION CREATIVITY
a colorado corporation

March 10, 1981

Dan Nidess, Merchandising Manager
Nutri-Books Corporation
P. O. Box 5793
Denver, CO 80217

Dear Mr. Nidess:

You remember The UNcook Book? Its goose is far from cooked!

Thought you'd be interested in these recent developments:

- Favorable review in Health Food Business magazine

- Nationally syndicated column devoted totally to the book,
  due to break April 5th

- Samples of orders coming to us that could be coming to
  NutriBooks

You indicated your mind was never set in concrete when we chatted on the phone a
while back. This book is really beginning to take off. We are continuing to support
it with ongoing promotion and media coverage, such as a Houston blitz the end of
this month and a Northwest author's tour scheduled for this summer.

Why don't you give The UNcook Book a try? It really is different from other books
on raw food!

Cordially,

Marilyn Ross

Marilyn Ross

MR:bb
Enclosures

those to major publishing houses for credit.)

You may encounter a distributor who wants exclusive rights to your book. If it happens, you must make a decision: whether to accept the distributor's stipulations or to stand up and negotiate. If you have already established several good local accounts, you might want to maintain control over the county in which you live. Just set up a relationship with one of the major chains? Then have the contract written to exclude sales to them. A contract is designed to facilitate *both* sides; don't be hesitant to speak your piece and insist that certain provisions be changed. The worst thing that could happen is to get a "no" and be back where you started.

One more bit of advice is to believe in yourself and your product enough to see that you get fair treatment. We had a frustrating experience with our first book, *Discover Your Roots*. Since it was released a few months after Alex Haley's television spectacular, the book was extremely timely. We stopped by a distributor with one of the first copies off the presses and left it for the buyer, who wasn't in at the time. Realizing it would take a while for reading, we didn't attempt further contact for a couple of weeks. But then our repeated phone calls got no further than a secretary. Finally, after six weeks, we were able to get through to the buyer herself, who casually informed us it would be another four weeks or so before she could evaluate the book and make a decision. That was like telling a jockey he could work in the stables but couldn't ride a horse. Our patience was gone. We ferreted out the general manager's name and looked in a city directory to track down his home address. A carefully worded letter politely explaining the situation was in the mail that night. Two days later the buyer called, set an immediate appointment, and subsequently ordered one hundred books.

Wholesalers and distributors come in all sizes, shapes, and dispositions. Some are a delight to work with. Others make you want to get out your horse whip. But they spell $-a-l-e-s for your book and should be wooed into your camp.

Tapping the lucrative library market

Library sales are to the self-publisher what the salmon spawning season is to a fisherman. In fact, some books reach the break-even point — or climb into profitable status — on library sales alone.

Why are they so great? Well, first of all, we recommend that library sales be at the full retail price for orders under five copies because many of them are single-copy orders. Why give away 40 percent when it isn't r.ecessary? Second, unlike bookstores, libraries involve no return hassle. Only in rare instances will a library refuse a book they have ordered. And third, some buy in nice quantities. Here's a sampling of orders we've received: The San Diego County Library bought thirty-five copies. The City of Chicago stocked their branches with twenty-eight copies. Fairfax Public Library ordered twenty-three, and the Nassau Library System purchased twelve. Not too shabby, eh? And we've gotten smaller orders from virtually every state in the Union.

Library patrons number in the millions each day. The U.S. has approximately 103,000 libraries, including elementary, high school, college, armed forces, public, and special libraries. According to the American Library Directory, there are currently 9,170 main libraries and 6,117 branches—a total of 15,287 public libraries.

Although recent citizen mandates for less governmental spending have tightened some library purse strings, this remains an ideal market for the small press. William Lofquist, the publishing industry's statistician at the Commerce Department in Washington, estimates it at about 10 percent of the entire book market. The overwhelming number of academic and public libraries have had *no* decrease in their materials budgets in the last five years.

Start your campaign by contacting the proper person in the local library system. Call the main branch and ask who is in charge of acquisitions (meaning ordering) for your type of book (children's literature, reference, adult fiction, etc.). This information can also be found in the *American Library Directory*. It's probably just as well to approach them as the author rather than the publisher, since librarians enjoy supporting local authors. You can do this by mail (see sample letters), or you can approach them in person. Send or leave a complimentary copy of the book to be circulated, plus plenty of promotional material. Potential library books are displayed for branch librarians to examine and order. Consequently, it may be a couple of months before you actually receive a purchase order.

Be sure you cover all local bases. In San Diego, for instance, the city and county are two separate entities. We received generous orders from both. Investigate the structure in your hometown so as not to neglect a nice sale.

Now that you've tapped the local resources, where to next? The whole country is your oyster! But librarians have one quirk. They are particularly impressed with reviewers' opinions and comments from nonpartisan experts. For that reason you would be wise not to approach them until a favorable review has appeared in one or more of the following: *Library Journal, Booklist, Publishers Weekly, Kirkus Reviews, Wilson Library Bulletin, School Library Journal* (if it is a work for children or young adults), or *Choice* (if a work slanted to college or research libraries).

These publications carry great weight with librarians. Once one of them has praised your book, library orders will begin to trickle in with no effort on your part. Notice the *Booklist* review we secured for the

COMMUNICATION CREATIVITY

October 20, 1977

Arthur E. Murray, County Librarian
San Diego County Library
5555 Overland Avenue, Building 15
San Diego, CA 92123

Dear Mr. Murray:

With "Roots" due to be re-run on television in January and the paperback edition of the book expected to be released soon, the interest in family history continues to mushroom.

Why not take this opportunity to expose the users of San Diego County libraries to the excitement of tracing their own roots? Our book, DISCOVER YOUR ROOTS, is an easy guide for climbing your family tree. It has been praised by the GENEALOGICAL HELPER (copy of review enclosed). This is the "Bible" of genealogists, and theirs is a high commendation for a book to receive.

I am hopeful that you have had a chance to review the copy we sent you previously and that it is making the rounds of other librarians. We have already filled a large order for the city libraries, and I hope we can do the same for residents who live in the county. By the way, the author is a local woman who is actively involved in speaking to various local groups.

We look forward to answering any questions for you and to filling your order promptly. Thank you for your interest in continuing to bring helpful and interesting reading materials to San Diego County residents.

Sincerely,

Ann Markham
Marketing Director

AM:111
Encl.

Ross, Marilyn and Ross, Tom.
The encyclopedia of self-publishing: how to successfully write, publish, promote and sell your own work. 1979. 191p. Communication Creativity, 5044 La Jolla Blvd., La Jolla, CA 92037, $29.95 (0-918880-02-5). Galley.

An encyclopedia it is not. A handbook stuffed with essential information on how to get into print, and beyond, it is. The authors are fully prepared; they have self-published and successfully marketed several books. With realism and extraordinary thoroughness, every practical topic is covered: how to organize for research and writing, mastering the ISBN, ABI, and CIP formalities, developing necessary business procedures, finding the right printer and format, advertising and promoting (including some very inventive approaches), and pushing distribution. Under the rubric "Other Alternatives" there are chapters on agents, conventional trade publishers, and vanity presses. Current lists of helpful organizations, reviewing media and syndicated columnists, bookstore chains, selected wholesalers, buyers of subsidiary rights, a bibliography, glossary, and index pack riches right up to the last page.

548.8'09 Publishers and publishing. Handbooks, manuals, etc. (CIP) 70-4054

CHOICE
JUNE '84
Biology
Zoology

JENNINGS, Dana C. (Dana Close). Buffalo management & marketing, by Dana C. Jennings and Judi Hebbring. National Buffalo Association (dist. by Communication Creativity), 1984 (c1983). 370p ill maps bibl index 83-19516. 19.95 ISBN 0-918880-03-3. CIP

A well-written, authentic, one-of-a-kind book that accurately describes buffalo management and marketing in today's economy. Even though obviously written by buffalo enthusiasts (who else would write a book about buffalo?) and the "selling of the buffalo" is paramount throughout, the work is authoritative and straightforward. The book is must reading for anyone interested in raising buffalo, and it will be of major interest to anyone seeking general information about the animal. There are chapters about every phase of the buffalo "industry," including history, health, handling, breeding, feeding, marketing, hunting, and an entire section on leading breeders. The pictures and illustrations are very well done. The authors, who know their subject well, have provided the major source of information concerning the current status of the buffalo industry in North America. Highly recommended as an acquisition for academic and public libraries.

Encyclopedia of Self-Publishing and what *Choice* had to say about a client's book, *Buffalo Management and Marketing*.

Wilson Library Bulletin is often overlooked by small presses. Yet it is a substantial source for reviews. Here's who covers what: "The Eclectic Eye" is a new column that focuses on unusual and offbeat books in the humanities (please *don't* send business, science, technology, poetry, history, sports, or workbooks with fill-in pages). The reviewer here is Patty Campbell, 1437 Lucile Avenue, Los Angeles, CA 90026. Young-adult fiction and nonfiction titles should go to Cathi Edgerton, "The Young Adult Perplex," 4546 Keswick Road, Baltimore, MD 21210. Current reference books go to the Earl Gregg Swem Library, College of William and Mary, Williamsburg, VA 23185; and art, autobiography, history, memoir, nature, science, sociology, theater, and women's studies are the specialties of Gail Pool, 75 Summitt Avenue, Brookline, MA 02146.

There is another aspect of timing to remember. Certain periods during the year will yield a better response than others. The best time to contact libraries is probably just before the end of their fiscal year (June 30 or December 30), as they may be in a hurry to use up unappropriated funds. (Or they can sit on the information until just after those dates when they have a fresh source of money at their disposal.) If you're making multiple contacts, get the first to them early in June or December, with the second thirty to forty-five days later.

By the way, ask your friends and relatives to help you by requesting your book at their local library. Most libraries keep track of such requests. Enough demand will result in their acquiring the title to meet the groundswell of requests. A good way to further spread the word about your book is to rent a mailing list. You can get information on prices and quantities available from the R. R. Bowker Company, which breaks its lists down according to the size of a library's appropriation budget. For *Discover Your Roots* we rented Bowker's list of the 620 libraries with the highest budgets. At that time it cost $33 and was a good investment.

We've since discovered *Marketing to Libraries Through Library Associations*, which is a treasure-trove of information. This directory shows you how to reach specialized markets such as medical or music librarians and contains data on each state (plus Canadian library associations). With it, you can pinpoint specifically targeted mailing lists to rent, journals in which to advertise, or conferences to attend.

To capture the attention of librarians, include excerpts—or the complete review, if it is short—from the strategic publications mentioned above. Also include other testimonials and comments, and highlight any timely tie-in. Make it easy for them to cooperate by providing an order form, which you have coded so you can keep track of results. See the adjacent flier to get an idea of how we pulled these elements together. Because library ordering tends to be a slow, bureaucratic process, there is no real advantage for the mailing to go out first-class. Bulk postage will cut costs and probably not reduce results.

You might also consider asking another publisher to advertise piggyback with you. For the same amount of postage, you include the other's promotional material. We invited an associate to include a catalog sheet in our mailing at no cost to her. The arrangement was we would get 40 percent on all orders received, and she would take care of the fulfillment.

HERE'S WHAT PEOPLE ARE SAYING ABOUT "DISCOVER YOUR ROOTS" ...

"Written in a new, easy format, this book guides the reader through unfamiliar genealogical surroundings."

GENEALOGICAL HELPER
July-August 1977 issue

"Immense help for those tracing their background."

Lee Harley, Reviewer
WOAD TV8

"Very comprehensive!"

Frederick G. Bohme, Chief
Census History Staff
U. S. Bureau of the Census

booklist

october 1, 1977

Heimberg, Marilyn Markham.
Discover your roots (a new, easy guide for tracing your family tree). 1977. 62p. Communication Creativity. paper, $4.95 (0-918880-00-9).

Playle, Ron.
How you can trace your family roots. 1977. 32p. R and D Services. paper, $1.99 (0-89511-005-9).
A slim booklet to supply root gatherers' needs, How You Can Trace Your Family Roots is for beginners. basic search calendars. and worksheets to keep names, dates, and sources straight. All the usual sources—military, court, and church census, are mentioned. together with advice on the etiquette of research, oral history. and the solicitation of relatives. Some addresses. Pedigree charts. Not indexed. A similar title, though better written, Discover Your Roots surveys the same ground but does not include work sheets. Different pedigree diagrams, an index, and a short bibliography make it equally, if not more, useful.

DID YOU KNOW...

* That a sequel to "Roots" will be televised in February?

* That a television special, "The Roots Phenomenon" will be broadcast early this year?

* That even more patrons will be asking for an easy how-to book for tracing their own ancestry?

* * * * * L I B R A R Y   S P E C I A L $3.95 * * * * *

Place your order today and save $1 per book! Clip & mail in enclosed envelope

Library name_____

Address_____

City_____State_____Zip_____

Acquisitions personnel_____Quantity ordered_____

NOTE: shipping charges will be added to all orders unless
       payment is enclosed with initial order.
COMMUNICATION CREATIVITY, 1340 Tourmaline St., San Diego Ca.
                                              92109

MEMBER
COSMEP
COMMITTEE OF SMALL MAGAZINE
EDITORS AND PUBLISHERS
BOX 703 SAN FRANCISCO CA 94101

Direct library mail piece.

That way we didn't spend anything additional, and she had no initial cash outlay; but both parties stood to benefit. It worked beautifully. We received enough orders for her book to cover all but a couple dollars of the entire mailing cost. This included list rental, printing, envelopes, and postage. The mailing was put out by manual labor, and since part of the deal was that our friend would help stuff and seal envelopes, we had fun in the process.

A discussion of libraries wouldn't be complete without explaining that there are about as many kinds of them as there are flavors of ice cream. For example, one intriguing possibility is military libraries. Unfortunately, there is no central way to sell to Defense Department Libraries. Each branch of the armed forces acquires its own titles.

The Army, for instance, sometimes orders as many as eight hundred copies of a book at a time. Federal procurement regulations require they buy through a jobber unless your book isn't available that way. Even so, you will still feel the happy end result. The Army Research and Development Center puts out a directory of military librarians. If your title especially suits this market, obtain a copy by writing Norman Varier, Army Research and Development Center, SMCAR-TSS, Building 59, Dover, NJ 70801-5001. To snap them to attention, send galleys of hardcovers six to eight weeks prior to publication. Paperbacks will be considered either before or after the publication date.

We received a favorable listing in the Air Force's review tabloid, which goes to hundreds of bases, thus generating orders from several. They do not centrally procure publications, but are especially interested in books on self-improvement, military history, and physical fitness. The Veterans Administration has 175 individual hospitals which also have book collections. Correspond with military libraries at the following addresses:

Headquarters
Department of the Army
Attn: DAAG-MSL
Hoffman Building #1
2461 Eisenhower Avenue
Alexandria, VA 22331

Acquisitions Librarian
Chief of Naval Education and
  Training Support
General Library Services Branch
  N32
Pensacola, FL 32509

Acquisitions Librarian
Air Force Libraries Section
HQ AFMPC/MPCSOL
Randolph AFB, TX 78150

Veterans Administration Library
810 Vermont Avenue N.W.
Room 976
Washington, DC 20420

Another library market which is often ignored is churches and synagogues. *Publishers Weekly* has noted that conservative estimates place the number at around fifty thousand libraries. And many carry inspirational and self-help books as well as religious titles. While some stock only a few dozen books, other collections number in the thousands and have generous annual budgets. You can reach them by contacting the national associations that represent each. Most have journals which carry advertisements, one of the best bargains around if this is a prime target for you.

Various specialized libraries may lead to further profit. Business, corporation, and technical library lists are available from Bowker. If you have a book about forestry, there are 1,361 libraries interested in the general field in which it falls. Is your tome a discussion of art? Then rent the art and architecture libraries list. And if you've done a book about easy ways to play the banjo, perhaps the almost 500 music libraries would like to hear about it. Don't overlook the possibility that there may be a group of libraries ideally suited to your specific subject matter. An excellent manual on the craft of writing for libraries and educational institutions is Nat Bodian's *Copywriter's Handbook: A Practical Guide for Advertising and Promotion of Specialized and Scholarly Books and Journals.*

There are also school and college libraries which buy everything from juvenile storybooks to university reference works. It's a good idea to approach them with a double-barreled mailing targeted to both the librarian and the appropriate department head. Let's explore this potential further.

Going after educational sales

Elementary and secondary schools, junior colleges, colleges, and universities all have potential as large-scale buyers. Orders will not pop into your office, however. They will dawdle in. Promotional material sent now may result in an order six months or a year downstream. But that order could be for dozens—even hundreds—of books. And it isn't necessarily a one-shot thing. Reorders are likely to roll in each new semester. Another reason this is an attractive market is that most sales are made on a "short discount," meaning that you only allow 20 percent off the retail price.

Perhaps you're thinking, "My book wouldn't sell to schools; it's not a textbook." You may be in for a nice surprise. The wide variety of titles that are appropriate in today's academic circles is amazing. For instance, the General Books Department of Harcourt Brace Jovanovich promoted the following for college use: *Hitler's Secret Service* (history and civilization), *Of Love and Lust* (psychology), *All Our Children* (sociology), *Zen Catholicism* (philosophy and religion), *The Company She Keeps* (women's studies), and the novels *The Voyage Out* and *Jacob's Room*. And because self-publishing is merely a microcosm of trade publishing, the book you're reading could serve as a text for university classes on publishing.

To help educators appreciate why your book would be appropriate, stress any features that make it more likely for adoption. These might include chapters arranged a certain way, inclusion of exercises and quizzes, or review questions at the end of each chapter.

Even if your work is not suitable as a text, it may be used as related material for course planning. Such books are called supplemental texts. We were fortunate in introducing *Discover Your Roots* to the San Diego Unified School District. This contact netted us ongoing sales as various junior and senior highs picked up the book as a supplementary text in history classes. Supplemental texts also find a fertile field in continuing education. Adult learning programs cover a lot of unlikely subjects, some of which may dovetail with your book.

Call the Board of Education at the nearest large city to determine who is in charge of curriculum for the subject area of your book. Get in touch with him or her. In our case the curriculum consultant was impressed with the examination copy we provided and invited us to supply him with a quantity of fliers to distribute to schools in the district. Needless to say, we were happy to cooperate.

Here again, the specialized mailing list is the perfect means of reaching your target market. There are several companies that provide computerized lists in very specific areas. If you're going after colleges and universities, several firms offer detailed breakdowns of faculty. One is CMG Information Services, 50 Cross Street, Winchester, MA 01890. The best time to mail to colleges is midterm—typically the beginning of March, May, August, and November.

If the book would appeal more to the younger age groups, K through twelfth grade, contact School Lists Mailings Corporation, 1710 Highway 35, Oakhurst, NJ 07755.

Educators will expect to receive an "examination copy" on which they can base a decision. That doesn't mean you automatically have to send books to everyone. Prepare a mailing piece and, as part of the qualification to receive a complimentary copy, require that the following information be provided:

• Title and nature of course
• Estimated number of students
• College upper or lower division course (Freshman and sophomore classes are larger and thus more profitable.)
• Starting date of the class
• Approximate date of "adoption" decision (Kids, pets, and books are adopted.)
• Source of the decision—person, committee, department (If commit-

tee or department, then also PR the faculty members.)

Because you can still end up giving away sizable quantities of examination copies in this way, some publishers indicate that they expect the book to be returned if it is not adopted. Or specify that it can be retained for the instructor's personal library by paying the regular price minus a 20 percent "professional" discount. If you take either of these stands, be prepared to send out a lot of statements for unreturned books — with very poor results. Even so, educational sales can boost your earnings. A good resource for selling to this market is John B. McHugh's *The College Publishing Market, Second Edition.*

Before we leave this subject, be aware that college bookstores may be interested in your book even if it is not adopted as a text or supplemental text. To get a feel for the kinds of books and merchandise they carry, send your ad agency rate letter to the *College Store Executive,* c/o Executive Business Media, Inc., Box 1500, Westbury, NY 11590. Browsing in the bookstore of your own local college or university will also be most revealing.

Using commissioned sales reps or exclusive distributors

While it will be difficult to interest a commissioned sales rep when you have only one title, we will discuss them briefly. These are independent salespeople who represent a given number of titles in a specific geographic area. They introduce new titles, take orders, straighten and restock bookstore shelves, and generally service the account for you. In return they expect a minimum of 10 percent of retail sales and 5 percent on wholesale accounts.

Most will also want a protected territory or all the "ledger accounts," which is another way of saying an exclusive. That means that on all books sold to the trade in their territory they receive a commission, whether you sell them or they do. Several small presses that have tried sales reps have abandoned the practice. Uncollectible billings is one big problem. The rep gets his or her commission, but downstream you may get returned books, on which you already forked over 5 or 10 percent. In spite of these warnings, if you want to try to line up a commissioned sales rep, you can find them in *LMP* under "U.S. Book Distributors and Sales Representatives." They also sometimes advertise in *Publishers Weekly* for new titles to represent. And talk with other publishers.

A different version of representation to the book trade is available to small presses. Several companies do exclusive distribution. They include Publishers Group West (PGW), Slawson Communications, Kampmann & Company, Consortium Book Sales, The Talman Company, Independent Publishers Group, Sun and Moon, and the National Book Network.

Whether they will take on a one-title publisher depends a lot on your persuasiveness. While they take a large hunk of the profits, they can provide you entry to such important wholesalers as Ingram, and to bookstores all across the country.

Remaindering

Remember that catalog you got in the mail a few weeks ago announcing publishers' closeouts that were reduced up to 83 percent? Have you noticed the bargain tables in bookstores? These are the graveyards of books. But not necessarily bad books. Today, best-selling hardcovers sometimes become candidates when they are replaced by a paperback edition. Discounting has also forced many recognizable titles by well-known authors into this status.

If you follow the pointers in this book, yours isn't likely to land there. But suppose you went astray. Several hundreds (or thousands) of books have taken up room in your garage or basement long enough. Visions of dollar signs no longer dance in your head. You simply want to salvage something out of the effort. Then consider the advice of the man who said, "If you're being run out of town, get in front of the crowd and make it look like a parade." Don't complain that none of your books sold. Do something. Contact remainder dealers. You can find them in *LMP* and the *American Book Trade Directory* and also in our Appendix.

These are specialized wholesalers who take all your books, dole out a token amount of money, and sell the books at drastically reduced rates — sometimes right back to the bookstores that returned them — or through mail-order channels. They will only be interested if you have at least 250 copies left. The pay? Somewhere between 3 and 15 percent of the retail price. No, it's not much. But there is one redeeming fact — when they're sold, they're sold. It's a nonrefundable transaction. They also pay the freight and usually remit a check within thirty days from your invoice date. They will want all copies; in effect, an exclusive.

This is the way it works. You send them a sample copy of the book along with a letter stating the quantity available, retail price, terms of payment, location of the inventory, and the closing date for accepting bids. Interested dealers will come back with a bid. The ball is then in your court. You pick the highest. If you decide to remainder, it is a customary courtesy to notify any wholesalers who still carry the book. (You may even be able to sell your overstock to them for a 70 or 80 percent discount.) Also notify your other accounts so they can return unsold books to be included in the remainders.

Authors who have been published by trade or vanity presses can sometimes pick up their own books in this way. Look at the fine print in your contract and see if you have the option of matching any remainder bid. (And if you don't, for heaven's sake be sure such a point is written into your next trade publishing contract!) With the creative marketing strategies you've learned in this guide, you may just turn a previous failure into a dynamic money-maker.

Another option is to donate slow-moving inventory to schools, hospitals, and other nonprofit groups. This allows you to take generous federal tax deductions. For information, contact Cruz A. Ramos, Director of Donor Relations, National Association of the Exchange of Industrial Resources, Box 8076, Galesburg, IL 61402. Yet another possible outlet for growth awaits in nontraditional special sales. Let's go on now and explore these intriguing possibilities.

CHAPTER 16

ADDITIONAL MONEY-MAKING STRATEGIES

In this chapter we'll be looking at innovative ways to increase sales and enlarge your marketing base. We'll explore retail outlets *other than* bookstores. And we'll talk about premiums and merchandise tie-ins, catalog opportunities, and ways to make large bulk sales. Additional maverick marketing ideas will be examined.

Creative thinking pays

Be a creative thinker. Only then will you come up with additional paths for merchandising your book. A good way to trigger new ideas is to play the "what if" game. Ask what if — then finish with some out-of-the-ordinary idea, situation, or condition. (You might say, "What if I gave away homemade chocolates with each copy of my book, *The History of Chocolate?*" "Too expensive and too unwieldy, not to mention spoilage." "What if, instead, I put a slip of dark chocolate-scented paper in each book?" "Now we're talking.")

This allows you to probe aspects thought to be impractical and impossible; things that lie outside the usual rules and guidelines. Not all of your brainstorms will be successful. So what? Keep at it! If one idea isn't a hit, try something else. Babe Ruth and Hank Aaron struck out many times, but that's not what they're remembered for.

Other retail outlets that will carry your product

There are numerous places besides bookstores where your product will sell. Major publishers call these "special sales." The Book Industry

Study Group released a study in 1988 titled *The Sale of Books Through Non-Bookstore Retailers*. Because it cost $650, not many people have had access to it. This unique compendium of facts shows that one out of every four books purchased by consumers today are bought in nonbookstore outlets. Such places as home-improvement centers, drugstores, discount stores, grocery stores, gift shops, liquor stores, even auto supply outlets are prime candidates. The study says that "While there are 20,000 bookstores in the United States, there is probably ten times this number of nonbookstore retail outlets also selling books." What a bonanza waits here! Think about your subject matter, then play with various connecting possibilities. Here are some equations of subject matter to retail outlets:

Plants—nurseries, florists
Crafts—hobby shops
Poetry—gift and specialty shops
Nutrition—health food stores, vegetarian restaurants
Wardrobe coordination—dress shops, fabric stores
Art book—museums, artist supply stores
Construction—building supply outlets
Hair or skin care—beauty shops
A political luminary—local party headquarters

A classic example of using nonbookstore retail channels is the wave of computer books distributed through computer stores. *Disco Dancing* is sold in record stores. A book of recipes using wild game tempts people who come into a sporting goods outlet to purchase hunting licenses. Thirty percent of all the books sold on how-to home improvements go out the doors of home improvement centers, says *National Home Center News*. The possibilities are endless.

And sometimes they're very unusual. The Pink Pony Cafe, a baseball hangout in Scottsdale, Arizona, sold fifteen copies of David Falkner's *The Short Season: The Hard Work and High Times of Baseball in the Spring* within the first few hours of the book's availability.

The meek may inherit the earth; but they won't sell many books. Assertiveness pays big dividends. Once your assertiveness has established a few good accounts among nonbookstore outlets—likely, in part, by offering the 50 percent discount rate they're used to getting from their other suppliers—and once the books are moving regularly, ask each store manager what wholesale supplier he or she deals with. By contacting the wholesaler and explaining your new product—which is "a real money-maker for Joe at XYZ"—you can convince him that this is a lucrative bandwagon which he will definitely want to climb onto. Do whatever it takes to convince him: bulldoze, charm, cajole. This is too big an opportunity to let slip by. Once convinced, the wholesaler will represent you to all similar outlets that are part of his territory. Presto! You've expanded your business by adding a whole new sales force—at no cost to you!

These wholesalers will need guidance. Usually, they haven't carried books before and will want encouragement and a simple plan for handling your title. Why not prepackage a few books and put them in an attractive point-of-purchase display stand? Supplying such displays, and whatever other attention-getters you can think of—posters made from photo blow-ups of your cover, easel-style advertising for a counter, maybe even just a colorful mylar balloon to tie to the display stand—is particularly important in selling to stores whose main business is not books. Offer your new business partner easy guidelines for reordering. You might even suggest in-store events like signings, demonstrations, slide shows, or lectures for certain of his best accounts.

Although, as mentioned, wholesalers are accustomed to a 50 percent discount, they're *not* used to being able to send back unsold merchandise. Take advantage of this. If your discount schedule is structured as we suggested in Chapter 5 on operating procedures, you can offer them the 50 percent discount for fewer books than usual by virtue of selling the books on a no-return basis.

Still another merchandising possibility hides in very unlikely places and is therefore frequently overlooked. National parks and monuments could be ideal sites for your book. One of the places we wanted *Discover Your Roots* to be carried was the Cabrillo National Monument in San Diego. Why? Because it is the most popular historical site in the United States, frequented by people from every state and dozens of foreign countries. Nice exposure for a book. Well, *DYR* didn't make it. Even though it dealt with history, it had nothing to do with the monument itself. That bit of information was filed away for future reference. When Marilyn was writing *Creative Loafing*, we decided to include national monuments as a leisure activity. Guess which specific one was used as an anecdote? (And guess which one agreed to carry the book?) The gift shops at these spots typically order like bookstores and expect a 40 percent discount. This kind of sensitivity to your market can be used to your advantage in editorial ways, too. Just like The Babe and Hank, we were determined, and consequently we profited from our mistakes.

Premium books and merchandise tie-ins

Sales that are anything but meager can be generated if your title lends itself to the premium market. Premium (also called "sponsored") books are given away—or sold at a fraction of their normal cost—to promote business. You've probably noted that savings and loans dole out calendars or books to entice new customers into establishing accounts. Other frequent premium buyers are insurance companies, investment brokers, manufacturers of various products, even newspapers who want to beef up their subscriber list. And you can sell and resell your book as a premium. All that is required is that exclusivity be assured for a given type of business in a given geographic area. For instance, if you were selling a premium edition to savings and loans, exclusivity would mean that no other bank in the city (or county, depending on the bank's range) would be offering the book.

We're talking about quantity here: 10,000, 20,000, 100,000 books at one swat. Of course, since the volume is so large, premium buyers expect (and rightly so) that you give them a very good deal. Even if you make much less per book, when you multiply the amount by 20,000 it adds up quickly. Plan on doing a customized promotional cover that includes the institution's name. This kind of personalization is what makes books such perfect premium items.

Approach prospective premium buyers with a well-thought-out sales package of your promotional materials. If these prospects show interest, send them a sample cover and folded and gathered pages (F & G's) of the book itself. Ideally, making such arrangements should be done far enough in advance of your print date to allow the extra books to be manufactured at the same time, allowing you to benefit from the reduced prices of the larger print run. But with a first book this may not be possible — you may need reviews and other post-printing aids to convince premium buyers that your book is one with which they want to associate themselves. But it can't hurt to try earlier, and if you've been careful to back off before a buyer can give you a definite "No," you can always reopen negotiations later, when you'll have a copy of the book in your hand and wonderful reviews to show him or her. And at that point, you can either arrange for a new run of appropriately-personalized covers or perhaps order a classy gold sticker you can attach, or have a special stamp made, to add the buyer's logo or other personalized information to your regular covers.

Suppose you want to find national wholesalers in a field well allied to your book that might be persuaded to take on your title as a merchandise tie-in. What do you do? Happily, there is a set of books that will lead you to just the right manufacturer if you're trying to match up with a product. It is called the *Thomas Register of American Manufacturers* and has some 80,000 headings covering more than 1.5 million sources. Because it is arranged alphabetically by product, this gigantic address book will help you track down virtually any American manufacturer. It's available in any major library. Think about who else goes to the market you're trying to reach with other products, then determine specific manufacturers in

Thomas Register.

That's what Marcella Smith, of St. Martin's Press, did. She sold *The Complete Handbook of Personal Computer Communications* to Hayes Microcomputer Products, Inc. The company purchased several tens of thousands to promote sales of its modems. What would you do with a book called *The Best of Everything?* If you were smart, you might contact Sylvania, as its Superset nineteen-inch color TV was voted "the best in its field." That's precisely what St. Martin's did . . . and sold them a premium edition of this book of lists. Dutton found a great premium home for the children's book *Winnie the Pooh.* They sold it to Lever Brothers, manufacturers of Mrs. Butterworth's syrup. Bottles of the pancake syrup featured a promotion telling consumers they could buy the book for half price with a proof-of-purchase label from Mrs. Butterworth's syrup. While the initial order was small, Lever Brothers forecasted selling forty thousand to eighty thousand books. Prentice-Hall does a lot of premiums as corporate gifts and for internal sales and learning tools. They recently did customized books for B. F. Goodrich, Getty Oil, and Manufacturers Hanover.

Better Homes and Gardens' special-sales division has gone into premiums in a big way. Mike Peterson, of BH&G, told us of selling 2 *million* booklets to the Nestlé Company for its *"Best You Can Bake" Chocolate Desserts.* BH&G extracted appropriate recipes from another book, packaged them in the familiar red-and-white-plaid cover of the BH&G coobook, tucked in some Nestlé advertising, and scored a supersale. Copies of the thirty-two-page booklet were given free to purchasers of Nestlé tollhouse morsels. They've put together similar little books with other companies. *Best Wok Recipes* was sold to West Bend; and Cribari wines gives complimentary copies of *Holiday Get-Together Recipes.*

In researching this subject and talking with special-sales people in major trade houses we were told, "There are only about ten of us going after premiums aggressively. It's an untapped resource for most publishers." If this avenue sounds intriguing, there are a couple of additional things you can do to stir the pot. Good ol' *LMP* comes to the rescue again. In the section on "Book Producers" there are some firms listed which deal primarily in premiums. Perhaps you can interest one of them in your book. Three trade publications are read by premium buyers in major corporations. To reach them, send a photo of your book and about a five-line blurb to Product Showcase Editor, *Potentials in Marketing,* 50 South Ninth Street, Minneapolis, MN 55402; to *Premium Incentive Business* magazine at 1515 Broadway, New York, NY 10036; and to *Incentive Marketing* at 633 Third Avenue, New York, NY 10017. If you are fortunate enough to be included, you'll probably get forty to fifty responses asking for details. One out of ten may jell, but it can take as long as a year. Discounts usually range from 60 to 70 percent off the retail price and purchases are nonreturnable. It's a great way to sell books!

If you've published a photography book, you might link up with a plastic camera housing company, for instance. Is your title *Play the Harmonica in Three Easy Lessons*? What a natural for a harmonica manufacturer. They cling together like brand-new dollar bills. A banana cookbook might interest Chiquita. If your message is about thwarting computer crime, contact computer manufacturers and suggest a mutual arrangement. Have a product that deals with being a better parent? You can reach a large number of pediatricians through distributors of medical supplies. They can be found in the *Hayes Directory of Physician and Hospital Supply Houses* or the *Directory of Medical Products Distributors*. Depending on your subject area, you might also look in the local yellow pages or contact trade and professional associations for names of suppliers.

Various service businesses might also yield opportunities for book sales. Let's suppose you have a book on how to interview effectively. Jeff Herman had just such a challenge with *Getting Hired: Everything You Need to Know About Resumes, Interviews and Job Hunting Strategies*. While *Time* magazine gave away a few thousand copies, he wasn't willing to stop there. Herman saw the book as a "natural" for college audiences. Who targets this market? Beer companies. So he solicited them for bids. His gusto resulted in Adolph Coors' purchasing no less than 164,750 copies! One of our students had good luck selling his booklet entitled *Locks: How They Work and How to Pick Them* to police departments. (Interesting correlation, that one!) Another unlikely alliance is Westphalia Press' *Tom's Remembrance*. They sold 1,000 copies of this title to the state funeral directors association. The association plans to give it to customers as "a salve for the soul." Writer's Digest Books worked with the Polaroid Corporation to carry one of their titles, *How to Create Super Slide Shows*, as a promotion for Polaroid's instant slide film system. Almost any book has premium potential if you are clever enough to determine where the fit is.

More bulk-sale opportunities

If we're to have large-scale successes, we must think big. That point was solidly brought home to us by our children one year. At Christmas, Marilyn typically bakes batches and batches of cookies. And most years the kids get into trouble because they sneak in and snitch them off the cookie sheets before they've even cooled, leaving tell-tale empty spots. One Christmas the sheets went untouched and we secretly rejoiced that the kids had finally outgrown their holiday mischief. It wasn't until weeks later, while cleaning the garage, that we learned the truth. There, stuck in a corner, was an empty cookie sheet. They had solved their problem by thinking big—taking the whole sheet—which we never missed!

Catalog marketing

One way you might think big is to place your book in a specialty mail-order catalog. These range from expensive gift and gadget books like the one Neiman-Marcus puts out, to ones covering more everyday fare like Miles Kimball, Lillian Vernon, and Walter Drake. There are also specialized catalogs for electronics, collectibles, clothing, gardening, appliances, hardware, and food. And if you have a book on boating, try Goldberg's Marine catalog. Want to place your title dealing with crafts? Maybe Lee Ward would be interested. And Brookstone, famous for its hard-to-find tools, just might cotton to your booklet on blacksmithing. *The Catalog of Catalogs* is the ultimate resource, including 8,000 listings in 450 categories. Those listed below account for about three-fourths of all the business in this field. You may want to write and request catalogs.

Miles Kimball Company
251 Bond Street
Oshkosh, WI 54901

Hanover House
340 Poplar
Hanover, PA 17331

Lillian Vernon
510 South Fulton Avenue
Mt. Vernon, NY 10550

Walter Drake & Sons, Inc.
Drake Building
Colorado Springs, CO 80901

Now browse through them looking for books or potential tie-ins with your title. When you find some that carry books, or you sense an innovative merchandising angle, send them a letter (see example in this section) and promotional materials offering a copy for their consideration. They are primarily interested in products that are not available in stores. An interesting paradox, however, is that after an item has succeeded in mail-order catalogs, it usually makes a smooth and profitable transition into retail stores.

Catalog houses expect discounts in the 55 to 60 percent range and, once an item establishes itself as being a good seller, will probably take five hundred to one thousand books at a time. To really learn the "ins and outs" of this form of merchandising, get a copy of Ron Payle's *Selling to Catalog Houses.*

Government sales

The government can also become your customer. Locking into the right agency or program can be a marvelous source of revenue. One way to get started is to call your nearest Federal Information Center and ask for advice on whom to contact. To learn more about the centers and how to use them, write the Consumer Information Center, Pueblo, CO 81009,

a colorado corporation

July 22, 1977

Re: New Products

Ted Leyhe, President
MILES KIMBALL
Kimball Building
41 West Eighth Avenue
Oshkosh, Wisconsin 54901

Dear Mr. Leyhe:

In reviewing your catalog, I notice you carry several "how-to" books. For that reason, you may be interested in our newest publication.

It is called Discover Your Roots: A New, Easy Guide for Tracing Your Family Tree. As you know, hundreds of thousands of Americans are intrigued by the concept of learning about their heritage. A post-Roots Gallup Poll showed that 29 percent of Americans were "very interested" in learning more about their ancestry. Another 40 percent were "somewhat interested." And the fascination is no passing fad. Interest continues to mushroom. In fact, the National Archives are currently beseiged with vacationers as reported in the July 4th issue of Newsweek.

Discover Your Roots differs from other genealogy books in two ways: Brevity is one of its strengths. The reader is not forced to wade through hundreds of pages of material. Rather, the material is offered in 14 short, information-packed chapters. Another asset is its light, entertaining style. We have had very favorable comments about its content from both general readers and experts in the field.

This book would fit in well with your gift line. And it is a natural marriage with the Ancestral Chart you have advertised in Volume 2, 1977.

The enclosed catalog sheet gives more particulars. I will be happy to provide you with a complimentary examination copy upon request. We look forward to establishing a mutually beneficial working relationship with you, so as to serve Miles Kimball customers more fully.

Sincerely,

Ann Markham

Ann Markham
Marketing Director

AM/lw
enclosures

415 Fourth Street, P.O. Box 213, Saguache, Colorado 81149-0213   303-655-2504

Catalog letter.

and ask for free brochure No. 621-E. (Also see the listing in the Appendix.)

Associations

National associations offer more rich veins to be mined. Go to the library and snuggle up with a copy of the *Encyclopedia of Associations*. No matter what your book is about, there is an association of people who would be interested in it. Find out who they are and contact the executive directors about quantity purchases.

Fund-raising

How about promoting your book as the ideal fund-raising tool? There may be groups of young, senior, or church folks who would love to help you sell copies for a percentage of the receipts. Anytime you can ally yourself with others who will serve as your sales force for a small percentage, it is worth serious consideration. Tom Davis, the author of *Be Tough or Be Gone,* whom you met earlier, is working on a nifty deal. He is talking with the national headquarters of 4-H to set up a program where local groups of young people sell his book as a fund-raiser.

Corporate sales

Many books lend themselves to being purchased by large companies. This is different from a premium sale where a book is customized for the individual company. In this case you simply sell a block of books—usually for internal use. Roger von Oech, whom we talked about earlier, did this with his *A Whack on the Side of the Head.* He told us IBM took two thousand, Hewlett Packard bought seven hundred, and Control Data reached into its corporate coffers for six hundred.

National syndication

While researching, we learned of another appealing road to bulk sales. There is an organization called National Syndication that buys remnant space in publications like *Parade* and *Family Weekly.* It uses this space to peddle books on very specific subjects to general audiences. Jess Joseph, of National Syndication, told us he is particularly interested in books on nutrition, health, exercise, needlecraft, and retirement that sell for $12.95 or less. He stresses that potential buyers can't browse through a book like they can in a bookstore, so everything about it (the title, jacket, and concept) must be very clear. Initially, Joseph buys 100 copies of a book he wants to consider. If it tests well, he'll take from 5,000 to 100,000 over the period of a year. He expects 65 to 70 percent off the retail price. You can reach National Syndication at 230 Fifth Avenue, Room 2010, New York, NY 10001.

Overseas sales

Your sales arena can be the whole world. Although book exports are not as brisk as they were in the 1950s, exporting your book may still find viable markets. Books published on the North American continent are in great demand in many English-speaking countries: England, New Zealand, South Africa, and Australia. And we've had reports that West Germany, India, the Philippines, Japan, Africa, Scandinavia, and Holland are not far behind. Don't overlook our neighbor to the North. While the Canadian market is only one-tenth that of the United States, it is still an excellent place to sell books through a distributor there. Of course, not all subject matter is appropriate. It must have universal appeal. If, for instance, you have a cookbook that includes recipes dependent on ingredients available only in the United States, it wouldn't work.

International book marketing can be a complicated undertaking. You will need information from the U.S. Department of Commerce and the Postal Service, plus guidance on currency exchange provisions and customs paperwork. Uncle Sam, in his efforts to increase exports, makes advertising and statistics available which can be quite helpful. Ask Commerce Department personnel to show you what nations bought the most books, and what type they were, etc. To avoid payment problems, insist that your sales be by Irrevocable Letter of Credit (ILOC). Under this plan, payment for your books is posted with a U.S. bank, to be released after your shipment reaches its destination.

What probably makes the most sense is to align yourself with an export agent. As you may have guessed, they, too, are listed in *LMP*. These distributors typically expect 55 to 65 percent off, but it's money well spent, as they are also responsible for all distribution and debt collection and can advise you in general about exporting. Some warn against signing an exclusive export agreement on a "best effort" basis. If they want such an arrangement, you want a minimum nonreturnable order before you grant exclusive rights to represent you. Catering to foreign markets can indeed boost your sales if it is done with good business judgment.

Additional marketing ideas

"Boldly go where no man has gone before," *Star Trek* used to challenge. And why not? The person clever enough to use imaginative ways to command attention or to expand sales is like cream . . . always rising to the top.

One way to move books is to hawk them personally. The author of *A War Ends* solds his $8.95 novel door-to-door. Fortunately for him, a reporter for a Los Angeles newspaper lived behind one of those doors. The reporter was so impressed with this unusual approach to bookselling that he wrote a story. Subsequent publicity focused a national spotlight on the author.

Gary Provost, who wrote and published *The Dorchester Gas Tank,* a book of offbeat humor, contends that the secret of selling self-published books is eyeball-to-eyeball contact with people. In the early days of his career, you could find him around the Boston Public Library, City Hall, subway stations, or any busy place almost every morning. He toted a suitcase full of books, a poster, and the knowledge that he was earning his living solely as a writer-publisher. Back then, Gary peddled between twenty and twenty-five books each day he worked.

While you may choose not to become this directly involved in selling, there is still a message here. Always carry books with you! As you meet new people and circulate in new places, fresh opportunities materialize. We've sold books to a gas station jockey who saw a copy in the car and to strangers waiting in line next to us. Keep your book visible and yourself verbal.

Speaking of visible, use your eyes to open new horizons. Marilyn noticed a Dell Purse Book in the market one day and picked up a copy to scan the publisher's list of titles in this series. There was nothing on genealogy. A letter proposing that Dell excerpt portions of our *Discover Your Roots* was soon on its way. The answer came back negative. They weren't interested in *DYR.* However, they were interested in contracting with her to write *another* book on genealogy for them. It was a quick and simple assignment, as all the research was complete. Two weeks later we were $700 richer.

In case you're wondering, we did give serious consideration to the question "Will a purse book detract from our book sales?" The answer came out no. Our prime buyers were libraries, schools, and individuals who frequent bookstores — not the same audience who impulsively picks up a small purse book at the grocery store.

Another nice spin-off for *DYR* occurred. We approached the Boy Scouts and the Girl Scouts to see if either would want to use it as a reference book for genealogy. The *Girl Scout Leader* ended up suggesting that tracing your roots would be a stimulating activity and gave our book top billing in a list of recommended resources. Many times being included in bibliographies leads to sales. If you become aware of one for your subject matter (and it does not already mention your book), write and request to be considered in the next revision.

Reading trade journals also leads to additional sales and promotional opportunities. "Small Things Considered," a daily New York City children's radio program, put out a call in *Publishers Weekly* for children's books to be awarded as prizes for various on-the-air contests. In exchange, publishers received a plug for their book.

As we go to press, BookMart, an on-line home-shopping service for books, is in the formative stages. This electronic publishing opportunity will sell or rent computerized listings for a year. It sounds interesting for those who publish specialty books and want to reach a national market without having to place inventory in bookstores nationwide. We're sure you'll be hearing more about them.

Along a similar line, some data bases—such as The Source, NewsNet, and CompuServe—may be interested in adding you to their offerings. This only applies if your information is especially timely, though. They have specific publishing agreements for electronic dissemination of your printed word.

Or you may even want to hire a programmer and set up your own data base. These sell anywhere from fifty dollars to several hundred dollars. John Kremer has done this with his marketing leads.

Through the efforts of William F. Buckley and Stuart W. Little, a new way to keep books alive has emerged. In 1984 they put out the first

Buckley-Little Catalogue, a listing of books available from authors. This catalog forges a new link in the book distribution chain. Authors whose books have gone out of print can often pick up the overstock their publishers intend to remainder, list their work in the catalog, and breathe fresh vitality into their title. It seems to us this is an innovative and courageous idea to keep good books in the marketplace. After all, 90 percent of new books are removed from bookstore shelves in less than twelve months — before they can possibly be expected to reach their full intended audience.

The *Buckley-Little Catalogue* contains listings for more than 750 titles. They run the gamut from fiction, literature, poetry, and juveniles to nonfiction topics such as psychology, business strategy, and travel guides. The subject index contains thirty-two different categories. Books listed are obtainable from their authors, who hail from every part of this country and Canada. The catalog is distributed to individuals, booksellers, and libraries. Authors who have out-of-print works they would like entered in future editions should write The Buckley-Little Book Catalogue Company, Inc., Kraus Building, Route 100, Millwood, NY, 10546, for more information.

One other way we found to move individual copies of books is to set up "drop-ship" arrangements. In this situation someone else — like a newsletter editor, allied organization, or magazine — advertises or recommends your book at full retail price. When the advertiser receives orders, he deducts a percentage, sends you the order plus his check and a mailing label, and you ship the book directly to the customer. Discounts usually range from 30 to 50 percent. Only books of ten dollars or more are practical to merchandise this way, however. Adjacent is a sample letter we used to set up several drop-ship plans for the forerunner of this book.

Having written a book and become an "expert," there may be another track open to you. Have you ever thought of becoming a consultant? This is simply another way of selling information, only instead of relying on the written word, you work in person, via mail or phone. While this isn't applicable to all authors and books, it may be a service that will open new horizons for you. Orchestrating a consulting service is challenging and fun. It can also be very profitable. If the idea appeals to you, we suggest getting three books: *The Consultant's Kit,* by Dr. Jeffrey L. Lant, *How to Succeed as an Independent Consultant,* by Herman Holtz, and *How to Set Your Fees and Get Them,* by Kate Kelly.

And as facsimile (fax) machines become more popular, some publishers of high-ticket books will no doubt be using this version of direct marketing to peddle their wares. Fax machines receive any document sent and have an aura of urgency. This could lead to a new phenomenon of fax "junk mail," as unsolicited letters creep into businesses around the country.

COMMUNICATION CREATIVITY

a colorado corporation

July 6, 1981

Elliot Young
Mail Order Council
P.O. Box 411
Kenilworth, IL 60043

Dear Elliot:

   Any self-respecting newsletter editor is an entrepreneur at heart. And an entrepreneur is always open to new ideas to increase the bottom line. Let me share an intriguing proposition with you...

> We have an award-winning book that is receiving high praise throughout the country. It's a vitally important book for anyone who has knowledge or information to sell. And you can make $12.00 on every single copy sold through your newsletter!
>
> The ENCYCLOPEDIA OF SELF-PUBLISHING: HOW TO SUCCESSFULLY WRITE, PUBLISH, PROMOTE, AND SELL YOUR OWN WORK retails for $29.95. We are offering it to you on a drop ship 40% discount basis.
>
> All you do is write a blurb recommending the book in your newsletter. All orders are sent to you. Simply deposit the purchaser's check -- keep your 40% ($12.00) -- and remit us $17.95, plus a completed mailing label. Upon receipt of your check and the label, we will promptly mail the book directly to your subscribers.
>
> If such a financial arrangement is against your policy, why not pass along these special savings to your sub- scribers? Simply instruct them to send their check or money order for $17.95 to Communication Creativity, P.O. Box 267, Saguache, Colorado 81149.

   We've tried to design this offer so that everybody wins. I hope you'll agree! I look forward to hearing from you soon and establishing a mutually rewarding relationship.

Sincerely,

Ann Markham

Ann Markham

AM/lw
enclosures

415 Fourth Street, P.O. Box 213, Saguache, Colorado 81149-0213   303-655-2504

Newsletter letter.

While we're talking about direct marketing, don't overlook your own mailing list as an additional money-making possibility. Once it reaches 3,000 names or so, you can rent (not sell) your own in-house list of book purchasers. You can expect to earn from $50 to $90 per 1,000 names for one-time use. If you're in search of Midas, this is a sure way to turn your list to gold. As we said before, it's a good idea to "seed" it with a name and address that will reach you so it is immediately apparent if someone misuses your trust and tries to recycle the names more than the one time they were rented for.

As you can see, there are dozens of innovative strategies for making money on your book. Perhaps you will want to play with one of the ideas we've presented here. Or maybe you will simply use these concepts to trigger something else. In either event, it will be an exciting adventure as you reach further out into the world and create your own destiny.

Good growing pains

Perhaps your destiny includes printing additional editions of your title . . . or growing from self-publisher status to producing the works of other writers . . . or doing a whole string of your own books. In all of these cases there are things to consider.

When you are ready to go back to the printer for a second edition, it's time to celebrate. You've obviously done something, or a lot of somethings, right! You probably weren't lucky; just plucky. Before you turn over your book to the manufacturer, determine if it should be revised or expanded. (Often this will open fresh doors for promotion.)

By using the same book manufacturer, you can save part of the initial setup costs. You will want to make some alterations to the copyright page of the book. It should read: "Second printing" and the year. Perhaps it makes sense to revise the cover, splashing good reviews on it. Take advantage of some free publicity and send a brief news release to *Publishers Weekly* for their "Back to Press" section.

If you've progressed to the point where you're producing three titles a year, get your press listed in *LMP, Publishers Directory, Writer's Market,* and *Book Publishers of the United States and Canada.* Once you've put together a catalog of books, submit it for a free listing in *Publishers' Catalogs Annual.*

Additional books of your own needn't necessarily be on different subjects. The author of *Life Extension*, Durk Pearson, filled his original book with complicated and scientific articles. And it sold over a million copies. Then he did a second edition for the layperson. Adapted for the average reader, it took the same information but slanted it to a less sophisticated reading audience. Same book: two ways. Just another route to experiencing happy growing pains.

Another possible outlet for growth awaits in the field of lecturing. Let's go on now and discover those tricks of the trade.

CHAPTER 17

LECTURES, SEMINARS, AND AUTHOR TOURS

The lecture circuit is a natural for certain authors. In selected cases author tours can focus attention on you and your book and boost sales in the process. Here we take time to look at lectures and readings, talk about seminars, and discuss how to develop a free author tour.

Giving lectures and readings

As an author you are an "expert" on your subject. People will be anxious to hear your opinions or of your work. Giving lectures and readings is one popular way to promote a book. It's gratifying for the ego, lets you meet interesting folks, and — when done selectively — sells books.

Any writer can find speaking engagements at church groups, the Y, PTAs, civic groups, libraries, women's clubs, professional organizations, adult educational institutions, or senior centers. You might also consider giving in-store demonstrations if your subject matter lends itself to a commercial tie-in. Constantly have your antenna out for possibilities to plant yourself in the midst of potential customers. The more specialized, the better. Sometimes, these contacts take a long time to develop, but when they ripen, look out!

Early in the history of our book on leisure, we decided it would make an ideal reference for retirement planning. Since this is the bailiwick of AIM (Action for Independent Maturity), we shot promotional letters, phone calls, and copies of the book off to their headquarters. To make a long story short, Marilyn was asked to serve as a resource authority on "meaningful use of leisure" at their regional conference. Since representatives from many Fortune 500 companies were there to learn how to organize preretirement planning programs in their firms, it was a perfect source of leads for bulk sales.

To maximize your exposure, here are a few dos and don'ts. If sales are your aim, it's a waste of time to talk about a specific subject (organic gardening) with a small general audience (the XYZ auxiliary). The few who would be passionately interested in your topic aren't worth the effort. Unless you just like to stand up and talk, that is.

Be selective and only accept engagements for highly specialized audiences or large groups where there is more likelihood that a reasonable number of sales will be generated. For instance, Marilyn spoke at a retreat for recreation majors, presenting a special education session for the California and Pacific Southwest Recreation and Park Conference. She also addressed a large audience at a College of the Emeriti lecture series.

Two of her invitations arrived out of the blue from people who had read *Creative Loafing* or had heard about her through our publicity campaign. One was instigated by a discreet phone call placed to the Conference Coordinator, alerting her to an authority in the field of leisure who could make a contribution to the delegates' insights. Marilyn received a complimentary pass to the conference (allowing her to mingle with the three thousand attendees anytime during the four days). The engagement was accepted on the condition that our book be displayed and sold, and promotional materials be made available.

Do be sure to go armed with sales materials whenever you speak. Fliers with self-contained order blanks work well. If you are donating your time, don't hesitate to pass out literature, or at the very least have it available at tables. Some authors even manage to get copies tucked into the next membership mailing. Naturally, you will have a box of books with you and lots more in your car. Get several of them out on display. If you accept credit cards, don't forget to take the machine and announce that credit cards are welcome. Of course, you'll need to take some change along. To avoid the difficulty of making loose change, many authors figure the sales tax, then round off to the nearest dollar to keep things simple. Some authors give a small discount—perhaps 10 percent—to induce immediate sales. In any event, be sure to weave into your presentation that books will be available afterward. It's also wise to show the book a couple of times as you speak.

And offer to autograph them. People like autographed editions in their personal libraries, and sometimes will buy your book for a gift if you'll autograph it. This brings up a point that is often overlooked by authors. What will you say? Think this through before you ever get books off the press. Devise a standard little "pat" comment such as the one Marilyn used for *Creative Loafing:* "May you find new adventures in these pages. Enjoy!" Naturally, you'll vary it for special people and circumstances. Always autograph for a person by name and if you have any doubt about how to spell it, ask.

Be sure there are quantities of books in the local bookstores. We often hear horror stories from writers published by the major trade houses. Many times when they give special lectures or appear for the media, there are no books available in the stores. This is self-defeating.

Before talking, find out what kind of turf you will be playing on. Who will the audience be: men or women? What is their average age? Educational level? Will it be a cozy group of two dozen or an auditorium of seven hundred? Also, give the person setting up the arrangements input from your end. Do you want a blackboard? Slide projector? Water? Would a lavaliere mike (which goes around your neck) give you more freedom for delivering your message? Professional speakers usually provide the person introducing them with a written introduction. This makes sure your credits are given correctly and starts you off with the expert status you deserve.

You can also ask the introducer to announce after the talk something like, "The speaker will be in the back of the room to autograph books." This reminder is a good sales stimulator. People who have enjoyed your talk will want to take something of you home, and your book satisfies that desire. Appropriately enough, this is known as "back of the room sales." Many authors have sold thousands of books this way; some professional speakers make more from their back of the room sales than they do from their lecture fees!

Establishing good communication with your sponsor and the person introducing you at the early stages yields a smooth presentation. Make each occasion a performance. Soon your fame will spread and paid engagements will be coming your way. (Not to mention hordes of single-copy book sales!) It may not be long before you're invited to be the keynote speaker for a major convention or meeting.

If your talk is of interest to the business community or has an important local news angle, you may be able to get even more mileage from it. Professional lecturers often provide the media with a copy of their speech. This should be a typed, double-spaced, word-for-word text of your address. (No, you don't have to stick to it exactly when you actually talk — in fact, please don't. The text is a guide, not a shackle.) Be sure your name, phone number, the name of the group you are addressing, and the date and time of the talk appear on the first page of all copies. It's a nice touch to also include a head-shot photograph, biographical sketch, and a news summary (a brief paragraph giving the basic facts of who, where, what, and why) of your talk.

Many who are getting rich giving seminars have their "pulling power" because of a book. The key to getting students is often a successful book. One Chicago author earned more than $2 million during a five-year span talking about his book's subject: real estate. And 130,000 people have attended Albert Lowery's lectures. He's the author of *How You Can Become Financially Independent by Investing in Real Estate*.

If you are a poet or novelist, there are many prime candidates for sharing your message at readings. All sorts of places sponsor such events. You could give a reading at a library, community center, church, or bookstore. University programs also sponsor such activities, as do museums and literary coffeehouses and bars.

Poets & Writers, in conjunction with the Literature Program of the New York State Council on the Arts, serves as a clearinghouse for such events in New York State (and at the time of this writing, they plan to begin a similar program in California in January 1989). In one year they were instrumental in 471 writers receiving over $200,000 in fees from readings and workshops.

Bruce Sievers takes a slightly different approach. He is billed as "An American in love with his country." Bruce is a poet who has produced patriotic booklets and tapes. He is also a showman. If a nonprofit organization pays his travel and hotel expenses, he will put on a presentation free of charge in exchange for the right to sell his materials. And sell them he does. Bruce makes $200,000 a year merchandising his poetry this way!

How to develop a free author tour

We have to be honest with you: It's much harder to get on shows than it was five years ago. At first we thought we'd lost our touch, as it was becoming increasingly more difficult to book our clients. (See the adjacent schedule of interviews for what it used to be like.) But it isn't just us; it's an industrywide enigma. *Publishers Weekly* noted that the bloom is off the rose for author tours: "Supply in excess of demand, too many similar books, and increased local emphasis are making radio and TV stations less receptive than they were." Publicists everywhere are complaining that authors have become a tough sell. Part of the problem is that everybody is competing for the same shows with the same kinds of books — stuff on nutrition, diets, and computers. And there's been such a spate of books by Hollywood celebrities, sports figures, and CEO's lately that the average author has slim pickings.

However, Becky Barker, who wrote and published *Answers* — a three-ring binder full of forms dealing with family, financial, property, insurance, and business issues — struck a vein of gold in national media. Her book came out of a tragedy. Becky's husband was killed, and she didn't know where to find any vital papers or information. She duplicated twenty copies of *Answers* for Christmas gifts, printed 1,000 in November of the next year and soon went back for printings totaling 50,000.

Becky has appeared on *Good Morning America, Hour Magazine,* and *Donahue. Good Morning America* had her back for a second time, as the response to her first appearance was one of the largest the show had ever received. What's the secret of her success? "They really liked the book. It was a different concept," she says. Becky had two friends who volunteered to contact the media for her. While they are poised and powerful women, she mainly attributes her acceptance by such top-notch shows to the unusual content of her book. Which goes to prove if you choose your subject carefully, first-rate things can happen!

So if you have a good subject, you may decide to put together a package of information that will provide an author tour with expenses prepaid. Impossible? Not really. We did it and you can, too.

After recognizing that we needed to reach people all over the nation through mass-media promotion, a strange sensation set in—fear. How could we afford to go truckin' all over the country to reach the media outlets we needed to promote *Creative Loafing*? Obviously, we would have to sell something. But what? Tom vetoed the house, Marilyn balked at losing her car, and our four teenagers refused to cooperate by working twelve-hour-days to fund the operation. This was a time for serious thinking.

What would create funds to offset expenses? Book sales would certainly be a factor. Sure enough, a publicity tour could be paid for by book sales. But one problem becomes immediately apparent. Books are typically sold on credit. While it would be nice to start getting checks after we got home, there is no front money in such an arrangement.

How about selling information? No, not another book—a seminar! After several months of developing a program, securing mailing lists, and designing and printing brochures, we were ready to hit the road. That was the birth of the "How to Get Successfully Published" conference program. As you can see on the letter and sample brochure, we typically offered a writers' workshop in the evening from seven to ten, then a self-publishing session the next day from ten until four. People could attend one or both. Here again, we offered the option of using credit cards to make it easy to partake.

For the next few months we roared around the country giving eleven sets of seminars and consulting with authors and self-publishers on an individual basis in most cities. At each stop Marilyn plugged *Creative Loafing* on TV, radio, and in newspapers. It was like running for the presidency—a very stressful time! But we were in a hurry; we wanted to get back to the typewriter and write *The Encyclopedia of Self-Publishing*. As it turned out, we became wiser in the process. Things that didn't work were jettisoned for those that did. We reworked and refined the tour and thus share what was learned.

To be sure, there are other ways to fund author tours besides teaching writing and publishing. You wrote a book; it must be on a subject that you're knowledgeable about. As an expert who has authored a book, why not give seminars or lectures to teach others that expertise? (And if you just can't stomach the idea of getting up in front of a bunch of people, you might use your author tour to do article or book research and interview national authorities for a future writing project.)

Some organizations will pick up the tab for travel and accommodations, as well as pay you a fee, in return for your giving a presentation to their group. The previous section gave tips on how to get started in public speaking. As you refine your speaking skills, you'll find the professional lecture circuit exciting and lucrative. One definite advantage of this method over the seminar loop is that *you* don't have to worry about facilities, advertising, scheduling, and coordination. The sponsor is responsible for all the details. You just show up, do your thing, get paid, and go about promoting your book.

There is much to be said for this approach. We presented two seminars at Folio's Face-to-Face Publishing Conference in New York: one on Special Sales Opportunities for Book Publishers; the other on Buying the Right Computer for Book Publishers. It was much easier to just walk in and give a presentation than it would have been to set up and promote the whole thing ourselves. Today we travel all over the country speaking at writer's conferences and publishing events. We're hired by colleges and universities, associations, writer's organizations, even a health spa.

Of course, with your own seminar the earning potential is greater. Even after spending up to 50 percent on expenses, a $50 seminar with fifty people nets $1,250. For a $100 admission fee it would cost you about 40 percent for expenses, yielding a net of $3,000. What you can charge depends a lot on your topic. If you have unique information that appeals to the business community, executives will pay hundreds of dollars for it. On the other hand, if your audience is housewives, the admission fee must be much smaller. There's one consolation, however: America has a lot more housewives than executives.

And author-publisher Beverly Nye certainly knows how to appeal to this group. To promote *A Family Raised on Sunshine,* Nye bought a thirty-day Greyhound bus ticket and visited the five cities where she had previously lived. Working with Mormon church groups and home-extension classes, she brought audiences together for homemaking lectures. Each time she finished, more than half of those present purchased her book. In a month's time, Nye sold fifteen hundred books. She also made money from the lecture admission fees.

 inc.   P.O. Box 9512   San Diego, CA 92109   (714)/459-3386

Dear Friend:

You can make a lot of money selling what you know! That's right. You possess special knowledge or ideas that others will gladly pay for. Everyone has salable information.

● What do you do better than most people? Notice I didn't say better than all people. If you do something better than half the citizen population of the U.S.A. . . . you have a potential market of 100 million people!

● What serious problem have you solved in your life? Do you really think you are the only one who ever had that problem? Tell others how to solve it and make money!

● What annoyance have you figured out a solution to? Put this knowledge into written form and reap new financial rewards!

Discover how to publish, promote and profit from your own book, booklet or newsletter. Many people have become wealthy entrepreneurs by starting their own self-publishing business writing and selling information. Some earn enough extra income to build their dream home or travel around the world. Others establish a comfortable retirement income. Here are a few of the success stories of self-publishing.

John Muir sold 1,000,000 copies of his How to Keep Your Volkswagen Alive. Carla Emery also cashed in on her knowledge. Her book, Carla Emery's Old Fashioned Recipe Book has gone into seven editions. Wayne Floyd saw a trend starting a few years ago. He brought out The Authentic Dictionary of CB Slang. And the list goes on . . . How to Form Your Own Corporation Without a Lawyer for Under $50, by businessman Ted Nicholas --- Touch for Health by chiropractor John Thie --- Four Minute Fun for Parent & Child by educator Elaine Hardt. These people all decided to capitalize on their specialized knowledge by privately publishing and promoting their own books.

Copy Concepts, Inc. is dedicated to helping people make money by publishing their own work. Our consultants have shown hundreds of people "How to Get Successfully Published." The conference program was developed to provide you easy access to proven methods for developing a salable topic, conducting market research and writing effectively. There will be heavy emphasis on how to get free publicity and use direct marketing techniques to implement a powerful sales program.

If you're tired of being in the dark about how some people, who are not any smarter than you, acquire fame and prosperity, you owe it to yourself to capitalize on this opportunity. Discover how to get results and earn good money by selling your ideas or specialized knowledge.

Read the enclosed brochure, learn what others are saying about our service, and take the first step toward launching your own successful publishing business --- today!

Sincerely,

Alana M. Klepper

Alana M. Klepper
Vice President, Educational Services

AMK:pl/Enclosure

P.S. Joe Karbo, one of today's superstars of self-publishing, has sold over 700,000 copies of his Lazy Man's Way to Riches for $10.00 each!

Seminar letter.

306

How to Get Successfully Published

- Do you have a book manuscript that should be published?

- Ideas or information others would pay for?

- Are you tired of collecting rejection slips?

- Disappointed in the sales of your already-published book?

- Aware of the opportunities in self-publishing?

WRITERS WORKSHOP

New Ideas to Help You Earn More Money from Freelance Writing

An information-packed look at effective non-fiction writing for today's marketplace. This workshop explores how to sharpen your writing skills and generate more sales. Now you can take the free out of freelance writing!

SELF-PUBLISHING WORKSHOP

How to Publish, Promote & Sell your Book, Booklet, Pamphlet or Report

Practical and broad-based, this workshop introduces you to all aspects of book production and marketing. Finally—the secrets of successful self-publishing are revealed!

Workshop letters.

Typical Participants' Comments

YOUR INSTRUCTORS

TOM ROSS is an editor and advertising executive. His business expertise spans 25 years, during which he served on the boards of directors for several corporations. He has conducted numerous business and management training sessions. Tom holds a degree from Pacific College and is frequently called upon as a consultant.

He has served as the senior editor for a book publishing house and currently is president of Copy Concepts, Inc., a San Diego-based advertising and public relations agency that specializes in working with the publishing industry.

Tom has masterminded nationwide publicity campaigns resulting in extensive author exposure on TV, radio and in print media.

A member of the Book Publicists of Southern California, he is known as an innovative and aggressive member of the business community.

MARILYN ROSS is an author, lecturer and publisher. *Creative Loafing*, her third book, was just released. Her work was sold to *Modern Maturity*, *Essence*, *Westways*, *National Enquirer*, *Coronet*, *NRTA Journal*, *Business Forum* and other national magazines and trade journals. Marilyn also has edited a newsletter, written a weekly newspaper column, and done advertising copywriting. Presently she heads her own publishing firm.

She has taught "Writing for Profit" in the San Diego Community College District. A gifted and dynamic teacher, Marilyn has earned the respect of students and associates alike. Her abilities have brought headlines in major newspapers, guest spots on radio and TV, and lecture engagements across the country.

Her professional affiliations include the Committee of Small Magazine Editors and Publishers (COSMEP), California Press Women—Southern District, and the Authors Guild.

Seize this opportunity to make more from your writing . . . apply for admission today!

Seminar strategy

There is no question about seminars being big business. They generate somewhere over $200 million each year in North America. And putting on seminars is a legitimate business expense, so everything is tax-deductible. (But that doesn't mean you can't have a wonderful visit with Aunt Minnie while in New York or renew an old friendship with John while doing Los Angeles.)

Here are a few specific suggestions: It works well if you have a liaison person assisting in each city. You can often find an enthusiastic helper by contacting other members of a national organization to which you belong. Reward this person with a small commission on seminar sales. The local can provide inside information on how to publicize your seminar, help arrange suitable meeting rooms, and assist during the actual function. Another thing we've used to build attendance is setting up referral fees with key people in various cities. If you know someone in your field who would have good contacts with people who could benefit from attending your seminar, let him or her in on the action. Everyone benefits this way. Pay the person a finder's fee of so much per head.

Be sure to arrive at the hotel where the seminar is scheduled at least an hour early. Go over everything you need with the meeting coordinator (a list should have been provided by mail earlier). Be sure the podium setup is to your liking; that microphones, screens, blackboards, slide projectors, are in place. Always ask for water, for both yourself and participants. If the seminar will run long, it's gracious to arrange for coffee, tea, and soft drinks for attendees. *Successful Meetings* magazine suggests upbeat music be played to greet people coming in the room. (The themes "Rocky" and "Chariots of Fire" are current favorites.) Bring name tags with you so that people can get acquainted. At some seminars the networking opportunities prove as valuable as the information dispensed. Get your books, ordering literature, and other paraphernalia set up. For display purposes many self-publishers have a poster made of a blowup of their book cover.

There may come a time when you face a difficult decision. Say it's a week or so before a scheduled seminar, and in a particular location registration is lagging way behind. If it appears the function will not pay for itself—and your trip to that city—do you go ahead or cancel? You must weigh the benefits of the author media exposure that's been arranged and any other considerations. It may make more sense to cancel than to run in the red.

Regardless which tack you take, a PR and advertising campaign is needed to promote your product—you. Seminars are advertised by direct-marketing techniques. (Refer to Chapters 11 and 12 for details.) If you choose the lecture circuit, create a package that consists of a cover letter and promotional material, plus testimonials emphasizing your speaking prowess. This can be sent to the list of lecture agents which appears in *LMP*. Or you can create your own specialized list by finding appropriate organizations in *National Trade and Professional Associations*.

As with most other programs, it's best to start at home and let the ripple of success carry you further and further. After the seminars or lectures prove themselves in your own backyard, try neighboring areas. Schedule a couple of sessions in nearby cities within driving distance to keep costs down. Then begin working your way further from camp. You can eventually cover the country from border to border and coast to coast.

Well, now we have succeeded in designing your program and exploring how you can take the show on the road. But don't forget your most important cargo. The point of this endeavor was to create a big clamor about your book. So let's tend to the matter of setting up the media package for our tour.

In previous chapters we shared how to create marketing plan lists and approach newspapers, radio, and television media. Those methods hold true for a tour as well as a local area. Check the previously mentioned comprehensive radio and television directories which give complete station information, network affiliation, audience profile, and the names of staff and special programs—in short, all the information you could possibly need to select programs for your campaign and tour. Some media contacts are also listed in *LMP*.

The best TV plums are the *CBS Morning News, Good Morning America, The Oprah Winfrey Show, Geraldo, Donahue,* and *Today*. Needless to say, it wouldn't hurt if Johnny Carson takes a personal interest, either. It has been reported that an appearance on *Donahue* can move fifty thousand books, and exposure on the *Today* show will sell three thousand. To help you in planning, be aware that *CBS Morning News, Good Morning America, Today,* and *Donahue* all originate in New York. Carson holds court in beautiful downtown Burbank (Southern California), and *Oprah* is produced in Chicago.

Before you even hope to crack one of these babies, get lots of media experience under your belt. As we said earlier, when you've had a particularly favorable interview, get a videotape of it. This will cost you, but rest assured that the producers of the abovementioned shows aren't about to let a rank amateur on the air. You'll have to prove that you're worthy of their precious airtime.

Review all your information sources carefully and build your mailing lists for the stations and programs you want to hit on your tour. Follow the procedures given under radio and TV interviews. For newspapers along the way, you can use the sources and techniques offered in the section on "Getting More Newspaper Coverage" in Chapter 14 and "Getting Reviewed" in Chapter 13. Or you might contact the phone company and get yellow pages for the cities on your route.

Once you've got your tour set, here are some ways you can make your life easier: In many major cities there are now people who function as publicity escorts. For around a hundred dollars a day, they shuttle authors to media appearances. While that may sound like a lot, consider what's involved if you have to rent a car, study maps, wrestle with traffic, allow for getting lost, and still arrive all fresh and vibrant to go on the air. If you want to use such an escort service, contact the Chamber of Commerce for referrals in cities you'll be visiting.

As you begin to put the author tour pieces together, leave yourself plenty of time. You'll want to schedule further in advance than for local coverage. Tours are not for everyone; yet they can be lucrative and fun under the right circumstances.

CHAPTER **18**

SUBSIDIARY RIGHTS

In this chapter we will concentrate on how to sell your book in "pieces" to magazines and newspapers. We'll also look at tapping into book clubs and merchandising paperback reprint rights to a major publisher. Lastly, film and TV plus foreign and translation rights will be examined.

What are subsidiary rights?

In trade publishing the *primary* sale is the actual sale or licensing providing for the initial publication of the book itself. *Subsidiary rights* (sub rights) follow and embrace all other rights. Perhaps an easier way to think of them would be as additional, spin-off sales which allow someone else to package and disseminate your material in a different form. This encompasses—but is not limited to—such things as selling the paperback rights to your hardcover book, selling the right to produce your book in motion-picture form, and selling the right to excerpt part of a book for a magazine.

It can be a dramatic avenue to profit, often producing greater revenue than the book itself. Selling subsidiary rights has another distinct advantage. It helps demonstrate your credibility. A book club that purchases a book or a respected national magazine that serializes it, for example, is in effect endorsing the book. This endorsement can be used in sales materials to influence other sub rights buyers, not to mention wholesalers, etc.

While such rights are more likely to be negotiated by large trade houses or literary agents, the self-publisher should nonetheless seek out any possibilities that might be to his or her advantage. And there are several.

Subsidiary rights run the gamut from paperback to book club to first and second serialization to foreign rights. They also cover such things as movies, dramatizations in the form of plays, television, and radio. And we've only just begun. There are also foreign rights, translation rights, condensation, anthology, and adaptation rights. In our high-tech world, new ones have emerged. Today there are videodisk, computerized data base, and microfilm possibilities. Someone might even be willing to pay you for the right to use your title commercially or to quote parts of your book or reproduce illustrations from it, so this could be construed as a subsidiary right.

Selling your book in "pieces" to magazines and newspapers

Selling first and second serial rights will not bring you megabucks. Oh sure, *Woman's Day* paid $200,000 for Rose Kennedy's memoirs. And the *National Enquirer* has been known to shell out $150,000 for a celebrity book. But that's certainly not the norm. What these rights *will* do is give your book tremendous exposure and help its sales.

First serial rights are those which appear *before* the official publication date rolls around. They are the most coveted. Just be sure to plan around the date when the material will appear in the periodical; since some first serial agreements prohibit you from publishing the book until a number of months have elapsed, you don't want to sign something that will hold up your pub date. Occasionally, a whole book will be serialized in installments in a single magazine, as was Norman Mailer's *An American Dream*. More often, a serialization contract will give the periodical the right to excerpt a stated maximum number of words or a specific portion of the work, such as a chapter.

Magazines, newspapers, and newspaper syndicates will expect an exclusive for the material they select. In some cases this is easy. When Patricia Breinen, of Holt, Reinhart & Winston, started peddling *Love Medicine,* she realized it could be easily divvied up among several takers. This was possible because the book—a saga of two Indian families—is written like a series of short stories, each story (chapter) concerning a member of one of the families at a critical moment in life. Breinen really outdid herself, however, and set a precedent by securing *ten* first serial sales. She sold parts of the book to *Atlantic, Ms., Kenyon Review, Chicago* (two excerpts), *Mother Jones, Mississippi Review, North American Review, North Dakota Quarterly,* and *New England Review.* Perhaps you have a novel that could be handled in a similar way, or a nonfiction book with chapters that will stand on their own.

To locate subsidiary rights buyers, first check the list provided in the Appendix. You will want to augment it by looking in *Book Marketing Op-*

portunities: A Directory and *Writer's Market* for additional names. Put together a sales package consisting of a letter, news release, and dust covers if you have them. Be prepared to send a copy of your typed manuscript or galleys to those who indicate interest.

One way to beef up your chances of making a sale is to preselect material to suggest to each magazine. Again, you're making it easy to buy. When you tailor the material to the individual needs of each—by recommending that particular attention be paid to a specific chapter or to a certain block of pages—you show that you respect the editor's busy schedule and understand the slant of the publication, and are offering something that will interest the readers of that publication. And it usually pays big dividends. We sold a small excerpt to the *National Enquirer* for one client, who pocketed an extra $300 from the transaction. The *Star* took two installments of another book we represented, giving the author access to 7 million readers. *New Woman* magazine, an excellent market, excerpted two other books of clients and *Woman* magazine took second serial rights to another one.

Second serial rights take place anytime after the pub date. While not considered such plums, they still have the potential of bringing your book to the attention of millions of new readers. And you can approach them at a more leisurely pace when the hubbub of initial publication activities has passed. The going rate is half or less of first-rights payments.

Trade-published authors can often get permission from their publishers to pursue second serial rights—and keep *all* the revenue they generate. This is just one more way *any author* can impact book sales by following the guidelines offered in these pages.

When you sell your book in pieces, there is one very important stipulation you should insist upon. At the beginning or end of the excerpt, you want the copyright notice to be printed. Don't run the risk of not being covered by the *magazine's* copyright. Require that ©, the year, and your name as copyright holder appear. It is also vital that readers be given ordering information about your book. It should include at least the following: book title, author, and publisher. Also try to include the publisher's address and the cost of the book so potential customers can get it easily.

Usually, the magazine or newspaper will have a standard agreement it uses to consummate the sale. Read it carefully and ask that the above provisions be included if there is any question. If there is no contract, as was the case with one of the serial rights sales we made back in 1980, create a letter of your own to outline the specifics. (See the adjacent sample.)

a colorado corporation

March 28, 1980

Ali Sar
Valley News
P.O. Box 310
Van Nuys, California   91408

Dear Ali:

I am pleased to confirm our recent telephone agreement on second
rights for Walt: Backstage Adventures with Walt Disney.

For a fee of $150.00 paid in advance, we hereby grant Valley News
the right to publish 10,000 words--one time only--for use in its
paper. No other rights are granted or implied.

Communication Creativity retains right of copy approval prior to
issue.

Valley News agrees, as part of the terms, to conspicuously
identify:
> 1. The author's name
> 2. The publisher
> 3. Communication Creativity
>   5644 La Jolla Blvd.
>   La Jolla, CA   92037

This letter represents the entire agreement between the two
parties and is in effect when approved by the authorized
representatives of each and one copy returned to Communication
Creativity.

T.M. Ross   _____
Rights & Permission Director
COMMUNICATION CREATIVITY   VALLEY NEWS

Date _____   Date _____

Second-rights letter.

Tapping into book clubs

Publishers Weekly reported on November 4, 1984, that annual sales of consumer books through book clubs were well over $500 million. Almost half the population has no easy access to a bookstore. And even if they did, many of the specialized titles carried by book clubs are not available in retail outlets. Considering these facts, book clubs are certainly to be cultivated. Placing a book with one or more of them will afford you both visibility and prestige.

Another plus is the "echo effect" which a book club's publicity often creates. This means that people will hear about your title through their book club, but may actually purchase it in a bookstore or through your direct-mail campaign.

What's the money picture like? You could receive as little as $600 . . . or as much as $250,000. Realistically, it will most likely be in the $2,000 to $3,000 range. The two Goliaths of the book club world are Book-of-the-Month Club (BOMC) and the Literary Guild. For a main selection they offer advances that average about $85,000. Alternate selections bring from $10,000 to $25,000. Troll Books is currently pestering these giants by topping offers from the established clubs.

The medium-sized and smaller clubs — of which there are some 150 — pay in the $5,000 to $10,000 range for a main selection. The clubs work on an "advance against royalty" basis; their royalties vary from a low of 6 percent to a high of 10 percent of the club price. (This royalty will be halved on books they offer at greatly reduced premium prices.) While negotiation always plays a role (study the techniques for this in the next chapter), normal advances are one-half of the club's total expected royalties. So you can guesstimate, eventually ending up with a total revenue of approximately double what the advance is. As we recommend in all cases, don't accept an offer over the phone. Ask that it be submitted in writing so you can mull over all the points and use it for leverage to solicit other bids.

Besides the Literary Guild and BOMC, which started this method of book merchandising in 1926, Doubleday and Macmillan both have a large number of specialized clubs under their respective wings. Quality Paperback Book Club is very receptive to small-press titles. Currently over 12 percent of their offerings are from this source. Then there are dozens and dozens of clubs tailored to virtually any interest. Got a book on maritime history? Try Sea Book Club. Your title on classic cars would appeal to the Wheels Book Club; a tome of professional interest to attorneys should capture the interest of the Lawyers' Literary Club. A book dealing with preparing unique appetizers might catch the fancy of the Professional Chef Book Club. And the Detective Book Club could be an ideal market for your new whodunit. This is but a sketchy sample of those listed in *LMP*.

As we mentioned in a previous chapter, you want to contact book clubs very early in the book creation process: six months before the pub date if possible. Most will even work from a typed manuscript if it is neat. All prefer to see a book at least in the galley stage. The reason for this is simple. The biggest clubs will print their own edition, but over 80 percent of the time, book clubs simply tag along on the publisher's print run, thus commanding a better unit cost for all involved.

Approach all likely candidates simultaneously with a letter describing the book and giving background information on the author. Also note any illustrative material that will be included. Spell out your publicity and marketing plans. Should you already have your covers, include one of them. Since you probably won't be that far along, at least send a color photocopy of the artist's sketch for the jacket design, or prepare a photo likeness. Most club editorial judging boards meet every three weeks to review the current crop of books. If yours has been in the pipeline for a month and you haven't heard anything, call or write to determine the status. This is too important a subsidiary rights sale to let slide through your fingers for want of basic sales follow-up. We cover this subject in great depth in our new title, *Marketing Your Book*.

Selling paperback reprint rights to a major publisher

Necessity may be the mother of invention, but ambition is definitely the father. And it's a wise writer-publisher who is ambitious when it comes to selling paperback rights to his or her book. This will most likely be the largest sale for a self-publisher. It often rakes in far more than the original book itself does, providing the gravy that makes the difference between profit and loss. Reprint rights sales have escalated to dizzying heights in the last few years. Bantam paid $3.2 *million* for Judith Krantz's second novel, *Princess Daisy*. The tragedy of such record-smashing buys is that dozens of "middle books" could be bought with that kind of money, thus spreading the wealth around a bit. Thank goodness such grandiose sales are few and far between. Most negotiation is for middle books.

It's an intriguing phenomenon that many writers who initially find trade publishers' doors closed to them are opting to self-publish strictly as a stepping stone. They realize that self-publishing can bring them forcefully to the attention of the conventional publishing community with highly profitable, fame-producing results. Their formula is to write the book, publish the book, make the book a success, then sell the book. And it's being done time after time.

It works one of two ways: Either a trade publisher comes knocking on your door with an offer, after perhaps learning of your book, or meeting you at the ABA, or you solicit bids from them, accepting the most promising offer.

In regular commercial publishing circles a hardcover house "auctions" reprint rights to the paperback publisher that promises to pay the highest guarantee against royalties. It is usually for a seven-year term. Often this auction takes place informally over the phone. Price is based on demand. The subsidiary rights director might negotiate vigorously, trying to get somebody up from $25,000 to $30,000; then a couple more biggies show interest and the amount leaps to $125,000 overnight.

A trade publisher markets paperback reprint rights for a book before the hardcover is ever off the presses. This is done amid much hoopla—and often commands six-figure advances. Here's an overview of the process. Copies of galleys are typically sent to perhaps half a dozen reprinters. These are followed up by announcements, such as first serial rights sold to *Redbook* or chosen as an alternate selection by BOMC. Soon a closing date is announced. That is the date of the actual bidding. Perhaps a "floor" will be set, meaning a minimum bid. The day of the auction things are frantic. To prime the pump, the sub rights director has no doubt placed ads in the *New York Times*. Calls start coming in early in the day. By day's end, that early caller may have to quadruple his or her bid to win the book. Reprinters who bid have what is termed "topping" privileges, meaning they have the right to bid 10 percent over any bid higher than theirs. It is like a ritualistic mating dance, with the favored suitor taking home the prize.

Auctions are normally reserved for bigger books, and they receive advances to match. New American Library forked over $250,000 for a nonfiction work, *Women Like Us,* and also picked up *The 100 Best Companies to Work for in America* for $357,500. Not all reprint sales go this high. Century paid $38,000 for the rights to *Amateur City,* a police procedural featuring a lesbian police detective. Pocket Books handed over $51,000 for *An Interrupted Life,* which tells of a young Dutch Jewish woman killed by the Nazis. A Civil War novel, *Unto This Hour,* was auctioned to Berkley for $66,000. But auctions are typically the ploy of the trade publisher.

For a self-published book you must first prove it can be a success in the marketplace. Then it is usually offered to one or several trade houses on a less structured basis than books which come under the auctioneer's hammer. There is no question, however, that reprint sales have swept many authors to national acclaim and healthy bank accounts.

Take the case of Kathy Coon, who originally published *The Dog Obedience Test* in her garage. She was so swamped with orders from pet owners across the country that it was impossible for her to fill all of the orders. Avon quickly solved that problem by purchasing the rights to her book and capitalizing further by sending her around the United States on an author tour.

John Wallace Spencer wrote and privately published *Limbo of the Lost,* which deals with the legendary Bermuda Triangle. By stumping across the country for four years, he captivated radio and TV audiences and managed to unload 200,000 copies of his book. Then the rooster at Bantam crowed into his ear. Under their imprint another million copies were snapped up by readers.

The companies that dominate this area are Avon Books, Bantam, Ballantine/Fawcett, Berkley, Dell, New American Library, Pocket Books, and Warner. While auctions aren't practical for most author-publishers, there definitely *are ways* to sell your book to the biggies, and we've devoted the next chapter to this strategy. "Attracting a Trade Publisher" gives you all the whys and wherefores for selling your book to a conventional publishing house.

More ways to profit from subsidiary spin-off sales

Television and film rights may also hold promise for your title, especially if it is fiction. Motion-picture and television producers buy "properties" (makes your book sound like a piece of real estate, doesn't it?) Most often they purchase "options" which give them the right to hold the property for six months to two years while they try to arrange for financing to produce it or sell the idea to an independent TV packager, network, or sponsor. Today you're not likely to get rich off options. That wasn't always the case. In the old days the public thirsted to see certain pet books brought to life on the silver screen. Formerly, a title that made the bestseller list was almost guaranteed to be produced by Hollywood. Lately, the only book people seemed anxious to experience as a movie was *The World According to Garp.* But while fiction has waned, new technology has opened more doors for nonfiction. With the advent of electronic publishing there are greater opportunities to exploit timely subjects with nonprint adaptations — transmitting directly from one screen to another.

The going option rate for unknown authors is from $500 to $5,000. *Publishers Weekly* announced two different options of $25,000 against a $250,000 pickup price, and another deal involving a $30,000 option that, if exercised, would yield $300,000 plus a percentage of net profits. Options are usually all there is, however. In an estimated 90 percent of the cases they are never exercised for the big bucks waiting.

Selling foreign or translation rights may also be practical if you have a book of universal interest. This is less difficult for fiction, as the range of human emotions is no different in China or Germany, for instance, from what it is in the United States. For nonfiction works there is more

319

to consider. First, it will help if your book has a good track record in the United States. Next, ask yourself if there is any reason it would not be of value or interest to folks in other countries.

A guide on how to homestead your house, thus protecting it from creditors, would be useless to someone in a foreign land where the laws are different. Yet a handbook describing how to cope with male menopause might be just as helpful to people in one country as in another. Your subject matter will dictate whether this subsidiary right is worth considering.

The R. R. Bowker Company publishes the *International Literary Market Place*, which covers 160 countries in full, giving you virtually any information you could conceivably need. The regular *LMP* also has two relevant sections: Foreign Rights & Sales Representatives and U.S. Agents of Foreign Publishers.

In these categories you can find agents who have representation abroad or who affiliate with a foreign literary agency. The main stomping ground for setting up foreign and translation rights is the Frankfurt Book Fair in Germany, held each year in early October.

Foreign rights are sold to publishers in English-speaking nations. You may sell an edition of perhaps one thousand bound books from your own print run or one thousand unfinished books in the form of flat sheets or F & Gs, which the buyer will have bound in the country of purchase. The alternative is simply to sell reproduction rights. Then the purchaser can make any minor changes and produce his or her own edition using your film (or at least camera-ready boards).

In this case the royalty is generally somewhere between 7 and 10 percent of the book's selling price. While most publishers use literary agents to negotiate such transactions (see Chapter 20), doing it yourself could provide a nice tax-deductible trip abroad. One word of caution on foreign rights sales, though: Insist on seeing a blue line of the book to be sure everything is okay before it rolls off the presses.

Translation rights for major languages—such as Spanish, German, French, Arabic, Chinese, and Japanese—usually bring at least $1,000 in an advance against royalties of 6 to 8 percent of the foreign publisher's receipts. Foreign publishers often request a two-month option period in which to consider a book. When a deal is consummated, all you have to do is supply a couple of copies of the book and any photographs or illustrations. They handle all the details of the translation, printing, and distribution.

While no one is likely to line up at your door with offers to purchase foreign or translation rights, they present just one more way to make additional money from your book project. And you may find a literary agent willing to handle them for you (see Chapter 20). Selling subsidiary rights can boost your book into national acclaim and give your bank account a fabulous influx of ready cash. To learn just how to attract the right trade publisher, keep reading.

CHAPTER **19**

ATTRACTING A TRADE PUBLISHER

Here you are—a self-publisher with a proven book. You don't have to fear getting a rejection that goes something like: "What you've submitted is both good and original. Unfortunately, what's good isn't original, and what's original isn't good." Reviews have been favorable, sales are brisk, and you'd like to turn control of this baby over to someone else. Or perhaps you're a trade-published author. You've gotten your rights back on a book which languished under the treatment it received, and you successfully turned it around. What now? In these cases, many authors elect to allow the giants on Publishers Row to take over their books ... for a price. That's what this chapter is about.

First, we will explore how to prospect for the right publisher. Then we will talk about maximizing that relationship. The fine art of negotiating will be unmasked, as will tips for getting your share—and more—of available marketing dollars. While our comments are directed primarily at self-publishers, authors aspiring to win a trade contract for their manuscripts will find valuable and seldom-disclosed gems here to help them triumph.

Insider's sources for determining the right publisher

If you're like most writers, you have little idea of how to select the most likely publishing houses. Oh sure, you've consulted *Writer's Market* and *LMP*. But do you start hunting in the A's and work on through the alphabet? No. We feel your market research should begin somewhere else.

A marvelous insider's source available for locating who publishes what is *Publisher's Trade List Annual (PTLA)*. It is a compilation of catalogs from virtually every major American publisher. Could you ask for a better place to browse for ideal publishing candidates? It's like judging a talent contest! How amazing that this prime resource for author-publishers remains such a well-kept secret.

This yellow pages of the publishing industry can be found at your main library—not, however, in any of the normal sections. *PTLA* is kept in the order department because it is a tool of the acquisitions librarian. You will need to request permission to go into the order department and peruse it there. Or perhaps a large bookstore will let you use its copy. By noticing the type of books each publisher puts out, you will soon become sensitive to who produces titles that are in the same category as your work. (Scanning the subject guide to *Books in Print* will also yield this type of information.) If you find a house that has a very similar book, steer clear. It won't want to compete with itself. On the other hand, if a house has books in the same general subject area but none quite like yours, it might be a very good prospect: Clearly, the house is interested in the subject and might well be looking for another book to add to its present titles. Also, note the quality of the house's book catalog. Is it professionally designed or hokey? Is it easy to read and well organized? Is the artwork clear or fuzzy? Does the information on each book make it sound appealing and interesting? Overall, does the catalog have, to your eye, that indefinable but necessary quality, *style?* Your book would probably reflect the same level of quality if they published it. Studying *PTLA* is also a super way to tune into emerging trends. If, page after page, there are titles dealing with the occult, holistic healing, or historical novels, you are finding the pulse of what is currently selling.

If your book is nonfiction, there is another unorthodox place to look for publishing leads. Check in the library card catalog under the subject that your manuscript revolves around. Notice which publishers have books out in that subject area, and who has recently released titles. Also talk to librarians: They know a lot about various publishers. They can tell you who keeps books in print the longest, who specializes in what type of books, etc. Bookstore owners and managers are an additional cherished source of who's who in the publishing industry. And by perusing a large bookstore, you can check out the current crop of who's publishing what.

And don't overlook the spring and fall "announcement" issues of *Publishers Weekly* and *Small Press*. Here you'll find a hefty collection of the titles publishers are proudest of, not to mention page upon page of advertisements that hold more clues. To further help solve the mystery, talk with other authors and self-publishers and ask for recommendations and past experiences. You can often track down an author via *Contemporary Authors* listings and other writers' directories or by reading their bio and calling information in the city of their residence for a phone number.

Of course, this is not to say you shouldn't look in *Writer's Market* and *LMP*. They will always be valuable resources. Both of them carry a subject index to publishers, so you can build a further list by researching them. After you've squeezed out leads for about a dozen houses, send a note to Customer Service requesting their most recent catalog so you can keep abreast of their upcoming titles. Also check listings in the two above books to learn specifics, such as the names of appropriate editors and the number of titles their houses publish each year.

This pinpoints their size. The largest trade hardcover publishers are Random House, Simon & Schuster, Harper & Row, and Doubleday. In the mass-paperback market Bantam leads the pack, with Pocket Books, New American Library, Dell, and Avon Books not far behind. Consider what kind of treatment you and your book want. As the large firms are absorbed by conglomerates, they become increasingly preoccupied with "name" authors. They introduce so many titles each season that an unknown writer can easily get left at the starting gate. Perhaps you'd be happier joining one of the smaller publishing houses. Ten Speed Press, for instance, published 28 titles in 1987—but it has had a book on the national best-seller lists almost half of the nineteen years it's been in existence. The Green Tiger Press puts out somewhat fewer titles, but is known in publishing circles for its beautiful books and assertive marketing stance. There are trade-offs either way. You'll usually get more personalized attention at a smaller house; but a big one may have national distribution that the little guy can't match.

There is still another possibility, especially if your book has merit but not much commercial appeal. Literary small presses, which publish from two to twenty books a year, encourage artists who write poetry, alternative fiction, or handle avant-garde subjects. You can find their requirements listed in the *International Directory of Little Magazines and Small Presses.*

Let us now assume that you will be taking the initiative and contacting potential trade publishers yourself, rather than having an agent represent you. Agents are covered in depth in the following chapter. Meanwhile, here are some significant pointers.

Launching a compelling sales campaign

Okay, you've identified a dozen or so publishers who seem likely targets for your book. Do you approach choice number one, then sit back with your fingers, toes, and eyes crossed? Never! Use a shotgun technique and spread the word to all of them at once. Nothing succeeds like excess.

It is far too costly for a writer-publisher to waste months—or even years—waiting for one publisher after another to pass judgment. If the book deals with a timely subject, this is plain suicide. Seven weeks is the average report time, but three months isn't unusual. Multiple submissions is the only businesslike approach to take. You are trying to sell your book, correct? Why should you have to operate by a different set of rules than a person selling any other product? Imagine how long a cement salesman would last if he approached only one contractor and attempted to sell his carload of cement, then went back to his office and patiently waited until that contractor placed an order. Such marketing is ludicrous! It is a courtesy, however, to tell your prospects that you are submitting to more than one publisher.

We recommend the query method. You send a carefully constructed query letter to all those prospects on your list.

Writing effective query letters

Your query letter had better be gussied up just right if it's to catch the perfect publisher. While there is no pat formula for successful query letters, a good one always gets off to a full gallop with a catchy lead. After you've hooked the editor's interest, briefly recount the book's history of success. Don't make an editor play guessing games. Provide insight into the book's treatment and scope. The more precisely and dynamically you communicate, the better your chances of establishing a rewarding relationship. After all, your query letter is your sales representative.

There are several other items that should be covered. Highlight any special qualifications you have for writing this book. If you are especially promotable and have appeared on some strategic shows, mention them. Do you give seminars or lecture professionally? Author promotability is a key factor in signing up a lot of books. If you've done extensive research, let its depth be known. Also be sure to note why readers are interested in this book. Is the topic timely or the slant unusual? It's also a good idea to stress subsidiary rights potential.

Know your competition. What other books are in print on the same subject? How does yours differ? Why is it likely to have long-range sales potential? Another zinger that will intrigue an editor is mention of any noteworthy personal or professional contacts you have who might be helpful in promoting the book. Perhaps you became friendly with an authority who assisted in the research or wrote the foreword. The publisher's marketing department would like to know of this. They will also be interested in what channels of distribution you've opened. No doubt you've established contacts they can pick up to add to their own marketing emphasis. Conclude with an offer to send a book.

To help you see how these elements can be incorporated into a query

July 2, 1984

Linda Price
BANTAM BOOKS
666 Fifth Avenue
New York, NY 10103

Dear Ms. Price   RE: REPRINT RIGHTS

     Are you aware that six of the ten leading causes of death in the U.S. have
been linked to our diet? Yet we have only to learn what, and how, to eat to
provide our bodies with all the essential maintenance and repair materials to
sustain -- or restore -- ourselves to good health. This is the theme of a very
successful title called The UNcook Book: Raw Food Adventures to a New Health
High. Originally published in early 1981, this book has gone into three
printings with only a limited promotional budget and word-of-mouth
recommendations. We are currently accepting bids for reprint rights on this
book.

     Ironically, the authors of The UNcook Book are the "Bakers". Elizabeth and
Dr. Elton Baker -- both in their seventies -- are living testimony that their
concepts work! He is a doctor, a trained chemist and a past advisor to the
National Institute of Nutrition in Bogota, Colombia. She cured herself of cancer
of the colon and has done extensive nutritional research, writing, consulting
and lecturing. Their unique combination of the academic and the practical yields
a detailed and thorough, yet very readable book.

     Disregarding the old adage, "Ignorance is bliss", the Bakers set out to
educate the public on the potential health hazards in much of the food on the
market today. Touching on such topics as what foods to buy and where to buy them
-- how to learn what things are good for you -- combining foods for proper
digestion -- how to sprout and grow seeds and grains -- tips to cut your grocery
bill -- body language tests to detect personal food allergies -- and how to
gather foods in the wild, they cover every aspect necessary for implementing a
healthy way of life. Additionally, the book describes ways to pack nourishing
and satisfying workday lunches and what to do when traveling and eating out.

     The last half of this guide is devoted to delicious recipes developed
through experimentation and creativity. By feasting on such delectable dishes as
Brazil Nut Louie, Raisin Carrot Bread, Asparagus a-la-king, Salad of the Sun and
Banana Date Pudding, a person doesn't even feel like sacrifices have been made
by giving up traditional harmful processed foods. But this is more than a
cookbook. More than a manual for America's seven million vegetarians. It's a
step-by-step guide to well-being and long life...complete with charts, tables
and extensive vitamin and mineral data.

     Should you be the publisher to obtain reprint rights of The UNcook Book,
you would have two articulate and very promotable authors. Elizabeth and Elton
are at home in all media. They've appeared on the Michael Jackson Show and
Stacie Hunt's syndicated radio program. Elizabeth's raw food demonstrations
delighted audiences on "Sun-Up" in San Diego and "Wake Up Houston" in Texas.
This dynamic couple were featured speakers at the National Health Federations'
annual convention the last two years and have been invited to participate in a
world-wide speaking tour plannned for this fall.

     In great demand by health food stores, The UNcook Book is one of Nutribooks
best sellers. This $5.95 238-page trade paperback is carried in many physician's
offices, by catalog houses, small press distributors and by a worldwide health
clinic. One especially rewarding aspect of The UNcook Book is it's extremely low
return history. Virtually everyone who carries this title re-orders it.

     By no means limited to vegetarians, The UNcook Book will appeal to all
readers interested in learning more about good health and nutrition. Please
contact me for an examination copy if you'd like to be considered as a reprint
house for this exciting title.

Sincerely,

Marilyn Ross
MR:sdw
encl.

Reprint-rights letter.

letter, a sample is shown. This letter was sent to thirteen major houses. Four responded by requesting books. At one point, we were negotiating with two of these for purchase of reprint rights.

Work with your query. Write and rewrite. You may want to present it over the aka name you use for promotion, so you can more gracefully say favorable things about yourself and your book. Refresh your writing skills by reviewing Chapter 3. Speak in specifics. By using actual statistics to quantify your market, you build a more dramatic case. "Ten million farmers" means more than "millions of farmers." Cut, tighten, pare, polish. Make it fit into two fast-moving, single-spaced pages. Its purpose is to wed you to a very sweet contract. This could be the most profitable letter you ever write!

Before sending it off, call each publisher and get the correct name for the editor responsible for your type of book. This is important. Otherwise, your query will end up in a slush pile for some junior editor to evaluate. By calling ahead and talking with the editor in chief, or his or her secretary, you make sure your message goes to the right person. (And also you can get the correct spelling of the editor's name.) You might include a self-addressed, stamped postcard the publisher can mail back to you so you'll know your materials have arrived.

One day a few weeks—or months—later, your phone will ring. Someone will say they're so-and-so from XYZ Publishing Company. Bells ring. Whistles toot. Your mouth gets dry; your eyes mist. It's finally happened! A major trade publisher is interested in your book! There are few natural "highs" more exhilarating. Somehow you'll muddle through the conversation with a promise to send a copy of your book. Now your really big guns go into action.

Certainly after all we've taught you, you'd never send *just* a book. You'll include copies of reviews. Lots if you've got 'em, so they sense a ground swell of interest about this title. Put the ones from prime sources on top. That way they'll realize you did your homework and scored. Include complimentary letters, copies of large orders, anything that gives the book credibility. When we put together the package for *The UNcook Book*, we included the flier we'd designed for Nutri-Books, which mentioned that *The UNcook Book* had been a top seller for two years. We also tucked in orders from doctors' offices and health professionals, many containing penned comments lauding the book. Letters commending the Bakers as articulate and knowledgeable speakers were enclosed, as were excerpts from reviews.

Negotiating contracts in your best interest

Chances are if one publisher thinks you have a good manuscript, others will, too. For that reason we feel you should exercise a bit of caution. When one of these publishers comes back and says they want to buy your book, *never*, NEVER agree to anything over the phone. Ask for their offer in writing. And as soon as you've hung up the telephone, get out your list of those who haven't already rejected the book, and give them a call. You might say something like, "We've had positive reactions from other interested publishers, but no response from you regarding our book. Thought I'd just touch base to be sure that wasn't an oversight before we make a final decision on whom to place the book with." This guarantees you won't miss out because the package was inadvertently set aside or misdelivered.

Here are some preliminary questions you should ask your potential publisher:

• How many copies do you typically print in the first run of this type book?

• What price would my book sell for?

• Would it be hardcover or paperback?

• How long do books in this genre usually stay in print?

• What amount would you budget to promote my book?

• What royalties are you offering for the manuscript? (Standard rates for hardcover are 10 percent on the first 5,000 copies, 12½ percent on the next 5,000, and 15 percent thereafter. On mass paperbacks it is 4 to 8 percent on the first 150,000 and a bit more thereafter. These same lower rates are common for children's books and school texts. Trade paperbacks usually bring 10 percent on the first 20,000 copies, 12½ percent up to 40,000, then 15 percent thereafter.)

• Are royalties based on the retail price or on the discounted (net) sales price? (It's greatly to your advantage to have them based on full retail catalog sales price. You give away a big chunk if they are determined by the discounted amount.)

In most cases you will be given an advance against future royalties. The Authors Guild notes that on original manuscript sales (not proven self-published books) the average advance is $5,000. Of course, to arrive at this "average," remember some writers get only a couple of hundred dollars, while big names capture advances of several hundred thousand or more. (When Norman Mailer gets a $4-*million* advance for *Ancient Evenings*, it plays havoc with averages . . . not to mention the morale of most authors.) The competition by publishers with deep pockets naturally works to the advantage of so-called brand-name authors. The theory is, it's wiser to invest $1 million or more in a best-selling author than to spend the same amount of money on a host of unknown writers.

Advances work this way: Typically, you receive one-half of the advance on acceptance of your book and signing of the contract; the other half when the revised and/or expanded edition is accepted. Another procedure used by some houses pays you in three increments: on signing, upon acceptance of the revised manuscript, and upon publication.

How much might you expect? Carla Emery, who self-published *Carla Emery's Old Fashioned Recipe Book*—and sold 70,000 copies herself—allowed Bantam's feisty rooster to take over the book for a cool $115,000 cash advance. That is unusually high. Most such advances run under $10,000. The reason for this? We feel most SP-ers are not knowledgeable on *how* to negotiate a more favorable contract. They take what's offered and are humbly grateful. Hogwash! You sweat blood and tears to turn out a quality book, then market it effectively. You deserve to be justly rewarded. Yet you don't have to be able to sell turquoise jewelry to the Navaho to get top dollar for your book. But don't blame the publisher if you settle for too little. In their shoes you'd handle things the same way.

We had an interesting experience concerning a book we wrote, published, and promoted to success. After a long courtship we finally had our chosen publisher committed to wanting the book. Before ever sitting down at the negotiation table, the two of us had discussed the project and determined what we felt would be a fair advance. After talking face-to-face with the editor in chief, however, it seemed our ideas of its value were far apart.

But Tom is an excellent negotiator. He believes that if both parties sincerely want to reach an agreement, something positive is bound to develop. He talked some more, this time including marketing and management personnel, constantly selling them on the idea of the book's track record and potential. They were reminded that we are promotable authors who would participate actively in book marketing. They compromised. We compromised. To make a long story short, he ended up securing a five-figure advance: over twice the original offer!

A good mental attitude is paramount to a productive negotiating session. If you go in expecting to sign a contract that is in the best interests of all concerned, that's most likely what will happen. A good negotiator strives to develop rapport; he or she is an open, informed, and flexible communicator.

Remember, as you discuss various points with editors, some things are high priorities for them; some low. Try to match your high priorities with their low ones, and vice versa. That way no one is forced to give up things each considers vitally important. If each side yields on issues of lesser concern, everyone benefits. Know ahead of time what you want ... and what you *must* have. Both parties to a negotiation should come out with some needs satisfied. Be open to alternate solutions. We also felt the royalty percentage was unacceptable in the above situation and proposed a different one. This proved unworkable for the publishers. But the publisher in turn suggested another approach—which ultimately met *our* goal—and everybody was happy.

Of course, advances and royalties are not the only aspects that warrant mediation. There are many other points—some of great significance—that should be considered.

Let's take a close look at the things you want included in (or omitted from) your book contract. The information we share has been gleaned from personal experience and research, plus interviews with authors who learned after the fact what they should have done to protect themselves. That is not to insinuate that publishers are vultures waiting to pounce on unsuspecting prey. But, as in any business, their standard contract is slanted toward their own best interests.

One important consideration is the book's actual publication date. The contract should stipulate that the book must be published within one year after acceptance. Otherwise, a sloppy house could take forever to get your work out to the public—and you have only the original one-half of the advance. On a more perverse level, it has happened that a book was bought by a publisher solely to keep it *out* of circulation because it directly competed with one of their other titles. Because the unsuspecting author didn't cover this point in the contract, the publisher was able to sit on the manuscript indefinitely.

Insist on getting at least 50 percent off the retail price on your own personal book purchases. That way you can profitably continue to sell copies to acquaintances, maintain drop-ship arrangements you may have established, or take a quantity along when you lecture. Ideally, you want full bookstore privileges (which also includes the right to return unsold inventory). Don't be surprised if they balk at this. We have one client who is negotiating a very aggressive deal with his publisher. He wants to buy one thousand books outright and is haggling for a discount considerably above the 50 percent. You, too, might want to consider doing this and setting yourself up as a jobber.

Free copies are another point for consideration. The usual amount is ten. But if you're going to help promote the book and send new review copies to important contacts, ten copies won't go anywhere. Twenty-five or fifty is much more like it.

Be sure that book sales on the second (or subsequent) edition start where the previous edition left off. In other words, don't let them reset the counter at zero and thus keep you in the lower royalty range, instead of picking up at 10,001 or whatever number is appropriate.

Seek the return of all rights if the book goes out of print and the publisher declines to reprint it within a reasonable period. As you know, excellent books sometimes die because they are not properly marketed. If this should happen to yours, you can always climb on the bandwagon again and breathe fresh life into it. Likewise, should your publisher decide to "remainder" or destroy the remaining copies of your book, you want the right of first refusal on the remaining stock. What a great way to acquire books for a fraction of what it cost to manufacture them! Also try to add a provision that allows you to pick up the negatives and plates so that additional books can be printed inexpensively.

Mail-order rights are something else you want to rally for. While no trade house will grant you these exclusively, most will be happy to let you sell single copies of the new edition of your book through the mail, if you ask. Don't be surprised if you're expected to refrain from selling copies of your self-published edition once the new trade edition is out.

Warranties and indemnities have to do with such things as the work's constituting no infringement of another's copyright, not being libelous, not misrepresenting facts, and so forth. This provision helps protect the publisher from lawsuits and typically puts all the financial responsibility on your shoulders, with little of the say-so. It is a clause that must be read very carefully. You may succeed in winning some changes, such as the author's having to give his or her consent regarding defense and settlement. Also insist that the clause refer to a "proven" breach. While most publishers won't sit still for much revision here, it is ideal to at least get the wording changed to the effect that "if the defendants do win, the publisher will pay at least half the cost of defense." On that point we simply wish you luck.

Typical publishing contracts also stipulate that a reserve to cover returns will be withheld from royalties. Since you are selling a proven book, this seems an unnecessary withholding of money due. Something else you should insist on is that the copyright be in *your* name. Most reputable publishers do this as standard procedure.

Remember, too, that you can negotiate the schedule of payment for the advance. We try to get the bulk of it up front, as that is where all our time is spent. If it is a two-pay advance, suggest a 75/25 split (and be ready to settle for 60/40). In a three-pay go for 50/25/25. One bit of strategy that may help you achieve more front money is to remind them you will supply negatives and plates (or computer keyboarded disks) if this is the case. By providing these, you cut their production costs dramatically. They should be willing to put part of that money in your pocket.

To avoid nasty disagreements — or costly court battles — the American Arbitration Association recommends that the following standard arbitration clause be inserted in all commercial contracts.

> Any controversy or claim arising out of or relating to this contract, or the breach thereof, shall be settled by arbitration in accordance with the Rules of the American Arbitration Association, and judgment upon the award rendered by the Arbitrator(s) may be entered in any Court having jurisdiction thereof.

During our research one of the most intriguing tips that emerged was from a woman who always writes her husband into her book contracts as an assistant for a few dollars a year. That way he can travel with her on research or promotion trips and all of his expenses are tax-deductible. If you are incorporated, it's to your advantage to have your advance and royalties paid to the corporation, thus sheltering them more.

Many contracts contain a clause stating that the publisher has the first option on your next work. This is often called the Right of First Refusal. Think carefully about this. Suppose you run into editorial or promotional snags with this house and find they don't give you a fair shake. Wouldn't it be too bad to automatically have to give them first dibs on your next book? They may be rather hard-nosed about giving up on this point. If they get a good author under contract, it is sound business practice for them to attach some strings to that author.

A couple of further references are available to help you with contract negotiation. Attorney Herb Cohen has written *You Can Negotiate Anything,* in which he counsels, "Be patient, be personal, be informed." In your public library or county law library there's a volume rich with information. Called *Entertainment, Publishing and the Arts,* by Alexander Lindsey and Clark Boardman, this masterpiece contains sample contracts and explanations of all sorts of legal documents relevant to publishing. Additionally, the Authors Guild (234 West 44th Street, New York, NY 10036) has a booklet called "The Recommended Trade Book Contract Guide." It is available only to members, however. To be eligible to join the Guild, you must have had a book published by a reputable American publisher within seven years prior to application, or have had three works (fiction or nonfiction) published by a magazine of general circulation within eighteen months prior to application.

How are publishers going to react to your assertiveness in wanting to modify their contracts? As predictably as fleas in a hot skillet. But after they've hopped around a bit—if your experience is typical—many of the things you want will be accommodated. Don't be afraid to stand up for your rights because you are a fledgling writer-publisher. Use chutzpah! Don't sell out too cheap. If they want your book, they will be open to compromise. There is nothing subversive about trying to strike the very best deal possible. Simply use your self-publishing knowledge to work with trade publishers. You're in a much better position than the average author to comprehend publishers' problems and to help find solutions acceptable to both sides.

Getting your share of a publisher's marketing dollar

We're all familiar with the old adage "The squeaky wheel gets the grease." It was never more true than in this industry. According to *Publishers Weekly*, there are some 53,000 books published each year. One out of 53,000 isn't very good odds. So it's up to you to make sure your book gets noticed. Oh, we know, that's the publisher's job. But if you want your books to move into people's homes rather than into a remainder dealer's warehouse, you have to squeak often and loudly. You want to keep publicity and sales personnel focusing on your book's case.

Ironically, one of the things you will probably need to do is hound the publisher to get books into the bookstores. It is especially disappointing when you are giving a lecture, reading, or appearing on television and none of the local bookstores have books. You should alert the publisher in a positive rather than a derogatory way, however. Call and tactfully say that someone inadvertently overlooked stocking the bookstores in such-and-such a town—as opposed to demanding, "Why are there no books available?"

Your publisher marketing campaign can really be lots of fun. It's simply a matter of being imaginative about getting your book noticed within the house—then within the world. Judith McQuown, author of *Inc. Yourself: Get Rich with Your Own Corporation*, decided that a button saying "Inc. Yourself" would be an attention-getter. So she called around and got some bids. She then passed the information along to Macmillan, who ordered the buttons. They were such a sensation around the offices—keeping everyone stirred up about her title—that the sub rights people sold the book to five book clubs and ordered another press run before it even reached its official publication date. Judith was creative. She was also smart. She made it easy for them to go along with her idea by doing the legwork and handing them a ready-made gimmick.

You can do legwork in other ways, too. While merchandising the book yourself, you no doubt tumbled into people or organizations very sympathetic to your cause. Have you alerted the publicity department to these names? Here is where you have impact. The marketing people aren't likely to have time to ferret out who they are. Create a mailing list of probable new review candidates. To keep tabs on how your campaign is progressing, save copies of any correspondence you send to the publisher.

Speaking of correspondence, shortly after signing your contract, you may be sent an author's questionnaire to fill out. Be as complete as possible and return it promptly. This information is used by the promotion department in several ways. And be sure to alert them to any new professional or personal contacts you've made in the field who may be willing to say something nice about the book.

Capitalize also on your specialized knowledge. Check with the local visitors and convention bureau or Chamber of Commerce to see what groups might be interested in your message. Seize every opportunity to speak before large audiences, as this can lead to terrific contacts, not to mention sales. Keep your editor and marketing representative apprised of these speaking engagements and of any positive feedback they generate. Of course, anytime you can get your hands on a list of the attendees, do so. Such lists come in handy for future mail-order blitzes and should be passed on to marketing personnel.

Subsidiary rights sales are another area where you can affect your book's track record. If you're especially qualified in some area—have contacts with movie companies, for instance, or with particular foreign publishers you've done business with before—you might suggest that you take over certain portions of sub rights sales so that you can give your whole attention to the chore, as a publisher's staff, with many books to promote, cannot do. But unless you're an expert yourself, you may do better to let the experts handle the whole job for you. In any event, suggest which chapters would match up with which periodicals, thus making it easy for the sub rights people to market excerpts or serial rights. If you previously came close to cinching a subsidiary rights sale, be sure to alert them to this. They may have the influence to consummate it this time around.

For additional exposure think through the manuscript to discover ways it might relate to various issues. Is the protagonist a crippled child? Organizations that work with the handicapped might be interested in having you as a guest speaker. A novel about terrorism? Perhaps you could get on a local TV show discussing terrorist tactics. Just as there are countless subtle ways to stay in front of your editor, there are vehicles for drawing public attention to yourself and your product. The more you use diplomatic means to assist your publisher's marketing department in promoting your book, the more likely it is to flourish. Study Chapters 14 and 16, on promotion and money-making strategies, for other ideas.

CHAPTER **20**

AGENTS

In this chapter we will consider the pros and cons of using agents. Agents are salespeople who market and negotiate the sale of literary properties. They represent an author not only in the United States but throughout the world as well. Writer-publishers sometimes use them to assist in selling subsidiary rights or to present their successful self-published book to major trade houses.

There is a paradox about agents. It goes like this: You have to be a selling author to get an agent, and you have to have an agent to sell. From the standpoint of agents it's all very logical. Since their revenue is generated solely from commissions (10 to 15 percent on domestic sales, 20 percent on foreign), unless you are producing quality books that are salable, it's not to their benefit to add you as a client. For the frustrated self-publisher, that can be downright discouraging . . . or it may be a blessing in disguise.

The pros and cons of using an agent

Be aware that you will be merely one of the many clients that the agent represents. Would you believe that the Scott Meredith agency handles seven thousand literary properties a year? It's true. While probably no other agency rivals this number, many are huge operations with separate departments for different functions. On the other end of the spectrum is the individual representing a roster of several authors.

Let's examine some of the reasons you might want an agent. A reputable agent—not a huckster—can open many doors. His or her job is to know who needs what and how to get top price. Many authors who use agents contend they don't really cost anything. The reasoning goes that the agent is able to intercede and get a higher advance than the author would be able to command. We've had an interesting experience in this area, however. When Tom sold the rights to one of our books to a trade publisher, the editor in chief commented he was the best negotiator she had ever dealt with. (And the sad truth is about half the manuscripts this publisher purchases are agented.)

It's a fact that agents develop contacts over the years that allow them to circulate in places you couldn't enter. Sales are often made over lunch or cocktails. Some publishers won't even look at material that comes in unsolicited "over the transom." It must be submitted through an agent.

Besides being a salesperson, your representative is a mediator between you and your editor, a business manager, and a contract negotiator. In this capacity an agent can help you to understand legal terminology, royalty statements, and can dicker with the publisher over things that should be included in—or excluded from—your contract. For some authors this point alone provides a compelling reason to use an agent. (Literary attorneys serve the same purpose.)

While this point isn't relevant for SP-ers, a good agent also offers editorial advice. He or she will point out if your protagonist gets out of character or if your writing becomes verbose. Don't expect nit-picking editing; do expect overall critiquing.

You might be better off, however, to bypass using an agent. A prominent one estimates that about a third of the books published in the United States, including some best-sellers, are negotiated without an agent. We have a friend who has tried it both ways and now markets all her own work. Before publishing her first book, she sent one-page query letters to twenty-five selected major New York publishing houses. Nine came back requesting outlines and sample chapters. After sending the outlines, she followed up with a trip East to negotiate the sale. Having had much success handling her own affairs for several books, she decided to try an agent. It was a brief association. Donna has gone back to representing herself. She reels out a couple of new craft or how-to books each year, which are eagerly gobbled up by major houses.

If you possess some flair for marketing—a sense of what might work where—can put together a powerful book proposal, and feel comfortable bargaining for the best deal, you may not need an agent. The Latin proverb says, "Fortune favors the bold." You *must* have a business head and be shrewd in negotiating your book contract. (This was covered in detail in the preceding chapter, on trade publishers.) On the other hand, if you abhor selling anything and the very idea of business negotiation puts a lump the size of a brick in your stomach, you're better off having someone represent you.

Sources of information

Let us assume you choose to use an agent. Where do you begin?

There are several scouting sources for names and addresses. We suggest you write the Society of Authors' Representatives, Inc., 39½ Washington Square South, New York, NY 10012, and request their pamphlet "The Literary Agent." It is available free when you send a #10 SASE. Author Aid/Research Associates International puts out a list called *Literary Agents of North America*. It includes 450 currently active agents in the United States and Canada. Also look in *LMP* where a list of the most active agencies indicates whether they specialize in literary or dramatic works.

If you're looking for someone to sell subsidiary rights or for a foreign representative, good clues wait here. *LMP* also notes memberships in various agent and literary associations. If motion-picture rights are your aim, many recommend that you use a West Coast agent (or at least an eastern firm that uses a subagent for California or has extensive experience in negotiating motion-picture rights.) To learn who handles TV and movie material, contact the Writers Guild of America West, 8955 Beverly Boulevard, Los Angeles, CA 90048.

In 1977 several agents who were concerned with ambiguities in royalty statements and other confusing information formed the Independent Literary Agents Association (ILAA). To get a list of the member agents of this trade association, send an SASE to 432 Park Avenue South, New York, NY 10016.

Another way to get leads on assertive agents is to regularly read the column "Rights" in *Publishers Weekly*. Here you'll learn who sold what to whom—and for how much. By charting this activity you'll soon have a feel for which individuals or agencies are most aggressive.

An even more resourceful way to determine who might be a conscientious agent is to scan the prefaces in books looking at author's comments. Those whose agents contribute a great deal to their growth are often verbal in their praise. Another go-getter we know tracked down a prominent local author from a story in the newspaper. After a congenial conversation the author agreed to look at the neophyte's work and subsequently put her in touch with a well-known New York agent.

When you think you're on the track of interesting quarry, feel free to check your prospective agent's references. You can simply ask for a list of clients, then write or call a few of these authors to determine if their experiences have been profitable, and the agents honest.

Become a "joiner" and develop contacts

One of the best ways to locate a really good agent is through word of mouth. But to be privy to this information, you usually have to be in the right place or know the right people. Hence, we suggest that you join any professional organization for which you are eligible. This might include the Authors Guild, the American Society of Journalists and Authors (ASJA), or Women in Communications, to name a few. Details about these groups can be found in the Appendix. Being able to cite your professional affiliations in query letters or author biographies is an additional fringe benefit of membership in such prestigious organizations.

Another great place to network is at writers' conferences which attract the more serious and professional types. The more you associate with writers, the better the chances of hearing about good—or bad—agent experiences.

When you have become acquainted with an author who is happy with his or her agent relationship, and you have proven that you are a worthy novice, your mentor may offer to contact the agent about representing you. This kind of referral is like finding a chunk of gold. No one gets more serious consideration from agents than someone suggested by a client whose work and opinion they respect.

How to approach an agent

Convincing an agent your book is a good risk is not much different from convincing a publisher. It all begins with a carefully created letter that describes your project and yourself. If you are corresponding because John Doe (whom the agent knows) said you should, be up-front about it. Start by saying something like, "I am writing you at the suggestion of John Doe. ..." Provide background on your writing history, promotability, and future goals. Include material about the book's past sales record and perhaps excerpt a couple of impressive reviews from key sources. Study the query letter in the previous chapter for specific techniques. Write, edit, rewrite, reedit. This is a sample of your ability. It had better be good!

But even if it is, arrangements don't always set up as fast as Jell-O. Sometimes an agent will circle and spar for several months before deciding whether to shake hands or bite. And this silence may continue to frustrate you through the relationship when you hunger for news of what's happening. More times than not, no contract is drawn up. This can be hazardous because moneys flow to the agent, who then doles out your share. Request a written agreement, but before signing, be sure you feel comfortable with this individual. Has a warm, personal rapport developed? Do you respect the comments and advice offered so far? Your book's literary life hangs in the balance, so be sure to entrust it to someone worthy.

CHAPTER 21

ANOTHER ALTERNATIVE? SUBSIDY (VANITY) PUBLISHERS

A subsidy publisher puts out books only when the author underwrites the entire venture. Vanity fare feeds the ego. That is not to insinuate that vanity presses serve no purpose. Suppose you have no time or inclination to go the self-publishing route, yet have a book of poems you want to distribute to friends or relatives at Christmas? Or perhaps a beloved family member just died and you want to preserve his or her writing for posterity. Maybe you've just finished tracing your ancestry and choose to distribute these genealogical findings to a wide circle of relatives. These circumstances, and any others where profit is *not* your motive, may be justification for subsidy publishing.

What does it cost?

Just what kind of financial commitment are we looking at? Charges to "publish" your book range from as little as $3,000 to more than $25,000, depending on size and quantity. According to *Writer's Digest*, the average return on subsidy investment is about twenty-five cents on the dollar. It's been said that the only way to profit from a vanity press is to buy stock in it. Being totally honest, this isn't always true. Occasional books do make money. But then, wouldn't a diamond gleam in a bucket of gravel?

Through the years Vantage Press and Dorrance & Company have been the front-runners in this industry. Others—many of which have come and gone—include Carlton Press, Pageant, Poseidon Press, Helios

Publishing Company, Wong, and William-Frederick Press (plus those listed at the end of this chapter). Not long after Ed Uhlan turned over the reins of his New York Exposition Press operation, it closed its doors. But Ed is a workhorse in the cause of vanity publishing. He has since opened up Exposition Press of Florida.

What to expect—and not to expect

The advertising copywriters hired by subsidy publishers are the best in the business. They could charm the lard off a hog. Brochures are cleverly worded to portray Utopia. Self-publishing successes are made to sound like vanity accomplishments with statements like, "It will probably surprise you to know that many prominent authors found it necessary to finance their entry into the literary world." You'll be led to believe that many dynamic leaders opt for this alternative. One promotional letter in our files reads, "Two of our authors, for example, are former Pulitzer Prize and Nobel Prize winners."

Another blurb says, "An Associated Press feature about the author and her book ran in hundreds of newspapers from coast to coast. Yes, imaginative and aggressive promotion paid off for the author of this book." Sounds like they were really out beating the bushes to hype this book, doesn't it? Read it again. Nowhere does it say *they* generated this AP spread. It could very well have resulted from the author's own efforts. Further, they allude to outsmarting the conventional trade houses when telling how an obscure businessman, whose work was rejected nine times, published his book through them and achieved sales of almost 100,000 copies.

If you send your manuscript to a subsidy publisher, expect to receive a glowing letter in return. Blandishments and flattery will be heaped upon you. You'll be praised for your flowing writing style, your choice of important subject matter, and/or your wisdom in contacting them. This letter—replete with superlatives and hyperbole—will probably also imply that wealth and fame are just around the corner. There are those who say that vanity publishers often praise writing that couldn't earn a passing grade in a junior high school English class. There is no question that quality control is missing in many of these publishing houses. Since they make their money "up-front" when writers pay to have their books printed, what incentive is there for producing well-written material or, for that matter, for selling it? Consequently, most of what rolls off the presses is wooden, trite, or overwritten.

Subsidy publishers are often the graveyards of white elephants. They don't tell you about the thousands who recoup only a fraction of their original investment. CBS's *60 Minutes* aired "So You Want to Write a

Book" in January 1979. They interviewed Martin Littlefield, president of Vantage Press, the biggest subsidy house in the country. Littlefield speculated that of the six hundred or so books his firm published in 1978, twenty-five to thirty of the authors might make money on their books. That's a *failure* ratio of 95 percent! Not very good odds.

Perhaps that's why Vantage Press was under attack by a number of its previous "customers." *Publishers Weekly* carried a news item about authors who won the right to sue Vantage in a class-action suit. In addition to charges of gross misrepresentation, the complaint alleged that "Vantage has frequently failed or refused to fill—and in some cases to even acknowledge—orders from booksellers." Vantage, the complaint continued, "has an uncompetitive return policy which discourages booksellers who might otherwise purchase books."

A major drawback is the lack of promotion. Book reviewers shun these titles. You'll never see a review for one in *Kirkus* or *Publishers Weekly*. In fact, one major reviewer commented, "They come in four at a time, and when I see the imprint, I throw them immediately in the wastebasket. I wouldn't even give them away."

While the conventional trade publisher employs sales representatives or has developed a national chain of distribution, and the self-publisher seeks out specialized markets and uses creative publicity to generate attention and sales, the subsidy publisher does virtually none of these things. Oh, maybe he adds the book to his catalog and runs what is known in the industry as a "tombstone" ad (where oodles of titles are lumped together and read like a laundry list). If you're really lucky you get a fourteen-line ad all to yourself. That sounds nifty, doesn't it? . . . until you realize that such an ad measures one column by one inch. Anticipating books to move from this kind of advertising would be like expecting a mechanic to overhaul a diesel rig with jeweler's tools.

In many cases—after paying thousands of dollars to print them—you don't own your books. You will be doled out a "royalty" on each copy sold. Alma Welch, author of *Always a Mimi*, learned this too late. "In order for me to acquire any books, even for promotion, I have to buy them," she laments.

Having climbed into the ring with a subsidy outfit, perhaps the most crippling blow is the realization that nobody wants these books. They are the orphans of the literary world. A subsidy imprint puts a stigma on a book much like quarantine signs once did on a house where plague had been diagnosed. Bookstores are not anxious to stock them. One vanity-published author reports receiving copies of invoices for a grand total of sixty-four books sold over a period of two years. Martin J. Baron quipped, "Vanity publishing is to legitimate publishing as loan-sharking is to banking."

How to check a subsidy publisher's credentials

Let us suppose you decide that a vanity house is your answer. How can you find out which is the straightest shooter? One thing you can do is write or call the Federal Trade Commission, Washington, DC 20540, and request copies of complaints or decisions filed against any company you are considering. Read these over and come to your own conclusion. You might also ask your banker to get an up-to-date Dun & Bradstreet report on them. (One California vanity press recently went bankrupt, leaving many writers dangling.)

Another smart move would be to contact the Better Business Bureau in the city where each is located. Be sure to inquire not only whether there are any unresolved complaints but also the nature of any previously settled problems. Another source of information is the state attorney general's office. And talk to the librarians or managers of your local bookstores to get their views.

There are some pointed questions you should ask any subsidy publisher. Inquire what percentage of books published last year sold over five hundred copies. Ask for a list of the bookstores that currently stock their titles. Request their catalog and randomly order two or three books from it. (Don't just settle for the prescreened samples they will provide.) Do these look like "real" bookstore books? Are they well written? Free of typographical errors? Is the printing quality good? What about the cover? Is it striking, colorful, clean, and packed with promotional zingers?

Something you might like to read is "Does It Pay to Pay to Have It Published?" This reprint is available from *Writer's Digest*, "Paying for It" Editor, 1507 Dana Avenue, Cincinnati, OH 45207. Include a #10 SASE with your request. Also read over the adjacent list of questions carefully. They were prepared by Charles Aronson, author of *The Writer Publisher*, in which he tells of his dismaying vanity publishing experiences.

Analyzing the contract

As in any contract, there are certain phrases and conditions that may not be to your advantage. Watch out for terminology that reads "up to" a given number. Instead, request that it say "not less than" that number. We are leery of statements that say the publisher will "consider" doing something. That gives you no guarantee that he will *actually* do it! Yet you have no leverage if he doesn't, as he can always say he considered the idea, but rejected it. These are all hedging statements that give you no real assurances.

Insist that specific production/delivery dates be stipulated. (And include a penalty clause that rapidly escalates if they aren't met. For instance, stipulate in the contract that for every fifteen days that delivery

CHECK LIST   SUBSIDY PUBLICATION

(Check each item with your subsidy publisher before you sign his contract)

1. Insist on bids and quotations being in writing.
2. Insist on specific numbers, not "up to."
3. Obtain up-to-date Dun & Bradstreet report, and Author's League report.
4. Things publisher agrees to do, have in writing WHEN he will do them.
5. Term of contract must date from delivery of MARKETABLE copies.
6. How many subsidized titles did publisher issue last year?
7. How many subsidized titles sold over 500 copies last year?
8. Is the agreed retail price of the book comparable to others like it?
9. Get example book signed that your book will be as good as the example.
10. Have exact physical specifications stipulated. (Not less than 50-lb inside paper, specific trimmed size, length of lines, lines per page, Smythe sewn, case bound hardcover, stamped cloth or morocco.)
11. There will be a dust jacket and it will be full four-color on cover.
12. There will be not less than 500 copies printed and bound—over and above specified complimentary copies and author's copies—in the house and ready for sale on official publication date.
13. There will be no less than enough page forms to produce 2000 copies of your book after publication date.
14. Publisher stipulates exactly when bound, salable books will be delivered.
15. Publisher stipulates the penalty he will pay to author for each day publisher is late beyond 30 working days past stipulated delivery date.
16. Author owns the page forms and can have them at termination, if he asks for them in writing at termination.
17. Author will receive 100 copies of his book on publication date, and these are over and above the 500 salable copies and all complimentary copies.
18. There will be no storage charge on books or forms.
19. Get a list of bookstores that stock this publisher's subsidized books.
20. How many book salesmen does publisher have, to actively sell your book?
21. Author can buy copies of his own book at 20% of retail.
22. Author gets 60% royalty on books publisher sells at retail.
23. On standard 40% discount sales to bookstores, author gets 40% royalty, publisher gets 20%; and this 2-2-1 ratio shall hold on all discount sales.
24. Publisher gives author copies of all sales accounted for each half year.
25. Author has complete and final O.K. of all editing and of page proofs.
26. Publisher will return to author all of author's manuscript and related material within 30 days of publication date, or forfeit $1,000.00.
27. "On an earlier page" will never be used in place of actual page number.
28. Author's name and address shall be on the book's dust jacket.
29. Author should not use publisher's envelopes for author's direct mailing because publisher will get all the orders and author loses 20% of retail price that way.
30. Publisher supplies list of reviewers who will get complimentary review copies, to number not less than fifty, and review copies will be sent out within three weeks of publication date.
31. Publisher supplies list of major booksellers and libraries that will get complimentary examination copies, to number not less than twenty-five, and these examination copies will be mailed out within four weeks of publication date.
32. Book's promotional circular will be on slick paper, in four-colors, produced in a quantity not less than 5000, 2000 of which will be mailed out within four weeks of publication date; author to get the balance.
33. Publisher stipulates minimum column-inches of advertising that will be devoted solely to your book, naming the media said advertising will appear in, and that none of the ads will be "tombstone."
34. Publisher and author will use certified mail for important communications.
35. At termination, all rights, including subsidiary rights, revert to author.

You have to be especially careful with a subsidy publisher because he does not have to sell any copies of your book in order to make his profit; he already has his profit when you pay him to print and bind and promote your book.

Have your subsidy publisher comment on the above statement.

Reprinted by permission from *The Writer Publisher* by Charles N. Aronson, 11520 Bixby Hill Road, Arcade, NY 14009.

Charles Aronson checklist.

of the books goes beyond the promised date, 5 percent will be deducted from the cost of the publishing. You may not be able to get a vanity publisher to agree to such a clause, but you can at least try.)

Be sure you know the exact number of *bound* books that will be available on the publication date. It is common practice to leave the majority of the books unbound and in flat sheets until they are needed (which is frequently never). Be aware that you will probably be assessed fees for storage of books, flat sheets, or promotional materials. Require that, upon termination of the agreement, all rights (including subsidiary rights) revert to the author. Before signing any contract, read the fine print carefully. Do not be carried away with the glamour of finally getting your book into print. Know *beforehand* what your situation will be if you agree to work with a subsidy publisher. If you do that, you're less likely to be confronted by the plight which one of our previous clients faced. As you can tell by reading the adjacent correspondence between Anna Ouellette and us, she couldn't even get her vanity publisher to talk to her! She hired an attorney to no avail. Still, Anna couldn't find out if review copies had gone out, if her book was listed in the company's catalog, "nothing like all the promises that were made before I signed the contract," she lamented. Upon our becoming involved in her predicament, Tom got on the phone and things started happening. As you can tell by the letters, Anna was soon released from her contract, received the unsold copies of her book plus royalties owed, and acquired the copyright and all original artwork. Unfortunately, it was a heart-wrenching ordeal for her before we intervened. It seems there's a good lesson here.

Working with subsidy publishers

Whether it's building a house or producing a book, production schedules do go haywire. If they do, somebody's work falls behind. See that it isn't yours. It's up to you to stay on top of the job and make sure that deadlines are met. (Remember that squeaky wheel.)

You can influence how much money you'll make. For one thing, insist that your name and address appear on the dust jacket cover and on the copyright page inside the book. Then people who see the book can order it directly from you, instead of going through the vanity publisher. There is another way you can steer more coins into your own coffers. Your publisher may encourage you to provide a mailing list of friends and relatives to whom it will send promotional material. Don't do it. Send to those people yourself! Why let the publisher collect the middleman commission? Recognize right away that if your vanity-published book is going to sell, it will be primarily because *you* hustle it. For detailed ways to generate publicity and sales, study Chapters 14 on promotion and 16

Oct. 5, 1979

Marilyn Ross:
Copy Concepts, Inc.
5644 La Jolla Blvd.
La Jolla, Ca. 92037

Dear Marilyn;
    Help!! — Now that I have your attention....
My book "An Affair of the Heart" is finished. I
like it, I think it will sell relatively well
for poetry. But..
    I don't seem to be making any headway with
the publisher, Mr.
Won't even talk to me. I've begged, threatened,
had an attorney contact them, I can't get to
first base. I've purchased 50 copies of my own book
and sold them all. A bookstore in Fountain Valley
ordered 50 copies. Thats all I know. They won't tell
me if the review copies have gone out, where they're
sending them, if I'm in their catalogue, what they
are going to do about publicity and promotion,
Nothing... Nothing like all the promises that were
made before I signed the contract and paid them
$2300⁰⁰. Art Work extra!!
    According to my contract they have me til up
for 2 years. If they aren't going to help me - who
will?
    Perhaps I could make an appointment to see you
and discuss possibilities. Thanks   Anne K

Letter about a subsidy publisher.

on money-making strategies.

Below is a list of subsidy publishers:

Dorrance & Company
Exposition Press
Mojave Books
Peter Randall, Publisher
Todd & Honeywell
Vantage Press
Vimach Associates

In addition to the foregoing, there are also several publishers who do both royalty and subsidy books. "Mum" is often the word on their subsidy activity, however, unless you happen to query them. These semisubsidy houses will then offer to do your book with you footing virtually all the bill. They don't necessarily turn out a product with any more merit than standard subsidy publishers, so be very cautious. This is sometimes the route taken for biographies, political stories, technical works, and business or industrial histories. University presses sometimes fall into this category, taking on a subsidy book if it is of excellent scientific or scholarly value. But university presses are by no means typical of subsidy publishers. As we've noted, there are situations when subsidy publishing makes sense for certain people. If that is your case, fine and good, but remember *caveat emptor*—let the buyer beware—and be aware.

Being self-publishers, we feel that if you want value for your money and a credible, quality product, self-publishing makes more sense.

PUTTING IT ALL TOGETHER

After reading through this book, if you've chosen to publish one of your own, you know you're in for a challenge — and lots of work — and lots of fun.

For most of us the process starts out as an idea, then ripens into a dream. It takes hold of our lives, dictates how we spend our time, compels us to capture our thoughts on paper, and tests our ingenuity in a hundred different ways. But dreams are the cartilage and muscle that make humanity strong. Suppose Edison hadn't been dedicated to his purpose? And what if Madame Curie had not been a woman of vision? Capturer of two Nobel Prizes, she is credited with isolating pure radium and discovering radioactivity. Humankind dreamed of orbiting the earth and landing on the moon. Yuri Gagarin and Neil Armstrong made those dreams reality. Big dreams beget big accomplishments.

True, few of us are likely to explore the galaxies . . . or expand the boundaries of scientific knowledge. A different adventure awaits us: birthing a book. And it can be the experience of a lifetime! Who is to say our dreams are less vital than the aspirations of people whose names have become household words?

But a dream without action is like a car with no gasoline. It can't go anywhere. To move our book from inception to completion we must fuel ourselves with education and study; we must conquer the craft of writing and publishing.

The undertaking is complex. The subject matter must be widely appealing — or tightly focused. A snappy title must be created. Sloppy writing must be sharpened and honed to a fine edge. A myriad of business procedures must be mastered: pricing, discounts, invoices, licenses, and taxes all clamor to be reckoned with. Unfamiliar numbers and listings must be conquered. The fine points of design and production seem infinite and incomprehensible. Typesetting decisions, paper weights, and binding options pull you in a dozen different directions. You feel as though you're drowning in a sea of details.

Then one day it all begins to fall into place and you gain a sense of how the whole process fits together. The mysteries of advertising and promotion begin to clear up. Your news releases find their mark. Requests for review copies pop up in each day's mail. A prestigious national magazine asks about first serial rights and an expert reader gives you a great blurb for the cover.

Finally comes The Day. Your books arrive from the printer. The dream has been given form. The Madame Curies and John Glenns have nothing on you. You had a goal and you reached it. And as your publishing venture matures, you'll mastermind merchandising techniques you never thought possible. Thousands of people have done it successfully. So can you.

Yes, we've traveled a long way together with this dream. We feel we've become friends through this book. And as with any friend, we offer you encouragement, wish you luck, and hope you will triumph!

AFTERWORD

We wrote *The Complete Guide to Self-Publishing* out of a sincere desire to help people put their knowledge and their dreams into print. We wanted to write the most comprehensive manual available on the subject. In writing it, we have withheld nothing as our "special secret." We've shared our victories and our disappointments.

Of course, growth is a never-ending process. And as our knowledge deepens, this volume will be updated appropriately. We'd be delighted to hear from you, our readers, for these future editions. Share your successes with us. Tell us what chapters were particularly helpful. Offer your suggestions for improvement. Let us know what still perplexes you.

Although we can't guarantee success, the principles offered here are tried and proven. They work for those who use them. We do extend this warning, however: Be careful . . . if you follow the guidelines set forth in this manual, you could outgrow the status of "self-publisher" — just as we did. Best of luck!

PUBLISHING TIMETABLE

We've tried to stress that for your self-publishing venture to have a good chance of success, you must plan and execute your actions carefully. This timetable will serve as a checklist to help you use your time wisely and do things in the most effective order. (Some of the steps in this timetable will not be clear before reading the book in its entirety.) Not all items apply to every book; use your own judgment. When you need specific details on any point, refer to the chapters noted and the Index, or check the appropriate listing in the Appendix.

I. Do Immediately

To set yourself up as a self-publisher, you must first "take care of business" — establish yourself as a commercial entity. For instructions on these steps, see Chapters 4, 5, and 7.

1. Read this book completely once. Read it through a second time, taking notes or highlighting sections.
2. Subscribe to *Writer's Digest* magazine, *Small Press,* and *Publishers Weekly.*
3. Order a copy of *Literary Market Place* from Bowker.
4. Review the Bibliography of this book. Request sample copies of any newsletters that interest you; borrow from the library, or purchase, any appropriate books from the Maverick Mail Order Bookstore.
5. Choose your publishing company name. Remember to research to see if it has already been used.
6. Write the Bank of America for its business booklets, and the Small Business Administration for its publications.
7. Contact Bowker for ABI information and listing forms and ISBN information and log sheet.
8. File a fictitious name statement (if required in your area).
9. Obtain a post office box.
10. Have letterhead, envelopes, and business cards printed.
11. Open a business checking account.
12. Contact the Chamber of Commerce and discuss local business license requirements, regulations, and procedures.
13. Write the Library of Congress to get CIP information for new publishers.
14. Review Chapters 2 and 3 on Choosing a Marketable Subject and Product Development.

II. Do Just After You've Finished Writing Your Book

With manuscript in hand, you're ready to think about the physical aspects of your book: page count, typeface, design, artwork, etc. Now is the time to file for important identifying numbers, such as ISBN. You also begin planning your marketing and distribution strategy. For specific advice on these steps, see Chapters 7, 8, 9, and 18.

1. Research your chosen title to see if it has been used already.
2. Get any needed permissions.
3. Wrap up last-minute research and verifications.
4. Ask competent friends or associates to read/critique/edit the manuscript. Revise accordingly.
5. Retype and proofread your manuscript—or enter changes on computer.
6. Make any corrections on manuscript; proofread them thoroughly.
7. Plan the interior design and mark the manuscript in readiness for typesetting.
8. Gather any interior artwork such as photographs or illustrations; size them.
9. Write cutlines for interior art and prepare a keyed list.
10. Prepare a cast-off to determine preliminary book length, specifications, etc.
11. Get author photo taken.
12. With professional help, design the cover.
13. Request price quotations from typesetters and printers.
14. Determine the tentative retail sales price using our guidelines.
15. Establish your publication date.
16. Photocopy your manuscript and send it out to authorities and key reviewers for advance comments and perhaps a foreword.
17. Assign an ISBN.
18. Complete the ABI form.
19. Obtain a Bookland EAN Scanning Symbol.
20. Send photocopies of your ABI form to Baker & Taylor, those on the "Suggested Galley Recipients" list, prime wholesalers and distributors, and other key contacts.
21. Send a copy of your ABI form, the title page, Table of Contents, the Introduction, any promotional literature, and the filled-in CIP data sheet to CIP to get your CIP data, which includes the Library of Congress preassigned catalog card number.

III. Do While Your Manuscript Is Being Typeset

At this point, you set up your promotional campaign and attend to the details of book production. For specific information on these steps, see Chapters 11, 12, and 13.

1. Research your Nationwide Marketing Plan. Track down names of reviewers, syndicated columnists, newsletters, associations, wholesalers, bookstores, special sales outlets, librarians, subsidiary rights buyers, local media people, etc. Think up innovative strategies. Prepare labels or envelopes.
2. Prepare the following promotional materials: news release, sales letter, mock-up review.
3. Contact appropriate book clubs and first serial rights buyers you have identified through market research to interest them in subsidiary rights.
4. Test mail-order ads if you're using direct marketing.
5. Prepare a personal mailing list from Christmas card recipients, business associates, club membership directories, students, etc.
6. Get business license (if needed).

7. Obtain your resale tax permit.

8. Proofread typeset galleys and have corrections made.

9. Paste up galleys if you're doing it yourself.

10. Double check that all corrections were made and that all pages, illustrations, etc., are in the correct places.

11. Prepare the index (if applicable).

12. Typeset and proofread index.

13. Photocopy F & G's or galleys and send to sources noted in this guide (see 1 above).

IV. Do While Your Book Is Being Printed

As you continue your promotional efforts, begin implementing your Nationwide Marketing Plan. Get ready for the arrival of your books. See Chapters, 5, 12, and 13 for more information on these steps.

1. Review bluelines carefully for any final corrections.

2. Set up warehousing space and a shipping area.

3. Order shipping and office supplies.

4. Prepare the following promotional materials: order flier, acknowledgment card for reviewers, discount schedule, and return-policy statement.

5. Implement your Nationwide Marketing Plan.

6. Follow up on book clubs and first serial rights potential buyers.

7. Mail your prepublication offer to your personal mailing list.

8. Write the copyright office for form TX.

9. Write Dustbooks for listing in their various directories.

10. Implement full-scale mail-order campaign (if applicable).

11. Coordinate freight delivery of books, making sure you'll be there to receive shipment and have payment ready (if needed).

V. Do When Books First Arrive

At last! You have books to sell. Begin filling orders and following up on marketing leads. Send copies of your book to important sources for promotion and copyright registration. See Chapters 5, 9, 13, 15, and 16 for more information.

1. Rejoice!

2. Take an inventory count and open several random cases to be sure books are not scuffed, bound upside down, etc.

3. Photograph book and order several 4 by 5 prints.

4. Fill complimentary copy requests that were generated by your Nationwide Marketing Plan.

5. Fill advance orders.

6. Pursue prime wholesalers and distributors who have not shown interest.

7. Go after second serial rights sales.

8. Implement special sales and innovative promotional ideas.

9. Don't forget to request the return of pertinent printing materials from your book manufacturer.

10. File your copyright registration.

11. Send a copy of the book to the CIP office.

12. Send a copy of the book to *Cumulative Book Index.*
13. Send a copy of the book to Baker & Taylor.
14. Always carry a copy of the book in your briefcase or purse, and have a case of books in the car.
15. Contact all bookstores in your area.
16. Set up a "revisions" file for noting typo corrections and new material for subsequent editions.

VI. Ongoing Promotional Activities

A self-publisher's work is never done — you must always be thinking of new ways to sell books. Now's the time to line up radio and TV interviews. See Chapters 14 and 17 for more information.

1. Implement special sales and innovative merchandising techniques.
2. Follow up on prime reviewers to be sure they received books.
3. Develop an "Available for Interview" sheet.
4. Contact local media for interviews and stories.
5. Expand your media focus to include regional print, radio, and TV.
6. Be on the lookout for new review sources and sales opportunities.
7. Consider giving lectures and/or seminars as promotional vehicles.

VII. After a Successful First Printing

Time to decide whether you want to reprint your book or offer it to a trade publisher. See Chapters 19 and 20 for more information.

1. Add favorable reviews to the cover or first page.
2. Revise the copyright page and correct any typos.
3. Revise, update, and/or expand the book as needed.
4. Review the back-page order form for price or other changes.
5. Get quotes on a second printing or —
6. Offer the book to major trade publishers.

APPENDICES

ORGANIZATIONS & OTHER INFORMATION SOURCES

About Books, Inc.
P.O. Box 1500, Buena Vista, CO 81211. Attn: Marilyn & Tom Ross; (719) 395-2459 or FAX (719) 395-8374.

ABI is a professional writing, publishing, and marketing service that specializes in working with authors, small presses, and independent publishers. Their expertise covers manuscript critiquing, editing, ghostwriting, interior layout and cover design, typesetting, and book production. They also develop and implement nationwide marketing and promotional plans.

American Bookdealers Exchange (ABE)
P.O. Box 2525, La Mesa, CA 92041. Attn: Al Galasso.

The ABE is an international marketing organization for independent publishers, small presses and mail-order book dealers. It offers members a wide variety of cooperative marketing opportunities.

American Booksellers Association (ABA)
137 W. 25th Street, #11, New York, NY 10001.

A trade association of some 5,300 retail booksellers. Sponsors the annual ABA Convention, where publishers exhibit their wares.

American Society of Journalists and Authors (ASJA)
1501 Broadway, Suite 1907, New York, NY 10036. (212) 997-0947.

ASJA is a 700-plus nationwide organization of nonfiction writers. It encourages high standards in the profession and maintains a listing of writers for hire, "Dial-a-Writer," which might be helpful.

The Association of American Publishers
2005 Massachusetts Avenue NW, Washington, DC 20036. Attn: Small Publishers Group

The AAP is the major trade organization of the publishing industry. It has seven major divisions. Although its fees and scope are not normally within the interest of the self-publisher, it is THE trade association in the field.

The Authors Guild, Inc.
234 West 44th Street, New York, NY 10036.

The Authors Guild is comprised of almost 5,000 professional writers, most with national reputations. Prospective members must meet certain professional publishing criteria to be admitted.

Book Publicists of Southern California
6430 Sunset Boulevard, Suite 503, Hollywood, CA 90028. Attn: Irwin Zucker; (213) 461-3921.

This is an organization of writers, publicity people, editors, and those of like mind who meet once a month to explore aspects of publicity in the publishing industry.

354

COSMEP
P.O. Box 703, San Francisco, CA 94101. Attn: Richard Morris; (415) 922-9490.
The largest association of independent book and periodical publishers in the U.S. Membership is $50 annually and includes their monthly newsletter. Any serious self-publisher should join this group.

Huenefeld Publishing Consultants
Box U, Bedford, MA 01730. Attn: John Huenefeld.
Offers sophisticated seminars and consulting for small publishers. They also publish *The Huenefeld Report* for managers and planners in middle-sized publishing houses.

Maverick Mail Order Bookstore
Box 1500, Dept MOBG, Buena Vista, CO 81211.
One-stop shopping. An extensive catalog of books for writers, small publishers, and speakers. Most of the titles mentioned in this guide are available from them. To receive a free catalog, send a #10 SASE with 45¢ postage.

National Federation of Press Women
Box 99, Blue Springs, MO 64015.
Comprised of writers, editors, and other communication professionals from across the country. They publish a monthly magazine, *The Press Woman,* and have chapters in most cities.

National Mail Order Association
5818 Venice Boulevard, Los Angeles, CA 90019.
Those who join the association receive the group's monthly newsletters, *Mail Order Digest,* and the *Washington Newsletter.* They also offer discounts on books and printing to members.

The National Writers Club
1450 South Havana, Suite 620, Aurora, CO 80012.
NWC was founded in 1937 to meet the need of freelance writers for authoritative help. They publish many informative reports, offer a complaint service, sponsor contests, give workshops, and have both regular and professional status memberships. They also publish a directory of their professional members available for hire.

PEN American Center
568 Broadway, New York, NY 10012.
PEN is the only worldwide organization of writers, and the chief voice of the international literary community. The 1,800 members have two or more published books of literary merit or one book of exceptional distinction.

Poets and Writers, Inc.
72 Spring Street, New York, NY 10012.
This group serves as an information center for the U.S. literary community. Poets and Writers publishes several reference guides, a magazine called *Coda,* subsidizes readings and workshops, and maintains an active information center.

R. R. Bowker Co.
249 West 17th Street, New York, NY 10011. (212) 645-9700.
They provide ABI Forms for listings in *Books in Print* and *Forthcoming Books in Print.* Also the source of ISBN logs.

Small Business Administration
1441 L Street NW, Washington, DC 20416. Toll-free line (800) 368-5855.

The SBA offers general business guidance. They have many free booklets and other inexpensive ones that are helpful to the new entrepreneur.

Women in Communications, Inc.
Box 9561, Austin, TX 78766.

Seeks to improve women's opportunities in the various communication professions. Approximately 13,000 members belong to this organization. They also publish a magazine.

There are also professional associations which invite writers working on specific subjects to join their groups (the Mystery Writers of America, Travel Writers of America, The Society of Children's Book Writers, etc.). You can find information about these specialized groups in *The Encyclopedia of Associations,* in writers' magazines, or through word of mouth.

Many small regional organizations are also springing up for self-publishers, such as the Marin Self-Publishers Association (Box 1346, Ross, CA 94957). Talk with other authors and small publishers in your vicinity to see if such a group exists — or start one!

FEDERAL INFORMATION CENTERS

Each state maintains one or more Federal Information Centers which provide a source of free information on a wide range of government-related topics.

ALABAMA
Birmingham (205)322-8591
Mobile (205)438-1421

ALASKA
Anchorage (907)271-3650

ARIZONA
Phoenix (602)261-3313
Tucson (602)622-1511

ARKANSAS
Little Rock (501)378-6177

CALIFORNIA
Los Angeles (213)894-3800
Sacramento (916)551-2380
San Diego (619)293-6030
San Francisco (415)556-6600
San Jose (408)275-7422
Santa Ana (714)836-2386

COLORADO
Colorado Springs (719)471-9491
Denver (303)234-7181
Pueblo (719)544-9523

CONNECTICUT
Hartford (203)527-2617
New Haven (203)624-4720

FLORIDA
St. Petersburg (813)893-3495
Tampa (813)229-7911

From elsewhere in Florida —
800)282-8556

GEORGIA
Atlanta (404)331-6891

HAWAII
Honolulu (808)546-8620

ILLINOIS
Chicago (312)353-4242

INDIANA
Gary/Hammond (219)883-4110
Indianapolis (317)269-7373

IOWA
Des Moines (515)284-4448

From elsewhere in Iowa —
(800)532-1556

KANSAS
Topeka (913)295-2866

From elsewhere in Kansas —
(800)432-2934

KENTUCKY
Louisville (502)582-6261

LOUISIANA
New Orleans (504)589-6696

MARYLAND
Baltimore (301)962-4980

MASSACHUSETTS
Boston (617)565-8121

MICHIGAN
Detroit (313)226-7016
Grand Rapids (616)451-2628

MINNESOTA
Minneapolis (612)349-5333

MISSOURI
St. Louis (314)425-4106

For other Missouri locations in
Area Code 314 — (800)392-7711

NEBRASKA
Omaha (402)221-3353

From elsewhere in Nebraska —
(800)642-8383

NEW JERSEY
Newark (201)645-3600
Paterson/Passaic (201)523-0717
Trenton (609)396-4400

NEW MEXICO
Albuquerque (505)766-3091
Santa Fe (505)983-7743

NEW YORK
Albany (518)463-4421
Buffalo (716)846-4010
New York (212)264-4464
Rochester (716)546-5075
Syracuse (315)476-8545

NORTH CAROLINA
Charlotte (704)376-3600

OHIO
Akron (216)375-5638
Cincinnati (513)684-2801
Cleveland (216)522-4040
Columbus (614)221-1014
Dayton (513)223-7377
Toledo (419)241-3223

OKLAHOMA
Oklahoma City (405)231-4868
Tulsa (918)584-4193

OREGON
Portland (503)221-2222

PENNSYLVANIA
Allentown/Bethlehem (215)821-7785
Philadelphia (215)597-7042
Pittsburgh (412)644-3456
Scranton (717)346-7081

RHODE ISLAND
Providence (401)331-5565

TENNESSEE
Chattanooga (615)265-8231
Memphis (901)521-3285
Nashville (615)242-5056

TEXAS
Austin (512)472-5494
Dallas (214)767-8585
Fort Worth (817)334-3624
Houston (713)229-2552
San Antonio (512)224-4471

UTAH
Ogden (801)399-1347
Salt Lake City (801)524-5353

VIRGINIA
Newport News (804)244-0480
Norfolk (804)441-3101
Richmond (804)643-4928
Roanoke (703)982-8591

WASHINGTON
Seattle (206)442-0570
Tacoma (206)383-5230

WISCONSIN
Milwaukee (414)271-2273

358

SELECTED BOOK MANUFACTURERS

Included here are some short-run book manufacturers. A few companies have been purposely omitted because the authors have had bad experiences with them. For more information, look in *LMP* or get a copy of John Kremer's *Directory of Book, Catalog and Magazine Printers*.

About Books, Inc.
425 Cedar Street, Box 1500
Buena Vista, CO 81211

Adams Press
30 W. Washington Street
Chicago, IL 60602

Arcata Graphics Book Group
Box 1977
201 West Market Street
Kingsport, TN 37662

BookCrafters
613 E. Industrial Dr.
P.O. Box 370
Chelsea, MI 48118

Delta Lithograph
28210 North Avenue Stanford
Valencia, CA 91355

Dickinson Press, Inc.
5100 33 Street SE
Grand Rapids, MI 49508

Dinner & Klein
600 S. Spokane Street
P.O. Box 3814
Seattle, WA 98124

R. R. Donnelley & Sons
2223 Martin Luther King Drive
Chicago, IL 60616

Edwards Brothers
2500 S. State Street
P.O. Box 1007
Ann Arbor, MI 48106

Griffin Printing & Lithography
544 West Colorado Street
Glendale, CA 91204

Harlo Printing
50 Victor Avenue
Detroit, MI 48203

Heffernan Press
35 New Street, Box 605
Worcester, MA 01613

Kingsport Graphics
Division of Arcata Graphics
P.O. Box 711
Kingsport, TN 37662

C.J. Krehbiel Company
3962 Virginia Avenue
Cincinnati, OH 45227

Malloy Lithographing, Inc.
5411 Jackson Road
P.O. Box 1124
Ann Arbor, MI 48106

Maple-Vail Group
Box 2695
Willow Springs Lane
York, PA 17405

Murray Printing Company
Pleasant Street
Westfort, MA 01886

Port City Press
1323 Greenwood Road
Baltimore, MD 21208

Thomson-Shore
7300 West Joy Road
P.O. Box 305
Dexter, MI 48130-0305

Walsworth Publishing Company
306 North Kansas Avenue
Marceline, MO 64658

MARKETING CONTACTS

Where to Send Galleys

For these prime sources, it's worth a phone call to learn the full name—and spelling—of the correct person and to update any address information. These sources also appear in *LMP*. (Address the galleys or folded and gathered sheets to the appropriate reviewer.)

BOOKLIST
%American Library Association
50 East Huron Street
Chicago, IL 60611

FORECAST MAGAZINE
Baker & Taylor
652 East Main Street
Bridgewater, NJ 08807

KIRKUS REVIEWS
200 Park Avenue South
New York, NY 10036

LIBRARY JOURNAL
205 East 42nd Street
New York, NY 10017

THE LOS ANGELES TIMES
Times Mirror Square
Los Angeles, CA 90053

NEW YORK TIMES
229 West 43rd Street
New York, NY 10036
(no how-to or self-help)

PUBLISHERS WEEKLY
249 West 17th Street
New York, NY 10011

SCHOOL LIBRARY JOURNAL
205 East 42nd Street
New York, NY 10017
(Only if your book is for
kindergarten—12th grade.)

SMALL PRESS MAGAZINE
11 Ferry Lane West
Westport, CT 06880

Send Finished Books

AMERICAN LIBRARIES
Source Department Editor
%American Library Association
50 East Huron Street
Chicago, IL 60611

CHOICE
%The Association of College &
    Research Libraries
100 Riverview Center
Middletown, CT 06457
(If the book's subject is appropriate to
    this academic publication.)

CUMULATIVE BOOK INDEX
c/o H. W. Wilson Co.
950 University Avenue
Bronx, NY 10452

THE BAKER & TAYLOR COMPANY
Publisher Contact Section
6 Kirby Avenue
Somerville, NJ 08876
Don't forget your own local and
    regional newspaper book review
    editors!

Book Clubs

LMP has an extensive list of book clubs noting areas of specialization. So does John Kremer's *Book Marketing Opportunities: A Directory*. Below are some random samples:

BOOK-OF-THE-MONTH CLUB
485 Lexington Avenue
New York, NY 10017

THE CHRISTIAN BOOKSHELF
40 Overlook Drive
Chappaqua, NY 10514

THE COMPUTER BOOK CLUB
TAB Books, Inc.
Blue Ridge Summit, PA 17214

DOUBLEDAY BOOK CLUB
245 Park Avenue
New York, NY 10167

GET RICH BOOK CLUB
The Putter Building, 7 Putter Lane
Middle Island, NY 11953-0102

LITERARY GUILD OF AMERICA
245 Park Avenue
New York, NY 10167

MACMILLAN BOOK CLUBS, INC.
866 3rd Avenue
New York, NY 10022

SELF-SUFFICIENCY BOOK CLUB
Sub of Rodale Press, Inc.
33 East Minor St.
Emmaus, PA 18049

SMALL PRESS BOOK CLUB
Box 100
Paradise, CA 95969
(Especially appropriate for some self-published titles, because they concentrate solely on small presses.)

THOUGHTFUL READER'S BOOK SOCIETY
P.O. Box 19207
Portland, OR 97219

WATSON-GUPTILL BOOK CLUB
1515 Broadway
New York, NY 10036

Selected Serial and Excerpt Rights Buyers

Both *Writer's Market* and *Book Marketing Opportunities: A Directory* are good places to prospect for possible serial rights sales. This list includes many of the major markets, but several others exist.

AMERICANA
29 West 38th Street
New York, NY 10018

AMERICAN HERITAGE
60 Fifth Avenue
New York, NY 10011

ARMY MAGAZINE
2425 Wilson Boulevard
Arlington, VA 22201

CATHOLIC DIGEST
Box 43090, St. Paul's Square
St. Paul, MN 55164

CHEVRON U.S.A. MAGAZINE
P.O. Box 6227
San Jose, CA 95150

COSMOPOLITAN
224 West 57th Street
New York, NY 10019

ESQUIRE
2 Park Avenue #1405
New York, NY 10016

ESSENCE MAGAZINE
1500 Broadway
New York, NY 10036

FAMILY CIRCLE MAGAZINE
488 Madison Avenue
New York, NY 10022

FIELD NEWSPAPER SYNDICATE
1703 Kaiser Avenue
Irvine, CA 92714

GLAMOUR MAGAZINE
The Conde-Nast Bldg.
350 Madison Avenue
New York, NY 10017

GLOBE
Cedar Square
5401 NW Braken Sound Boulevard
Boca Raton, FL 33431

GOOD HOUSEKEEPING MAGAZINE
959 8th Avenue
New York, NY 10019

HARPER'S BAZAAR
1700 Broadway
New York, NY 10019

INDEPENDENT NEWS ALLIANCE
Division of United Feature Syndicate
200 Park Avenue
New York, NY 10166

KING FEATURES SYNDICATE
235 East 45th Street
New York, NY 10017

LADIES' HOME JOURNAL
3 Park Avenue
New York, NY 10016-5902

LOS ANGELES TIMES SYNDICATE
Times Mirror Square
Los Angeles, CA 90053

McCALL'S MAGAZINE
230 Park Avenue
New York, NY 10169

MODERN MATURITY MAGAZINE
215 Long Beach Boulevard
Long Beach, CA 90801

MS. MAGAZINE
119 West 40th Street
New York, NY 10018

NATIONAL ENQUIRER
600 South East Coast Avenue
Lantana, FL 33464

NEW WOMAN
New Woman, Inc.
215 Lexington Avenue
New York, NY 10016

NEW YORK TIMES SYNDICATE
Sales Corp.
130 Fifth Avenue, 9th Floor
New York, NY 10011

OUI
Laurant Publications
300 West 43rd Street
New York, NY 10036

OUTSIDE MAGAZINE
Burke Communications Industries
1165 North Clark Street
Chicago, IL 60610

PARENTS MAGAZINE
685 3rd Avenue
New York, NY 10017

PENTHOUSE
Penthouse International
1965 Broadway
New York, NY 10023

PLAYBOY
Playboy Enterprises
919 N. Michigan Ave.
Chicago, IL 60611

PSYCHOLOGY TODAY
1200 Seventeenth Street NW
Washington, DC 20036

READER'S DIGEST
Pleasantville, NY 10570

REDBOOK
959 Eighth Avenue
New York, NY 10019

THE SATURDAY EVENING POST
The Saturday Evening Post Society
1100 Waterway Blvd.
Indianapolis, IN 46202

SATURDAY REVIEW
Saturday Review Publishing Co.
214 Massachusetts Avenue NE #460
P.O. Box 6024
Washington, DC 20002

SELF MAGAZINE
Conde-Nast Bldg.
350 Madison Avenue
New York, NY 10017

SMITHSONIAN
900 Jefferson Drive NW
Washington, DC 20560

THE STAR
660 White Plains Road
Tarrytown, NY 10591

UNITED FEATURE SYNDICATE, INC.
200 Park Avenue
New York, NY 10166

UNIVERSAL PRESS SYNDICATE
4900 Main Street, 9th Floor
Kansas City, MO 64112

UTNE READER
The Fawkes Building
1624 Haromon Place
Minneapolis, MN 55403

WEEKLY WORLD NEWS
600 South East Coast Avenue
Lantana, FL 33462

WOMAN'S DAY
1515 Broadway
New York, NY 10036

Selected Wholesalers and Distributors

The *American Book Trade Directory* is a great source for more names. Look at it in a large library, where it will be kept in the reference section. You may also want to check *LMP*. (Address your query to either the hardcover or paperback and nonfiction or fiction buyer: e.g., hardcover nonfiction buyer.)

Associated Booksellers
562 Boston Avenue
Bridgeport, CT 06606

The Baker & Taylor Co.
Publisher Contact Services
Box 6920, 652 East Main Street
Bridgewater, NJ 08807
(largest wholesaler)

Baker & Taylor Regional Centers:

Eastern Division
Buying Manager
The Baker & Taylor Company
50 Kirby Avenue
Somerville, NJ 08876

Midwestern Division
Buying Manager
The Baker & Taylor Company
501 South Gladiolus Street
Momence, IL 60954

Southeastern Division
Buying Manager
The Baker & Taylor Company
Mount Olive Road
Commerce, GA 30599

Western Division
Buying Manager
The Baker & Taylor Company
380 Edison Way
Reno, NV 89564

Book Carrier
19534 Club House Road
Gaithersburg, MD 20879

Bookpeople
2929 Fifth Street
Berkeley, CA 94710

Bookslinger
502 North Trior Avenue
St. Paul, MN 55104
(literary titles)

Brodart Company
500 Arch Street
Williamsport, PA 17705

Cicero Bible Press
Box 160, Industrial Park Road
Harrison, AR 72601
(religious-book jobber)

Coles Book Stores, Ltd.
90 Ronson Avenue
Rexdale, Ontario
Canada M9W 1C1

Coutts Library Service, Inc.
736 Cayuga Street
Lewiston, NY 14092

Crown Books
3301 Pennsey Drive
Landover, MD 20785

De Vorss and Co.
Box 550
Marina Del Rey, CA 90294
(metaphysical books)

The Distributors
702 South Michigan
South Bend, IN 46618

East Coast Christian Distributors
P.O. Box 4200, 35 Readington Road
Somerville, NJ 08876
(religious-book jobber)

E.B.S. Inc. Book Service
290 Broadway
Lynbrook, NY 11563

Golden-Lee Book Distributors, Inc.
1000 Dean Street
Brooklyn, NY 11238

Independent Publishers Group
814 North Franklin Street
Chicago, IL 60610

Ingram Book Company
Box M266
347 Reedwood Drive
Nashville, TN 37217

Inland Book Company
Box 261
East Haven, CT 06512
(emphasis on small and self-
  publishing)

Key Book Service, Inc.
425 Asylum Street
Bridgeport, CT 06610

Midwest Library Service
11443 St. Charles Rock Road
Bridgeton, MO 63044

Nutri-Books
P.O. Box 5793
Denver, CO 80217
(health related books)

Pacific Pipeline
19215-66th Avenue S.
Kent, WA 98032-1171

Publishers Group West
5855 Beaudry Street
Emeryville, CA 94608

Quality Books
918 Sherwood Drive
Lake Bluff, IL 60044
(reps. small presses)

Spring Arbor Distributors
10885 Textile Road
Belleville, MI 48111
(religious and children's titles)

Unilit, Inc.
5600 Hassalo Street
Portland, OR 97213
(religious-book jobber)

Samuel Weiser
Box 612
York Beach, ME 03910
(metaphysical books)

Selected Bookstore Chains

There are oodles of bookstore chains; this is a sampling of some of the largest. Others (and their specialties) can be located in the *American Book Trade Directory*. (Address your query to either the hardcover or paperback and nonfiction or fiction buyer.)

Barnes and Noble
105 5th Avenue
New York, NY 10003

Bookland
2512 Commerce Square W
Birmingham, AL 35210

Crown Books
1275 K Street
Washington, DC 20005

B. Dalton
P.O. Box 317
Minneapolis, MN 55440
(will buy only from distributors, not
     directly from small presses)

Doubleday Book Shops
673 5th Avenue
New York, NY 10022

Follett College Stores
103 Myrtle
Elmhurst, IL 60126

Hunters Books
420 North Rodeo Drive
Beverly Hills, CA 90210

Waldenbooks Company, Inc.
P.O. Box 10218
Stamford, CT 06904

Large Library Systems

This is a representative sample of library districts that purchase large quantities
of our books. Check the yellow pages to contact your local library. You can also
rent specialized library mailing lists from the R. R. Bowker Company. (Address
your query to the acquisition librarian for your specific type of book, e.g., acquisitions librarian, fiction, or acquisitions librarian, sports.)

Atlanta Public Library
10 Pryor Street, SW
Atlanta, GA 30303

Buffalo & Erie County Public Library
     System
Lafayette Square
Buffalo, NY 14203

Chicago Public Library
425 North Michigan Ave.
Chicago, IL 60611

Cuyahoga County Public Library
4510 Memphis Avenue
Cleveland, OH 44144

Denver Public Library
1357 Broadway
Denver, CO 80203

Free Library of Philadelphia
Logan Square
Philadelphia, PA 19103

Houston Public Library
500 McKinney Avenue
Houston, TX 77002

Los Angeles Public Library
361 South Anderson Street
Los Angeles, CA 90033

Nassau Library System
900 Jerusalem Avenue
Uniondale, NY 11553

New York Public Library
8 East 40th Street
New York, NY 10016

San Diego County Library
555 Overland Avenue, Bldg. 15
San Diego, CA 92123

San Diego Public Library
820 "E" Street
San Diego, CA 92101

Selected Book Review Sources

This is a listing of key newspaper and magazine book reviewers. You will want to choose those publications most suitable to your subject. Additional sources can be found in *LMP, Writer's Market,* and the *Standard Periodical Directory,* among other reference guides. (Address your query to either the hardcover or paperback, and nonfiction or fiction book review editor if no contact name is listed.)

About Books
American Library Association
50 East Huron Street
Chicago, IL 60611

American Library Association
Public Information Officer
50 East Huron Street
Chicago, IL 60611

Bestsellers
401 North Broad Street
Philadelphia, PA 19108

The Bloomsbury Review
1028 Bannock
Denver, CO 80204

The Book World
P.O. Drawer 112
Macon, MS 39341

Christian Science Monitor
One Norway Street
Boston, MA 02115

ERC Reviews
1107 Lexington Avenue
Dayton, OH 45407

Feature News Service
2330 South Brentwood Boulevard
St. Louis, MO 63144-2096

Hearst Community Newspaper, Inc.
128 Kenwood St., #9
Burbank, CA 91505

King Features Syndicate
Division of Hearst Corp.
235 East 45th Street
New York, NY 10017

New Book Information
Baker & Taylor Company
P.O. Box 6920
652 East Main Street
Bridgewater, NJ 08807-0920

New Pages
4426 South Belsay Road
Grand Blanc, MI 48439

Newsday
780 Third Avenue
New York, NY 10017

New York Review of Books
250 West 57th Street
New York, NY 10107

New York Times Book Review
229 West 43rd Street
New York, NY 10036

Parade
750 Third Avenue
New York, NY 10017

San Diego Union
P.O. Box 191
San Diego, CA 92112

San Francisco Chronicle Books
901 Mission Street
San Francisco, CA 94103

San Francisco Review of Books
1117 Geary Street
San Francisco, CA 94109

Small Press Book Review
P.O. Box 176
Southport, CT 06490

Small Press Review
P.O. Box 100
Paradise, CA 95969

Star Magazine
1729 Grand Avenue
Kansas City, MO 64108

Time Magazine
Book Editor
Rockefeller Center
New York, NY 10020

Wall Street Journal
% Dow Jones & Company
200 Liberty Street
New York, NY 10281

Washington Post Book World
1150 - 15th Street NW
Washington, DC 20071

Weekly Record Department
R. R. Bowker
245 West 17 Street
New York, NY 10011

Western Publisher
San Francisco Publishing Company
1111 Kearny Street, Suite 4
San Francisco, CA 94133
(Only for Western publishers or
   Western connected books)

Selected Syndicated Columnists

Included here are columnists who are especially interested in books. To locate other syndicated columnists appropriate to your subject matter, check *Working Press of the Nation*.

Sid Ascher
Book Review
Sidney Ascher Syndicate
214 Boston Avenue
Mays Landing, NJ 08330

John Austin
Box 49957
Los Angeles, CA 90049

Joseph Barbato
40-13 82nd Street, Room 203
Elmhurst, NY 11373

John Barkham Reviews
27 East 65th Street
New York, NY 10021

Millicent Braverman
1517 Schuyer Road, Suite A
Beverly Hills, CA 90210

Marion Benasutti
Book Talks
885 North Easton Rd.
Apt. 6A3
Glenside, PA 19038

Alan Caruba
Box 40
9 Brookside Road
Maplewood, NJ 07040

Feature News Service
2330 South Brentwood Blvd.
St. Louis, MO 63144

Sidney Goldberg
United Feature Syndicate
200 Park Avenue
New York, NY 10166

Richard Heeler
Gannett News Service
P.O. Box 7858
Washington, DC 20044

Charles Lee
Presidential Apartments
Apt. D-1203
Philadelphia, PA 19131

Jerry Mack
Box 5200
San Angelo, TX 76902

E. T. Malone, Jr.
The Literary Lantern
103 Carl Drive, Route 4
Chapel Hill, NC 27514
(emphasis on Southern books and
   authors)

Win Pendleton
Box 665
Windermere, FL 32786

San Francisco Review of Books
1117 Geary Street
San Francisco, CA 94109

Phil Thomas, Book Editor
Associated Press
50 Rockefeller Plaza
New York, NY 10020

Church and Synagogue Library Associations

Association of Jewish Libraries
% National Foundation for Jewish
   Culture
122 East 42nd Street
New York, NY 10168

Catholic Library Association
Parish and Community
Library Section
461 West Lancaster Avenue
Haverford, PA 19041

Church and Synagogue
Library Association
P.O. Box 19357
Portland, OR 97219

Lutheran Church Library Association
122 West Franklin Avenue
Minneapolis, MN 55404

Church Media Library Department
Sunday School Board of the Southern
   Baptist Convention
127 Ninth Avenue, N
Nashville, TN 37234

Cokesbury Church Library Association
Room 248
201 8th Avenue S.
Nashville, TN 37202

Evangelical Church
Library Association
P.O. Box 353
Glen Ellyn, IL 60138

Selected Large Paperback Reprint Houses

When your self-published book has achieved a level of success, you may want to approach a major trade publisher to sell them reprint rights. These are the larger paperback houses. Call and get the name of the proper editor.

Avon Books
105 Madison Avenue
New York, NY 10016

Ballantine Books
201 East 50th Street
New York, NY 10022

Bantam Books
666 5th Avenue
New York, NY 10103

Berkley Publishing Group
200 Madison Avenue
New York, NY 10016

Dell Publishing Company, Inc.
1 Dag Hammarskjold Plaza
New York, NY 10017

Little, Brown and Company
34 Beacon Street
Boston, MA 02108

New American Library
1633 Broadway
New York, NY 10019

Pocket Books
1230 Avenue of the Americas
New York, NY 10020

Times Books
201 East 50th Street
New York, NY 10022

Warner Books, Inc.
666 5th Avenue
New York, NY 10103

Literary Review Sources

Books of poetry, novels, and other literary works will find better reception here than in general review sources. To prospect for more possibilities, study the *Small Press Review*.

ACM (Another Chicago Magazine)
Box No. 11223
Chicago, IL 60611

The American Poetry Review
1704 Walnut Street
Philadelphia, PA 19103

Antaeus
The Ecco Press
26 West 17th Street
New York, NY 10011

Callaloo (Black Poets)
University of Kentucky
English Department
Lexington, KY 40506

The Chattahoochee Review
2101 Womack
Dunwoody, GA 30338

Confrontation
English Department
C.W. Post
Greenvale, NY 11548

Conjunctions
33 West 9th Street
New York, NY 10011

Crawl Out Your Window
4641 Park Boulevard
San Diego, CA 92116

Evergreen Review
Grove Press, Inc.
920 Broadway
New York, NY 10010

Ferro-Botanica
P.O. Box 1122
Hoboken, NJ 07030

Graham House Review
Box 5000
Colgate University
Hamilton, NY 13346

Grand Street
50 Riverside Drive
New York, NY 10024

Granta
13 White Street
New York, NY 10013

Hambone
132 Clinton
Santa Cruz, CA 95062

Hungry Mind Review
A Midwestern Book Review
1648 Grand Avenue
St. Paul, MN 55105

Lips
P.O. Box 1345
Montclair, NJ 07042

Manhattan Poetry Review
36 Sutton Place
% 11D
New York, NY 10022

Mississippi Review
Southern Station
Box 5144
Hattiesburg, MS 39406

The North American Review
Cedar Falls, IA 50614

North Dakota Quarterly
Box 8237
Grand Forks, ND 58202

The Paris Review
45-39 171st Place
Flushing, NY 11358

Parnassus
Herbert Leibowitz
205 W. 89th Street
New York, NY 10024

Ploughshares
Box 529
Cambridge, MA 02139

Poet Lore
% The Writer's Center
7815 Old Georgetown Road
Bethesda, MD 20814

Poetry
Joseph Parisi, Acting Editor
60 West Walton Street
Chicago, IL 60610

Raritan
165 College Avenue
New Brunswick, NJ 08903

Second Coming
P.O. Box 31249
San Francisco, CA 94131

Seneca Review
Smith Colleges
Geneva, NY 14456

Small Press News
Weeks Mills
New Sharon, ME 04955

Small Press Review
Len Fulton
P.O. Box 100
Paradise, CA 95969

Southwest Review
Box 4374
Southern Methodist University
Dallas, TX 75275

South Atlantic Quarterly
6697 College Station
Durham, NC 27708

The Southern Review
43 Allen Hall
Louisiana State University
Baton Rouge, LA 70803

Theater
222 York Street
New Haven, CT 06520

Third Rail
P.O. Box 46127
Los Angeles, CA 90046

Village Voice Literary Supplement
842 Broadway
New York, NY 10003

The Yale Review
Yale University Press
302 Temple Street
New Haven, CT 06520

Zone
Johns Hopkins Press
Journals Division
70 West 40th Street
Baltimore, MD 21211

ZYZZYVA
55 Sutter
San Francisco, CA 94104

Libraries with Small Press Collections

The libraries noted below have a keen interest in the small press literary movement. Study the list to determine which libraries might be most interested in your book.

ACADEMIC LIBRARIES

ARIZONA

Arizona State University
  Hayden Library
  Tempe, AZ 85287
  Marilyn Wurzburger, Head
    Focus: "Contemporary literature in English and materials requiring special selection."

University of Arizona
  Poetry Center
  1086 North Highland Avenue
  Tucson, AZ 85719
  Lois Shelton, Director
    Focus: Contemporary poetry

CALIFORNIA

California State University Library
Dissent and Social Change
Collection
2000 Jed Smith Drive
Sacramento, CA 95819
John Liberty, Librarian
Focus: Right- and left-wing
presses

University of California at Berkeley
Bancroft Library, Social Protest
Project
Berkeley, CA 94720
Gerda Kornfeld, Librarian
Focus: Political and social move-
ments, 1960 to the present.

University of California At Los Angeles
Research Library
Department of Special Collections
Los Angeles, CA 90024
James Davis, Librarian
Focus: "English fiction (1750-
1900), Western Americana, children's books, popular literature,
area and ethnic studies, photography, printing and graphic arts,
mountaineering."

University of California at San Diego
Library
Department of Special Collections
La Jolla, CA 92093
Michael Davidson, Curator of
Archive for New Poetry
Focus: "English-language poetry
published since World War II."

University of California at Santa
Barbara Library
Department of Special Collections
Santa Barbara, CA 93106
Christian Brun, Head
Focus: "20th-century major
English and American writers."

University of San Francisco
Richard A Gleeson Library
Donohue Rare Book Room
San Francisco, CA 94117
D. Steven Corey, Special Collections
Librarian
Focus: "Fine presses."

University of Southern California
Library
Department of Special Collections
University Park
Los Angeles, CA 90089
William Jankos, Curator
Focus: "American literature."

COLORADO

University of Colorado Libraries
Special Collections
Boulder, CO 80309
Nora Quinlan, Head
Focus: "Colorado printing, works
of authors we collect—
Colorado authors."

CONNECTICUT

Trinity College Library
Watkins Library
300 Summit Street
Hartford, CT 06106
Jeffrey H. Kaimowitz, Curator
Focus: "Private presses, graphic
arts, printing bibliographies, some
poetry."

University of Connecticut Library
Special Collections
U-5SC
Storrs, CT 06268
Richard H. Schimmelpfeng,
Director
Focus: "Primarily literature,
poetry, and little magazines."

Yale University
Sterling Memorial Library
1603 A Yale Station
New Haven, CT 06520
Susan Steinberg, American and
Commonwealth Studies
Bibliographer
Focus: "Current American,
British, and Canadian fiction and
poetry."

FLORIDA

Florida State University
  Strozier Library
  Shaw Collection
  Tallahassee, FL 32306
  Frederick Korn, Curator
    Focus: "20th-century English and
  American poetry, poetry about
  childhood."
University of Florida
  Parkman Dexter Library of
  American Literature
  531 West Library
  Gainesville, FL 32611
  Carmen Russell, Curator
    Focus: "Parkman Dexter Howe
  Collections of New England Litera-
  ture, seventeenth to twentieth cen-
  tury, curated by Sidney Ives, univer-
  sity librarian for rare books and
  manuscrips."

GEORGIA

University of Georgia Libraries
  Special Collections Division
  Athens, GA 30602
  Mary Ellen Brooks, Rare Books Bibliographer
    Focus: "We aim to collect at least
  one example of every American
  small press . . . and representative
  examples of quality book arts from
  abroad."

ILLINOIS

Northwestern University Library
  Special Collections Department
  Evanston, IL 60201
  R. Russell Maylone, Curator
    Focus: "American, British, Cana-
  dian, 1945-1980."
Southern Illinois University
  Morris Library
  Special Collections
  Carbondale, IL 62901
  David D. Koch, Curator
    Focus: "English-language presses
  in Europe, 1920s-1940s; American
  private presses; Illinois imprints (ex-
  cept Chicago)."

INDIANA

Ball State University
  Bracken Library
  Muncie, IN 47306
  Peter W. Hart, Chief Bibliographer
    Focus: "Across the board—
  extensive collections for some first
  editions, and modern American
  poetry."

MAINE

Colby College
  Miller Library
  Special Collections
  Waterville, ME 04901
  Fraser Cocks, Curator
    Focus: "20th-Century American
  poetry; contemporary Irish poetry
  and prose."

MASSACHUSETTS

Amherst College Library
  Amherst, MA 01002
  Michael Kasper, Reference
  Librarian
    Focus: "Contemporary poetry."
Harvard College
  Lamont Library, Woodberry
  Poetry Room
  Cambridge, MA 02138
  Stratis Haviaras, Curator
    Focus: "20th-century poetry in
  English or English translation."
Salem State College Library
  Alternatives Library
  Lafayette Street
  Salem, MA 01970
  Margaret Andrew, Adviser
    Focus: "Poetry, politics, women's
  movement, Third World."

MICHIGAN

Michigan State University Libraries
  Special Collections Division
  American Radicalism Collection
  East Lansing, MI 48823
  Jannette Fiore, Head of Special
  Collections
    Focus: "20th-century anti-
  Establishment presses."

University of Michigan at Ann Arbor
711 Hatcher Library
Labadie Collection
Ann Arbor, MI 48109
Edward C. Weber, Head
Focus: "Social protest literature: anarchism, underground press, recent liberation movements, etc."

MISSOURI

Washington University
Olin Library
Special Collections
St. Louis, MO 63130
Holly Hall, Head
Focus: "Poetry, fiction, printing and publishing history, local history."

NEW HAMPSHIRE

Dartmouth College Library
Special Collections
Hanover, NH 03755
Stanley W. Brown, Chief
Focus: "American presses, printers, and publishers of the 20th century."

NEW JERSEY

Monclair State College
Harry A. Sprague Library
Upper Montclair, NJ 07043
Norman Stock, Librarian
Focus: "Representative small-press titles in poetry and fiction."
Princeton University Library
Graphic Arts Collection
Princeton, NJ 08548
Dale Roylance, Curator
Focus: "Fine printing."

NEW MEXICO

University of New Mexico General Library
Special Collections Department
Albuquerque, NM 87131
James Wright, Acting Head
Focus: "Covers a wide range of small-press printing. Inclusive of all types of private, small, fine, or hobby presses that are operated for the joy of printing as a craft and as a means of self-expression."

NEW YORK

State University of New York at Buffalo Library
Poetry/Rare Book Collection
420 Capen Hall
Buffalo, NY 14260
Robert J. Bertholf, Curator
Focus: "20th-century English poetry."
State University of New York at Stony Brook Library
Department of Special Collections
Stony Brook, NY 11794
Evert Volkersz, Head
Focus: "Literature and poetry, primarily mid-20th century and on."
Syracuse University
George Arents Research Library
600 Bird Library
Syracuse, NY 13710
Mark F. Weimer, Rare Book Bibliographer
Focus: "Local, regional presses, Syracuse authors, specimens of various presses."

NORTH CAROLINA

University of North Carolina at Greensboro
Walter Clinton Jackson Library
Greensboro, NC 27412
Emilie W. Mills, Special Collections Librarian
Focus: Literature and poetry.

OHIO

Bowling Green State University
Jerome Library
Center for Archival Collections
Thomas F. Eckman Memorial Collection
Bowling Green, OH 43403
Nancy Steen, Rare Books Librarian
Focus: Modern poetry.
Kent State University Library
Department of Special Collections
Kent, OH 44242
Dean H. Keller, Curator
Focus: "19th- and 20th-century English and American literature; history."

University of Cincinnati
   George Elliston Poetry Collection
   646 Central Library
   Cincinnati, OH 45221
   James Cummins, Curator
      Focus: "Modern and contempo-
   rary (20th century) poetry."
University of Toledo Libraries
   Ward M. Canaday Center
   2801 West Bancroft
   Toledo, OH 43606
   David J. Martz, Jr., Director
      Focus: "20th-century Anglo-
   American literature: heavy poetry
   emphasis."

PENNSYLVANIA

Carnegie-Mellon University Libraries
   Special Collections
   Schenley Park
   Pittsburgh, PA 15213
   Mary Catherine Schall, Librarian
      Focus: "19th- and 20th-century
   English and American literature,
   graphic arts, history of science."
Temple University Library
   Contemporary Culture Collection
   Philadelphia, PA 19122
   Patricia J. Case, Curator
      Focus: "Publications from social-
   change movements; alternative and
   small-press publications."

RHODE ISLAND

Brown University
   John Hay Library
   Harris Collection of American
   Poetry and Plays
   Providence, RI 02914
   Rosemary L. Cullen, Curator
      Focus: "We collect comprehen-
   sively in American and Canadian
   poetry and plays."

SOUTH CAROLINA

Wofford College
   Sandor Teszler Library
   Spartanburg, SC 29301
   Frank J. Anderson, Librarian
      Focus: "A broad selection of art-
   ists' books, private presses, etc."

TEXAS

University of Texas at Austin
   Humanities Research Center
   Austin, TX 78712
   Decherd Turner, Director
      Focus: "19th- and 20th-century
   British, American, and French literature, sizable small-press holdings in
   poetry and short stories by contemporary American and British
   writers."

VIRGINIA

Virginia Commonwealth University
   James Branch Cabell Library
   Special Collections and University
   Archives
   901 Park Avenue
   Richmond, VA 23284
   Dan Yanchisin, Special Collections
   Librarian
      Focus: "Modern American
   poetry (post-1945)."

WISCONSIN

University of Wisconsin-LaCrosse
   Murphy Library
   Special Collections Department
   La Crosse, WI 54601
   Edwin L. Hill, Librarian
      Focus: "Contemporary Midwest-
   ern littles, private presses, contem-
   porary poetry."

University of Wisconsin-Madison
   Memorial Library
   728 State Street
   Madison, WI 53706
   Deborah Reilly, Assistant Curator of
   Rare Books
      Focus: English-language little
   magazines and holdings in the
   Humanities.

CANADA

McMaster University Library
   1280 Main Street West
   Hamilton, Ontario, Canada L85 4L6
   Bruce Whiteman, Research
   Collections Librarian
      Focus: "Canadian poetry, 1945-
   present."

University of Waterloo Library
  Waterloo, Ontario, Canada N2L 3G1
  Susan Bellingham, Head of
  Special Collections
    Focus: Small and private
    presses.

PUBLIC LIBRARIES

ARIZONA

Phoenix Public Library
  12 East McDowell Road
  Phoenix, AZ 85004
  Meredith Julian, Librarian,
  Humanities Department

CALIFORNIA

Berkeley Public Library
  2090 Kittridge Street
  Berkeley, CA 94704
  June Nash, Library Services
  Coordinator
San Diego Public Library
  820 E Street
  San Diego, CA 92101
  John Vanderby, Librarian,
  Literature Section
San Francisco Public Library
  Civic Center
  San Francisco, CA 94107
  Johanna Goldschmid, Librarian,
  Special Collections Department

DISTRICT OF COLUMBIA

Library of Congress
  Washington, DC 20540
  Peter Van Wingen, Head,
  Reference and Reader Services
  Section

ILLINOIS

Chicago Public Library
  78 East Washington Street
  Chicago, IL 60602
  Laura Linard, Curator,
  Special Collections

MARYLAND

Enoch Pratt Free Library
  400 Cathedral Street
  Baltimore, MD 21201
  Faye Lawry, Humanities
  Department

MICHIGAN

Detroit Public Library
  5201 Woodward
  Detroit, MI 48202
  Ann Rabjohns, Chief,
  Language and Literature

NEVADA

North Las Vegas Public Library
  2300 Civic Center Drive
  North Las Vegas, NV 89030
  Thomasine Carson, Librarian

NEW JERSEY

Newark Public Library
  5 Washington Street
  Box 630
  Newark, NJ 07101
  William J. Dane, Supervising
  Librarian,
  Art and Music Department

NEW YORK

New York Public Library
  Research Libraries
  5th Avenue at 42nd Street
  New York, NY 10018
  Stephen Green, Librarian
Brooklyn Public Library
  Grand Army Plaza
  Brooklyn, NY 11238
  Ann P. Miller, Literature Specialist

OHIO

Public Library of Cincinnati and
  Hamilton County
  800 Vine Street-Library Square
  Cincinnati, OH 45202
  Donna S. Monnig, Head,
  Literature Department

TEXAS

Houston Public Library
  500 McKinney
  Houston, TX 77027
  Donna Grove, Curator

WISCONSIN

Milwaukee Public Library
  814 West Wisconsin Avenue
  Milwaukee, WI 53203
  Orval Liljequist, Humanities
  Specialist

Remainder Dealers

Remainder dealers buy overstock books and titles that are not moving well. They are a last resort option for disposing of your books. More detailed lists can be found in *LMP*.

Booksmith Promotional Co.
432 Park Avenue South
New York, NY 10016

Bookthrift
45 West 36th Street
New York, NY 10018

Book Sales, Inc.
110 Enterprise Avenue
Secaucus, NJ 07094

Daedalus Books
2260 25th Place NE
Washington, DC 20018

Marboro Books, Inc.
205 Moonachie Road
Moonachie, NJ 07074

Outlet Book Company
225 Park Avenue South
New York, NY 10003

Publishers Central Bureau
One Champion Avenue
Avenel, NJ 07001

Publishers Marketing
  Enterprises, Inc.
386 Park Avenue South
New York, NY 10016

Sunflower Books
Division of W. H. Smith
  Publishers, Inc.
112 Madison Avenue
New York, NY 10016

Western Book Distributors
2970 San Pablo Avenue
Berkeley, CA 94702

Other Helpful Information

Bookland EAN Scanning Symbol Suppliers

George Goldberg
GGX Associates
11 Middle Neck Road
Great Neck, NY 11021

George Wright
Product Identification & Processing
  Systems (PIPS)
436 East 87th Street
New York, NY 10128

Scott Puckett
Precision Photography, Inc.
1150 North Tustin Avenue
Anaheim, CA 92807

Marc Landy
Landy & Associates
5311 North Highland
Tacoma, WA 98407

Clip Art Sources

Art Direction Book Company
10 East 39th Street, 6th Floor
New York, NY 10016
(212)889-6550

ArtMaster * Art-Pak
500 North Claremont Boulevard
Claremont, CA 91711
(714)626-8065

Creative Media Services
P.O. Box 5955
Berkeley, CA 94705
(415)483-3408

Dover Publications, Inc.
31 East 2nd Street
Mineola, NY 11501
(516)294-7000

Graphic Products Corporation
3601 Edison Place
Rolling Meadows, IL 60008
(312)392-1476

Letraset USA
40 Eisenhower Drive
Paramus, NJ 07652
(201)845-6100

The Printers Shopper
111 Press Lane
Chula Vista, CA 92012
(800)854-2911
California
(800)522-1573

Point-of-Purchase (POP) Suppliers

Beemak Plastics
7424 Santa Monica Boulevard
Los Angeles, CA 90046

Bookstore Fixtures of America
6856 Gulfport Boulevard
South Pasadena, FL 33707

Clinton Plastics
5133 West 65th Street
Chicago, IL 60638

Commercial Wire and Display
    Products
P.O. Box 3121
Rockford, IL 61106

Diversified Display
5600 North County Road 18
Minneapolis, MN 55428

Elite Marketing Ltd.
4215 Crescent Street
Long Island City, NY 11101

Siegel Display Products
P.O. Box 95
Minneapolis, MN 55440

BIBLIOGRAPHY/ RECOMMENDED READING

Writing and Editing

BEGINNING WRITER'S ANSWER BOOK edited by Kirk Polking and Rose Adkins
Writer's Digest Books: 1984. Completely revised and updated edition answers nearly 900 questions about writing.

THE BUSINESS OF WRITING FOR BUSINESS by Don Cook
Darcy Publications. A system for improving your writing skills and marketing them to make more money.

THE CAREFUL WRITER by Theodore M. Bernstein
Atheneum: 1965. A modern guide to English usage.

CHICAGO MANUAL OF STYLE
University of Chicago Press: 1982. Standard style guide for publishers and editors. Covers fundamentals of printing and typesetting, as well as grammar and style.

COPYEDITING: A PRACTICAL GUIDE by Karen Judd
William Kauffman, Inc.: 1982. How it's done from the publisher's point of view. An especially helpful book.

EDITING YOUR NEWSLETTER by Mark Beach
Coast to Coast Books, distributed by Writer's Digest/North Light Books, third edition, 1988. A guide to writing, design, and production of newsletters . . . but also contains good general information.

THE ELEMENTS OF STYLE by William Strunk, Jr., and E. B. White
Macmillan Publishing Co., Inc.: 1978. A small but uniquely comprehensive book on the fundamentals of writing.

GETTING THE WORDS RIGHT by Theodore A. Rees Cheney
Writer's Digest Books: 1983. How to revise, edit, and rewrite. Contains many useful examples of text with the revised versions.

HOW TO CHOOSE A WINNING TITLE by Nat G. Bodian
Oryx Press: 1988. A unique guide for writers, editors, and publishers.

HOW TO WRITE A COOKBOOK AND GET IT PUBLISHED by Sara Pitzer
Writer's Digest Books: 1984. A good step-by-step discussion of the type of cookbook to write and how to make it sell.

HOW TO WRITE AND SELL YOUR PERSONAL EXPERIENCES by Lois Duncan
Writer's Digest Books: 1979. How to turn everything that happens to you into salable writing.

HOW TO WRITE THE STORY OF YOUR LIFE by Frank P. Thomas
Writer's Digest Books: 1984. Useful information to help the memoirist remember, research, and write.

HOW YOU CAN MAKE $25,000 A YEAR WRITING (NO MATTER WHERE YOU LIVE) by Nancy Edmonds Hanson

Writer's Digest Books: 1980. How to build a successful freelance career by writing for newspapers, businesses, and government.

IF I CAN WRITE, YOU CAN WRITE by Charlie Shedd
Writer's Digest Books: 1984. Bestselling inspirational writer shares his rules for good writing.

INSTANT ORAL BIOGRAPHIES by William Zimmerman
Guarionex Press, Ltd.: 1981. How to interview people and tape the stories of their lives.

IS THERE A BOOK INSIDE YOU? by Dan Poynter and Mindy Bingham
Para Publishing: 1985. How to pick a topic, break in, do research, etc.

KNOWING WHERE TO LOOK by Lois Horowitz
Writer's Digest Books: 1984. The ultimate guide to research by a librarian who really knows her subject.

MAKE EVERY WORD COUNT by Gary Provost
Writer's Digest Books: 1980. A guide to the basic techniques of good writing.

THE NEWSLETTER EDITOR'S DESK BOOK by Marvin Arth and Helen Ashmore
Parkway Press: 1981. A concise review of journalism principles applied to special-audience periodicals.

ON WRITING WELL, Third Edition, by William K. Zinsser
Harper & Row: 1985. An outstanding book for every nonfiction writer.

ONE WAY TO WRITE YOUR NOVEL by Dick Perry
Writer's Digest Books: 1981. A step-by-step method for writing and selling a novel.

A PRACTICAL STYLE GUIDE FOR AUTHORS AND EDITORS by Margaret Nicholson
Holt, Rinehart, and Winston: 1967. Good general format information.

RESPONSIBILITIES OF THE AMERICAN BOOK COMMUNITY edited by John Y. Cole
Library of Congress: 1982. Private and public responsibilities as a writer.

STET! TRICKS OF THE TRADE FOR WRITERS AND EDITORS by Bruce O. Boston
Editorial Experts, Inc.: 1986. A remarkable editing tool, plus fun reading for anyone who loves words.

THE 29 MOST COMMON WRITING MISTAKES AND HOW TO AVOID THEM by Judy Delton
Writer's Digest Books: 1985. This little book will help you improve your writing by avoiding often-made mistakes.

WORDS INTO TYPE, 3rd edition, edited by M. Skillin and R. Gay
Prentice-Hall: 1974. Resource for fine points of grammar, usage, style, and production methods.

WRITING CREATIVE NON-FICTION by Theodore A. Rees Cheney
Writer's Digest Books: 1987. Explores the use of fiction techniques to make nonfiction more interesting, dramatic, and vivid.

WRITING THE NOVEL: FROM PLOT TO PRINT by Lawrence Block
Writer's Digest Books: 1979. A perceptive handbook on how to handle the questions that plague prospective novelists.

WRITING TO INSPIRE by William Gentz, Lee Roddy, and others
Writer's Digest Books: 1982. A guide to writing and publishing for the expanding religious market.

Business Procedures

AUTHOR LAW AND STRATEGIES by Brad Bunnin and Peter Beren
Nolo Press: 1983. A legal guide for the working writer. This is a thorough and fascinating book.

BUSINESS LETTERS FOR PUBLISHERS by Dan Poynter
Para Publishing: 1981. Sample letters for various aspects of the publishing business.

THE CONSULTANT'S KIT by Jeffrey L. Lant
Jeffrey Lant Associates Publishing, Inc.: 1981. Establishing and operating your successful consulting business. A must for anyone entering this field.

DIRECTORY OF BOOK, CATALOG, AND MAGAZINE PRINTERS by John Kremer
Ad-Lib Publications: 1988. This fourth edition lists 1,000 printers with full details.

FINANCIAL FEASIBILITY IN BOOK PUBLISHING by Robert Follett
Alpine Guild: 1988. Designed to determine what makes sense to publish; by a real pro.

HOW TO BORROW YOUR WAY TO A GREAT FORTUNE by Tyler G. Hicks
Parker Publishing Company: 1970. Ideas on accumulating much-needed capital using the magic of OPM: other people's money.

HOW TO SET YOUR FEES AND GET THEM by Kate Kelly
Visibility Enterprises: 1982. Seldom-seen information on how to charge the right rates for your consulting services.

HOW TO START, FINANCE, AND MANAGE YOUR OWN SMALL BUSINESS by Joseph R. Mancuso
Prentice-Hall, Inc.: 1978. The ABC's of making a go of it in your own small business.

HOW TO SUCCEED AS AN INDEPENDENT CONSULTANT by Herman Holtz
John Wiley and Sons: 1982. Advice on consulting services.

INCORPORATING YOUR BUSINESS by John Kirk
TPR Publishing Co., Inc.: 1981. Step-by-step guide to the ins and outs of incorporation.

INCORPORATING YOUR TALENTS by Robert A. Esperti and Renno L. Peterson
McGraw-Hill Book Company: 1984. A guide to the one-person corporation.

LAW AND THE WRITER, third edition, edited by Kirk Polking and Leonard S. Meranus
Writer's Digest Books: 1985. A handbook of good advice on how to recognize and avoid legal problems.

MEDIA LAW by Katherine M. Galvin, attorney
Nolo Press: 1984. A legal handbook for the working journalist.

SMALL TIME OPERATOR by Bernard Kamoroff, C.P.A.
    Bell Springs Publishing: 1987. How to start your own business, keep books, pay taxes, and stay out of trouble. The leading book in its field.

VENTURE CAPITAL SOURCES FOR BOOK PUBLISHERS compiled by John Kremer
    Ad-Lib Publications: 1988. Tips on how to apply for venture capital plus a listing of nineteen firms interested in investing in publishing.

WHAT THEY DON'T TEACH YOU AT HARVARD BUSINESS SCHOOL by Mark H. McCormack
    Bantam Books: 1984. A discussion of the street knowledge that comes from the day-to-day experiences of running a business and managing people.

YOU CAN NEGOTIATE ANYTHING by Herb Cohen
    Bantam Books: 1982. The how-tos and whys of negotiating to get what you want.

Computer Information

BEACHAM'S WORDPERFECT 5.0 HANDBOOK by Walton Beacham and Deborah Beacham
    Bantam Books: 1988. A most useful guide, which goes from basic functions to advanced applications for WordPerfect.

A DESKTOP PUBLISHER'S GUIDE TO PASTEUP by Tony Middleton
    Plusware, Inc.: 1987. A step-by-step illustrated book on preparing mechanicals for printing.

DESKTOP PUBLISHING WITH WORDPERFECT by Roger C. Parker
    Ventana Press, Inc.: 1988. This unique book introduces you to WordPerfect's new features, which let you create attractive printed materials quickly and inexpensively.

THE ILLUSTRATED HANDBOOK OF DESKTOP PUBLISHING AND TYPE-SETTING by Michael L. Kleper
    TAB: 1987. A fat sourcebook with much valuable information on computerized print and graphics production.

LOOKING GOOD IN PRINT by Roger C. Parker
    Ventana Press, Inc.: 1988. A guide to basic design for desktop publishing no matter which software you use.

MASTERING DOS by Judd Robbins
    Sybex: 1987. A complete tutorial and up-to-date user's guide to DOS.

THE NEW WRITER by Joan P. Mitchell
    Microsoft Press: 1987. Contains many techniques for writing well with a computer.

PAGEMAKER by Kevin Strehlo
    Scott, Foresman and Company: 1987. Tells how to use PageMaker to do desktop publishing on your IBM PC or compatible.

USING WORDPERFECT 5 by Charles O. Stewart III
    Que Corporation: 1988. An essential, comprehensive guide for users of WordPerfect software.

VENTURA PUBLISHER FOR THE IBM PC by Richard J. Jantz
John Wiley & Sons: 1987. A handy guide to mastering desktop publishing using Ventura Publisher software.

WORD PROCESSING POWER WITH MICROSOFT WORD by Peter Rinearson
Microsoft Press: 1986. Many tips for beginners, intermediates and power users.

Design and Printing

BUSINESS GUIDE TO PRINT PROMOTION by Marlene Miller
Iris Communication Group: 1988. Logos, stationery, brochures, plus many other forms of business printing.

DELTA'S PUBLISHER'S PLANNING KIT
Delta Lithographic Co. A helpful kit explaining printing requirements.

THE DESIGN OF BOOKS by Adrian Wilson
Peregrine-Smith Books: 1974. A guide to the design of books.

THE DESIGNER'S GUIDE TO TEXT TYPE by Jean Callan King and Tony Esposito
Van Nostrand Reinhold Company: 1980. Provides leaded samples of the fifty-one most popular typefaces. Legibility, color, and the character of each face may be thoroughly examined and compared with other faces.

DIRECTORY OF SHORT RUN BOOK PRINTERS compiled by John Kremer
Ad-Lib Publications: 1984. An extremely useful evaluation of who does what for what price in the book manufacturing industry.

GETTING IT PRINTED by Mark Beach, Steve Shepro, and Ken Russon
Coast to Coast Books: 1986. Offers a fresh, clear explanation of how to work with printers and graphic art services.

GRAPHICS MASTER by Dean Phillip Lem
Dean Lem Associates, Inc.: 1983. A workbook of planning aids, reference guides, and graphic tools for the design and preparation of printing. A rather technical, but extremely useful, book.

A HISTORY OF GRAPHICAL DESIGN by Phillip B. Meggs
Van Nostrand Reinhold. A history of graphic designs throughout the world.

HOW TO UNDERSTAND AND USE DESIGN AND LAYOUT by Alan Swann
North Light Books: 1987. A wonderful, easy-to-follow book that helps you produce professional results.

MANUALE TYPOGRAPHICUM by Hermann Zapf
The M. I. T. Press: 1970. One hundred typographic pages with quotations from the past and present on types and printing in sixteen different languages.

METHODS OF BOOK DESIGN by Hugh Williamson
Yale University Press: 1983. A tool for book cover design.

POCKET PAL, 13th edition
International Paper: 1983. A graphic arts production book with many handy visuals and tips.

PRINTING IN ASIA by Bill Dalton
Moon Publications. An introduction to what is involved in printing books in Asia.

STUDIO SECRETS FOR THE GRAPHIC ARTIST by Lorraine Dickey
North Light Books: 1986. A sophisticated explanation of graphic equipment and techniques.

TYPE PROCESSING by Dean Phillip Lem
Dean Lem Associates: 1986. Tells how to use your word processing keyboard to turn text into type and save on typesetting costs.

Publishing Information

THE BOOK MARKET: HOW TO WRITE, PUBLISH, AND MARKET YOUR BOOK by Aaron Mathieu
Andover Press: 1981. Full of detailed information about commercial publishing and self-publishing.

BOOK PUBLISHING; A WORKING GUIDE FOR AUTHORS, EDITORS, AND SMALL PUBLISHERS by Donald R. Armstrong
Bookman House: 1979. Covers the industry, alternatives, manuscript preparation, book design and production, and marketing.

BOOK PUBLISHING: WHAT IT IS, WHAT IT DOES by John P. Dessauer
Dessauer Continuum Publishing Corp.: 1989. This new third edition provides an excellent overview of the industry.

A CANDID CRITIQUE OF BOOK PUBLISHING by Curtis G. Benjamin
R. R. Bowker Company: 1977. An insider's look at the publishing industry.

COLLEGE PUBLISHING MARKET by John B. McHugh
McHugh Publishing Reports: 1988. Discusses the methods of marketing, acquisition and editorial management for the college market.

DIRECTORY PUBLISHING by Russell Perkins
Morgan Rand: 1987. A practical guide on how to succeed in this entrepreneurial kind of publishing.

FORMAIDS FOR DIRECT RESPONSE MARKETING
Ad-Lib Publications: 1985. Forms, records, sample letters, etc., to ensure your success as a small publisher.

HOW TO GET HAPPILY PUBLISHED by Judith Applebaum
Harper and Row Publishers, Inc.: 1988. The ways and resources with which to get the very best deal for yourself and your writing.

HOW TO MAKE BIG PROFITS PUBLISHING CITY & REGIONAL BOOKS by Marilyn and Tom Ross
Communication Creativity: 1987. Everything you need to know to research, write, produce, and sell books with an "area" tie-in.

IN COLD TYPE by Leonard Shatzkin
Houghton Mifflin Company: 1982. An excellent book on the whys and wherefores of book publishing.

INTO PRINT by Mary Hill and Wendell Cochran
William Kaufmann, Inc.: 1977. A practical guide to writing, illustrating, and publishing.

ONE BOOK/FIVE WAYS
   William Kaufmann, Inc.: 1978. An unusual behind-the-scenes look at the publishing procedures of five university presses.

PUBLISH IT YOURSELF by Charles J. Chickadel
   Trinity Press: 1978. Helpful information on putting out your own book, including technical printing tips.

PUBLISHING: A COMPLETE GUIDE FOR SCHOOLS, SMALL PRESSES, AND ENTREPRENEURS by Robert Lawrence Holt
   California Financial Publications: 1982. A thorough description of how to establish your own publishing track record.

THE PUBLISH-IT-YOURSELF HANDBOOK, revised edition, edited by Bill Henderson
   Pushcart Press: 1987. Good for inspiration; the self-publishing stories of Walt Whitman, Anais Nin, Virginia and Leonard Woolf, Alan Swallow, Stewart Brand, and others.

PUBLISH YOURSELF WITHOUT KILLING YOURSELF by L. A. Tattan
   InPrint: 1981. A complete guide to the economics of book production for self-publishing authors.

THE SELF-PUBLISHING MANUAL by Dan Poynter
   Para Publications: 1984. A thorough and useful guide on the subject.

SMALL PRESS RECORD edited by Len Fulton
   Dustbooks. An annual compendium of trends, small press profiles, reviews, etc. A mainstay of self-publishing and small press news.

WHAT HAPPENS IN BOOK PUBLISHING edited by Chandler Grannis
   Columbia University Press: 1972. Some of the experienced people in the book business give suggestions and tips for self-publishers.

THE WRITER/PUBLISHER by Charles N. Aronson
   C. N. Aronson: 1976. A discussion of the author's experiences with a vanity press and other publishing information.

A WRITER'S GUIDE TO BOOK PUBLISHING, 2nd edition, by Richard Balkin
   Hawthorn/Dutton: 1981. One of the best books on all aspects of book publishing.

THE WRITER'S SURVIVAL MANUAL by Carol Meyer
   Crown Publishers, Inc.: 1982. The complete guide to getting your book published by a commercial publisher.

Marketing and Publicity

ALL-IN-ONE DIRECTORY edited by Amalia Gebbie
   Gebbie Press. This annual lists more than 21,000 daily and weekly newspapers, magazines, TV, and radio.

ALL TV PUBLICITY OUTLETS
   Nationwide Public Relations Plus, Inc. An annual that lists local, syndicated, network, and cable TV opportunities.

BOOK FAIRS by Dan Poynter
Para Publishing: 1986. A handy exhibiting guide for publishers.

BOOK MARKETING OPPORTUNITIES: A DIRECTORY by John Kremer
Ad-Lib Publications: 1987. Lists more than 2,500 key contacts for publicizing and selling books.

BOOK PROMOTION AND MARKETING by Marilyn and Tom Ross
Communication Creativity: 1987. A six-hour audio cassette program that describes success strategies to increase your sales. Learn while you drive, fill book orders, collate mailings, etc.

CABLE CONTACTS YEARBOOK
Larimi Communications Assoc. Ltd. An annual listing of cable systems, satellite networks, independent producers, and multi-system operators.

CABLE TV PUBLICITY OUTLETS
Public Relations Plus, Inc. Directory of publicity outlets for cable TV.

THE CATALOG OF CATALOGS compiled by Edward Palder
Woodbine House: 1987. Lists over 8,000 catalogs in 450 different categories.

CHASE'S ANNUAL EVENTS by William D. and Helen M. Chase
Contemporary Books, Inc. An annual publication listing special days, weeks, and months each year. Useful for promotion.

COPYWRITER'S HANDBOOK by Nat G. Bodian
ISI Press: 1984. A practical book covering advertising and promotion of specialized and scholarly books.

CREATING EFFECTIVE RESPONSE ADS IN PUBLICATIONS by Rene Gnam
Rene Gnam Consultation Company: 1984. Guidelines and helpful hints on positioning, research, testing, and copywriting by a real pro.

DIRECTORY OF RELIGIOUS BROADCASTING 1984 edited by Ben Armstrong
National Religious Broadcasters. A guide to what is available in religious broadcasting opportunities for promotion.

DOLLARS IN YOUR MAILBOX by Ernest P. Weckesser, Ph.D.
The Green Tree Press: 1977. A handy how-to book on mail order techniques.

ENCYCLOPEDIA OF MAILING LIST TERMINOLOGY AND TECHNIQUES by Nat G. Bodian
Bret Scot Press: 1986. Enables mail-list users to communicate more easily and effectively.

FORMAIDS FOR DIRECT RESPONSE MARKETING by Ad-Lib Consultants
Ad-Lib: 1983. Forms and time-saving information.

GETTING YOUR MESSAGE OUT by Michael M. Klepper
Prentice-Hall, Inc.: 1984. How to get, use, and survive radio and television air time. A superior book.

HOW TO CREATE SMALL-SPACE NEWSPAPER ADVERTISING THAT WORKS by Ken Eichenbaum
Unicom Publishing Group: 1987. An excellent guide containing examples of what works and why in small-space advertising.

HOW TO GET RICH IN MAIL ORDER by Melvin Powers
    Wilshire Book Company: 1980. An excellent, beginner's guide to direct marketing.

HUDSON'S NEWSLETTER DIRECTORY compiled by Howard Penn Hudson
    Hudson's Newsletter Directory: 1988. A detailed listing of newsletters from A-Z.

LMP (LITERARY MARKET PLACE)
    R. R. Bowker Company. A comprehensive list of prime contacts published annually. This book should be in every self-publisher's library.

MARKETING TO LIBRARIES THROUGH LIBRARY ASSOCIATIONS compiled by Sandy Whitley
    American Library Association: 1987. A survey that identifies marketing opportunities through area and specialized library associations.

MARKETING YOUR BOOK by Marilyn and Tom Ross
    Communication Creativity: 1989. A collection of profit-making ideas for authors and publishers. Highly recommended.

METRO CALIFORNIA MEDIA
    Public Relations Plus, Inc. A directory of media listings for the "hot" California cities.

NATIONAL RADIO PUBLICITY OUTLETS
    Public Relations Plus, Inc. The publicist's annual guide to radio, with separate listings for network shows and syndicated shows.

NATIONAL SURVEY OF NEWSPAPER OP-ED PAGES edited by Marilyn Ross
    Communication Creativity: 1986. One-of-a-kind information on op-ed (opposite editorial) pages in newspapers around the country.

NATIONAL TRADE AND PROFESSIONAL ASSOCIATIONS OF THE U.S.A. edited by Craig Colgate, Jr.
    Columbia Books, Inc.: 1982. A very useful guide to numerous associations.

NEW YORK PUBLICITY OUTLETS
    Public Relations Plus, Inc. A directory of media listings in the Big Apple.

1984 DIRECTORY OF LITERARY MAGAZINES prepared by the Coordinating Council of Literary Magazines
    Compiled list of magazines that publish literary work.

1001 WAYS TO MARKET YOUR BOOKS by John Kremer
    Ad-Lib Publications: 1989. A new, revised edition of his excellent 101 ways to market your book.

POETRY MARKETING by Lincoln B. Young
    Fine Arts Press: 1982. How and where to sell your poetry.

PROFESSIONAL GUIDE TO PUBLICITY by Richard Weiner
    Public Relations Publishing Co., Inc.: 1981. How to work with publicity and the working press.

PUBLICITY FOR BOOKS AND AUTHORS by Peggy Glenn
    Aames-Allen Publishing Company: 1985. An ideal source of information for authors and publishers alike.

THE PUBLICITY MANUAL by Kate Kelly
Visibility Enterprises: 1980. A leading book on the subject, which tells how to develop good publicity relationships.

THE PUBLISHER'S DIRECT MAIL HANDBOOK by Nat G. Bodian
ISI Press: 1987. Chock-full of case studies, examples, and illustrations. Especially for selling professional, scholarly, or reference books.

RADIO CONTACTS
Larimi Communications Assoc., Ltd. An annual directory on local, network, and syndicated radio programming.

THE SECRETS OF PRACTICAL MARKETING FOR SMALL BUSINESS by Herman R. Holtz
Prentice-Hall, Inc.: 1982. The "Betty Crocker cookbook" on marketing techniques for the small entrepreneur.

SELLING TO CATALOG HOUSES by Ron Playle
R & D Services: 1982. How you can sell thousands of books or other products to the large mail-order catalog houses. Chock-full of useful tips.

THE STANDARD PERIODICAL DIRECTORY
Oxbridge Communications, Inc.: 1988. Guide to U.S. and Canadian periodicals. Information on 60,000 publications.

SUCCESSFUL DIRECT MARKETING METHODS by Bob Stone
NTC Business Books: 1988. The fourth edition of his masterful book covering all aspects of direct marketing.

TELEVISION CONTACTS
Larimi Communications Assoc., Ltd. An annual directory of national, syndicated, and local TV programs.

TRADE BOOK MARKETING, an anthology
R. R. Bowker Co.: 1983. Explains effective book-selling techniques.

TV NEWS
Larimi Communications Assoc., Ltd. An annual publication that cites news directories, assignment editors, and news programs on local TV stations and networks throughout the country.

TV PUBLICITY OUTLETS NATIONWIDE
Public Relations Press. A directory of outlets for television exposure.

ULRICH'S INTERNATIONAL PERIODICAL DIRECTORY
R. R. Bowker Co.: 1986. Information on more than 55,000 magazines listed under some 200-plus subject headings.

WHICH AD PULLED BEST? by Phillip Ward Burton and Scott C. Purvis
NTC Business Books: 1987. Fifty case histories of how to write display ads that work.

WORDS THAT SELL by Richard Bayan
Caddylak Systems: 1984. A thesaurus of powerful words, phrases, and slogans.

WORKING PRESS OF THE NATION
National Research Bureau: 1988. A five-volume reference work containing the names and addresses of book reviewers, freelance professional journalists, syndicated columnists, etc.

WRITER'S MARKET
Writer's Digest Books. This annual volume contains excellent marketing sources. Also hints on writing, submitting, trade book publishers, etc.

General Reference and Miscellaneous

AMERICAN BOOK TRADE DIRECTORY
R. R. Bowker Company. The most complete list available of individual bookstores and chains, published annually.

BODIAN'S PUBLISHING DESK REFERENCE by Nat G. Bodian
Oryx Press: 1988. Nearly 4,000 terms, ideas, and techniques for book selling.

THE BOOKMAN'S GLOSSARY edited by Jean Peters
R. R. Bowker Company: 1975. A glossary of terms for the writer-publisher.

BOOKS IN PRINT
R. R. Bowker Company. An annual publication listing all in-print titles from more than 7,000 publishers.

THE DICTIONARY OF PUBLISHING by David M. Brownstone and Irene M. Franck
Van Nostrand Reinhold Company: 1982. Reference dictionary of publishing language.

ENCYCLOPEDIA OF ASSOCIATIONS
Gale Research Company. This annual series lists societies, associations, and groups representing virtually any subject.

FOUNDATION GRANTS TO INDIVIDUALS, 4th edition. Edited by Claude Barilleaux.
The Foundation Center: 1984. The most comprehensive listing available of private U.S. foundations that provide financial assistance to individuals.

GRANTS AND AWARDS AVAILABLE TO AMERICAN WRITERS edited by John Morrone
PEN American Center: 1988. More than 500 American and international grants for writers of all kinds.

THE GUIDE TO WRITERS CONFERENCES
Shaw Associates: 1988. Covers more than 800 annual conferences, plus information on twenty-two colonies and retreats.

R. R. BOWKER CATALOG
R. R. Bowker Company. This free catalog contains a description of all Bowker publications.

THE RANDOM HOUSE COLLEGE DICTIONARY
Random House: 1982. An excellent and easy-to-use dictionary.

SMALL PRESS RECORD OF BOOKS IN PRINT edited by Len Fulton
Dustbooks: annual. Lists by author, title, publisher, and subject.

WEBSTER'S NINTH NEW COLLEGIATE DICTIONARY
Merriam-Webster: 1984. A comprehensive, useful dictionary.

A WHACK ON THE SIDE OF THE HEAD by Roger Von Oech, Ph.D.
Creative Think: 1983. How to unlock your mind for innovation. A fun book leading to new avenues of creativity.

THE WRITER Magazine
Heavy on how-to articles especially for poets and fiction writers; some marketing tips.

WRITER'S DIGEST Magazine
Writer's Digest Books. Has market information, getting-published aids, and how-to articles.

WRITER'S ENCYCLOPEDIA edited by Kirk Polking
Writer's Digest Books: 1983. A fascinating reference book filled with facts and figures about the profession of writing.

WRITER'S RESOURCE GUIDE, 2nd edition, edited by Bernadine Clark
Writer's Digest Books: 1983. More than 1,500 sources of research information—associations, companies, government agencies, and special interest groups as well as how to get available information/services from that source.

THE WRITER'S YELLOW PAGES edited by Steve Davis
Steve Davis Publishing: 1988. Lists over 23,000 U.S. companies, groups, and individuals of interest to writers.

Note: Most of the aforementioned titles can be ordered from the Maverick Mail Order Bookstore. For their current catalog, send a #10 SASE with 45¢ postage to Box 1500, Dept. MOBG, Buena Vista, CO 81211.

Newsletters

Over the last several decades, the newsletter industry has flourished. Newsletters provide abbreviated, timely information for quick reference. Those listed below are of particular interest to writers and publishers.

ALPS MONTHLY
Pacific Arts & Letters
P.O. Box 99394
San Francisco, CA 94109

AUTHOR'S NEWSLETTER
Arizona Author's Association
3509 East Shea Boulevard
Suite 117
Phoenix, AZ 85028

AUTHORSHIP
The National Writers Club
1450 South Havana
Suite 620
Aurora, CO 80012

BOOK DEALERS WORLD
American Bookdealers Exchange
Box 2525
La Mesa, CA 92041

BP REPORT
Knowledge Industry Publications
701 Westchester Avenue
White Plains, NY 10604

COMMUNICATION BRIEFINGS
140 South Braodway
Pitman, NJ 08071

COSMEP NEWSLETTER
Cosmep, Inc.
P.O. Box 703
San Francisco, CA 94101

THE DIGEST OF INFORMATION
ON PHOTOTYPESETTING
Graphic Dimensions
134 Caversham Woods
Pittsford, NY 14534

EPB
ELECTRONIC PUBLISHING
& BOOKSELLING
T & B Computing, Department EPB 5
1100 Eisenhower Place
Ann Arbor, MI 48104

FREELANCE WRITER'S REPORT
Cassell Communications, Inc.
P.O. Box 9844
Fort Lauderdale, FL 33310

THE INDEPENDENT PUBLISHER
Cosmep
P.O. Box 703
San Francisco, CA 94101

KEY NEWSLETTER
Boice Publications
1016 South Fly Avenue
Goreville, IL 62939

LITERARY MARKETS
P.O. Drawer 1310
Point Roberts, WA 98281

PMA
Publishers Marketing Association
2401 Pacific Coast Highway
Suite 206
Hermosa Beach, CA 90254

POETS & WRITERS MAGAZINE
Poets & Writers, Inc.
72 Spring Street
New York, NY 10012

TEACHER-WRITER
EdMart International Dept 60-F
177 White Plains Road
Tarrytown, NY 10591

TOWERS CLUB USA NEWSLETTER
Towers Club Press
P.O. Box 2038
Vancouver, WA 98668

WESTERN PUBLISHER
111 Kearny Street
San Francisco, CA 94133

WRITERS CONNECTION
The Writers Connection
10601 S. De Anza Boulevard
Suite 301
Cupertino, CA 95014

WRITER'S WORLD
Bhakti Press
P.O. Box 5119
Hilo, HI 96720

WRITING UPDATE
4812 Folsom Boulevard, #250
Sacramento, CA 95819

GLOSSARY

A

AA — author's alterations: changes by author on typeset galleys. *See also* PE, Printer's error.

ABA — American Bookseller's Association. A trade association of major publishers and booksellers.

ABI form — Advance Book Information form. A form filed by publisher with Bowker, who uses the information to list books in their directories; e.g., *Books in Print.*

Accounts receivable — money owed a company by credit customers.

Acknowledgment — the author's expressed appreciation to those who helped in producing the book. Usually a part of a book's FRONT MATTER.

Acquisition editor — a person in a publishing house who is responsible for acquiring new manuscripts.

Acquisition librarian — the librarian who orders new library books.

Adoptions — books accepted for use as textbooks in schools and universities.

Advance — money paid an author before a book's publication: an advance installment against ROYALTIES.

Afterword — part of a book's back matter; the author's parting remarks to the reader. *See also* Back matter; Foreword; Front matter.

AKA — "also known as": a term referring to another name used for self-promotion or advertising agency business. *See also* DBA.

ALA — American Library Association. The trade association of libraries.

Anthology — a collection of writings by one or more authors published as a single work.

Antiquarian bookseller — One who specializes in buying and selling old or rare books.

Appendix — that part of a book's back matter that includes lists of resources or other specialized reference material. *See also* Back matter.

Art work — a catch-all phrase of book production that refers to a photograph, illustration, chart, graph, or ornament: anything other than straight text.

As-told-to — a book produced by a writer in collaboration with a non-writer, the latter often a celebrity. The writer is credited as co-author: i.e., *The Story of My Life* by Famous Person as told to Pro Writer. *See also* Ghost writer.

Autograph party — a gathering, usually at a bookstore, where the author signs customers' copies of his or her book(s).

B

Back flap — the back inner fold of a dust jacket. It often has a continuation of copy from the front flap, as well as a photo and a brief biography of the author. *See also* Flap copy; Front flap.

Backlist — previously published books that are still in print and available from a publisher, as contrasted to frontlist (newly published) books.

Back matter—all pages in a book after the main text. Included may be an AFTER-WORD, APPENDIX, BIBLIOGRAPHY, COLOPHON, GLOSSARY, INDEX. *See also* Front matter.

Backorder—a book order waiting to be filled when a new supply of books becomes available.

Backup—printing the second or reverse side of a sheet or page already printed on one side.

Bad break—an illogical or unpleasant-looking beginning or end of a page or line of type. Also, an incorrectly broken word at the end of a line.

Bastard title—*See* Half title.

Belt press—an expensive and sophisticated printing press (e.g., Cameron), which prints and binds a book in one pass.

Best-seller—a nationally popular book. Best-seller lists are compiled weekly by the *New York Times* as well as by *Publishers Weekly* and *Time* magazines and others.

Bibliography—the part of a book's BACK MATTER listing other books or articles the author either cited or consulted in preparing the book or wishes to bring to the reader's notice.

Binding—the way the leaves or signatures of a book are held together. *See also* Case binding; Comb binding; Perfect binding; Saddle stitching; Signature; Smythe sewn; Spiral binding; Velo binding.

Blank—an unprinted page that is part of a signature.

Bleed—printing where the ink color goes all the way to one or more edges of the paper. A bleed is achieved by trimming the edge(s) to eliminate any MARGIN. Most magazines have covers that bleed.

Blueline—a proof the printer provides to catch any errors before a book is actually printed: consists of white letters on a blue background (or blue letters on a white background). Also called "blues," or sometimes a "brownline," in which case the background is brown.

Blue, nonreproducing pencil—a colored pencil or pen whose marks will not photograph. They "wash out" and disappear; thus, this kind of pencil is ideal for marking camera-ready copy because the marks will not reproduce in the printed book.

Blue penciling—a term used to refer to correcting or indicating rewrites of copy.

Blurb—a promotional phrase, announcement, or advertisement.

Boards—the stiff board used to reinforce the covers of a hardcover book. The term also refers to the heavier paper on which galleys are pasted up.

Boldface—heavy bold type which gives emphasis. *See also* Display type.

Book—a nonperiodical publication containing 49 or more pages.

Book fair—an event where publishers rent tables or booths to display and sell their wares.

Booklet—a small, softcover publication that usually has fewer than 49 pages.

Book packager—an individual or company contracting with publishers to handle book functions at least through camera-ready copy, and frequently beyond. Also called a "book producer."

Boxed—a technique for drawing attention to a certain paragraph or feature by enclosing it within a ruled box.

Bulk — the thickness of paper in number of pages per inch (PPI); also the thickness of the pages of the book, not counting the cover. Used as a verb, to make a book appear longer (thicker) than the amount of text would otherwise require by using thick, light paper.

Bulletin board — a computer term referring to an electronic communication program allowing the sending and storing of information between or among computers. *See also* Telecommunications.

Bullets — small black dots used to set off items in a list and make them easier to read.

Burnish — a paste-up term meaning to rub the boards with a tool to smooth and firmly affix the galleys to them.

C

C1S — coated one side. Refers to book cover stock.

Calligraphy — hand lettering, often ornate, which is sometimes used for poetry, cookbooks, etc.

Camera-ready copy — text or art ready to be shot by the printer's camera. It should be free of smudges and of unclear, broken, or faint type. *See also* Mechanicals; Repro.

Cameron belt press — *See* Belt press.

Capitalization expenditures — purchases of items by a business with a useful life over several years whose cost is more than $100 and not fully deducted in the calender year purchased. These purchases are depreciated over their useful life. *See also* Expensed purchases.

Caps — short for capitals or upper case (u.c.) letters.

Caption — *See* Cutline.

Captured keystroke — a computer term meaning that information, once entered, is retained by the computer and therefore doesn't need retyping.

Case binding — hard cover.

Cast-off — an estimate of the length a manuscript will be when typeset.

Catalog sheet — a low-key promotional page including contents, author, and ordering information, often used as a flier.

CBA — Christian Booksellers Association. A trade association of religious bookstores and suppliers.

Center spread — the pair of facing pages in the center of a magazine or book.

Chapbook — a small book or pamphlet of popular tales, ballads, or poems.

Chapter head — the chapter title printed before the text in each new chapter.

Character — a letter of the alphabet, numeral, or mark of punctuation.

CIP — Cataloging in Publication. A process which aids librarians in ordering and cataloging a book. Predesignated reference numbers provided by the Library of Congress are included in the front matter of a book.

Clean copy — a manuscript or galley free from corrections, deletions, and other unnecessary marks. *See also* Dirty copy.

Clip art — inexpensive visuals that can be purchased and pasted up in a book instead of using custom-drawn illustrations.

Clipping service — a firm which, for a fee, collects articles, reviews, and notices about a specific subject a customer is interested in. Also called a clipping bureau.

Cloth — a material used for binding, or casing, of books.

Coated paper — paper stock surfaced with white clay to provide a smooth printing surface. Enamel-coated glossy papers are used for book covers.

COD — Cash on Delivery. A form of payment in which money is received before, or when, merchandise is delivered.

Cold type — typesetting accomplished without the use of molten lead or "hot metal." Cold type includes offset, rub-on, direct-impression, etc. It is the most popular method currently in use. *See also* Hot type.

Collating — gathering sheets together into proper order.

Colophon — a Greek term meaning "finishing touch." A brief listing of production details (typeface, etc.) that occasionally appears in a book's BACK MATTER.

Color correction — any method such as masking, dot etching, re-etching, and scanning, used to improve color rendition.

Color printing — usually any printing color, other than black, on white paper. For instance, a work with three different colored inks is referred to as three-color printing.

Color separation — the camera technique of "separating" each of the four primary colors for the four necessary printing plates; each color is printed by preparing art on separate acetate overlays.

Comb binding — a plastic multipronged binding that allows a book to lie flat. *See also* Binding.

Composition — the process of setting type, or the set type itself.

Compositor — another term for typesetter. A person who sets type.

Condensed — a narrow and more compact version of a given typeface.

Content editing — the process of evaluating a manuscript for style, organization, and large general revisions. *See also* Copy editing.

Co-op advertising — a program in which the publisher and the bookstore share the cost of book advertising, the publisher paying the major share.

Co-op publishing — also called co-publishing. Several people — or more than one company — work together to put out a book.

Co-operative publishing — *See* Subsidy press.

Copy — the text of a book.

Copy editing — technical editing of a manuscript for spelling, grammar, punctuation, clarity, and overall correctness. *See also* Content editing.

Copyright — the right of persons to retain or to sell copies of artistic works which they have produced. *See also* Copyright notice; Copyright infringement; Fair use; Universal Copyright Convention.

Copyright infringement — unauthorized and illegal use of copyrighted material. Commonly known as, but not identical to, PLAGIARISM. *Also see* Fair use.

Copyright notice — a notice required by law to protect publicly distributed information. It must include the symbol ©, the word "copyright" or the abbreviation "copr."; the first year in which the work is published; and the name of the copyright holder.

COSMEP — Committee of Small Magazines, Editors, and Publishers. A trade association of small presses and self-publishers.

CP/M—the forerunner of personal computer operating systems. CP/M was the standard until IBM entered the fledgling PC marketplace.

CPU—Central Processing Unit. Generally refers to the microprocessor and memory. A term carried over from the mini computer world.

Credit memo—a statement that shows customers they have credit for returned merchandise.

Cropping—placing pencil (or crayon) marks at the margins and corners to indicate what portion of a photo or illustration is to be reproduced.

Cross reference—a reference made from one part of a book to another.

Cutline—a legend or explanation which identifies an illustration or photograph. Also known as "caption."

D

Daisy wheel printer—a computer peripheral that employs a process whereby a daisy-shaped typing element with characters on its "petals" spins to produce fine, letter-quality type. *See also* Dot matrix printer.

Database—data stored and managed by a database management system (DBMS). Can be as simple as a mailing list or as complex as needed to provide management of the data for easy access.

DBA—"doing business as," used when a name other than one's own is the business' name. *See also* AKA.

Deadline—the cut-off date by which a task must be completed.

Dedication—the inscription honoring the person(s) who inspired the work. Part of a book's FRONT MATTER.

Defamation—a legally actionable attack (either written or spoken) that tends to injure a person's reputation. *See also* Libel.

Delete—a proofreading term directing the removal of certain characters or material.

Demographics—a profile of a group (readers, listeners, viewers, etc.) documenting such things as age, sex, marital status, education, socioeconomic level, hobbies, and so forth.

Desktop publishing—a publishing system based on microcomputers and 300-DPI printer output to produce near-typeset-quality publications and thus supplanting the complicated and expensive photo typesetting process.

Die cut—the creation of openings, shapes, or folds by cutting away part of the paper stock.

Direct mail—letters or promotional material mailed directly to potential customers.

Dirty copy—heavily edited or marked-up copy that is difficult to read. *See also* Clean copy.

Disc drive—a storage device for holding electronic text.

Display ad—a print advertisement that uses graphics.

Display type—larger or bolder type for heads, subheads, etc., as compared with type used in the text as a whole. *See also* Boldface.

Distributor—*See* Jobber; Wholesaler.

Dot matrix printer—a computer peripheral that fires pins against a print ribbon to create an impression made up of dots. Usually produces fast, but lower-quality, printing. *See also* Daisy wheel printer.

Down time—time when a supplier is not busy and may give better prices; also, the time during which a given piece of equipment is inoperable and/or under repair.

Dummy—a rough layout of how the finished book is to appear.

Dump—a display unit used in bookstores. *See also* Point-of-purchase display.

Dun and Bradstreet rating—a profile of a company's financial stability, etc., prepared by Dun and Bradstreet.

Duotone—a process for producing an illustration in two colors from a one-color original. It gives a quality of added depth and texture.

Dust cover—*See* Dust jacket.

Dust jacket—a protective and attractive cover for hardback books. It provides space for visual display and promotional copy. Also called a "dust cover."

E

Editing—making or suggesting changes in a manuscript.

Edition—one or more printings of a work that are basically the same. A revised edition contains substantial changes. *See also* Revised edition; First edition; Limited edition; Simultaneous editions.

Editor in Chief—the top editorial executive in a publishing program, setting policy for that program and directing acquisitions.

Electronic publishing—a general term embracing all forms of computerized publication, particularly those that deliver text or other materials directly to the consumer's (TV or computer) screen.

Elite type—a common, smaller typewriter face with 12 characters to the inch. *See also* Pica type.

Em—approximately the width of the letter "m" in any given typeface, used to measure such things as indents and dashes. An em-dash, for instance, is twice as wide as an en-dash (hyphen). *See also* En.

En—approximately the width of the letter "n" in any given typeface. *See also* Em.

Endpapers—the heavy sheets of paper, one at the beginning and the other at the end, of a hardbound book. They fasten the book to its cover.

Engraving—the cutting of a design into a block of material, resulting in a pattern from which a print can be made.

Enlargement—the photographic process of creating an image larger than the original. *See also* Reduction; Scale.

Epilogue—a concluding section that rounds out a story and often updates the reader. Part of the text, not of the back matter.

Errata—errors found in printed books. They are commonly corrected, prior to the book's next printing, by the insertion of a loose sheet (an "errata sheet") with revised text in each copy of the book.

Estimate—*See* Price estimate.

Excerpt—a portion taken from a longer work. Also called an "extract."

Exclusive—a news or feature story, or TV appearance, printed or aired by one media source substantially ahead of its competitors.

Expanded type—a wider-than-usual typeface.

Expensed purchases—any business expenditure under $100 for items whose useful lives are one year or less and are fully deducted (expensed) in the year purchased. *See also* Capitalization expenditures.

Expert reading—a reading of the book done by an authority on the book's subject to determine accuracy and completeness prior to publication.

F

Facing page—any page forming a double spread with another.

Fair use—the allowable and legal use of a limited amount of copyrighted material without getting permission.

First edition—the entire original run of copies of a work from the same plates.

First serial rights—the right to serialize a forthcoming work prior to the publication date. Often sold to only one magazine or one newspaper. *See also* Rights; Second serial rights.

Flap copy—the material describing a book and its author which appears on the inside folds of dust jackets. *See also* Back flap; Front flap.

Flat fee—a one-time payment for a job or task, such as the preparation of text or artwork.

Flier—an inexpensive promotional piece often printed on an 8½×11 sheet of paper.

Flop—to flip a photo negative over so it will be printed facing the opposite way.

Flush—meaning to be even with. Usually refers to the left margin, as in "flush left." *See also* Justify; Ragged right.

FOB—Free on Board. When books are shipped from the manufacturer F.O.B., the publisher must pay shipping cost to the destination.

Folded and gathered pages—abbreviated as "F & G's," these are unbound book pages. They are often sent to prime reviewers. *See also* Galleys, Proofs.

Folio—a page number of a book.

Font—complete set of type, including letters, numbers, and punctuation marks, in one face.

Forecasting—using mathematical computations to predict business trends.

Foreign rights—subsidiary rights allowing a work to be published in other countries and/or translated into other languages. *See also* Rights.

Foreword—introductory remarks about a book and its author. Often written by an expert (other than the author) to give a book greater promotability and authority. Part of a book's FRONT MATTER. *See also* Afterword.

Format—designation of typeface, margins, boxing, or any other special treatment of copy. Also used to indicate the trim size and physical layout of the book.

Formatting—the process of designing a publication.

Freelance—skilled creative people (writers, editors, graphic artists, consultants, *et al.*) who sell their services as independent contractors.

Front matter—all pages before the main text. It may include DEDICATION, FOREWORD, FRONTISPIECE, HALF TITLE, INTRODUCTION, TABLE OF CONTENTS, TABLE OF ILLUSTRATIONS, TITLE PAGE.

Front plate—*See* Frontispiece.

Frontispiece—an illustration preceding and facing the title page. Also called a "front plate." Part of a book's FRONT MATTER.

FTC—Federal Trade Commission. A governmental regulatory agency.

Fulfillment—the filling and shipping of book orders.

G

Galleys — proofs from the typesetter usually before they are in page format, copies of which may be sent to important book reviewers. *See also* Folded and gathered pages; Page proofs; Proofs.

Genre — a category or specific kind of writing, such as historical, science fiction, mystery, etc.

Ghost writer — a professional writer who produces books attributed to others. *See also* As-told-to; Work for hire.

Glossary — a body of definitions relevant to the work. Part of the BACK MATTER.

Glossy — a photograph with a shiny rather than a matte finish.

Grant — an outright gift of money to subsidize a specific project.

Graphics — the illustrative elements in a work.

Gutter — the inside center margin of a book.

H

Half title — a page on which the title stands alone with no other information; precedes the complete TITLE PAGE. Also known as "Bastard title."

Halftone — a photograph or illustration that has been "converted" into a pattern of tiny dots so it can be printed.

Hardback — *See* Hard cover.

Hard cover — a book bound in BOARDS. Casebound.

Headband — a piece of material affixed to a book's spine for reinforcement.

Headline — a large bold caption appearing at the top of an advertisement or article.

Heads — short for chapter titles. *See also* Running heads; Subheads.

Hickey — a speck or blotch in a photographic negative.

Hot type — an older typesetting process utilizing hot metal cast in relief. Not used in offset printing. However, black-and-white "proofs" of hot type may be pasted up for photographic reproduction. *See also* Cold type.

House organ — periodical or newsletter issued by a firm or organization for its members, employees, customers, or prospects.

Hyperbole — also known as "hype." Exaggerated claims intended to sell a product or promote a person.

I

Illustrations — visual material such as photographs, drawings, graphs, and tables. *See also* Art work.

Image area — the printable area of a page where an image has been, or will be, produced.

Imprint — the identifying name of a publishing company carried on a published book.

Index — an A to Z list giving the location of specific material in a book. Part of the BACK MATTER.

India ink — dense, black ink preferred for drawing and ruling in preparing art work for photographic reproduction.

In-house—those functions performed within a publishing company rather than by outside contractors. Also, the term used to indicate that the finished books have been delivered to the publisher.

In-house ad agency—the setting up by a firm of its own advertising agency, of which it is the sole client.

In print—books that are currently available from publishers.

Insert—additional material added to a manuscript by an author or editor.

Insertion order—a form advertising agencies use to place advertising in various media.

Inventory—books on hand available for sale.

Invoice—a bill sent with a book order.

ISBN—International Standard Book Number. An essential identifying number used for ordering and cataloging purposes.

Italics—type with a right-hand slant like *this*. Often used for quotations, titles, and special emphasis.

J

Jacket—*See* Dust jacket.

Jobber—in the book business, one who buys in large lots to resell to retailers or libraries. Also called a "wholesaler" or "distributor."

Justify—the setting of type so that the end of each line is flush right and aligned perfectly. *See also* Flush; Ragged right.

K

Kern—that part of a letter that projects in any direction beyond its own body, or over/under adjacent letters.

Kerning—removing space between letters.

Key—an identifying explanation of coded material, e.g., a color-coded map and its accompanying key indicating what each color stands for.

Keyline—essentially the same as a PASTE-UP. The original composite art for offset printing.

Kill fee—money paid to a writer in compensation for time spent working on assignment on a piece the publisher decides not to accept. Kill fees range from 20 percent to 50 percent of the agreed-upon price, as stipulated in the original terms of assignment between writer and publisher.

L

Laser Printer—a nonimpact output device that burns an image on paper through the use of a small laser. Laser printers generally have much higher resolution and faster speed than typical dot matrix or daisy wheel printers.

Layout—the working template of the proposed design for a printing job. *See also* Mechanical; Sample pages.

LCCN—Library of Congress Card Number. An important coding process used by libraries in cataloging.

Leading—(rhymes with "wedding") the amount of space between lines of type.

Letterhead—company stationery that is printed with the name, address, telephone number, and any LOGO.

Letterpress — printing from raised letters or type, rather than from photographic plates.

Libel — written defamation of character, for which one can be sued. *See also* Defamation.

Light table — a table with a diffused light underneath to facilitate paste-up of text and art work.

Limited edition — a specified and limited quantity of books, often numbered and signed by the author.

Line art — a black-and-white original illustration that does not require halftone reproduction. In line art there are no in-between tones of gray. *See also* Halftone.

List — all of the titles a publisher has in print and for sale; or, the official or "listed" retail price of a book. *See also* List price.

List broker — someone who handles direct mail list rentals for use in direct marketing efforts.

List price — the full retail price of a book, without discounts. *See also* List.

LMP — *Literary Market Place.* An important overall publishing reference work: a comprehensive compilation of publishers, agents, book clubs, printers, and everyone else relevant to the book publishing industry. With names, addresses, and phone numbers.

Logo — a symbol or illustration used as an identifying mark by an individual or business.

Lower case — ("l.c."): small letters as opposed to either CAPITALS (u.c.) or SMALL CAPITALS (s.c.).

M

Macintosh — a non-IBM-compatible, Motorola 68000-based microcomputer that pioneered 32-bit processing, bit-mapped graphics displays, and a user interface based on icons, windows, and a pointing device called a mouse. Combined with the Apple Laserwriter, the Mac became the basic engine for the first desktop-publishing systems.

Mail fulfillment house — a company that handles envelope-stuffing, addressing, and mailing for a direct mail campaign. Some will also provide copywriting and list acquisitions.

Mail order — a method of merchandising books directly to the consumer using ads in magazines and newspapers.

Make-ready — all preparations of a press to get ready for a specific print run.

Margin — the unprinted edge that surrounds the printed image on a page. *See also* Bleed; Gutter.

Marketing plan — a publisher's total advertising and promotional plan designed to generate reviews, merchandise subsidiary rights, and sell books.

Market research — information gathering and analysis relating to any aspect of marketing.

Mass market paperback — the smaller 4x7-inch paperbacks designed for the widest possible distribution. *See also* Trade paperback.

Master — original camera-ready art work.

Measure — the length of a full line of type on a page. It is expressed in PICAS.

Mechanical – either a detailed layout diagram, with guides to all elements of copy and art work (present only as simulations), to guide the engraver or printer; or the actual pasted-up, camera-ready layout, with actual copy and art work in place, from which photographic negatives are made. *See also* Layout, Repro.

Media – all print, TV, radio, and other electronic sources for advertising and promotional exposure.

Microcomputer – any small computer designed for use in small business. Also called a "personal computer."

Microfiche – one of three major microforms (microfilm, microfiche, microcards) in which information is stored in greatly reduced form on photographic film and read through a special enlarging device.

Mock-up – a visual presentation of a proposed page or piece of promotional material.

Model release – a form giving permission to use a photograph of an individual for publication.

Modem – a device used with a microcomputer and a telephone to facilitate TELE-COMMUNICATIONS.

Monitor – a video display unit on which information typed into a computer appears.

Monograph – a short written report covering a single specific subject.

Ms – an abbreviation for "manuscript."

MS-DOS – generic version of PC-DOS distributed by Microsoft Corp. for use on non-IBM PCs.

Multiple submission – the offering of a work to more than one publisher at the same time.

N

Nationwide marketing plan – *See* Marketing plan.

Negative – a film replica of the original in which the gradations of light and dark are reversed.

Net receipts – moneys received by a publisher on a book's sale after all discounts and returned copies have been deducted. Some authors' contracts specify that royalties are calculated on the basis of net receipts rather than the book's retail (list) price.

News release – a one- or two-page story used for promotion, covering the five w's: who, what, when, where, and why.

Nonreturnable – merchandise that may not be returned for credit or a cash refund.

Nth name – randomly selected names in a mailing list – often every tenth – used to test the value of the total list.

O

Offset printing – any one of several printing processes which print type from a flat, rather than a raised or incised, surface. Also called "offset lithography" and "photo offset."

OOP – out of print. A book that is no longer available through the publisher. As contrasted with OOS, out of stock.

Opaque—not admitting light; also, to paint portions of a negative so they will not reproduce.

Operating system—a group of controlling programs that govern the functioning of a whole computer system.

OPM—other people's money. A business term meaning to borrow capital elsewhere rather than using one's own.

Option—the right to purchase or sell something—such as movie rights—for a specified price and within a certain length of time; also, the right a publisher may have, by previous contract, to bid on an author's subsequent books.

Ornament—a decorative device in book design, such as a larger initial letter, rule line, border, etc.

OOS—out of stock. A book not available because its publisher's supply has been temporarily exhausted. *See also* OOP.

Orphan—the first line of a new paragraph that appears alone at the bottom of a page.

Overrun—an extra amount of finished copies of the book the printer may produce above the stipulated order (should never exceed 10 percent); also, an additional quantity of book covers a publisher may order for promotional purposes. *See also* Underrun.

Over the transom—unsolicited material sent to a publisher directly by the author rather than through an agent or at the request of an editor. *See also* Slush pile.

P

Page proof—a duplicate of the actual layout of the pages exactly as they will appear in the compiled book, as contrasted with long "GALLEYS." *See also* Proofs.

Pagination—the numbering or order of pages in a book.

Paperback—or paperbound. A book bound with a flexible paper cover.

Paper stock—the paper used for printing a book.

Paste-up—the camera-ready original for offset printing; also, the making of that original.

PC—personal computer. *See* Microcomputer.

PC-DOS—a disk operating system created by Microsoft Corp. for use exclusively on IBM PCs operating on the 8088/8086 family of microprocessors.

PE—a printer's error on typeset galleys. *See also* AA.

Pen name—*See* Pseudonym.

Perfect binding—a flat or squared spine achieved by gluing the sheet ends together; used for hard covers, good paperbacks, and some magazines. *See also* Binding.

Periodical—a magazine.

Peripherals—devices that are attached to a computer system to increase its usefulness and functions, such as a printer or a modem.

Permission—an authorization from a copyright holder to quote material or reproduce illustrations taken from the copyrighted work. Often requires a fee.

Photo offset—*See* Offset printing.

Photostat—a copy of an illustration, printed page, etc., which is of suitable quality for printing reproduction.

Phototypesetting—a common form of typesetting in which each character and word is a photographic image. Major advantages are crispness, economy, and speed.

P.I. ads—per inquiry ads, where the advertiser shares a percentage of revenue from all sales with the media carrying the ad, instead of buying ad space outright.

Pica—a printer's measurement. Approximately ⅙ of an inch.

Pica type—the larger typewriter type which runs 10 characters to the inch, as contrasted to ELITE TYPE.

Plagiarism—copying or imitating another author's work and passing it off as one's own. *See also* Copyright; Copyright infringement; Fair use.

Plate—the final printing master which contains the image to be reproduced. It may be metal, plastic, or other material.

PMS color—(Pantone Matching System) specially mixed colors used in printing.

Point—a unit of vertical measurement. In typesetting, one point equals 1/72 of an inch.

Point-of-purchase display—book display racks, posters, bookmarks, and other sales materials given to bookstores to promote a book. *See also* Dump, Slit-card.

Point size—the height of a letter, expressed in point units (e.g., 8-point type, 32-point type, etc.).

Positioning—strategic placement of an ad where it will get maximum exposure; also, the place within a list where a book falls in relation to other titles in the subject area.

PPI—pages per inch. A term used to measure the thickness of paper stock.

Preface—introductory remarks (usually by the author) telling the reason the book was written and giving its aims and scope. Part of a book's FRONT MATTER.

Premium—a book which will usually be given away free as part of a promotional campaign for a product or service. Premium books are typically bought in large quantities.

Prepack—a point-of-purchase (P.O.P.) temporary countertop or floor display unit, often made from cardboard, designed to hold and bring extra attention to merchandise.

Prepublication copies—copies of a book which are circulated or sold prior to the publication date. Sometimes a discount is offered to stimulate early orders.

Prepublication price—a special lesser price offered on books bought before the official publication date.

Press kit—a collection of publicity materials used to promote a book or an author to the media. They are usually presented in a cardboard folder with pockets.

Press proof—a proof drawn just before the press run begins. It is sometimes used to check the cover colors, etc., of the printing job.

Press release—*See* News release.

Press run—the number of usable copies produced in a single printing.

Price estimate—an educated guess of how much a job will cost.

Price quote—a firm commitment on how much a job will cost.

Printer—another term for a book manufacturer. *See also* Dot matrix printer; Daisy wheel printer; Laser printer.

Promotional material—any printed matter (such as fliers, catalog sheets, letters, review excerpts, etc.) which is designed to publicize and sell a book.

Proof—a direct impression of type or a photographic reproduction of what the printed job should look like. *See also* Blueline; Galleys; Folded and gathered pages; Page proofs; Press proofs; Repro.

Proportion wheel—a small device used to determine enlargements and reductions for art work. *See also* Scale; Scaling.

Proportional spacing—a method of spacing in most typeset copy in which the width of a letter is determined by the actual amount of space it needs.

Proposal—a detailed plan of a proposed new enterprise that is used to sell that project; also, a package consisting of an outline, sample chapters, author bio, and other supporting materials used by a writer to persuade a publisher to offer a contract for a book.

Pseudonym—an assumed name used to conceal an author's identity; a pen name.

Publication date—a date, typically set about three months after books are actually in house, when a book is officially launched and available for purchase.

Public domain—material that is not protected by copyright.

Publicist—one who prepares promotional materials and/or schedules media appearances either as an independent contractor or as part of the staff of a publisher, advertising agency, or PR firm.

Q

Quality paperback—*See* Trade paperback.

Query letter—a one- or two-page letter created to interest an editor or agent in a book project or magazine article. It displays the author's writing ability and is meant to sell an idea. Also known as a "query."

Quote—a statement, often from a celebrity or key reviewer, used in advertising or for book cover copy; also, an exact copy of original wording from another source reproduced in one's own writing, enclosed in quotation marks; also, an offer to do work for a specific sum: a PRICE QUOTE.

R

Ragged right—a right-hand margin that does not align evenly. *See also* Justify.

Rate card—a price sheet giving the costs of media time or space advertising.

Recto—a right-hand page, as opposed to a VERSO, a left-hand page.

Recto-verso—two-sided printing.

Reduction—the photographic process of creating an image smaller than the original. A half-size image is expressed as a 50 percent reduction or "scale 50 percent." A three-fourths size image is "scale 75 percent." Oversize copy is thus scaled for reduction. *See also* Enlargement; Scale.

Register—the correct positioning of print on a page or, in color process printing, proper positioning of separations relative to each other.

Remaindering—a publisher's selling of the remaining stock of unsuccessful books for a fraction of their list price.

Remnant space—random advertising space, often in regional editions, which has not been sold when the magazine or newspaper is ready to go to press, usually available at a reduced rate.

Reprint—a general term used in publishing to describe any new printing of a book. *See also* Edition; First edition; Limited edition; Revised edition.

Repro—"reproduction proof": CAMERA-READY COPY on photosensitive paper to be pasted up on MECHANICALS to be photographed. *See also* Layout.

Retouching—touch-up of a photograph to correct flaws or to improve appearance.

Returns—books which have not been sold and are sent back to a publisher for credit or a cash refund.

Review—a critical evaluation of a work, citing its strengths and weaknesses.

Review copy—a complimentary copy of a book sent to reviewers or potential wholesale purchasers.

Revised edition—a new edition of a previously published book containing updated or supplementary material. *See also* Edition; First edition; Limited edition.

Rights—the various rights to reproduce or publish a work in any form, in whole or in part, which its author may sell or retain. *See also* Copyright; First serial rights; Foreign rights; Second serial rights; Subsidiary rights; Universal Copyright Convention.

Roll-fed press—*See* Web press.

Royalties—the money paid to authors by publishers for the right to use their work, usually computed as an agreed percentage of the price per copy sold. *See also* Advance; Net receipts.

Rule—a line. Rules can be made in many different thicknesses, either with a pen, by machine, or with graphic tape.

Runaround—when typeset words are set to accommodate art work; a more costly form of typesetting than straight copy.

Running copy—text, as opposed to headlines.

Running heads—the title and/or chapter headings that often appear on the top of each page in a book. *See also* Heads.

Run in—proofreader's notation directing that an existing break (such as a paragraph) be ignored and the text continued without break as one paragraph.

S

Saddle stitching—binding a booklet or magazine by driving staples through the fold at the very center; not practical for publications of more than 72 pages. *See also* Binding.

Sales rep—also called a "traveler." An individual who represents a publisher's books to retailers, wholesalers, etc., in exchange for a commission.

Sample pages—typeset examples of a book's intended design.

SAN—Standard Account Number. Sometimes used in order fulfillment. A code for identification of book dealers, libraries, schools, and school systems. Assigned by Bowker.

Sans serif—refers to type faces which do not have SERIFS.

SASE—a self-addressed, stamped envelope.

Scale—the percentage of enlargement or reduction based on same size reproduction at 100 percent. A piece 4x6 inches scaled 150 percent becomes 6x9 inches; scaled 50 percent, it's 2x3 inches. *See also* Enlargement; Reduction.

Scaling—using a PROPORTION WHEEL to determine enlargement or reduction proportions.

Scoring—creasing or incising paper or card stock in a crisp line in order to facilitate folding.

Screen—a masking device used to create various tints of the same color; 10 percent being very pale, 100 percent being the darkest tint possible.

Search and replace—a word processing function that automatically finds and replaces words or text throughout a document.

Second serial rights—the rights for a magazine excerpt or serial which will appear after the publication date. *See also* Rights.

Self-cover—a cover consisting of the same paper stock as that used for the inside pages.

Serif—the "tails" on typographic characters that make them easier to read. *See also* Sans serif.

Sheet-fed press—a press that requires paper cut into separate sheets, rather than a continuous roll. *See also* Web press.

Short rate discount—any discount less than the usual 40 percent. Schools often buy on a 20-percent short rate.

Short rated—when advertising contract obligations are not met and the advertiser is rebilled at the higher actual usage rates.

Short run—small printing jobs of a few hundred (for neighborhood printing) or a few thousand (for book manufacturers) books or booklets.

Shrink wrap—a clear plastic covering used in shipping from the manufacturer to avoid books' being marred.

Signature—the multiples of pages (4, 8, 12, 16, or 32, depending on the press used), in which books are normally printed.

Silk-screening—a printing method whereby ink is forced through a stencil, thus creating a design. A more expensive process used for imprinting heavy stock paper.

Simultaneous editions—the printing of hard cover and paperback editions of a book at the same time.

Single copy order—when only one copy of a book is ordered. Many publishers do not give any discounts on single copy orders.

Sinkage—the extra white space above a display such as at a chapter opening.

Slipcase—a protective box-like container, open at one end, for books.

Slit-card—a display poster designed to fit into or around a book. *See also* Point-of-purchase display.

Slug—spacing between lines of type wider than the usual two or three points of LEADING.

Slush pile—the accumulation of unsolicited material submitted to a publisher. It's scanned by junior editors when time allows. *See also* Over the transom.

Small caps—("s.c."): proofreader's direction to set material in capital letters the same size as the lower case letters being used.

Smythe sewn—a form of binding used for many hard-cover books. The signatures are first sewn together, then glued into the hard cover. It's a sturdy but costly form of binding. *See also* Binding.

Software—individual computer programs, such as word processing or spreadsheets, which make a computer system perform specific functions.

Sp—a proofreader's mark meaning to spell out, rather than abbreviate or use initials.

Special order—on the retail level, an order by a consumer for a book not in stock. On the wholesale level, an order received from a bookseller that requires special handling, such as a rush order.

Specs—an abbreviation of "specifications." The physical details of a publishing project, such as type choice and size, binding, trim size, number of pages, etc.

Spine—that part of a book that connects the front to the back.

Spine out—books placed on shelves so that only the spine shows.

Spiral binding—a continuous wire binding, usually used only on paperbacks. *See also* Binding.

Split runs—different ads run in regional editions of the same magazine issue; an ideal tool for mail order testing. Also, an edition of a book printed simultaneously in paperback and hardbound.

Sponsored book—*See* Premium.

Spreadsheet—a programmable balance sheet commonly used for accounting functions planning and forecasts.

SRDS—Standard Rate and Data Services, Inc. A group of reference books designed especially for ad agencies, but useful in other marketing efforts, as well.

Stamping—imprinting lettering or a design on a book cover.

Standard trim size—any of a variety of page measurements standard to a particular kind of book (i.e., 4¼x7, mass market paperback; 5½ × 8½, 6 × 9, 6 × 9¼, trade books; 8½ × 11, illustrated books and workbooks, etc.)

Statement—a chronological listing of all charges and credits to date for a specific account.

Stet—from the Latin term "to stand." A mark meaning that a proofreader's symbol should be disregarded, and the text left as is.

Strip in—to combine a photographic negative with one or more others in preparation to making a printing plate.

Stripping—the process of preparing a negative or series of negatives for plate making.

Style sheet—a guide to editorial specifications, or selected typographical details, for a particular book.

Subsidiary rights—additional rights, such as book club, serial rights, or paperback rights, which can be sold in addition to the book itself. *See also* Rights.

Subsidy press—a company that charges writers to publish their work, then usually retains ownership of the books and does little, if any, promotion. Also called a "vanity press" or "co-operative publisher."

Subtitle—a second or additional title further explaining a book's content and scope.

Syndication—the simultaneous release of written or broadcast material to many outlets.

T

Table of contents—includes the title and beginning page number of each section of the book; sometimes includes descriptive material for each chapter. It is part of a book's FRONT MATTER.

Table of illustrations — a list noting illustrations used in the text. It is part of a book's FRONT MATTER.

Tail-piece — a small ORNAMENT — at the end of a chapter.

Tear sheets — newspaper or magazine reviews, ads, or stories cut from the periodicals they appeared in.

Telecommunications — electronic communication between one computer and another using a telephone and a MODEM.

Thesaurus — a program which stores words, specifically an electronic book of synonyms and antonyms.

Tipping in — the insertion of additonal material, by pasting, into a bound book. Fold-out maps are often tipped in, for instance.

Title — any one of the books a publisher currently has in print. Also, the name of a particular book.

Title page — the page in a book's FRONT MATTER, on the right, which usually gives the title, author(s) or editor(s), publisher, and place and date of publication. *See also* Front matter.

Trade paperback — the larger paperback (5x8 to 7x10 inches). Also called a "quality paperback."

Trade publisher — a conventional publishing house, publishing books for a mass audience, which typically pays authors advances and royalties, as opposed to a self-publisher or a subsidy publisher.

Transpose — to accidentally reverse the order (such as of two letters).

Traveler — *See* Jobber; Sales rep.

Trim size — the finished size of a book after the signatures have been trimmed and folded. *See also* Standard trim size.

Two-up — pieces printed side-by-side.

U

Underrun — when a printer manufactures fewer copies than were ordered. *See also* Overrun.

Unit cost — the production cost to print each individual book.

Universal Copyright Convention — an agreement, ratified by 90 nations, to offer the copyrighted works of citizens of other nations the same protections as are extended to those of their own citizens. *See also* Copyright; Copyright infringement; Plagiarism.

Universal discount schedule — a system that gives everyone the same discounts, whether wholesaler, bookstore, individual, or library.

UNIX — a multi-user DOS system developed by Bell Labs of AT&T. Has not gained wide acceptance in the PC marketplace.

Up-charge — an additional fee incurred over and above a stated price.

Upper case — ("u.c."): the capital letters of a font. *See also* Lower case; Small caps.

V

Vanity press — *See* Subsidy press.

Varnishing — a coating process that results in a hard, glossy surface. Used for protection and eye appeal on book covers.

Velo binding — an inexpensive fused plastic binding. *See also* Binding.

Vendor — a supplier who sells goods or services.

Verso — a left-hand page, as opposed to a RECTO, a right-hand page.

Visuals — *See* Art work.

W

Web press — a fast, sophisticated printing press that uses roll-fed paper rather than sheets. *See also* Sheet-fed press.

Wholesaler — a person or company who buys from a publisher, then resells to a bookstore or library. Also sometimes referred to as a "jobber" or a "distributor."

Widow — the last line of a paragraph that appears alone at the top of a new page.

Wire service — a news-gathering organization that sells information to its subscribers. UPI and AP are the leading ones.

Word-of-mouth — an informal, but important, kind of advertising in which a book is praised by one person to another.

Word processing — the electronic manipulation of text that allows a document to be monitored and corrected prior to the printing of a final document.

Work for hire — work done for a fee in which the author has no copyright or ownership. Under current law, work for hire must be covered by a written agreement. *See also* Ghost writer.

Working title — a preliminary title used while a book is in preparation.

Writer's Market — a publishing reference work important to authors; a comprehensive annual compilation of publishers' names, addresses, current needs, and general policies and contract terms. *See also* LMP.

Wrong font — ("wf"): a proofreader's mark indicating that in one or more words, the printer has used the wrong font (face) of type.

About the authors

After self-publishing four books, the husband and wife team of Tom and Marilyn Ross began giving nationwide writing and publishing seminars to share what they had learned about the process. A flood of requests for individual guidance for a variety of publishing ventures led to the creation of their consulting service, About Books, Inc.

Over the last decade they have helped hundreds of authors, entrepreneurs, associations, and professionals successfully self-publish. These busy professionals continue to be in demand as speakers. They've been on the faculty of Folio's New York Face-to-Face conference, spoken at colleges and universities, and are often called upon to present seminars for national writing and publishing conferences.

Tom Ross has masterminded promotional campaigns which created extensive print, radio, and TV coverage, and opened doors for national book distribution. As a consultant, Tom specializes in helping clients with project analysis, editing, production, computerizing, and developing nationwide book marketing campaigns. Trained as a computer engineer, he is a respected leader in the publishing industry and is listed in *Who's Who in the West*.

Marilyn Ross is the award-winning author of nine nonfiction books. She has also served as a corporate director of marketing and owned and operated her own advertising/PR agency, which qualifies her to address the area of publicity and sales. Marilyn is a member of ASJA, was recently elected chairperson of COSMEP, and is listed in *Who's Who of American Women*. She also heads Communication Creativity—the Rosses' publishing imprint—which distributes Marilyn and Tom's audio cassette program titled *Book Promotion & Marketing*.

About Books, Inc., the publishing and book marketing firm founded over a decade ago by Tom and Marilyn Ross, serves as a consulting firm that assists authors to successfully publish and promote their books. The Rosses do everything from hourly consulting by phone to handling all aspects of book editing, production, and marketing. Since ABI works strictly as a consultant, authors retain all rights and own all copies of their book.

Marilyn and Tom have a proven track record of producing attractive books and result-getting promotion and publicity. You can contact them by writing Box 1500, Buena Vista, CO 81211 or by calling (719) 395-2459.

A

Q

R

S